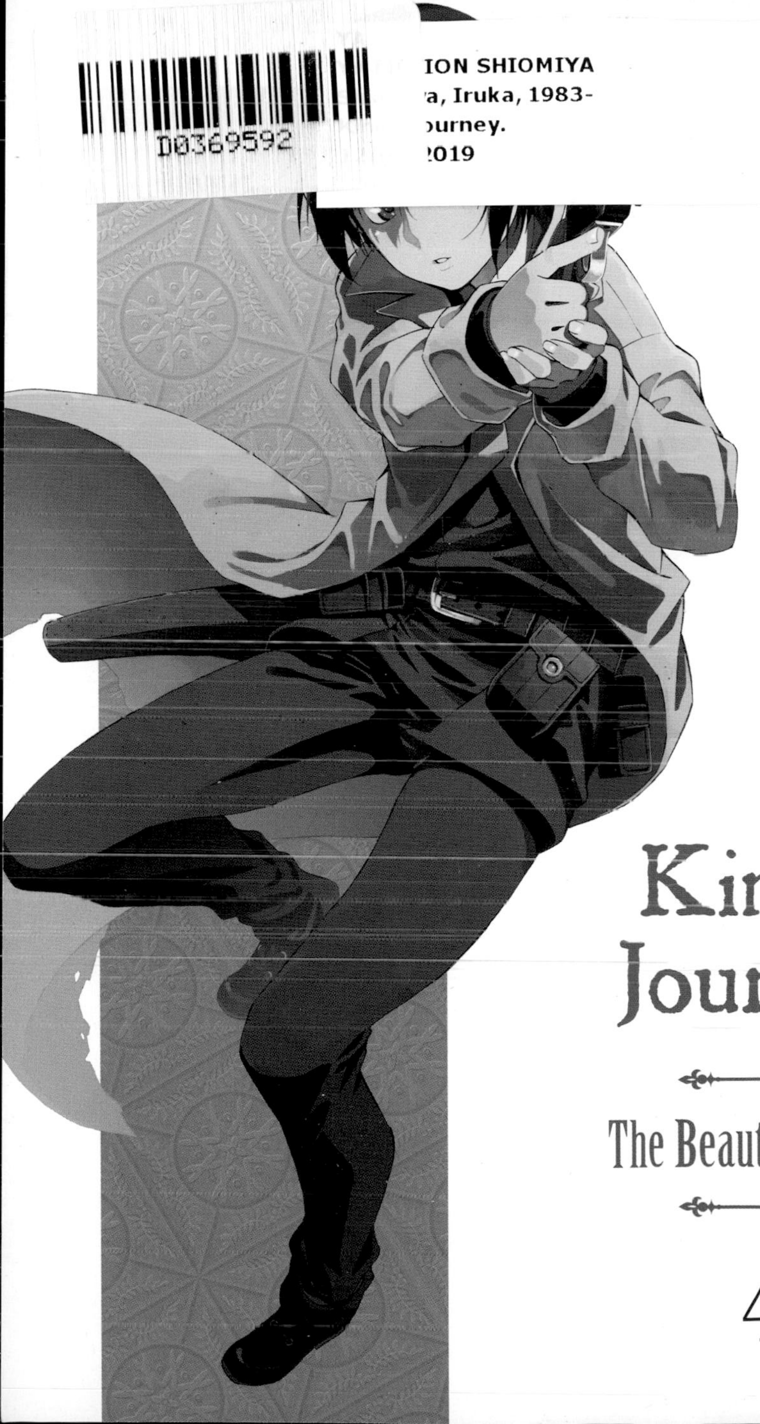

Iruka Shiomiya

Original Story:
Keiichi Sigsawa

Original Character Design:
Kouhaku Kuroboshi

Kino's Journey

The Beautiful World

4

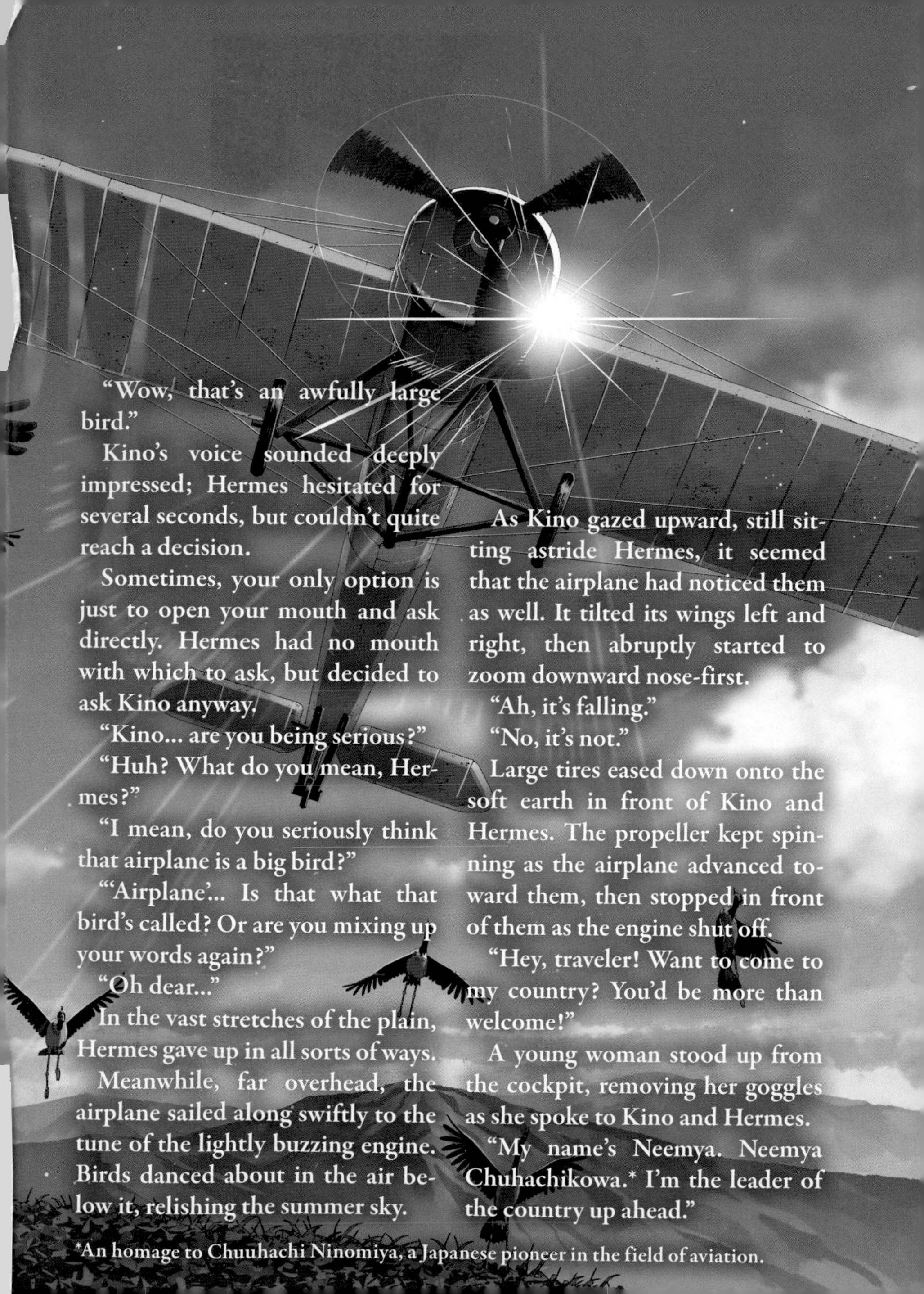

"Wow, that's an awfully large bird."

Kino's voice sounded deeply impressed; Hermes hesitated for several seconds, but couldn't quite reach a decision.

Sometimes, your only option is just to open your mouth and ask directly. Hermes had no mouth with which to ask, but decided to ask Kino anyway.

"Kino... are you being serious?"

"Huh? What do you mean, Hermes?"

"I mean, do you seriously think that airplane is a big bird?"

"'Airplane'... Is that what that bird's called? Or are you mixing up your words again?"

"Oh dear..."

In the vast stretches of the plain, Hermes gave up in all sorts of ways.

Meanwhile, far overhead, the airplane sailed along swiftly to the tune of the lightly buzzing engine. Birds danced about in the air below it, relishing the summer sky.

As Kino gazed upward, still sitting astride Hermes, it seemed that the airplane had noticed them as well. It tilted its wings left and right, then abruptly started to zoom downward nose-first.

"Ah, it's falling."

"No, it's not."

Large tires eased down onto the soft earth in front of Kino and Hermes. The propeller kept spinning as the airplane advanced toward them, then stopped in front of them as the engine shut off.

"Hey, traveler! Want to come to my country? You'd be more than welcome!"

A young woman stood up from the cockpit, removing her goggles as she spoke to Kino and Hermes.

"My name's Neemya. Neemya Chuhachikowa.* I'm the leader of the country up ahead."

*An homage to Chuuhachi Ninomiya, a Japanese pioneer in the field of aviation.

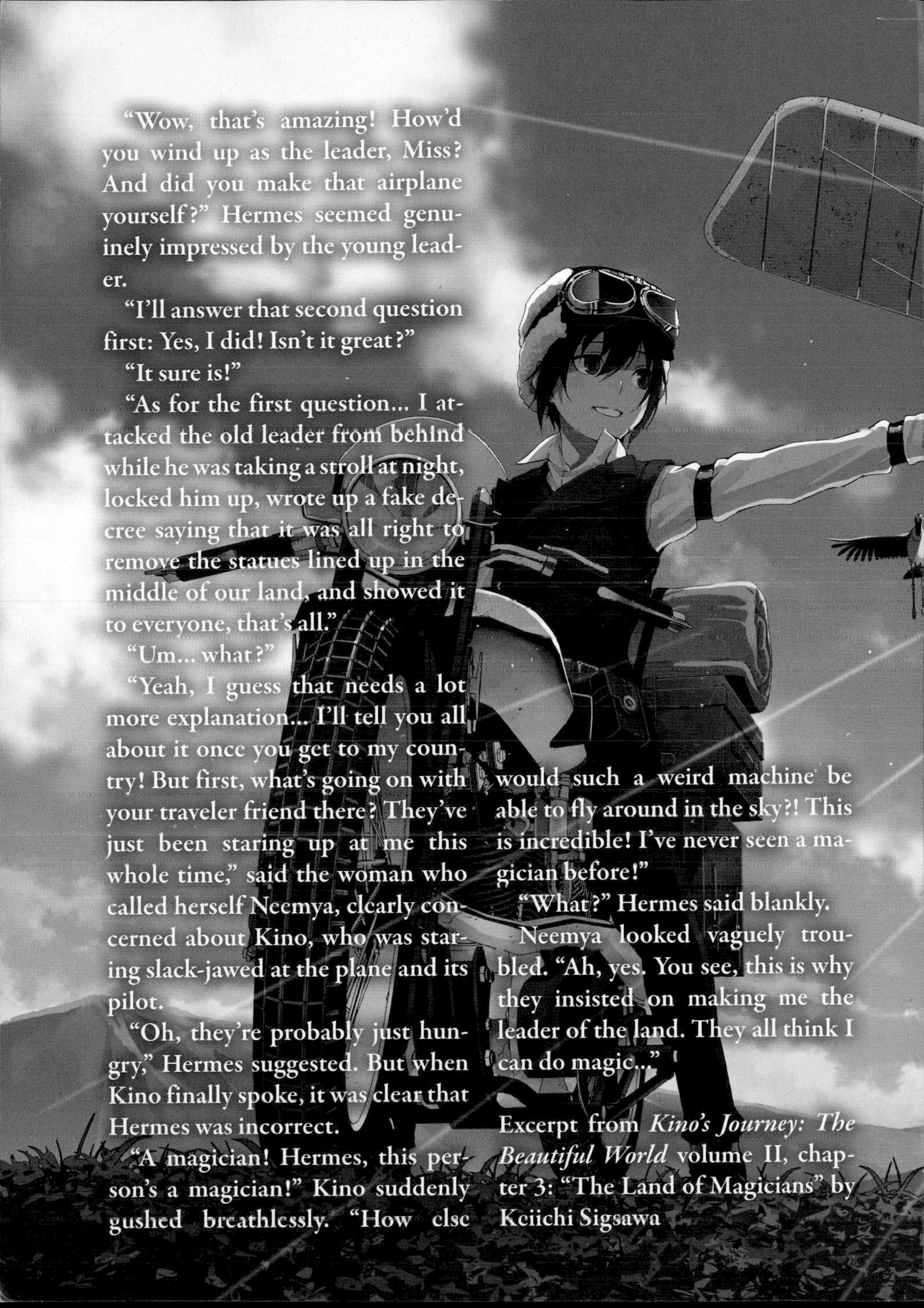

"Wow, that's amazing! How'd you wind up as the leader, Miss? And did you make that airplane yourself?" Hermes seemed genuinely impressed by the young leader.

"I'll answer that second question first: Yes, I did! Isn't it great?"

"It sure is!"

"As for the first question... I attacked the old leader from behind while he was taking a stroll at night, locked him up, wrote up a fake decree saying that it was all right to remove the statues lined up in the middle of our land, and showed it to everyone, that's all."

"Um... what?"

"Yeah, I guess that needs a lot more explanation... I'll tell you all about it once you get to my country! But first, what's going on with your traveler friend there? They've just been staring up at me this whole time," said the woman who called herself Neemya, clearly concerned about Kino, who was staring slack-jawed at the plane and its pilot.

"Oh, they're probably just hungry," Hermes suggested. But when Kino finally spoke, it was clear that Hermes was incorrect.

"A magician! Hermes, this person's a magician!" Kino suddenly gushed breathlessly. "How else would such a weird machine be able to fly around in the sky?! This is incredible! I've never seen a magician before!"

"What?" Hermes said blankly.

Neemya looked vaguely troubled. "Ah, yes. You see, this is why they insisted on making me the leader of the land. They all think I can do magic..."

Excerpt from *Kino's Journey: The Beautiful World* volume II, chapter 3: "The Land of Magicians" by Keiichi Sigsawa

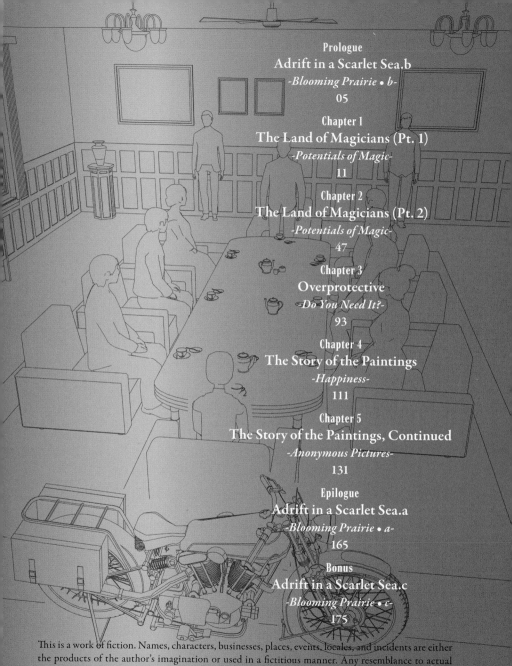

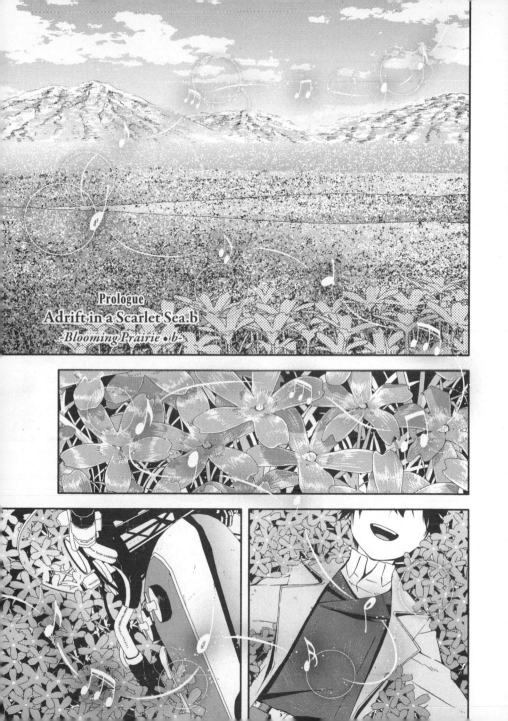

Prologue
Adrift in a Scarlet Sea.b
-Blooming Prairie ●b-

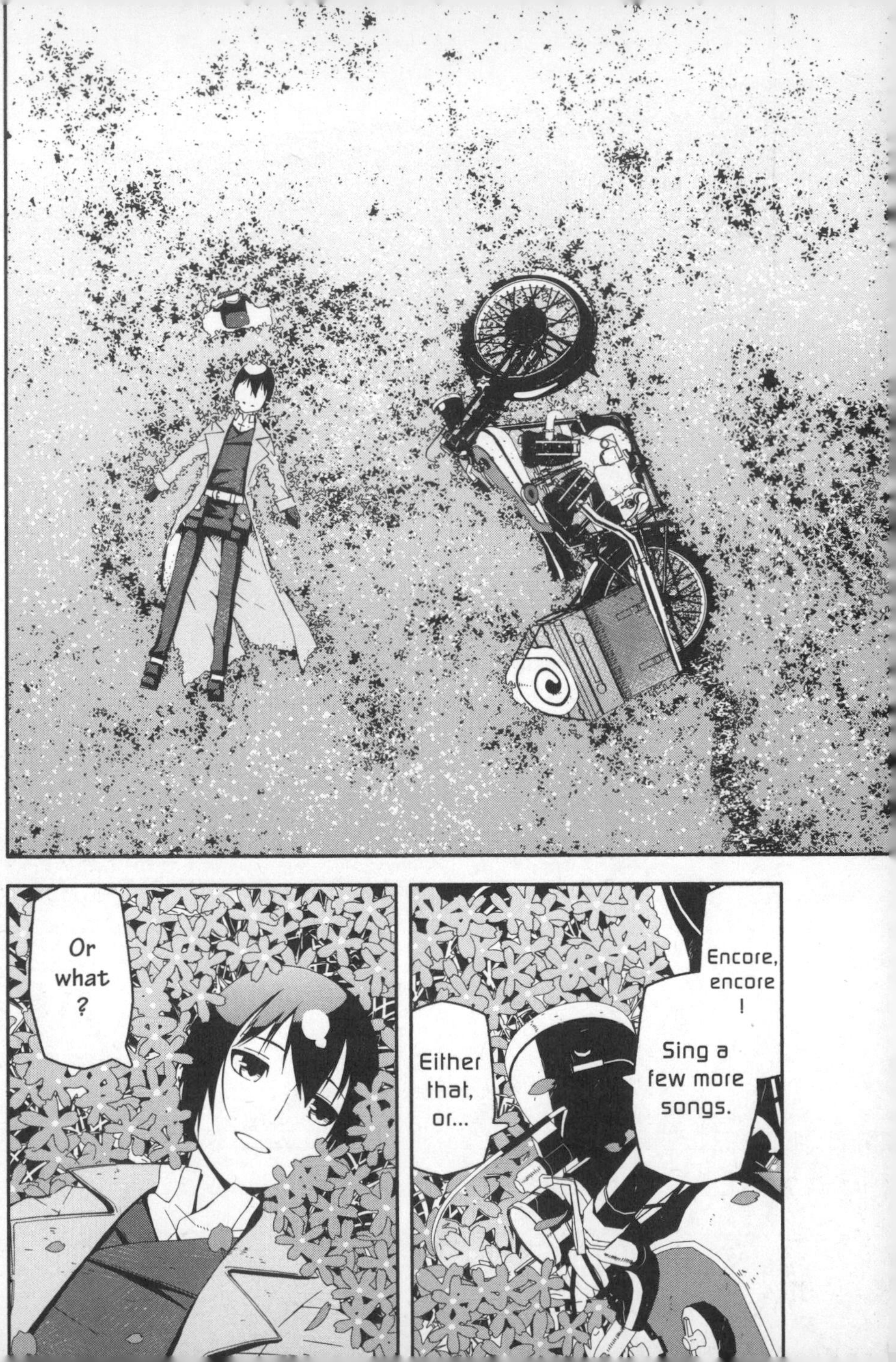
Encore, encore !
Sing a few more songs.
Either that, or...
Or what ?

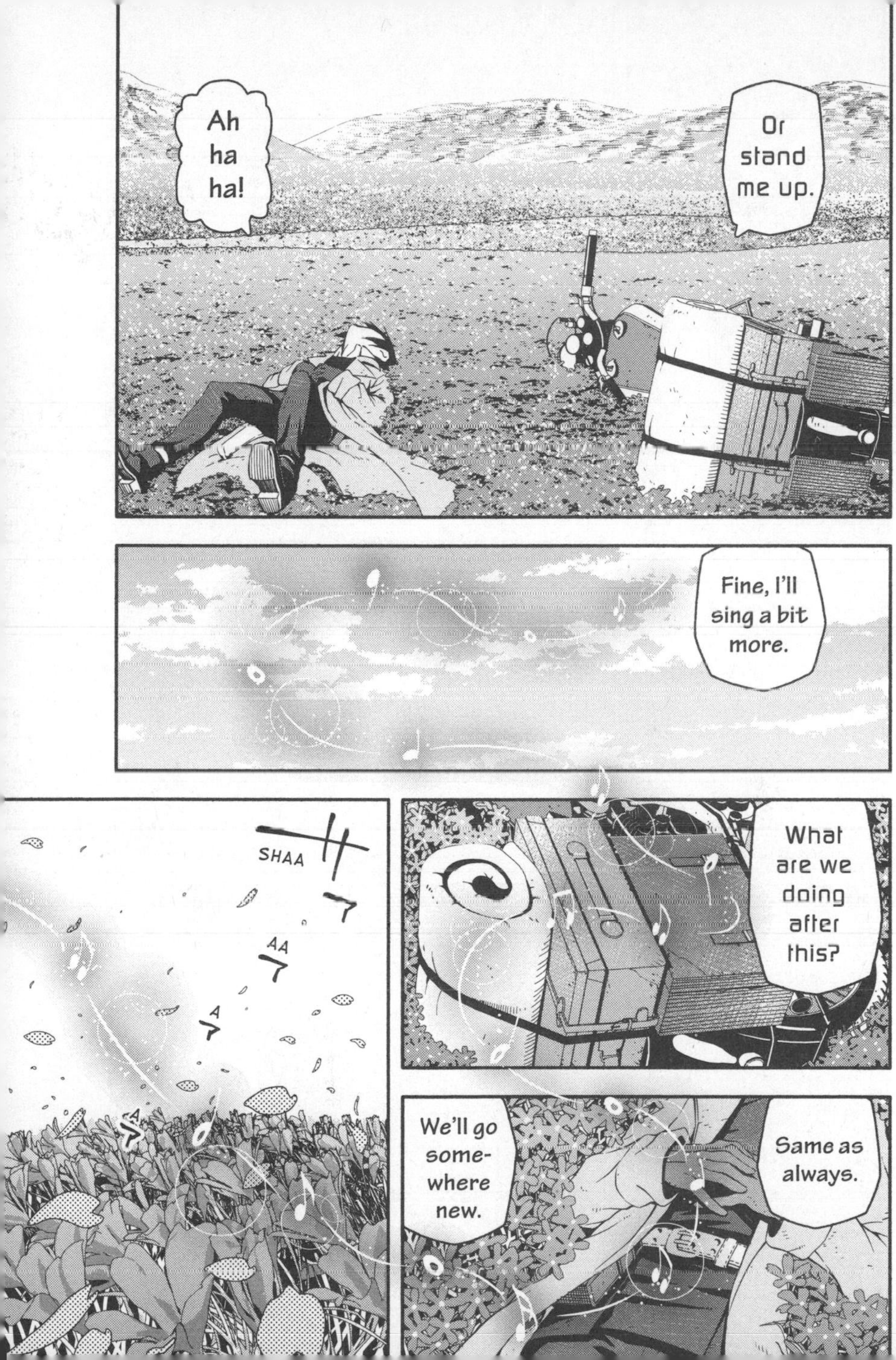

Or stand me up.
Ah ha ha!
Fine, I'll sing a bit more.
What are we doing after this?
Same as always.
We'll go somewhere new.
SHAA
AA
A
A

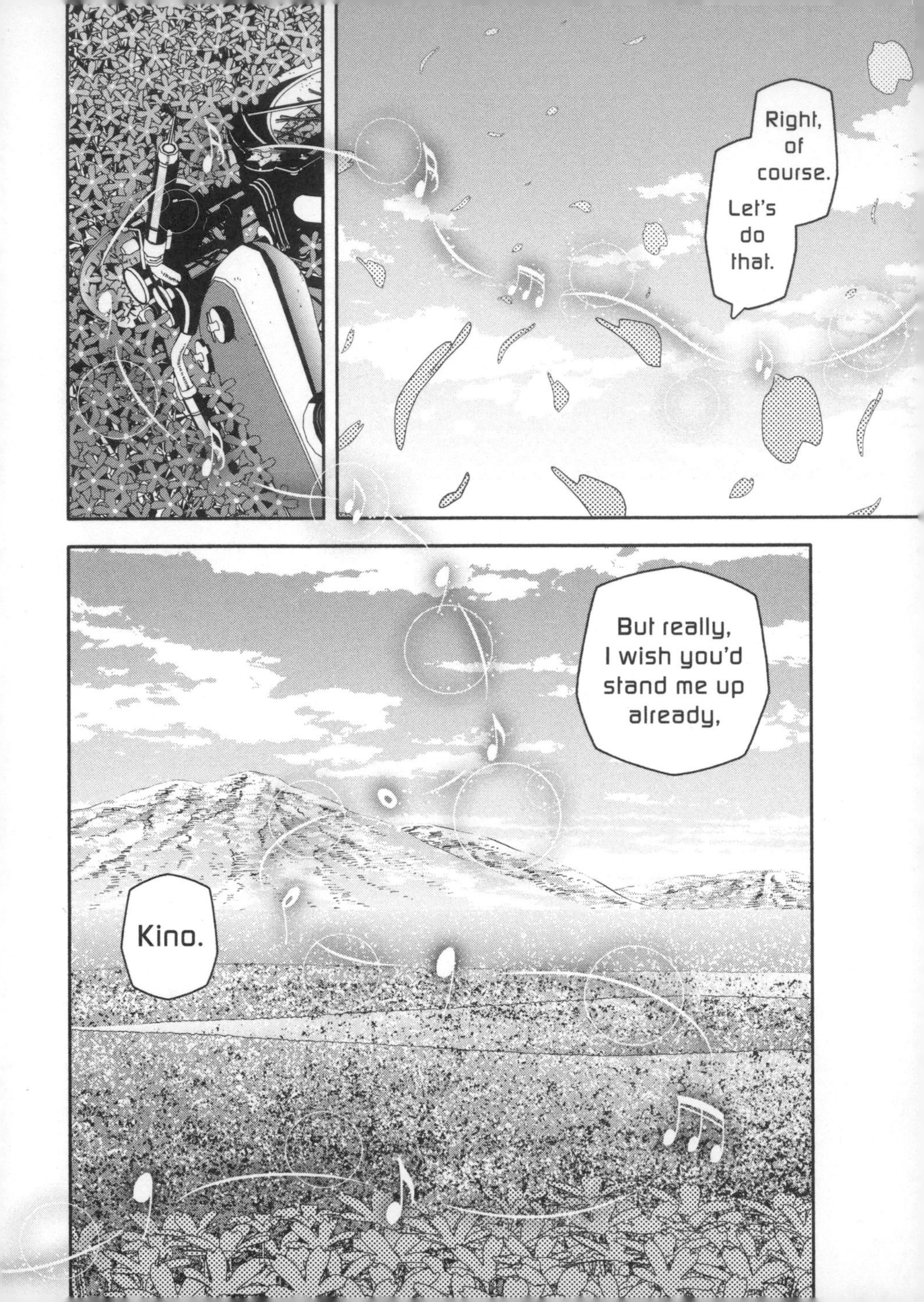
Right, of course.
Let's do that.
But really, I wish you'd stand me up already,
Kino.

Kino's Journey

— The Beautiful World —

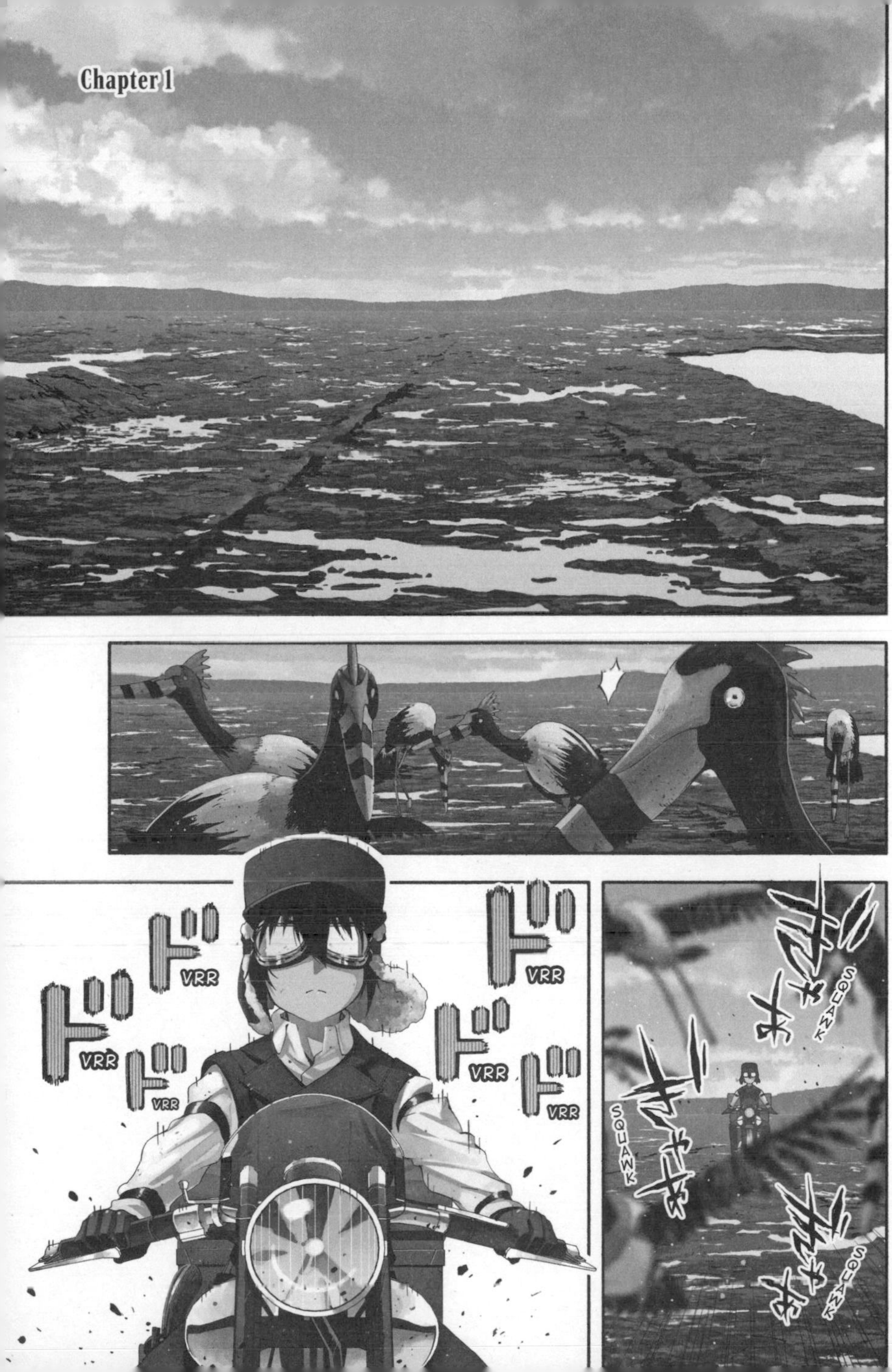
Chapter 1
SQUAWK
SQUAWK
SQUAWK
VRR
VRR
VRR
VRR
VRR
VRR
VRR

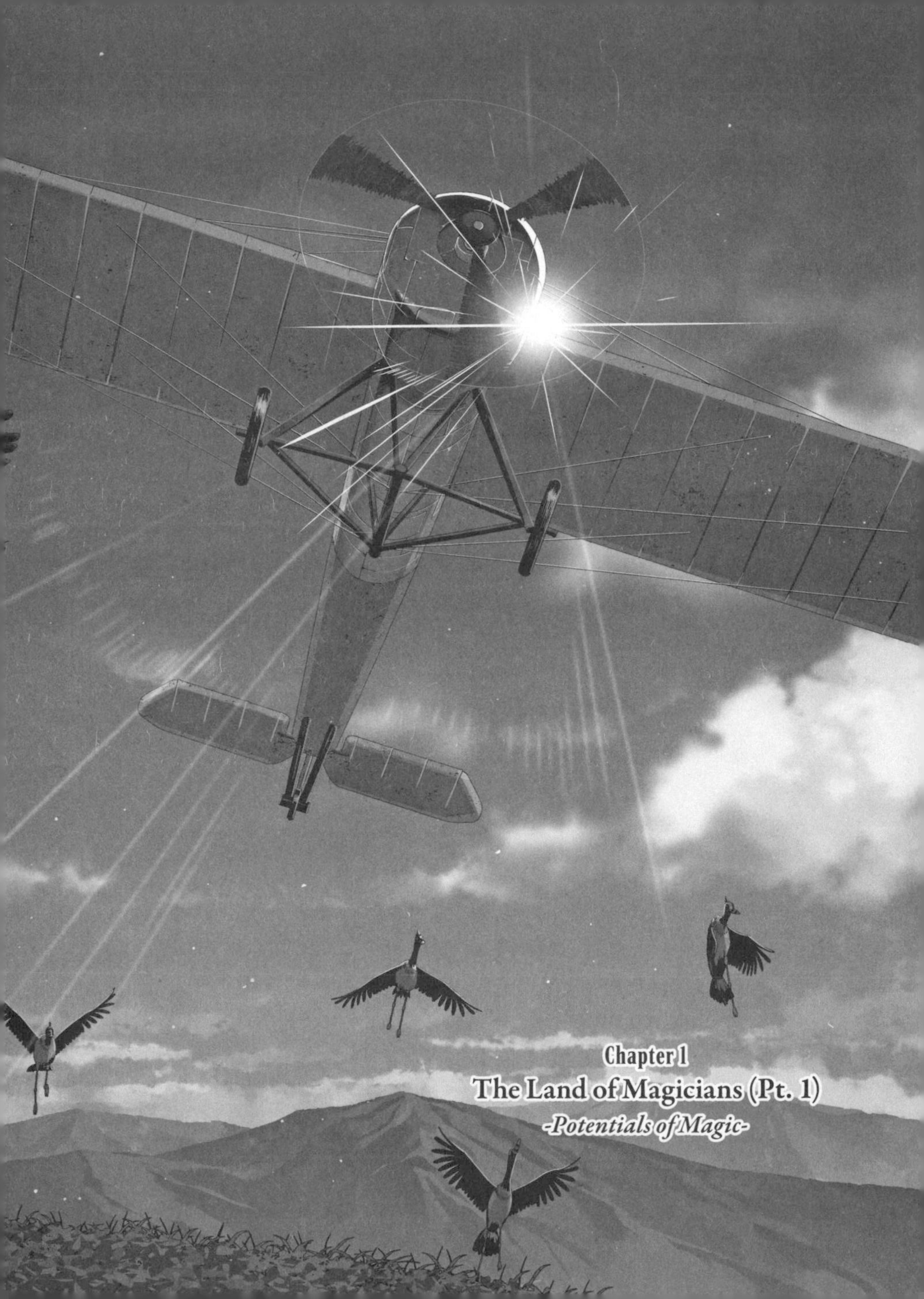
Chapter 1
The Land of Magicians (Pt. 1)
-Potentials of Magic-

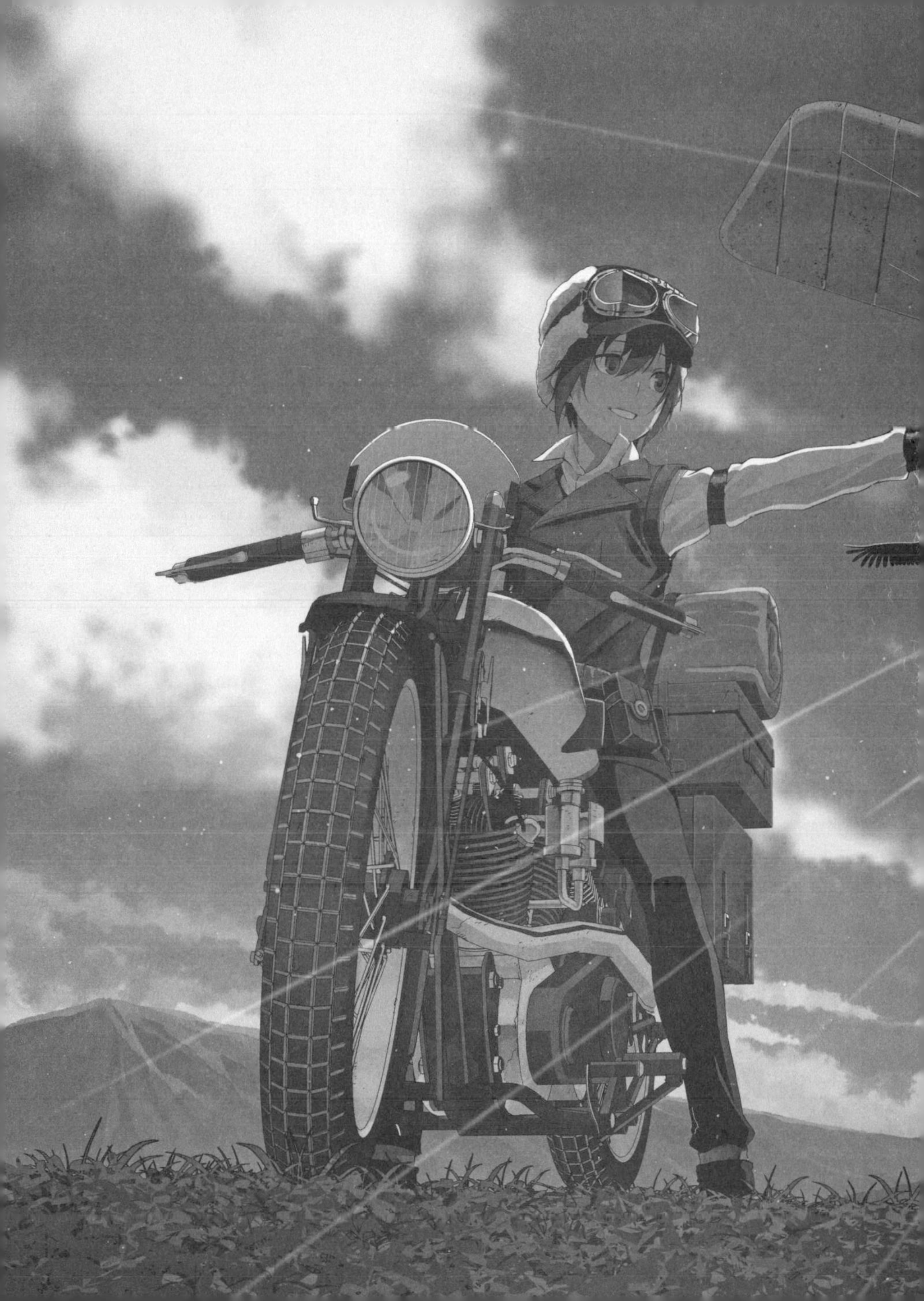

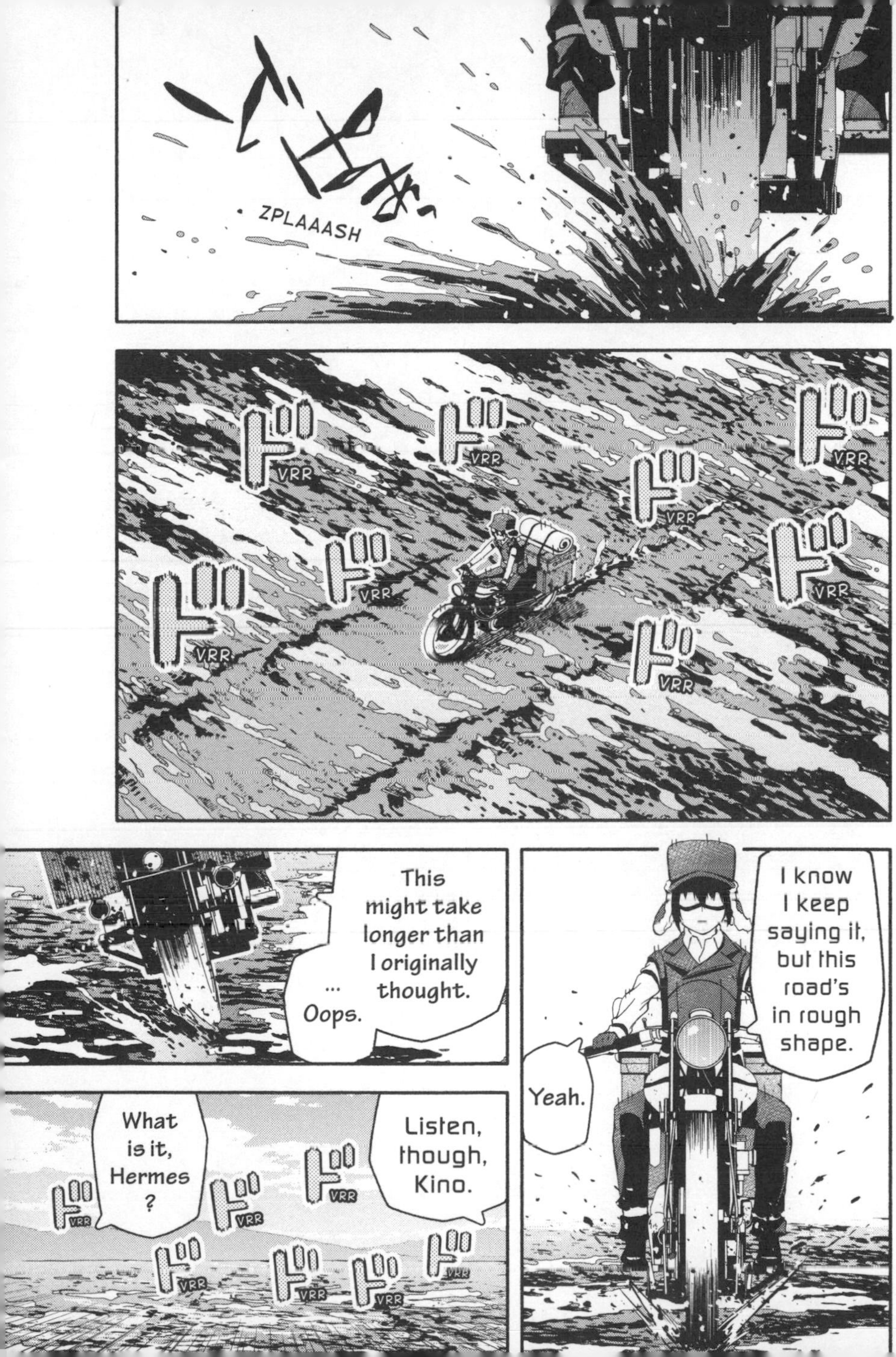
ZPLAASH
VRR
VRR
VRR
VRR
VRR
VRR
VRR
VRR
I know I keep saying it, but this road's in rough shape.
Yeah.
This might take longer than I originally thought.
... Oops.
Listen, though, Kino.
What is it, Hermes?
VRR
VRR
VRR
VRR
VRR
VRR
VRR

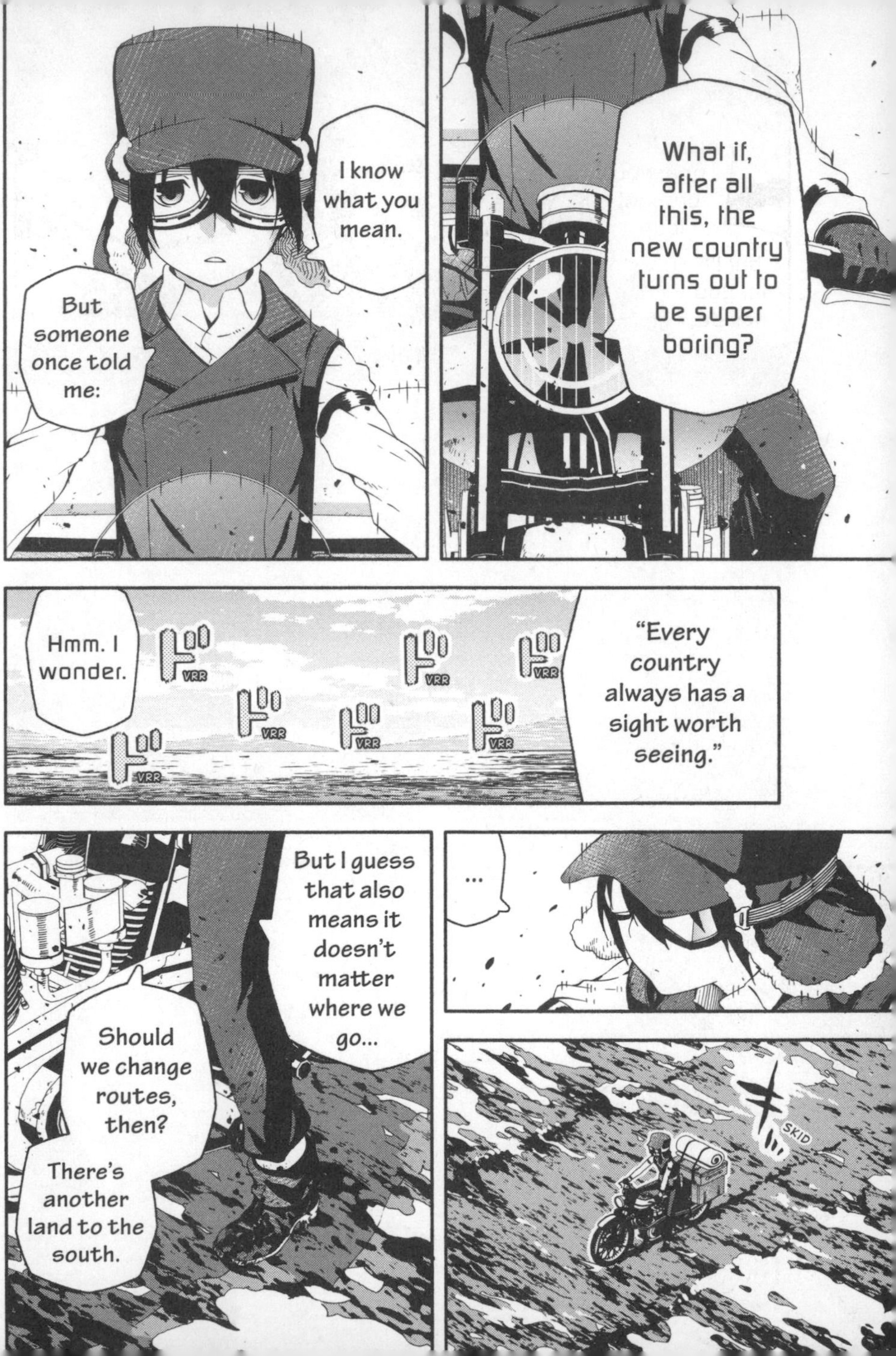
What if, after all this, the new country turns out to be super boring?
I know what you mean.
But someone once told me:
“Every country always has a sight worth seeing.”
ド VRR
ド VRR
ド VRR
ド VRR
ド VRR
ド VRR
ド VRR
Hmm. I wonder.
...
SKID
But I guess that also means it doesn't matter where we go...
Should we change routes, then?
There's another land to the south.

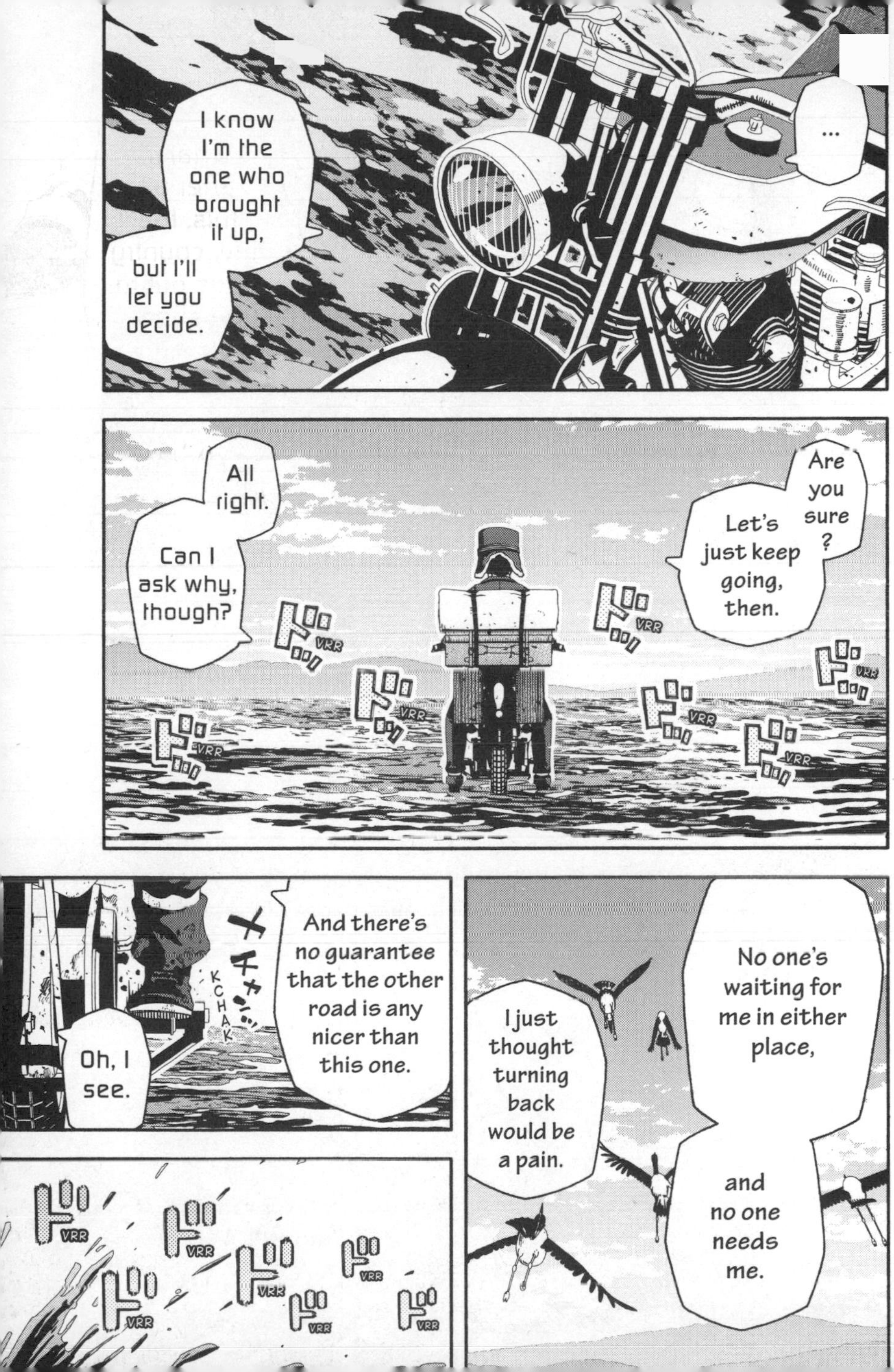
...
I know I'm the one who brought it up,
but I'll let you decide.
Are you sure?
Let's just keep going, then.
VRR
VRR
VRR
VRR
VRR
All right.
Can I ask why, though?
VRR
VRR
VRR
No one's waiting for me in either place,
and no one needs me.
I just thought turning back would be a pain.
And there's no guarantee that the other road is any nicer than this one.
KCHAK
Oh, I see.
VRR
VRR
VRR
VRR
VRR
VRR
VRR
VRR

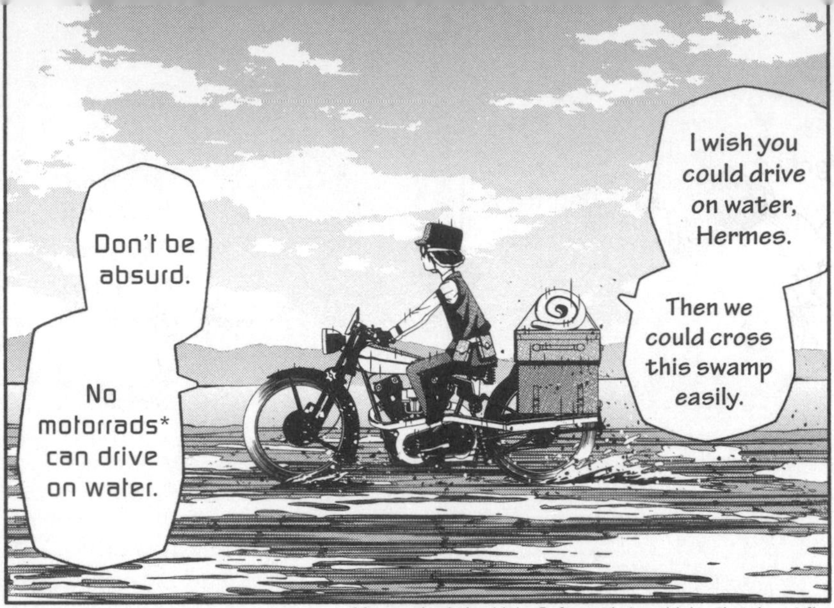
I wish you could drive on water, Hermes.
Then we could cross this swamp easily.
Don't be absurd.
No motorrads* can drive on water.

*A two-wheeled vehicle. Refers only to vehicles that do not fly.

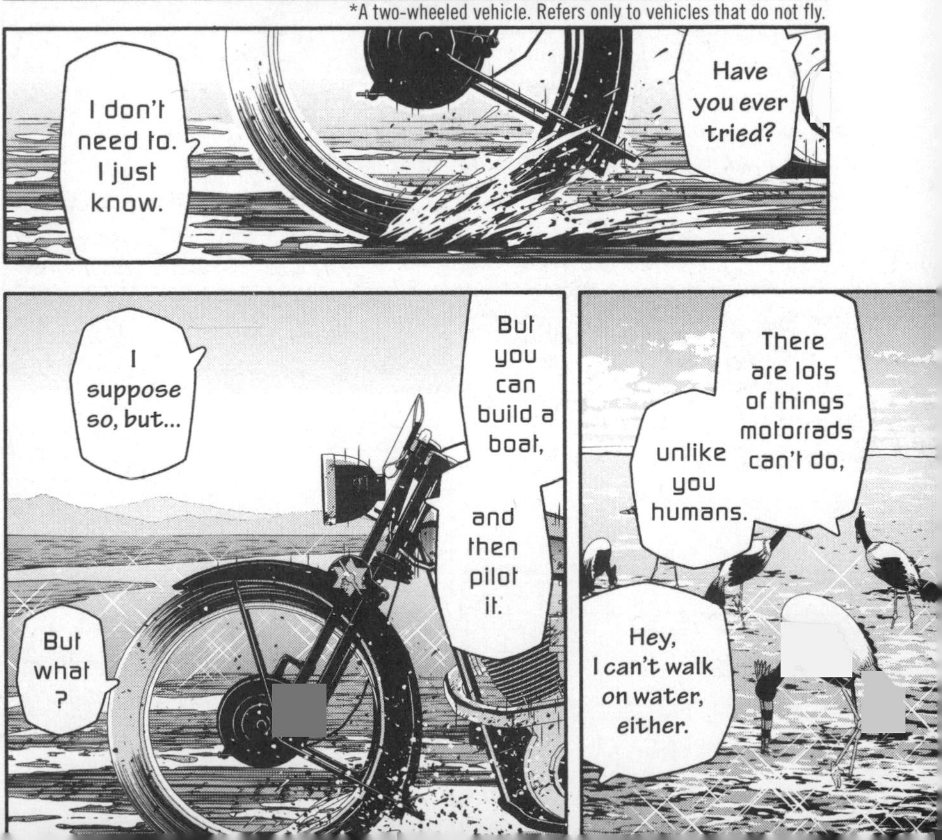
Have you ever tried?
I don't need to. I just know.
There are lots of things motorrads can't do, unlike you humans.
Hey, I can't walk on water, either.
But you can build a boat,
and then pilot it.
I suppose so, but...
But what?

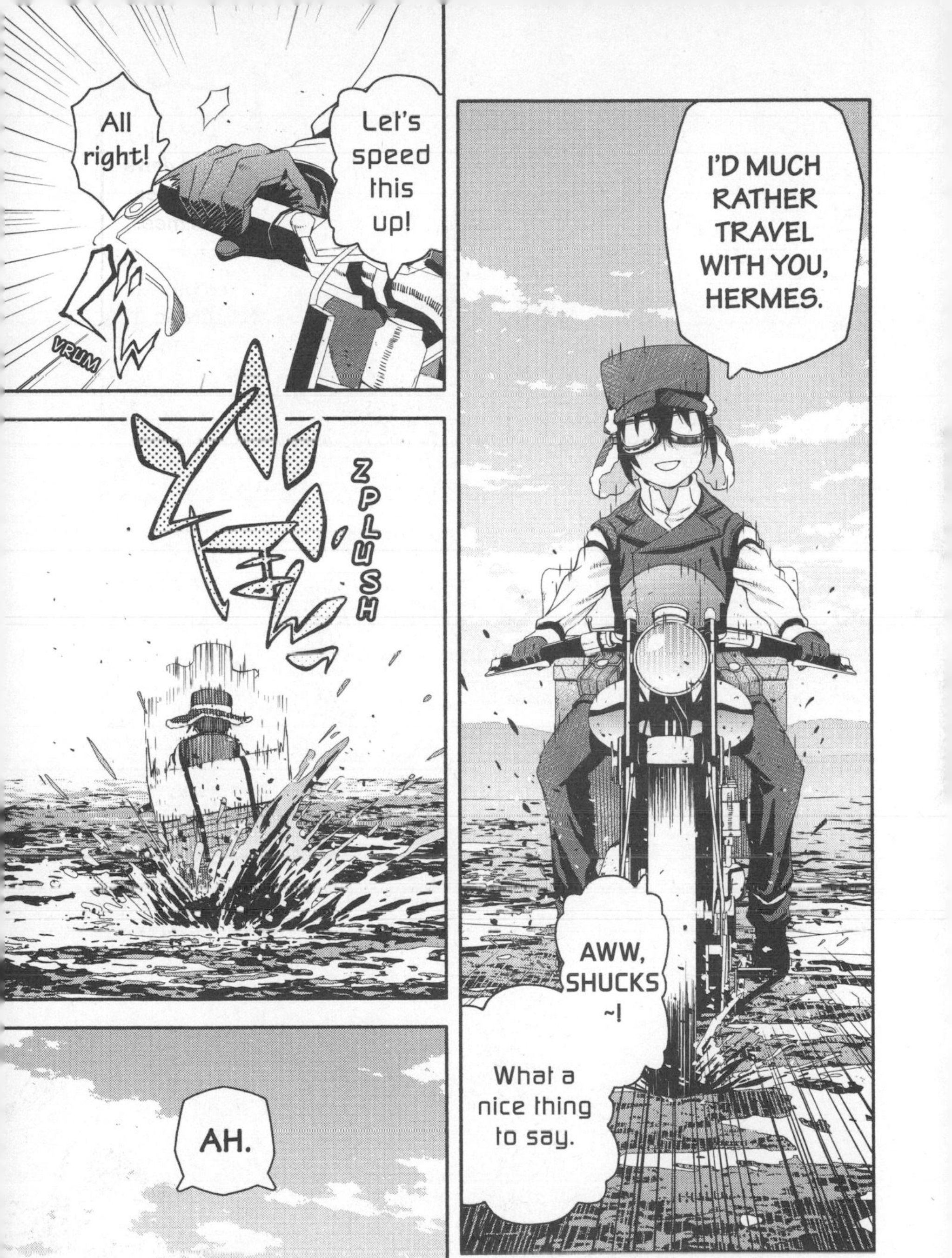
I'D MUCH RATHER TRAVEL WITH YOU, HERMES.
AWW, SHUCKS ~!
What a nice thing to say.
Let's speed this up!
All right!
VRUM
ZPLUSH
AH.

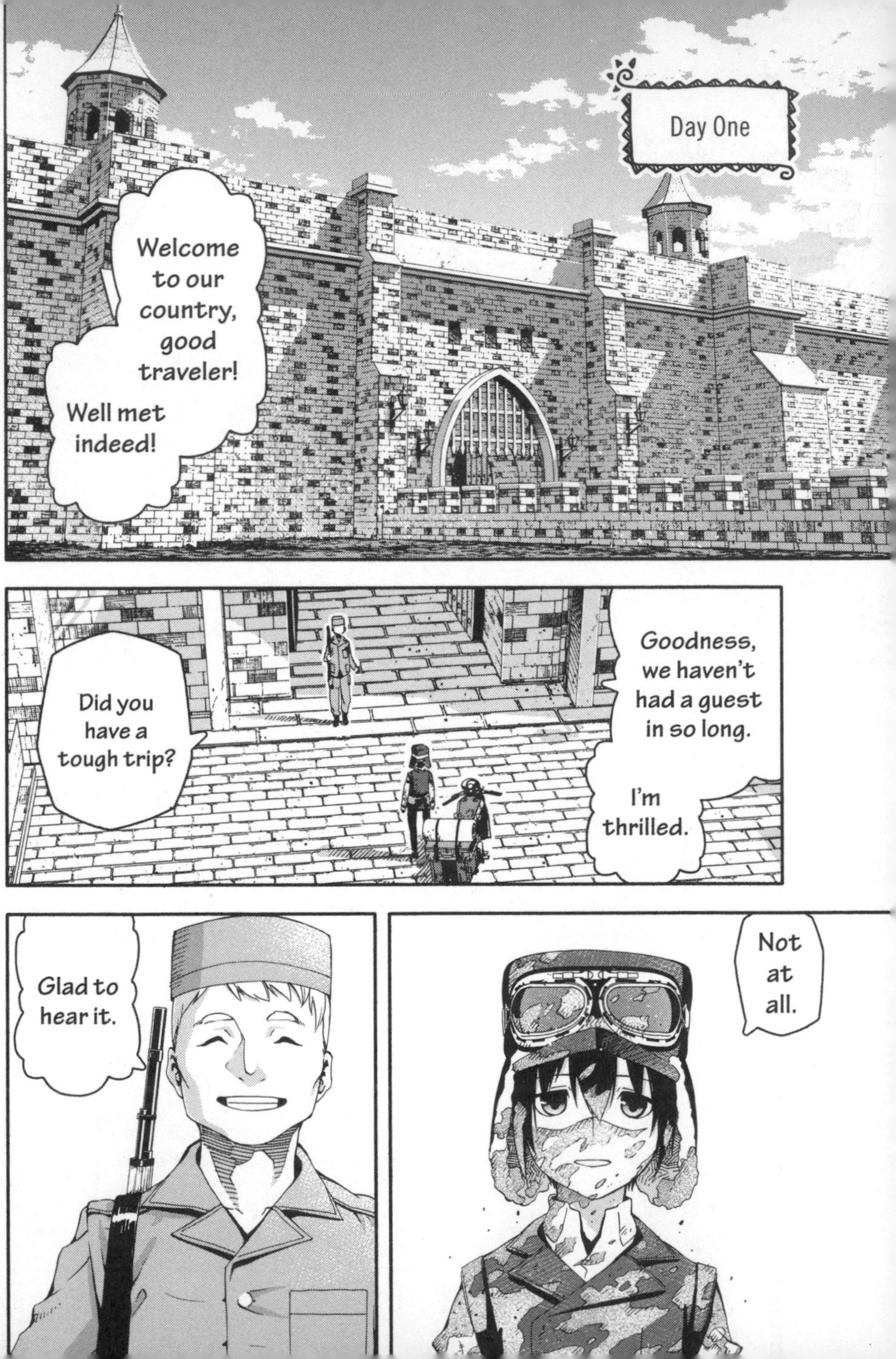
Day One
Welcome to our country, good traveler!
Well met indeed!
Goodness, we haven't had a guest in so long.
I'm thrilled.
Did you have a tough trip?
Not at all.
Glad to hear it.

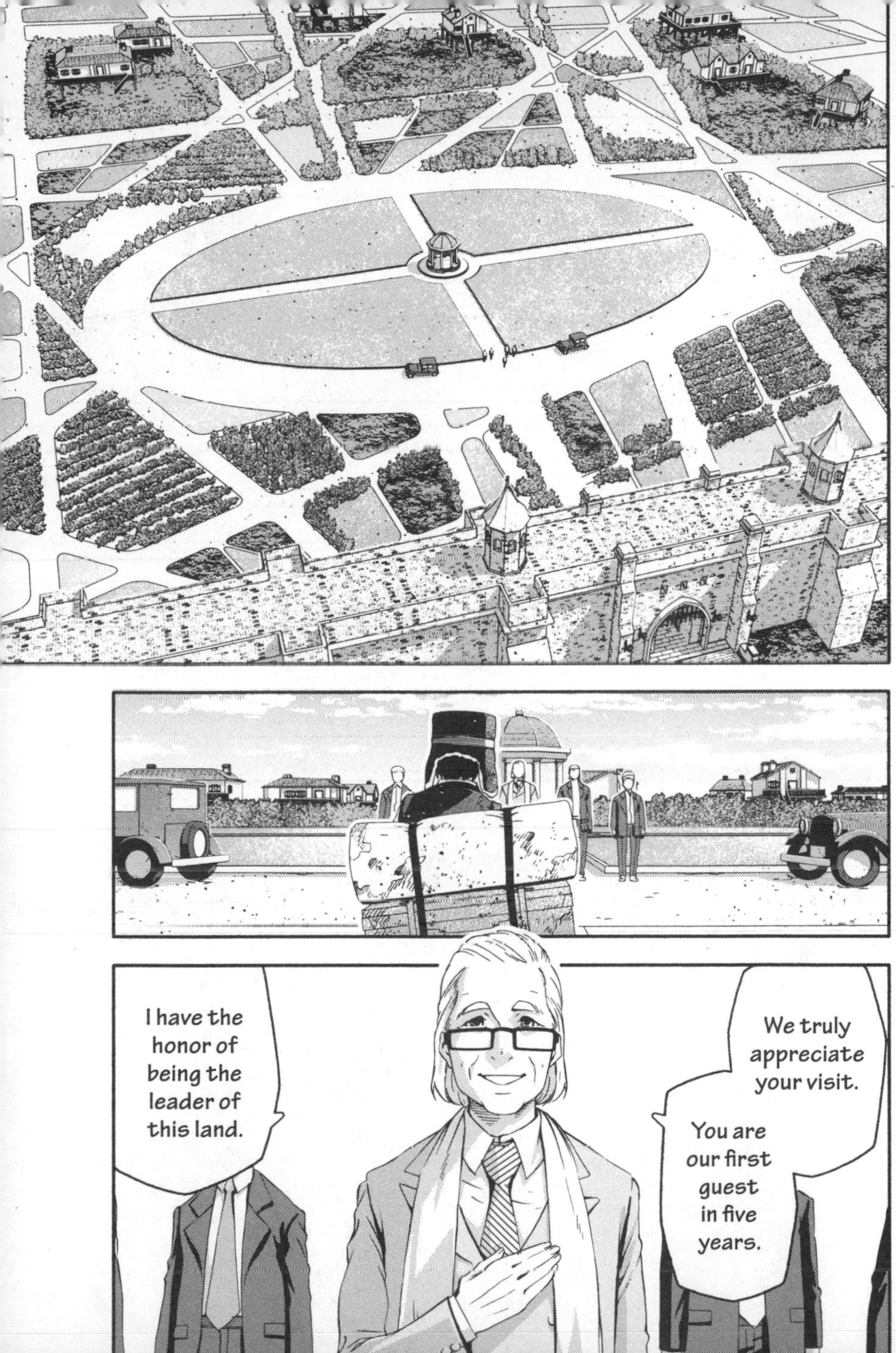

We truly appreciate your visit.
You are our first guest in five years.
I have the honor of being the leader of this land.

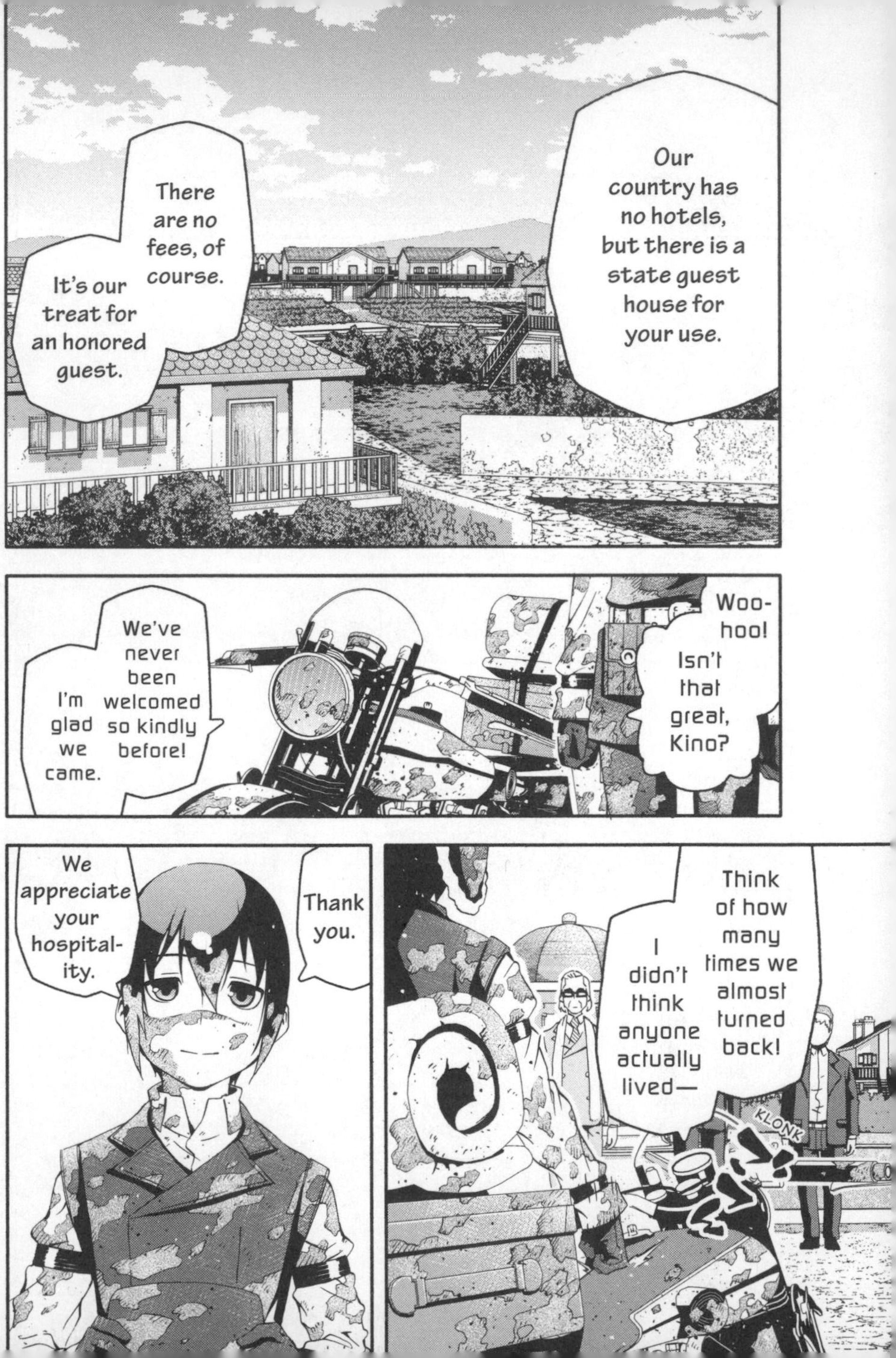
Our country has no hotels, but there is a state guest house for your use.
There are no fees, of course.
It's our treat for an honored guest.
Woo-hoo! Isn't that great, Kino?
We've never been welcomed so kindly before!
I'm glad we came.
Think of how many times we almost turned back!
I didn't think anyone actually lived—
KLONK
Thank you.
We appreciate your hospital-ity.

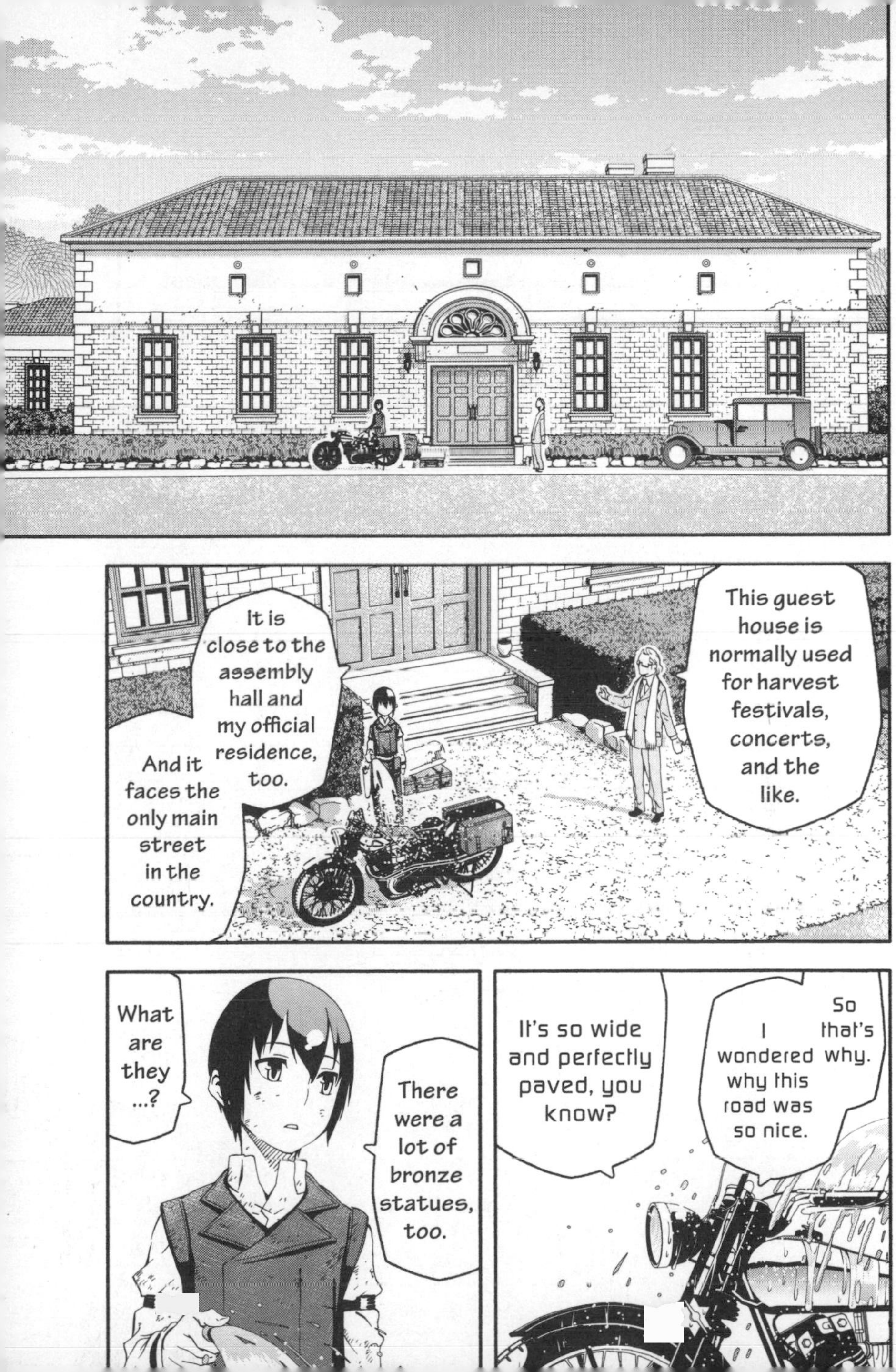
This guest house is normally used for harvest festivals, concerts, and the like.
It is close to the assembly hall and my official residence, too.
And it faces the only main street in the country.
So that's why.
I wondered why this road was so nice.
It's so wide and perfectly paved, you know?
There were a lot of bronze statues, too.
What are they ...?

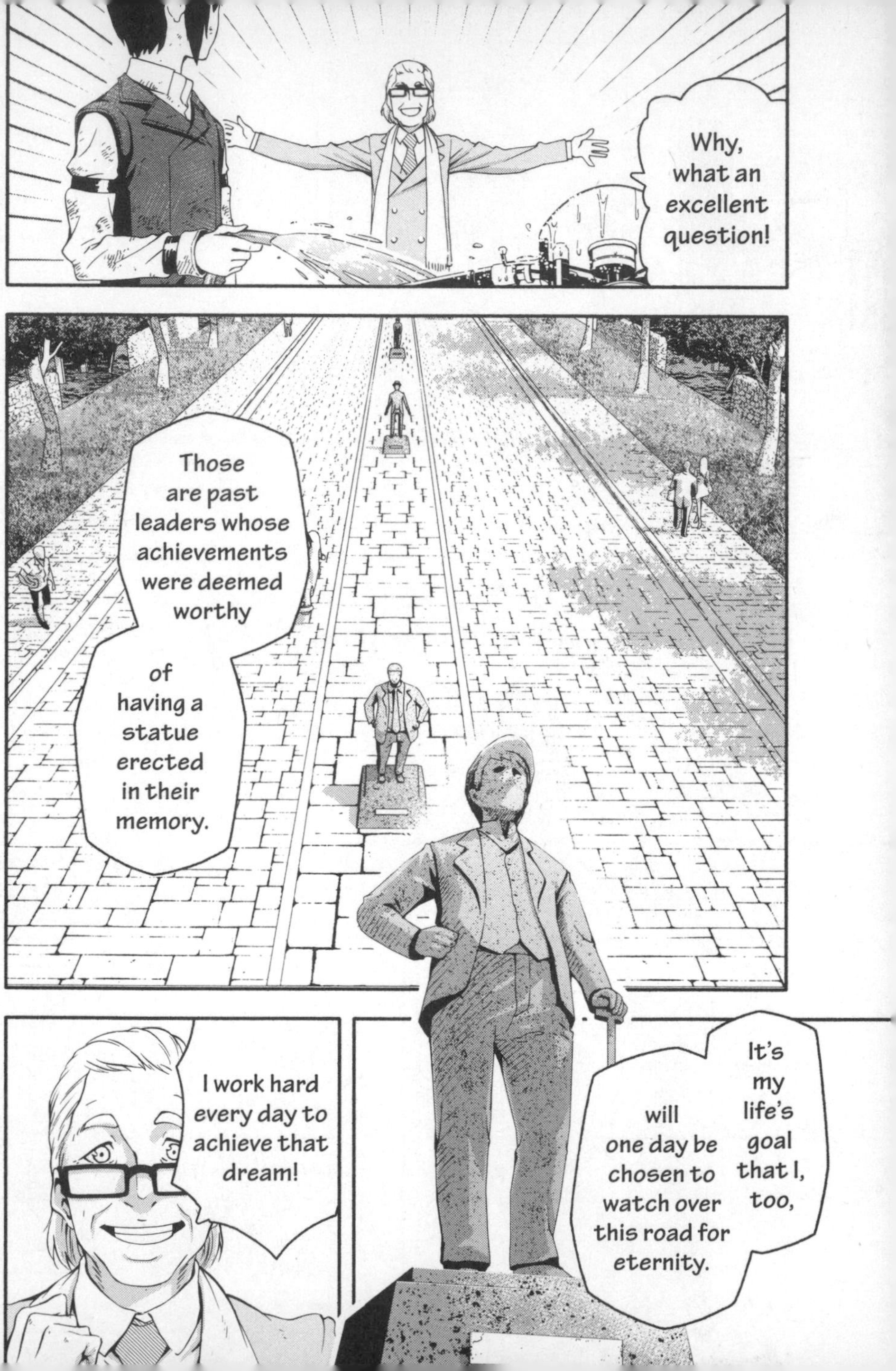
Why, what an excellent question!
Those are past leaders whose achievements were deemed worthy
of having a statue erected in their memory.
It's my life's goal that I, too,
will one day be chosen to watch over this road for eternity.
I work hard every day to achieve that dream!

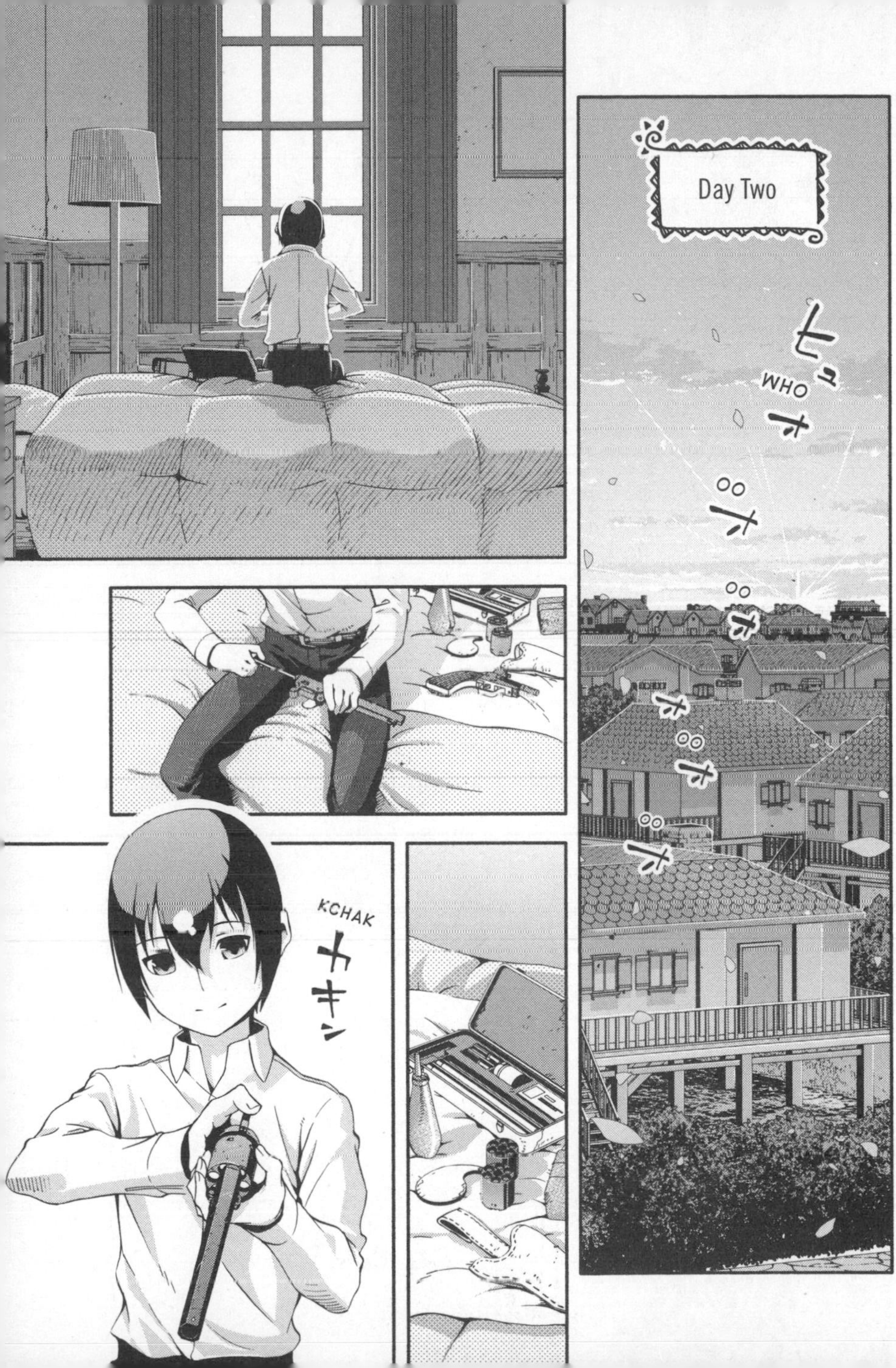
Day Two
ヒュオオオオオオ
WHO
oo
oo
oo
oo
KCHAK
カキン

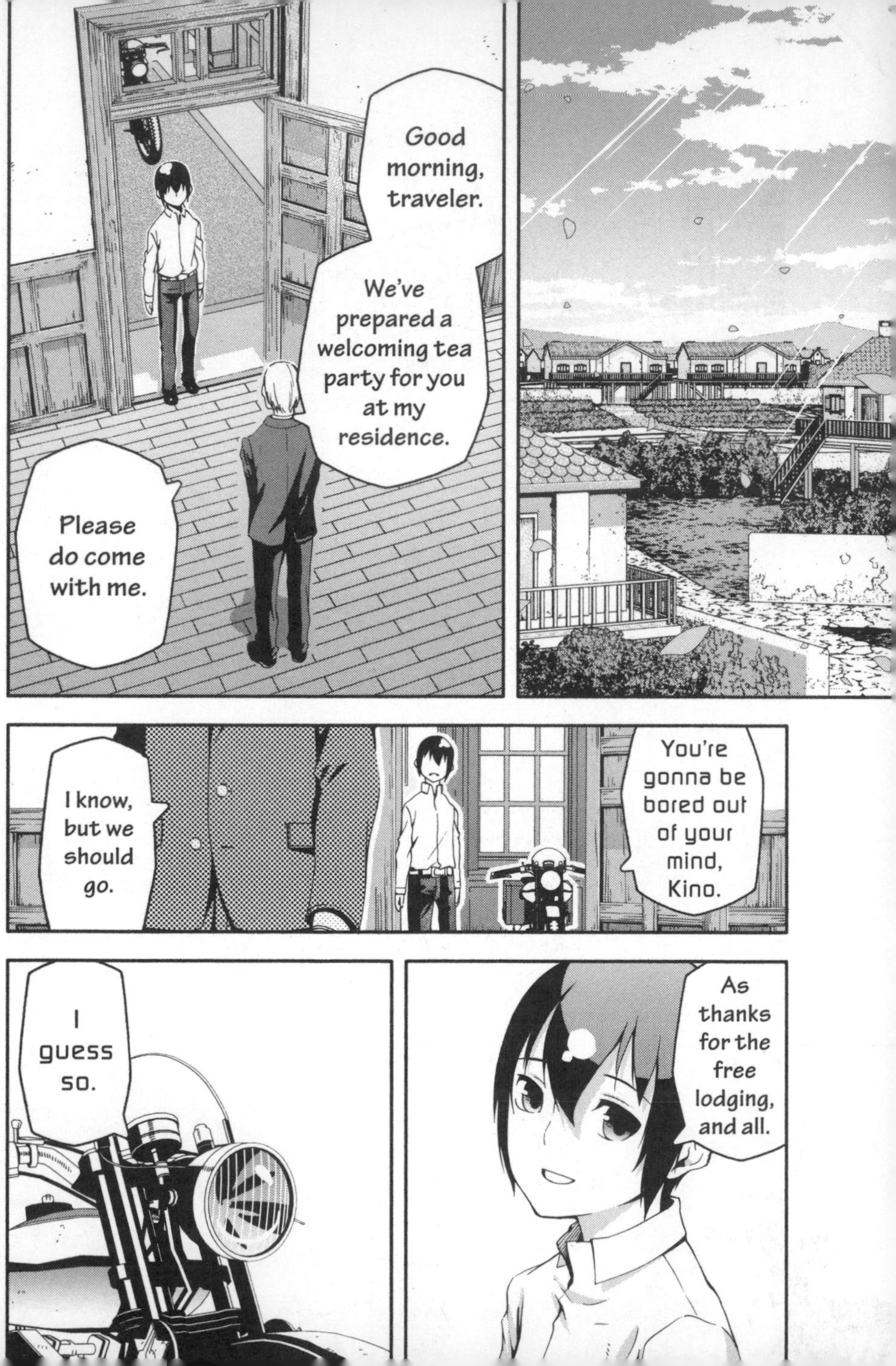
Good morning, traveler.
We've prepared a welcoming tea party for you at my residence.
Please do come with me.
You're gonna be bored out of your mind, Kino.
I know, but we should go.
As thanks for the free lodging, and all.
I guess so.

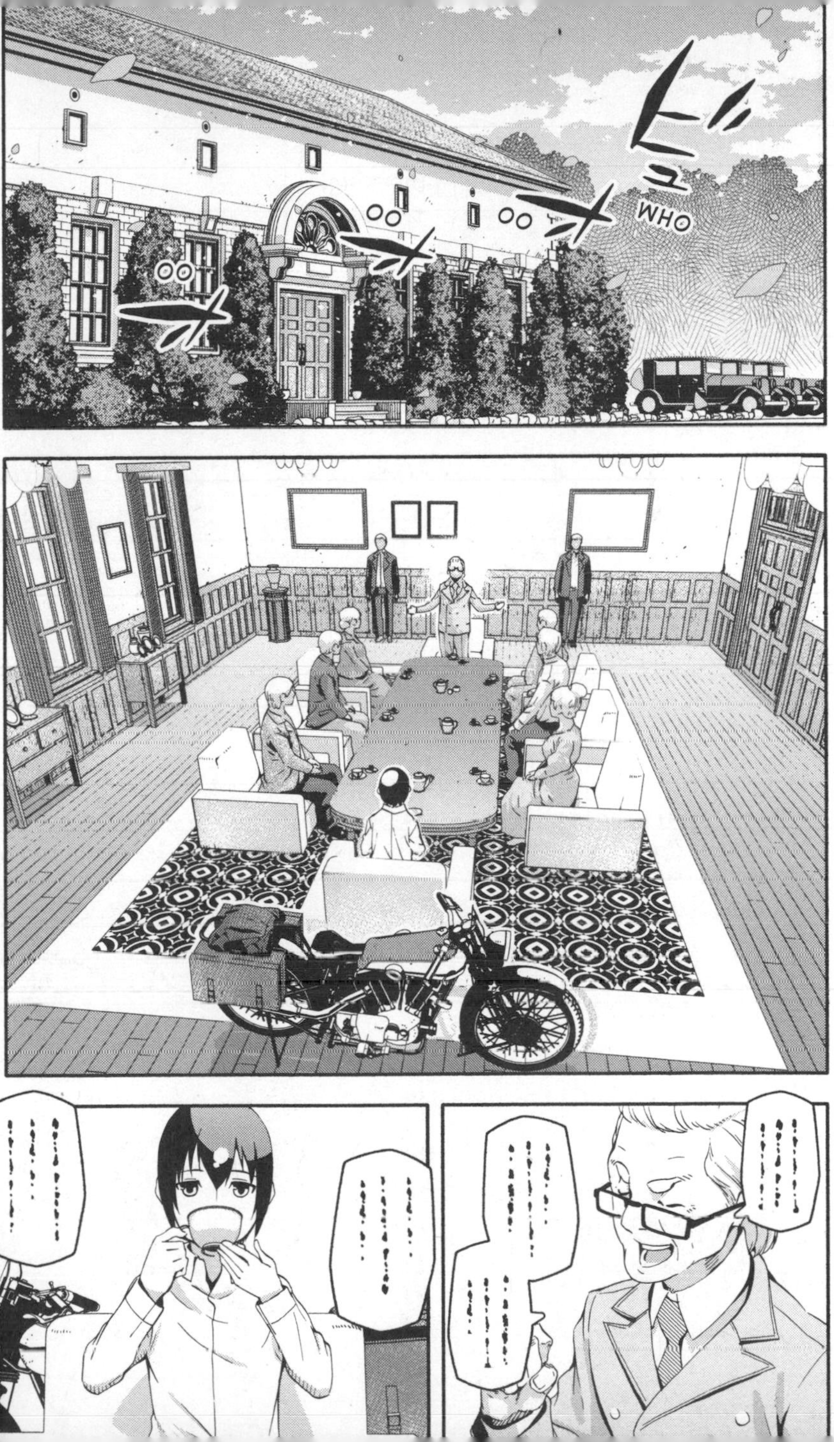
WHO

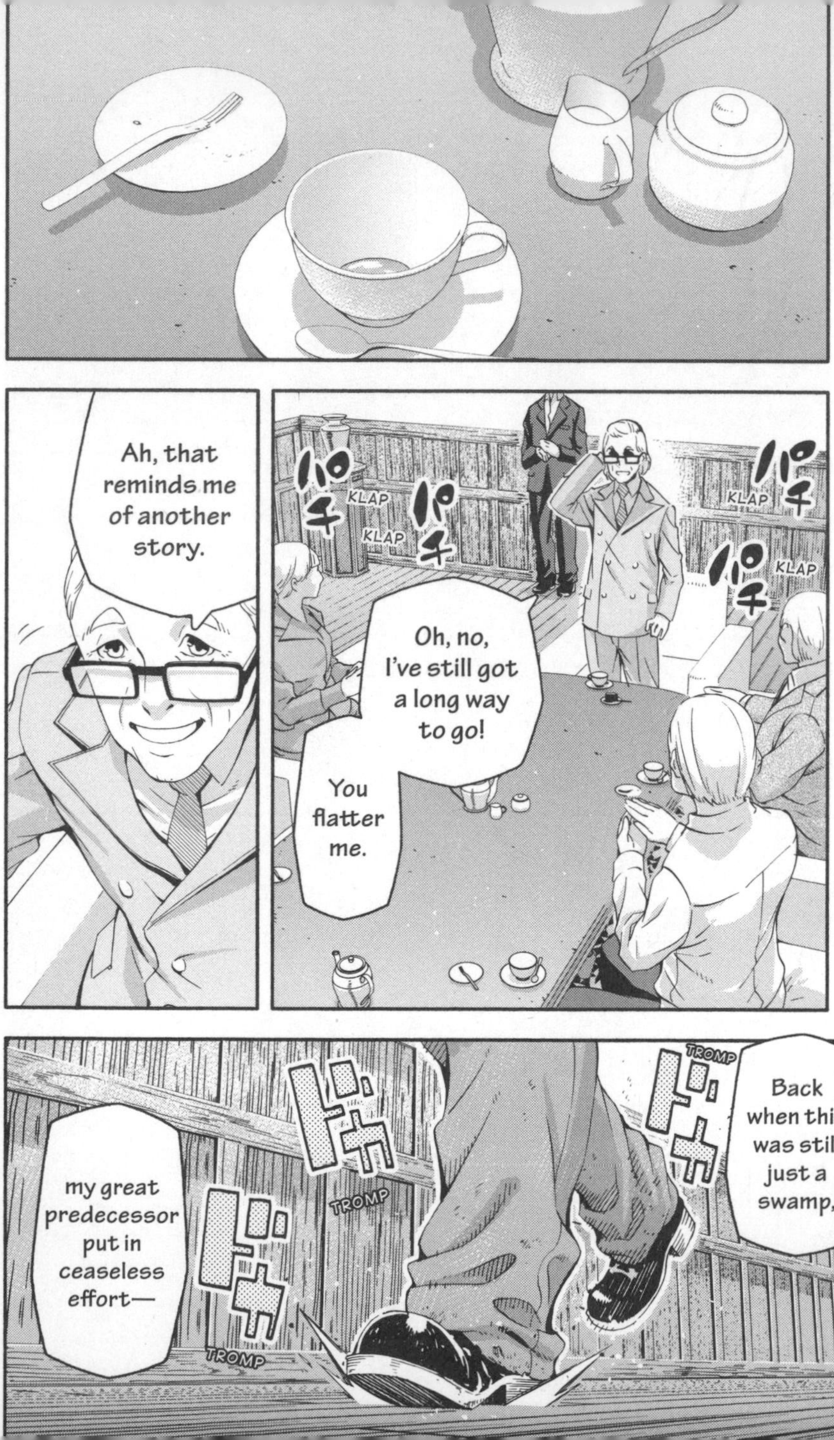
パチ
KLAP
パチ
KLAP
パチ
KLAP
パチ
KLAP
Oh, no, I've still got a long way to go!
You flatter me.
Ah, that reminds me of another story.
TROMP
Back when this was still just a swamp,
TROMP
my great predecessor put in ceaseless effort—
TROMP

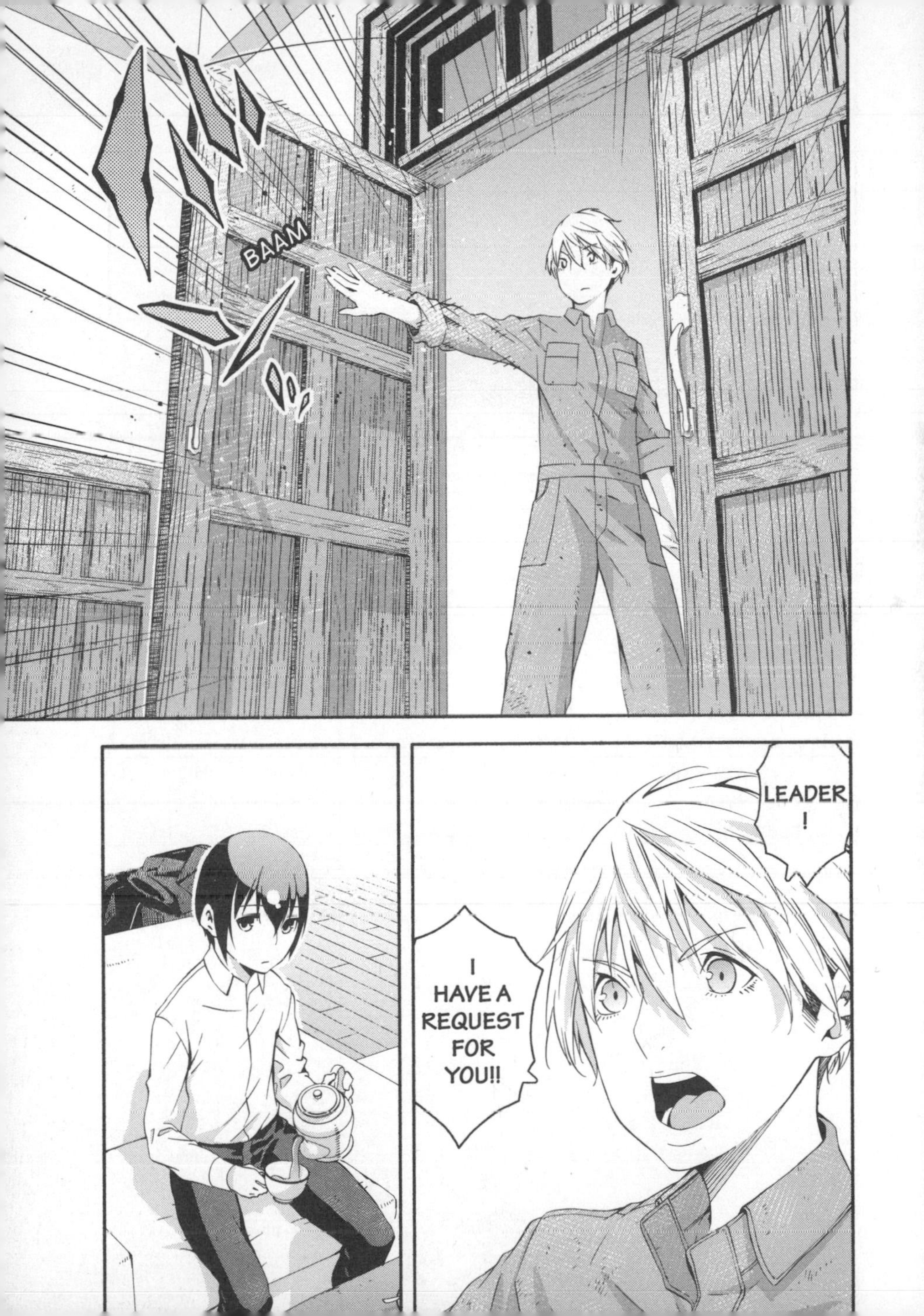
BAAM
LEADER!
I HAVE A REQUEST FOR YOU!!

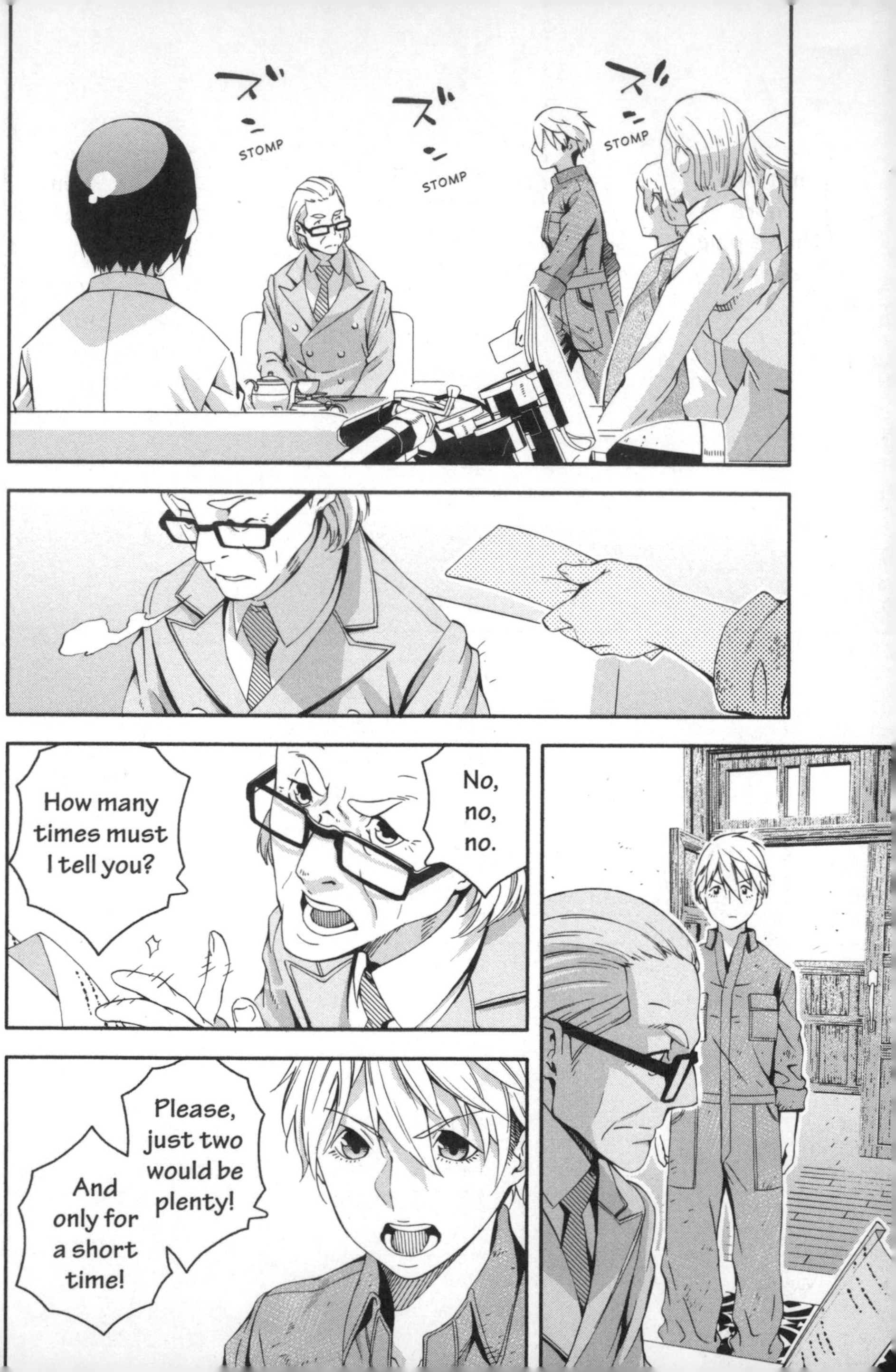
ズ
STOMP
ズ
STOMP
ズ
STOMP
No, no, no.
How many times must I tell you?
Please, just two would be plenty!
And only for a short time!

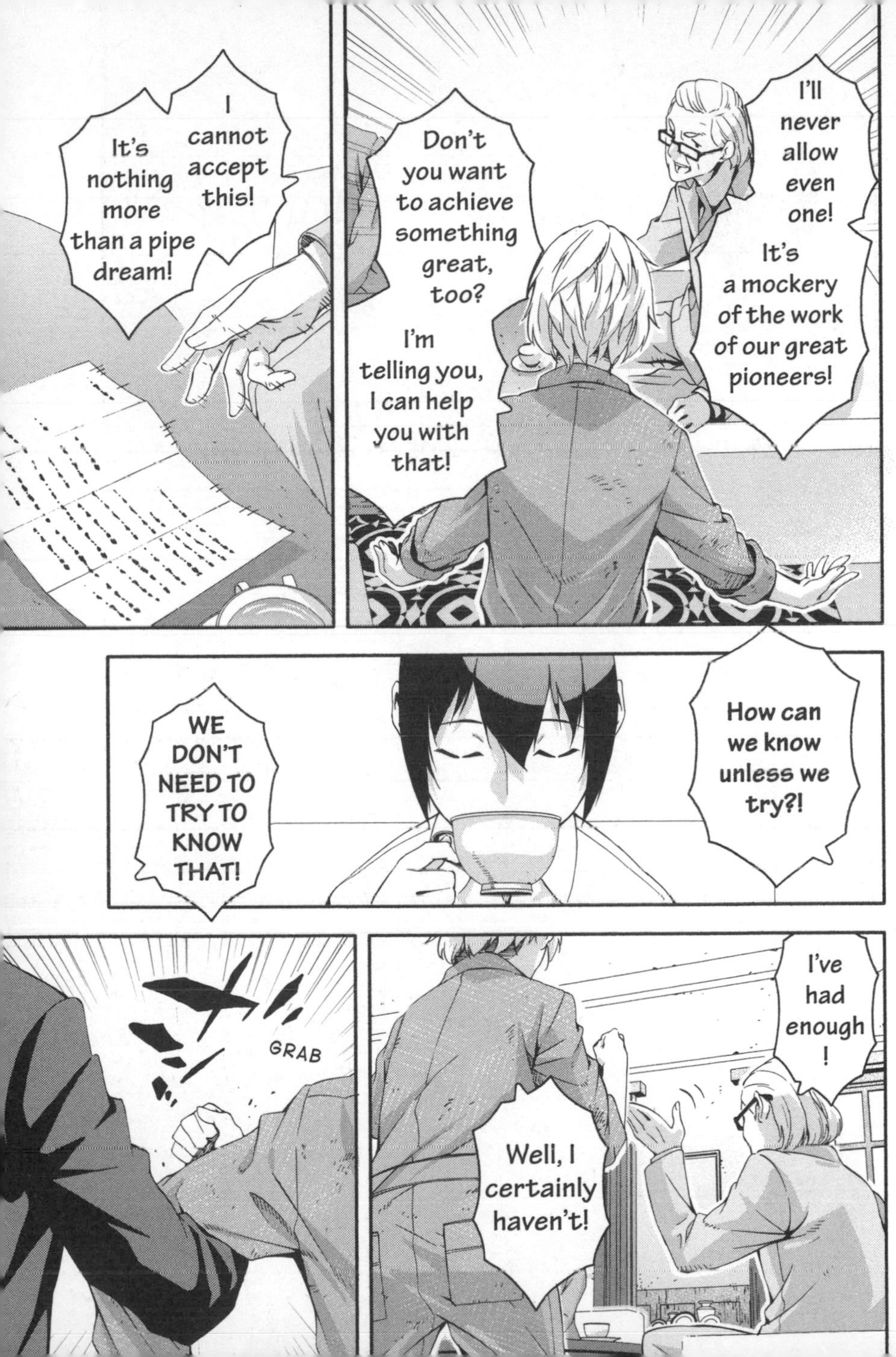
I'll never allow even one!
It's a mockery of the work of our great pioneers!
Don't you want to achieve something great, too?
I'm telling you, I can help you with that!
I cannot accept this!
It's nothing more than a pipe dream!
How can we know unless we try?!
WE DON'T NEED TO TRY TO KNOW THAT!
I've had enough!
Well, I certainly haven't!
GRAB

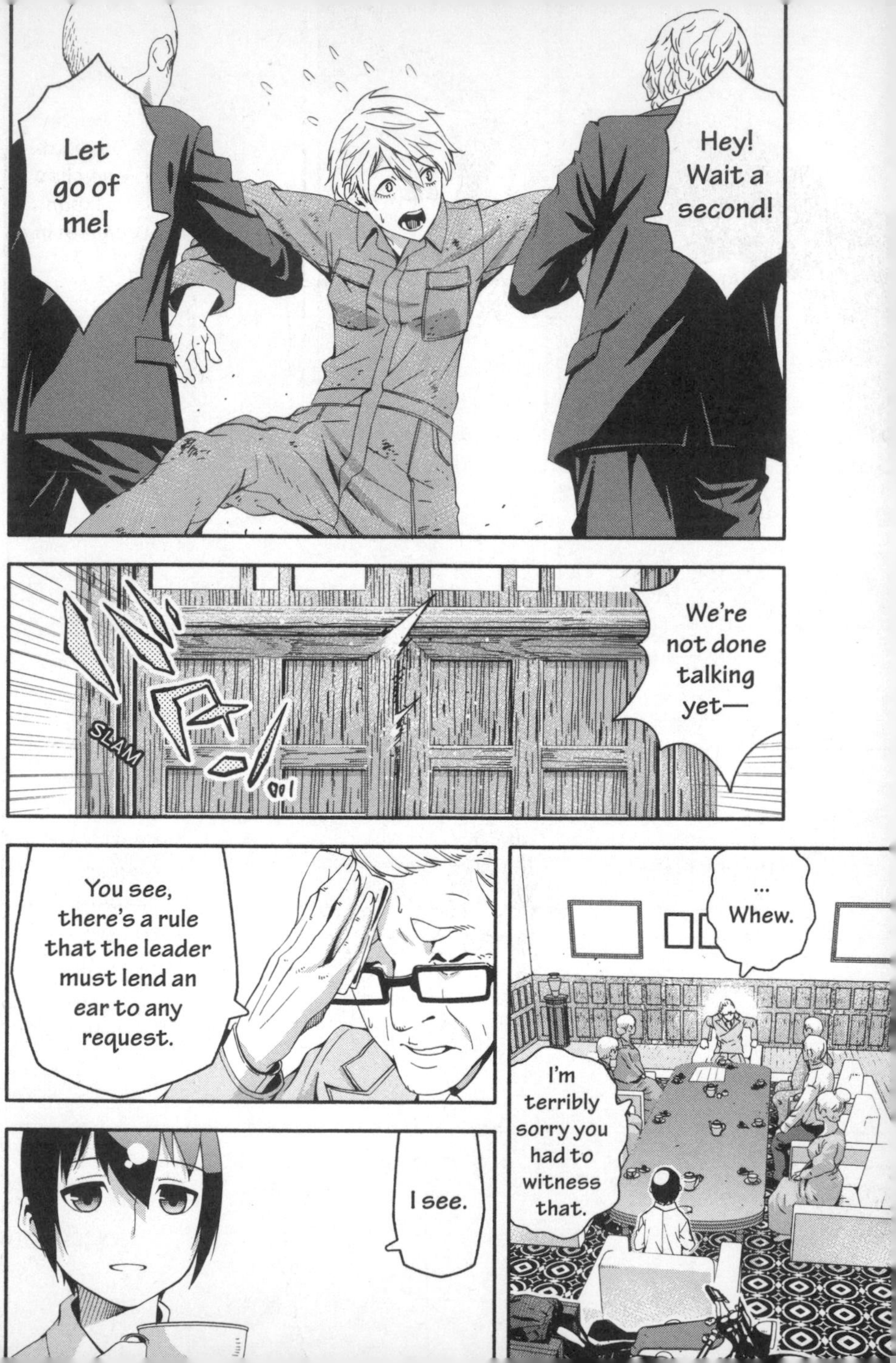
Hey! Wait a second!
Let go of me!
We're not done talking yet—
SLAM
... Whew.
I'm terribly sorry you had to witness that.
You see, there's a rule that the leader must lend an ear to any request.
I see.

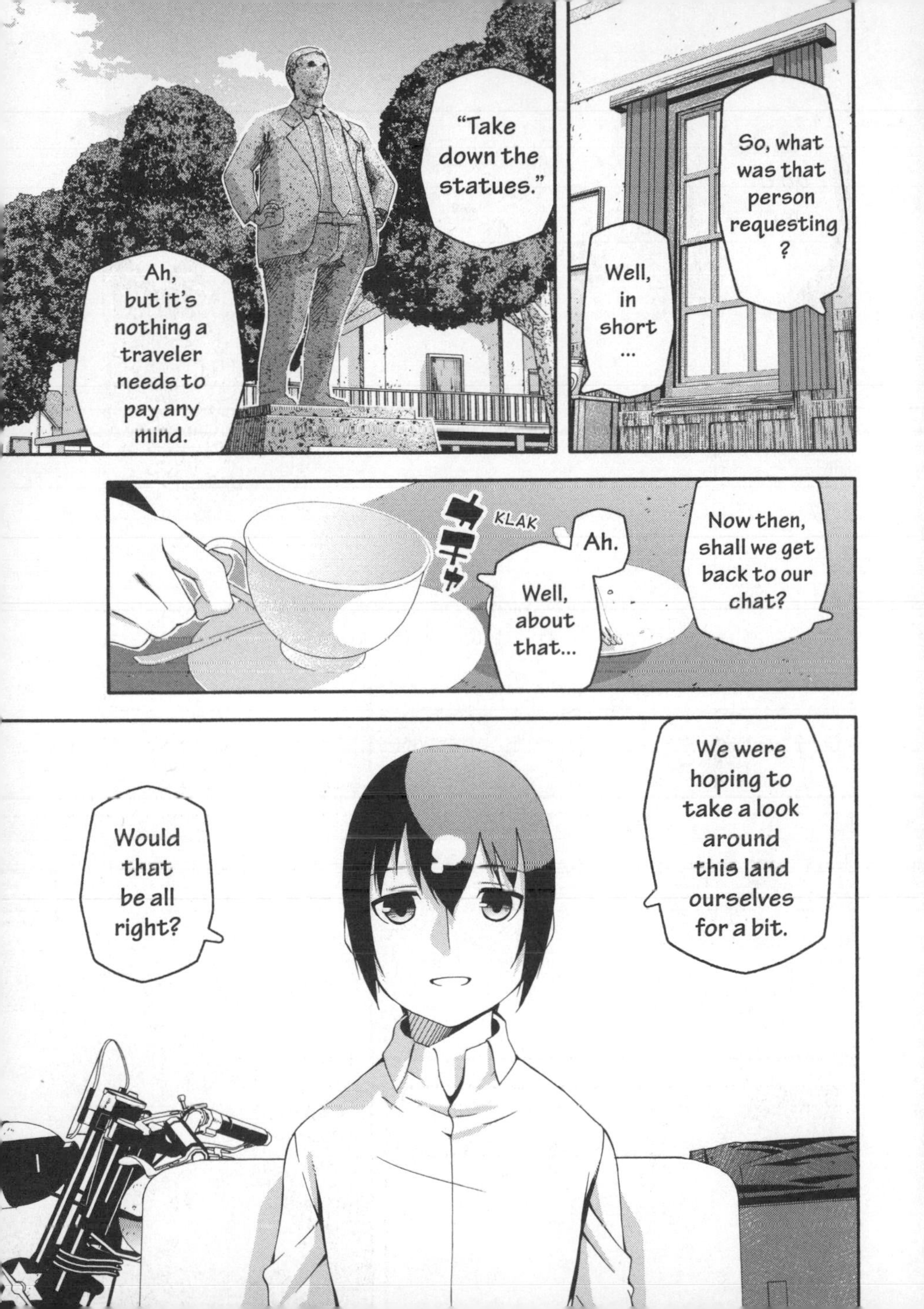

So, what was that person requesting?
Well, in short...
“Take down the statues.”
Ah, but it’s nothing a traveler needs to pay any mind.
Now then, shall we get back to our chat?
Ah.
KLAK
Well, about that...
We were hoping to take a look around this land ourselves for a bit.
Would that be all right?

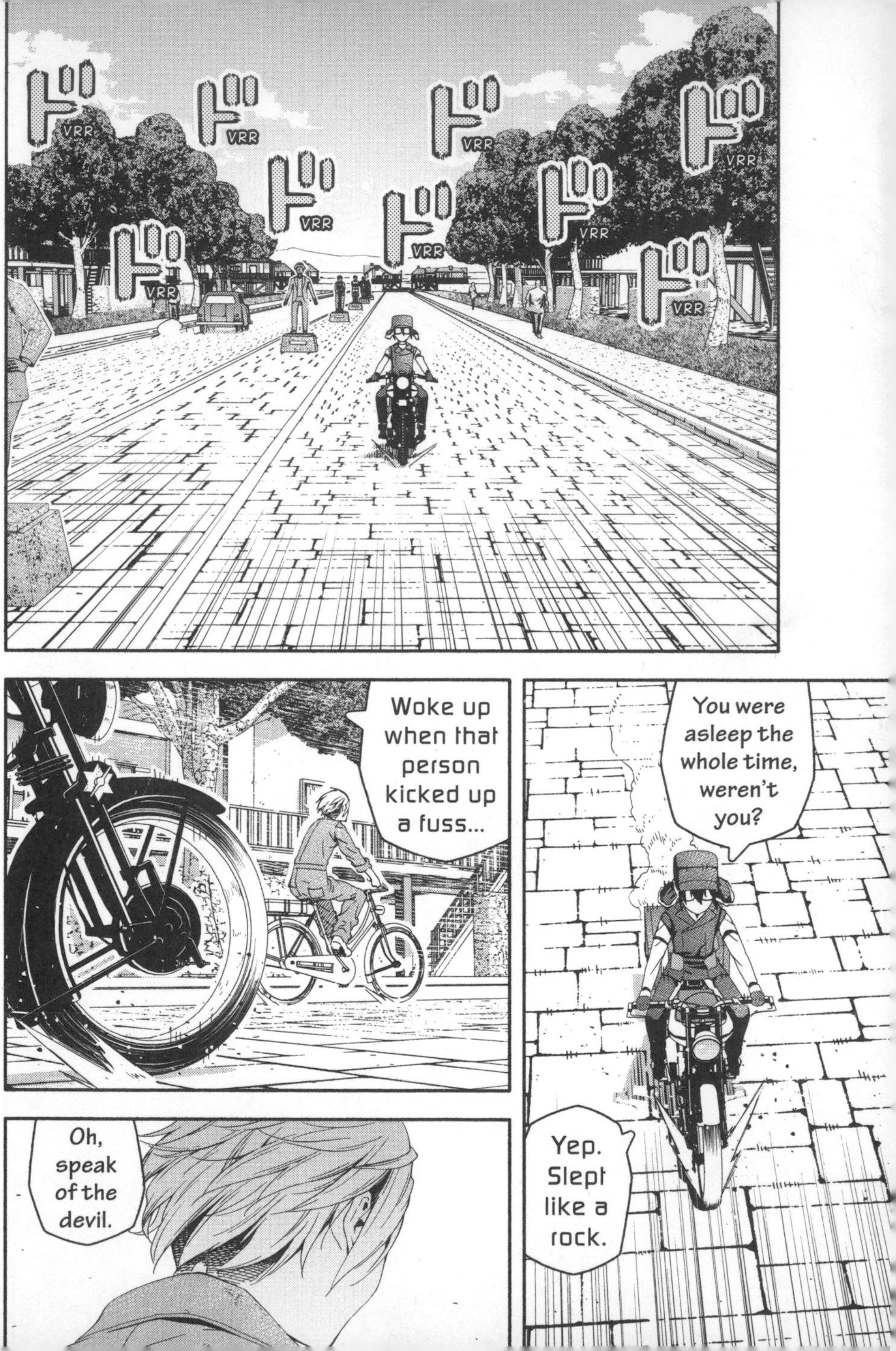
ド VRR
ド VRR
ド VRR
ド VRR
ド VRR
ド VRR
ド VRR
ド VRR
ド VRR
ド VRR
You were asleep the whole time, weren't you?
Woke up when that person kicked up a fuss...
Yep. Slept like a rock.
Oh, speak of the devil.

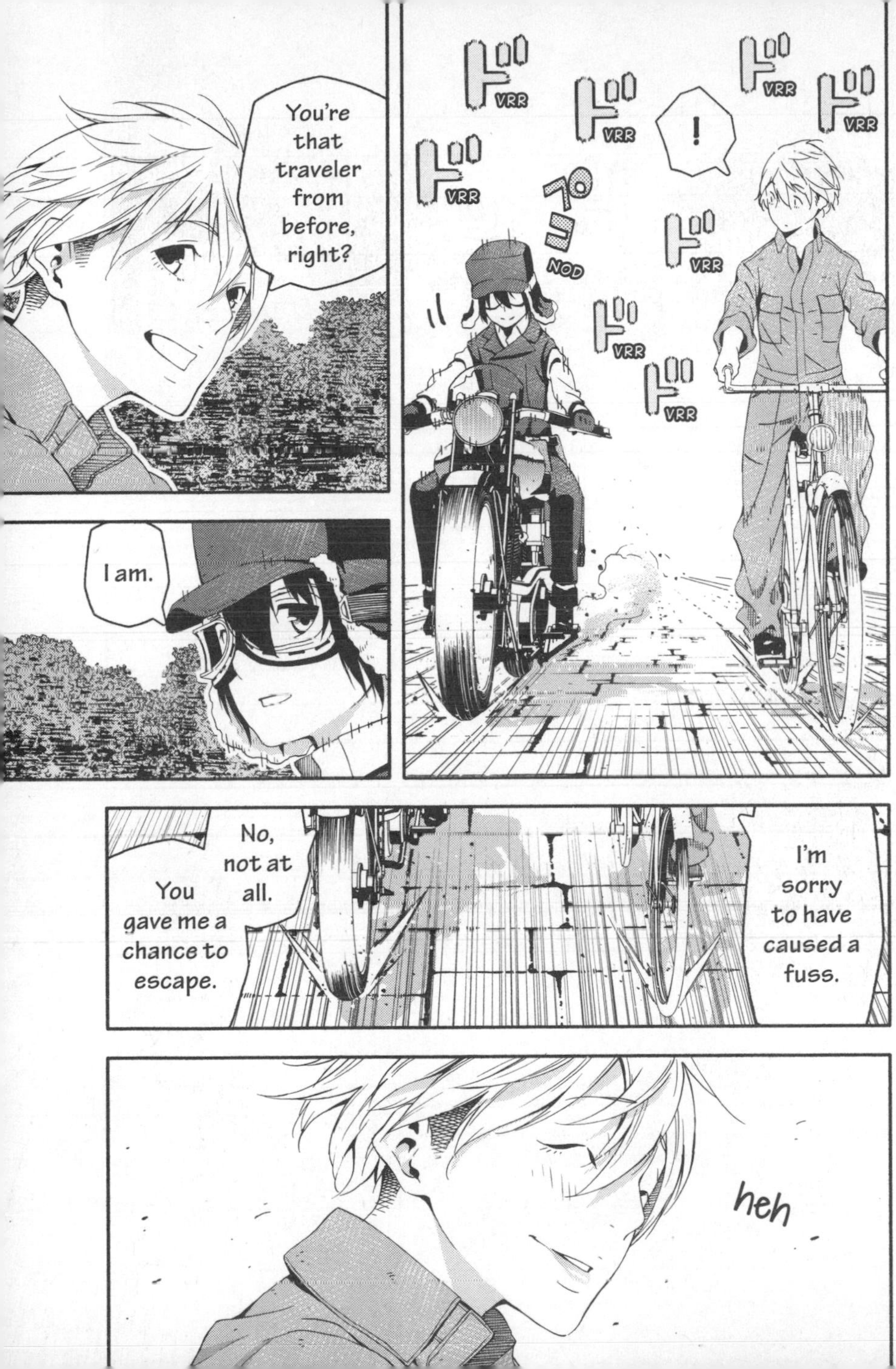
VRR
VRR
VRR
VRR
!
VRR
NOD
VRR
VRR
VRR
You're that traveler from before, right?
I am.
I'm sorry to have caused a fuss.
No, not at all.
You gave me a chance to escape.
heh

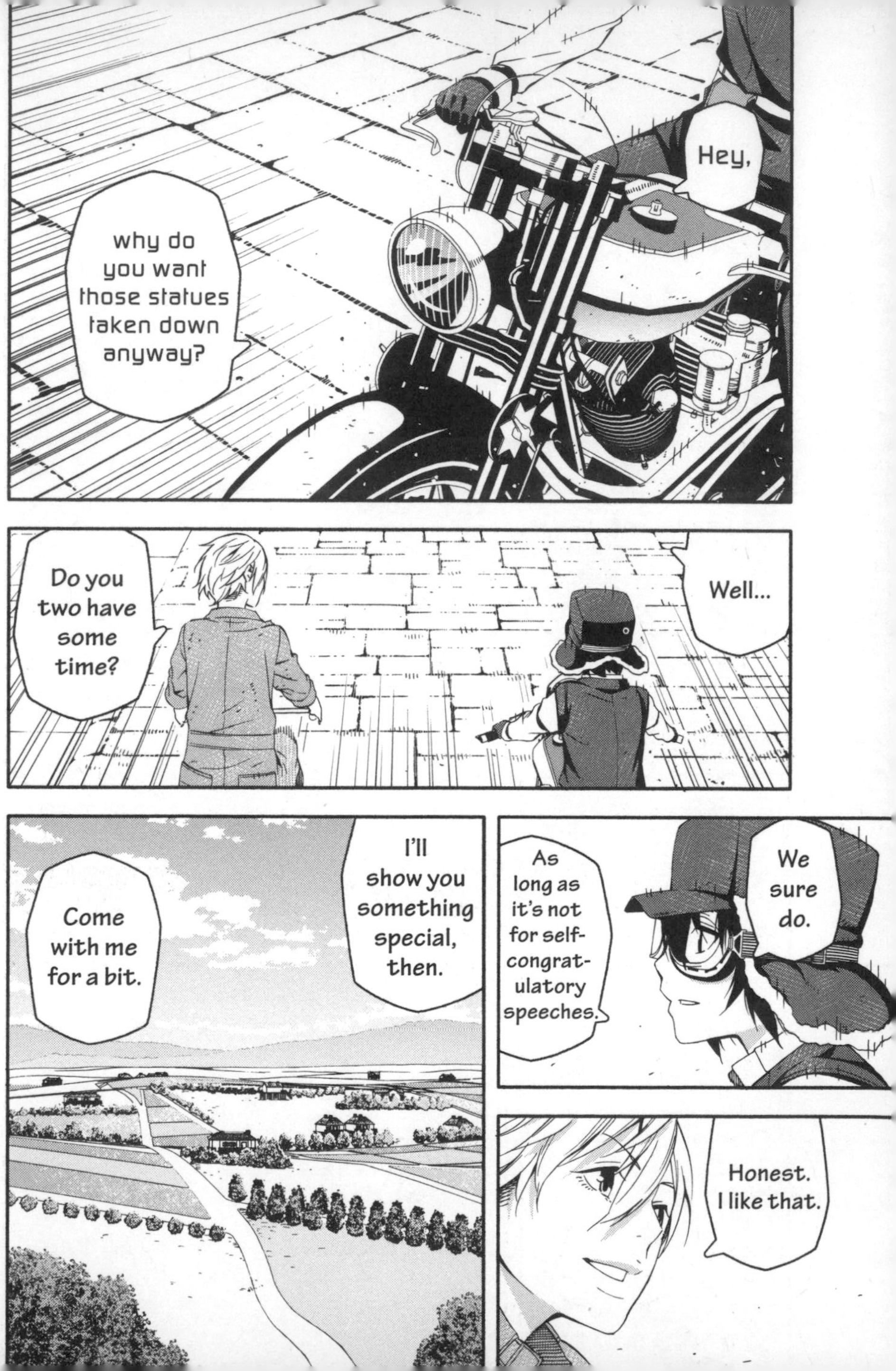
Hey,
why do you want those statues taken down anyway?
Well...
Do you two have some time?
We sure do.
As long as it's not for self-congrat-ulatory speeches.
Honest. I like that.
I'll show you something special, then.
Come with me for a bit.

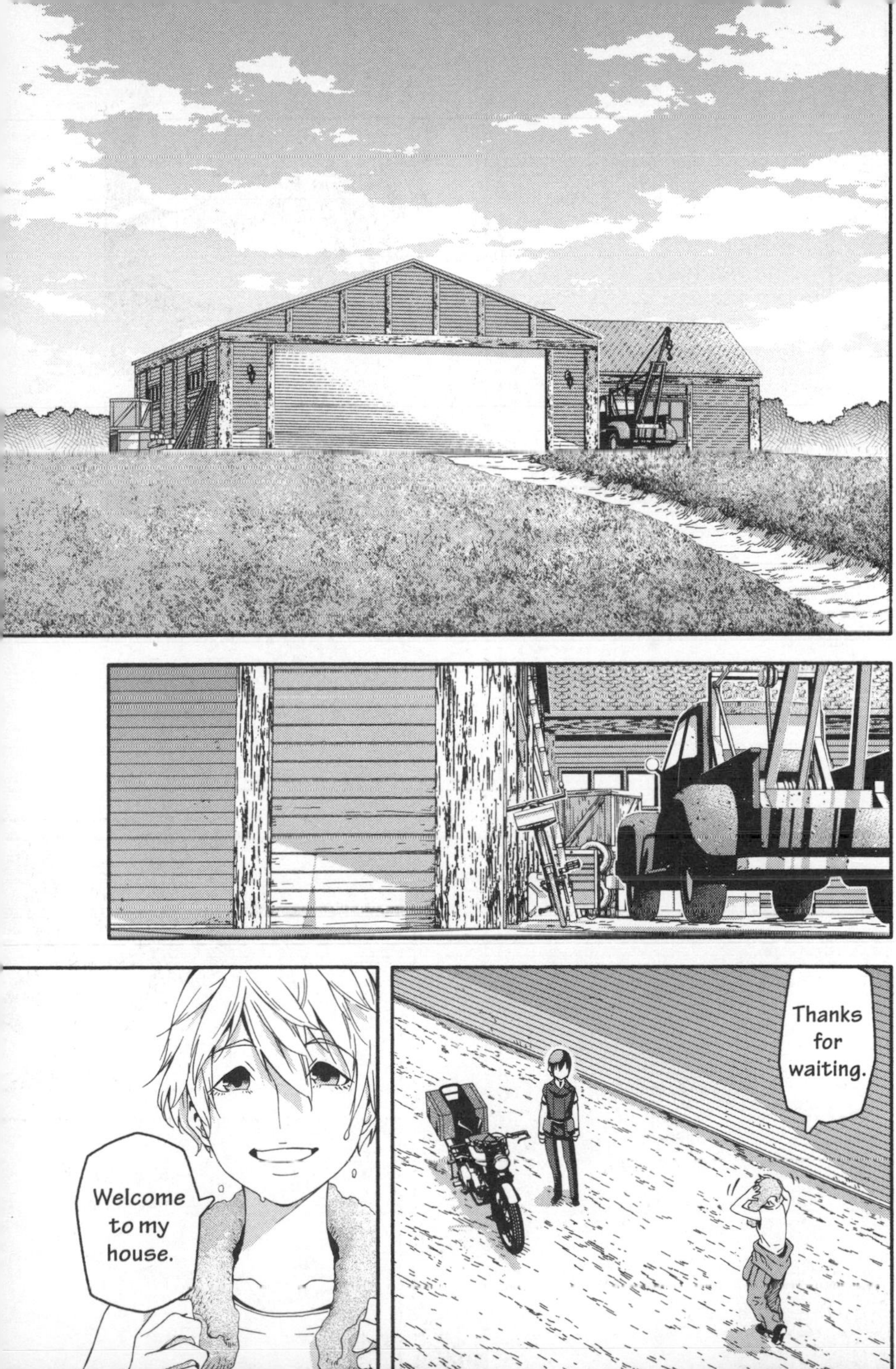
Thanks for waiting.
Welcome to my house.

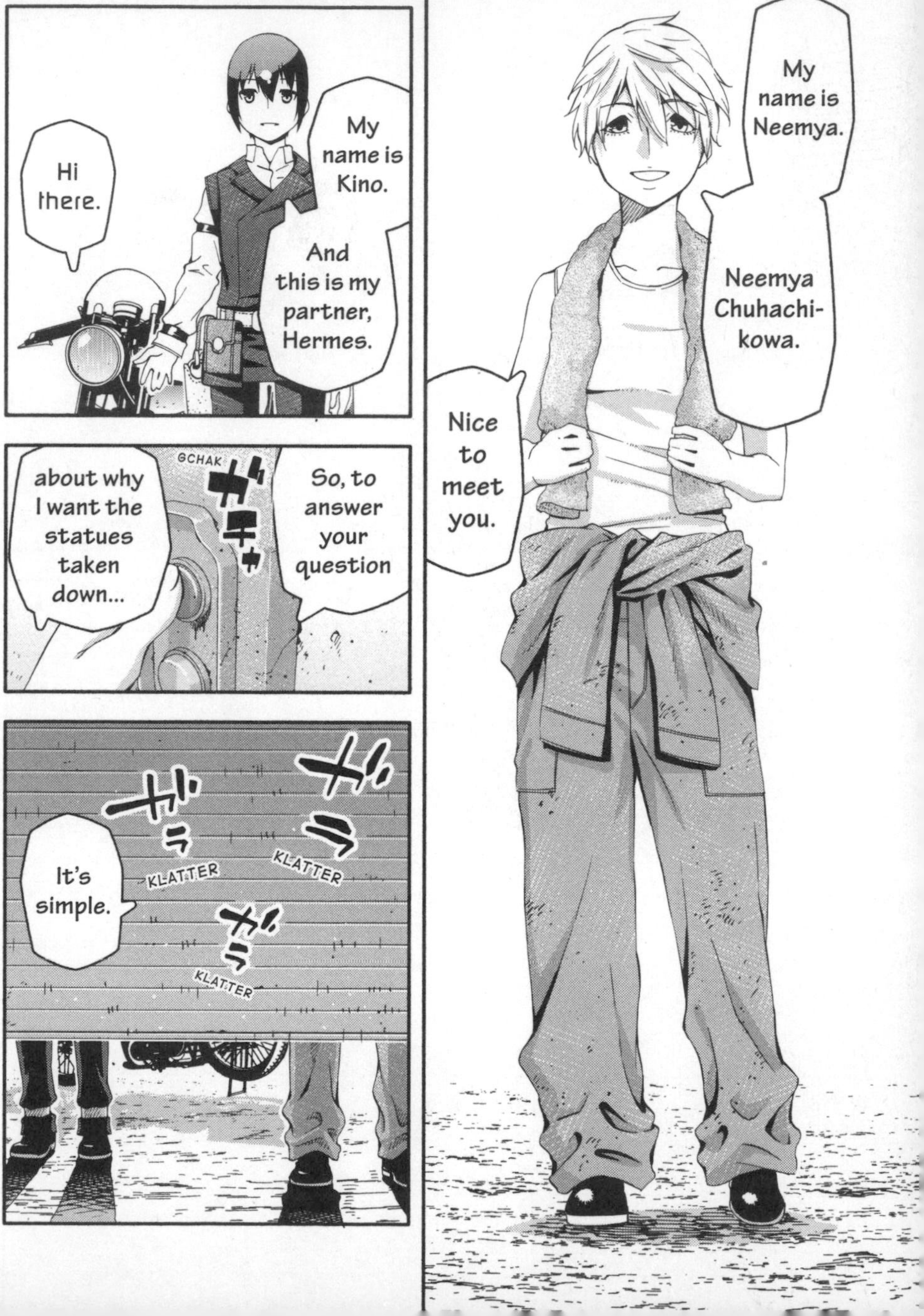
My name is Neemya.
Neemya Chuhachi-kowa.
Nice to meet you.
My name is Kino.
And this is my partner, Hermes.
Hi there.
GCHAK
So, to answer your question
about why I want the statues taken down...
KLATTER
KLATTER
It's simple.
KLATTER

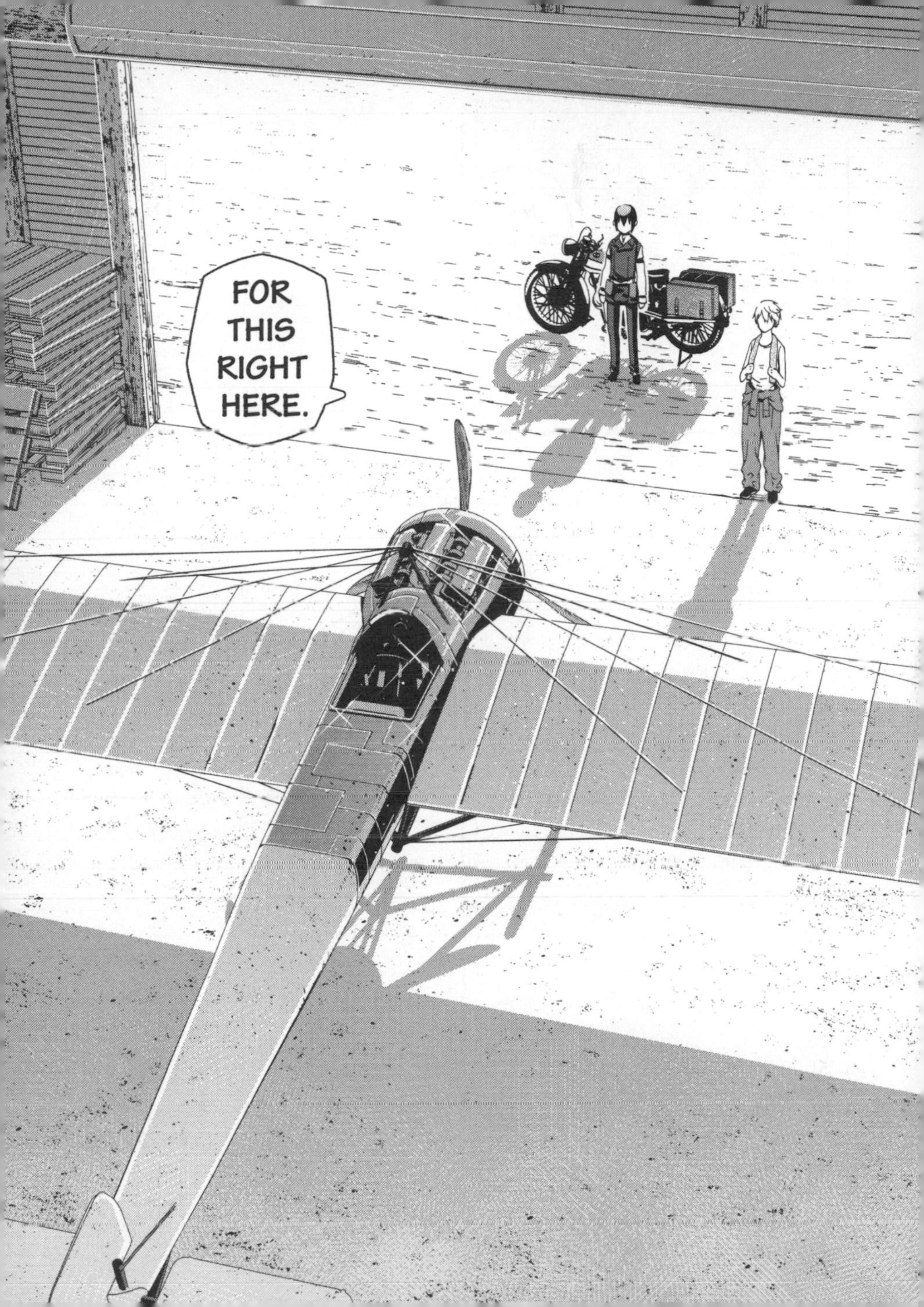
FOR THIS RIGHT HERE.

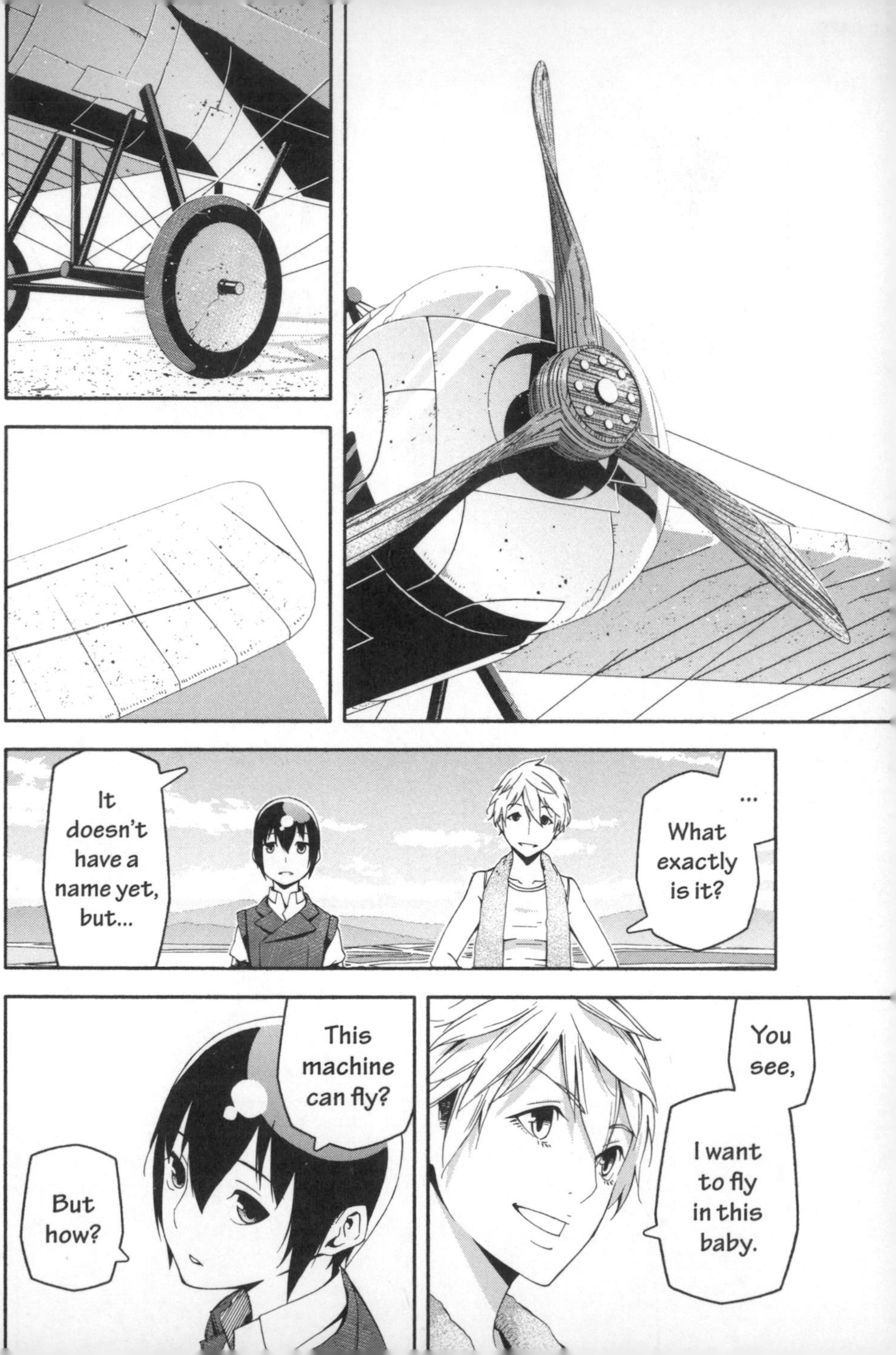
... What exactly is it?
It doesn't have a name yet, but...
You see,
I want to fly in this baby.
This machine can fly?
But how?

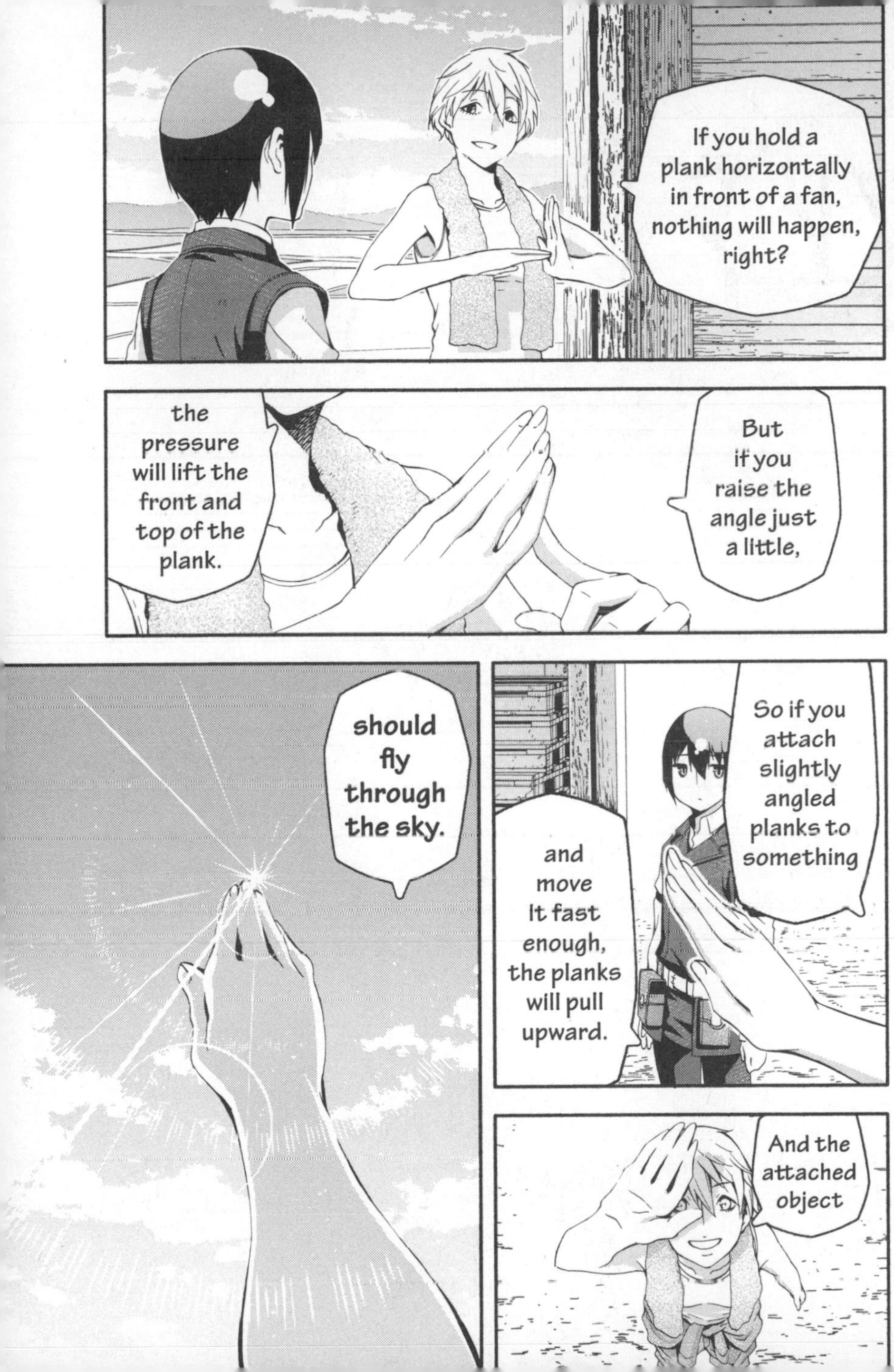
If you hold a plank horizontally in front of a fan, nothing will happen, right?
But if you raise the angle just a little,
the pressure will lift the front and top of the plank.
So if you attach slightly angled planks to something
and move it fast enough, the planks will pull upward.
And the attached object
should fly through the sky.

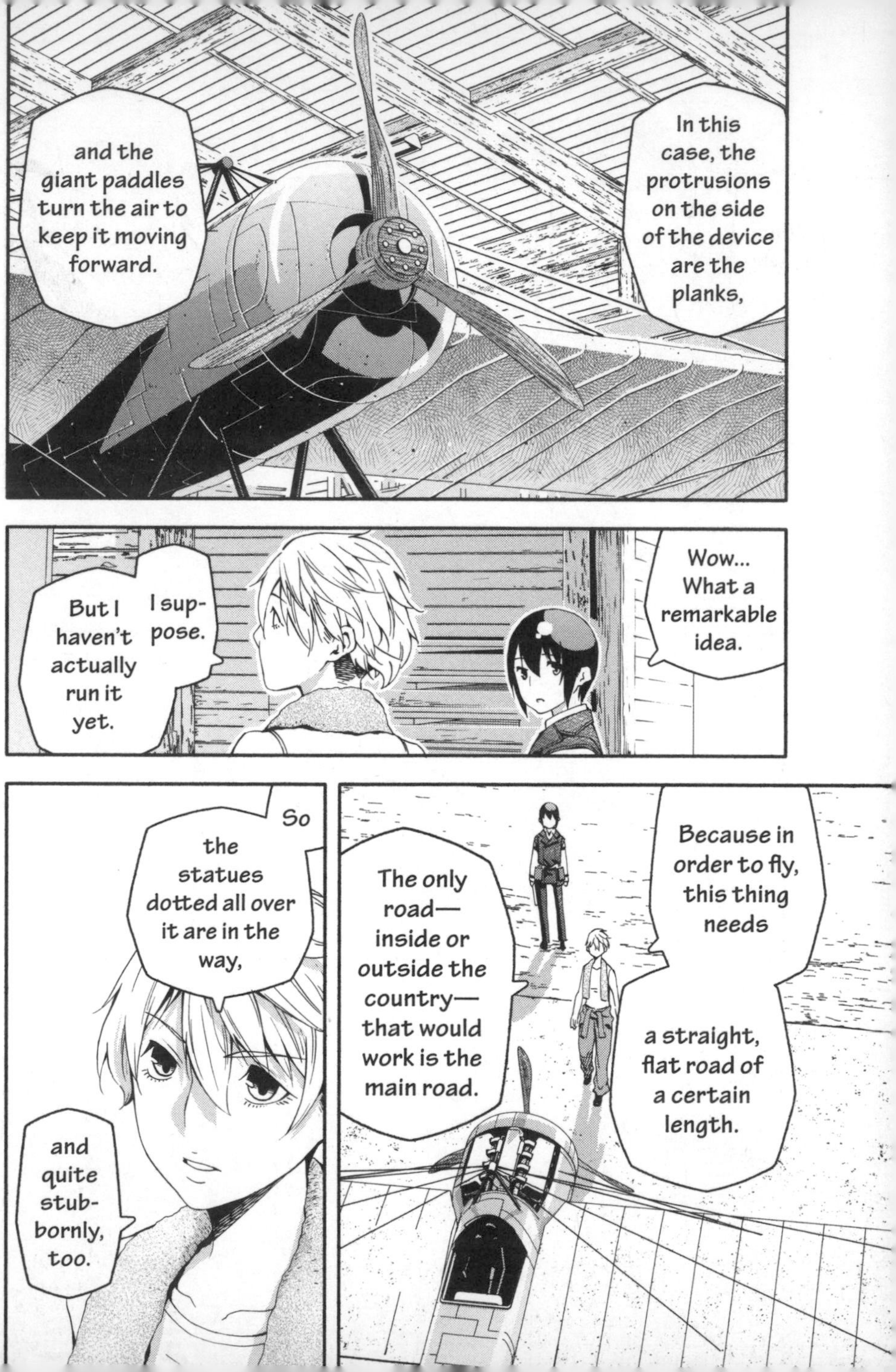
In this case, the protrusions on the side of the device are the planks,
and the giant paddles turn the air to keep it moving forward.
Wow... What a remarkable idea.
I suppose.
But I haven't actually run it yet.
Because in order to fly, this thing needs
a straight, flat road of a certain length.
The only road—inside or outside the country—that would work is the main road.
So the statues dotted all over it are in the way,
and quite stubbornly, too.

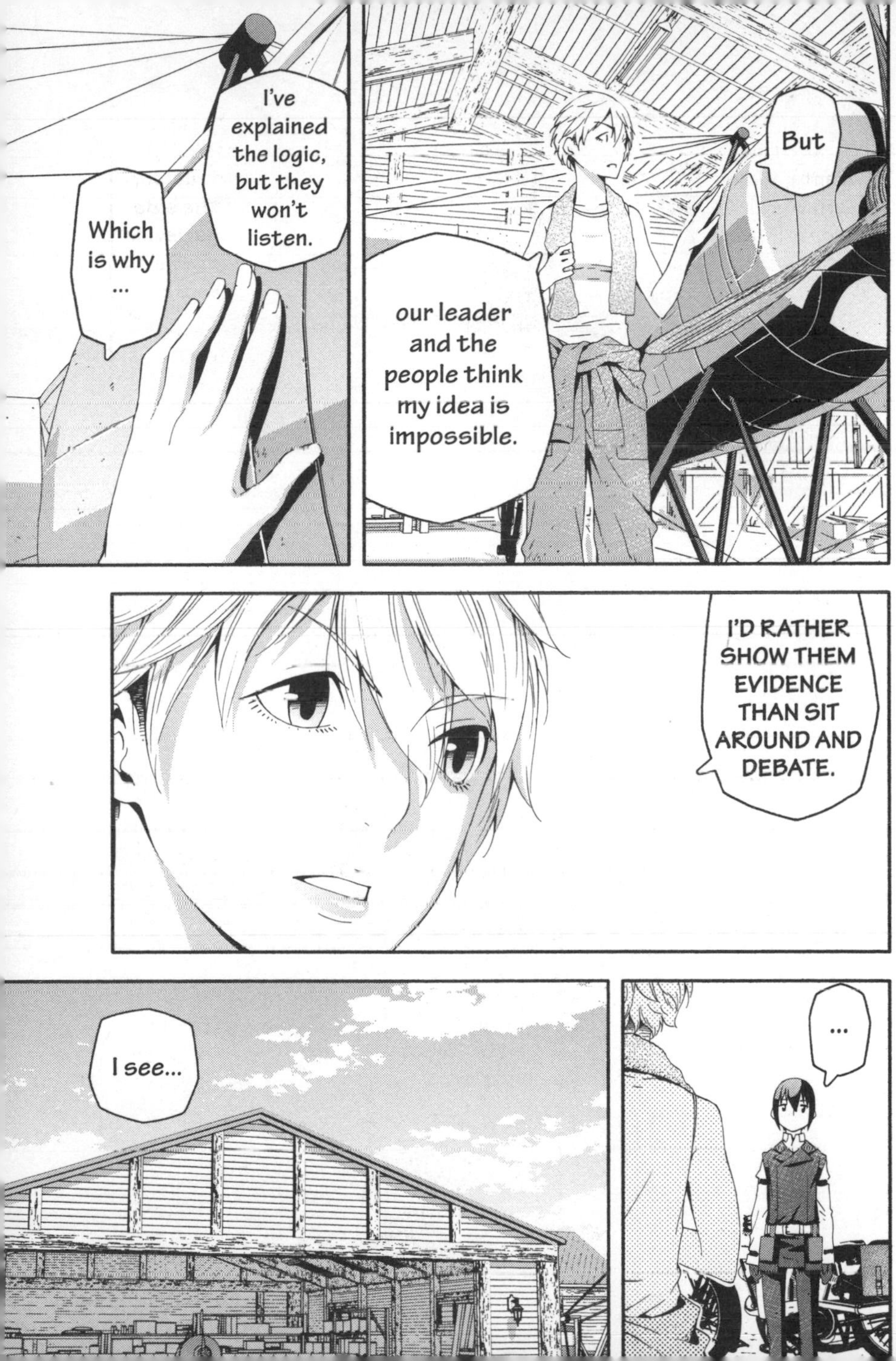
But
our leader and the people think my idea is impossible.
I've explained the logic, but they won't listen.
Which is why ...
I'D RATHER SHOW THEM EVIDENCE THAN SIT AROUND AND DEBATE.
...
I see...

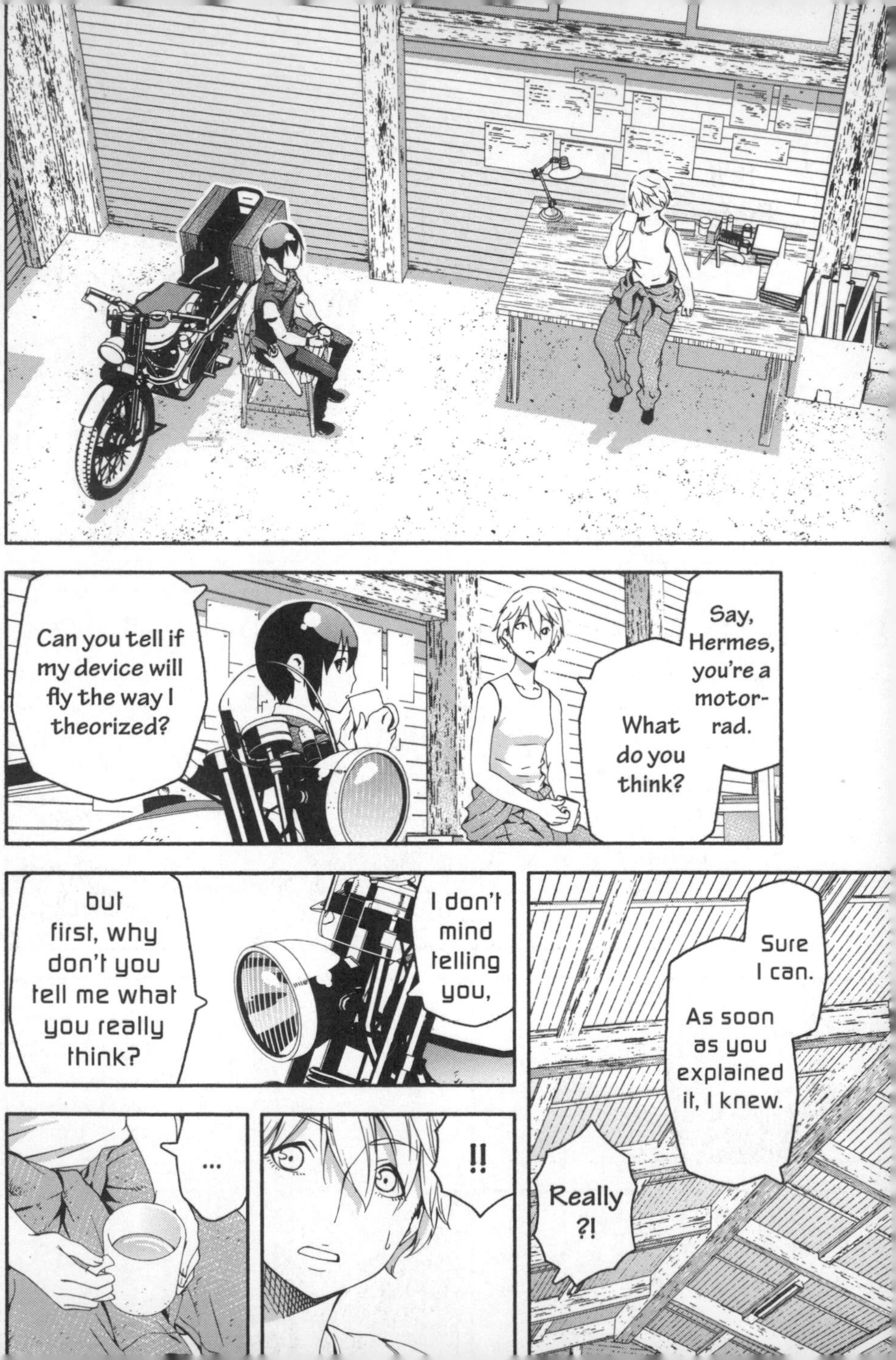
Say, Hermes, you're a motor-rad.
What do you think?
Can you tell if my device will fly the way I theorized?
Sure I can.
As soon as you explained it, I knew.
Really?!
I don't mind telling you,
but first, why don't you tell me what you really think?
!!
...

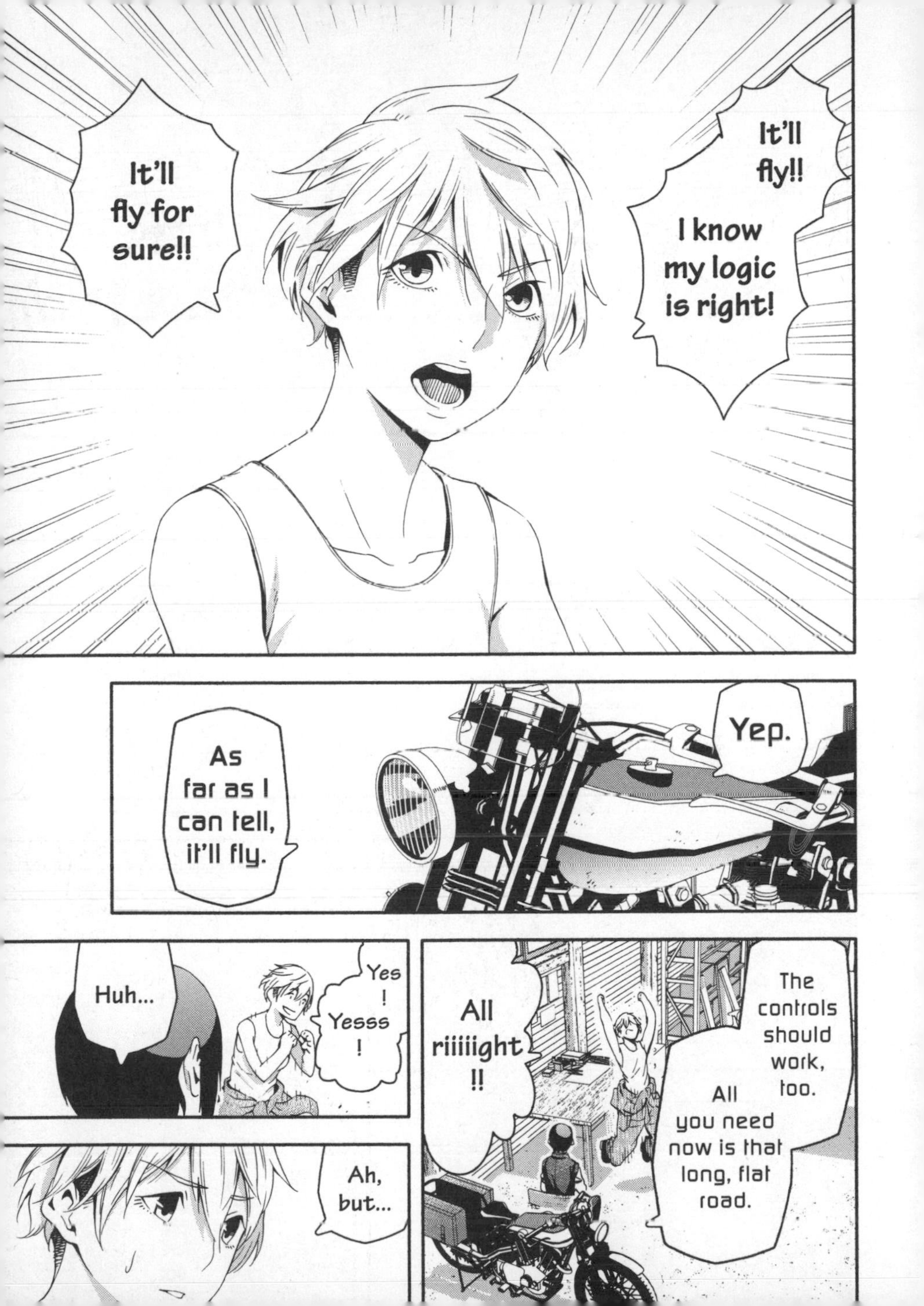
It'll fly!!
I know my logic is right!
It'll fly for sure!!
Yep.
As far as I can tell, it'll fly.
The controls should work, too.
All you need now is that long, flat road.
All riiiiight!!
Yes! Yesss!
Huh...
Ah, but...

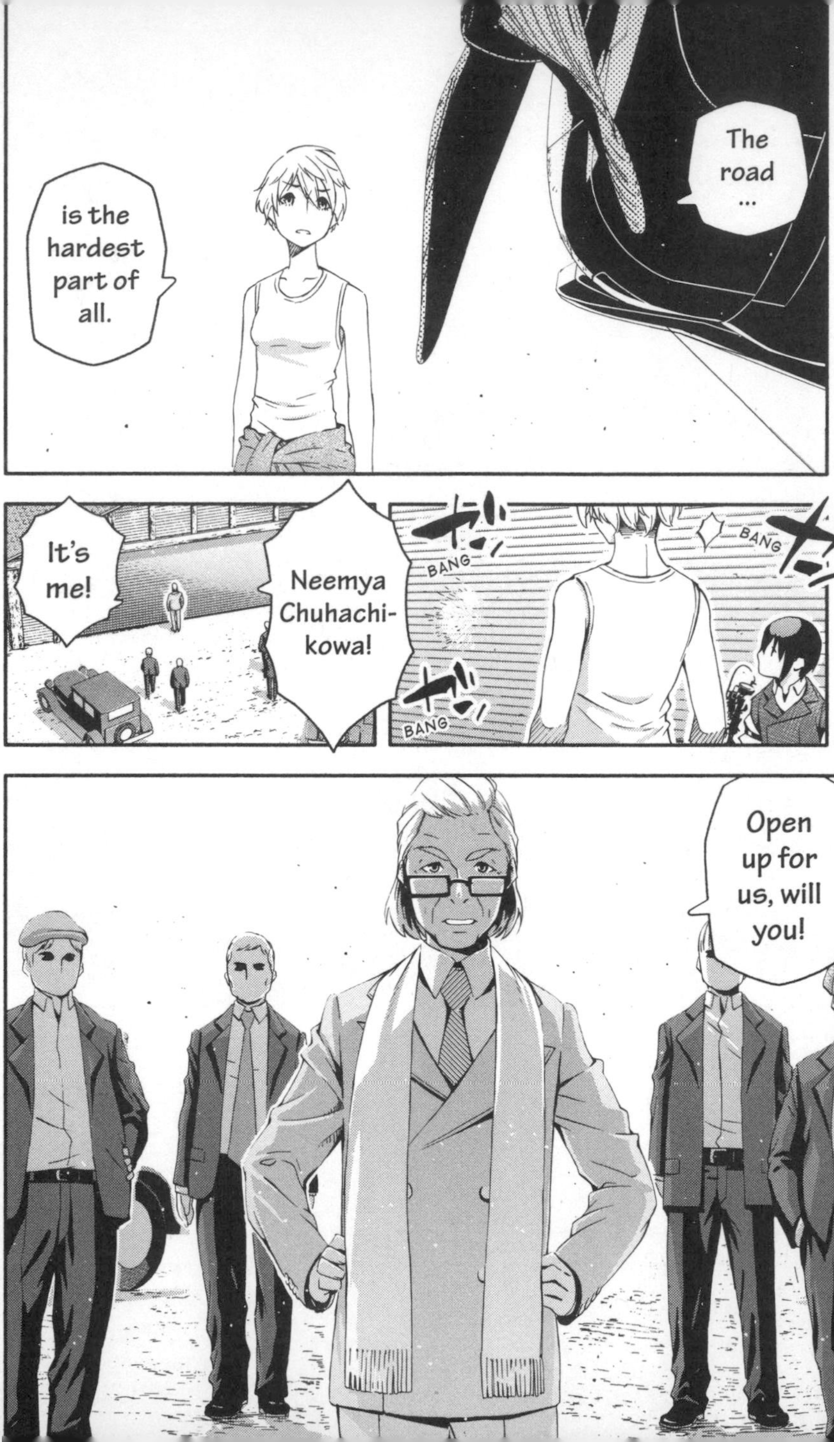
The road ...
is the hardest part of all.
BANG
BANG
BANG
Neemya Chuhachi-kowa!
It's me!
Open up for us, will you!

Chapter 2
The Land of Magicians (Pt. 2)
-Potentials of Magic-

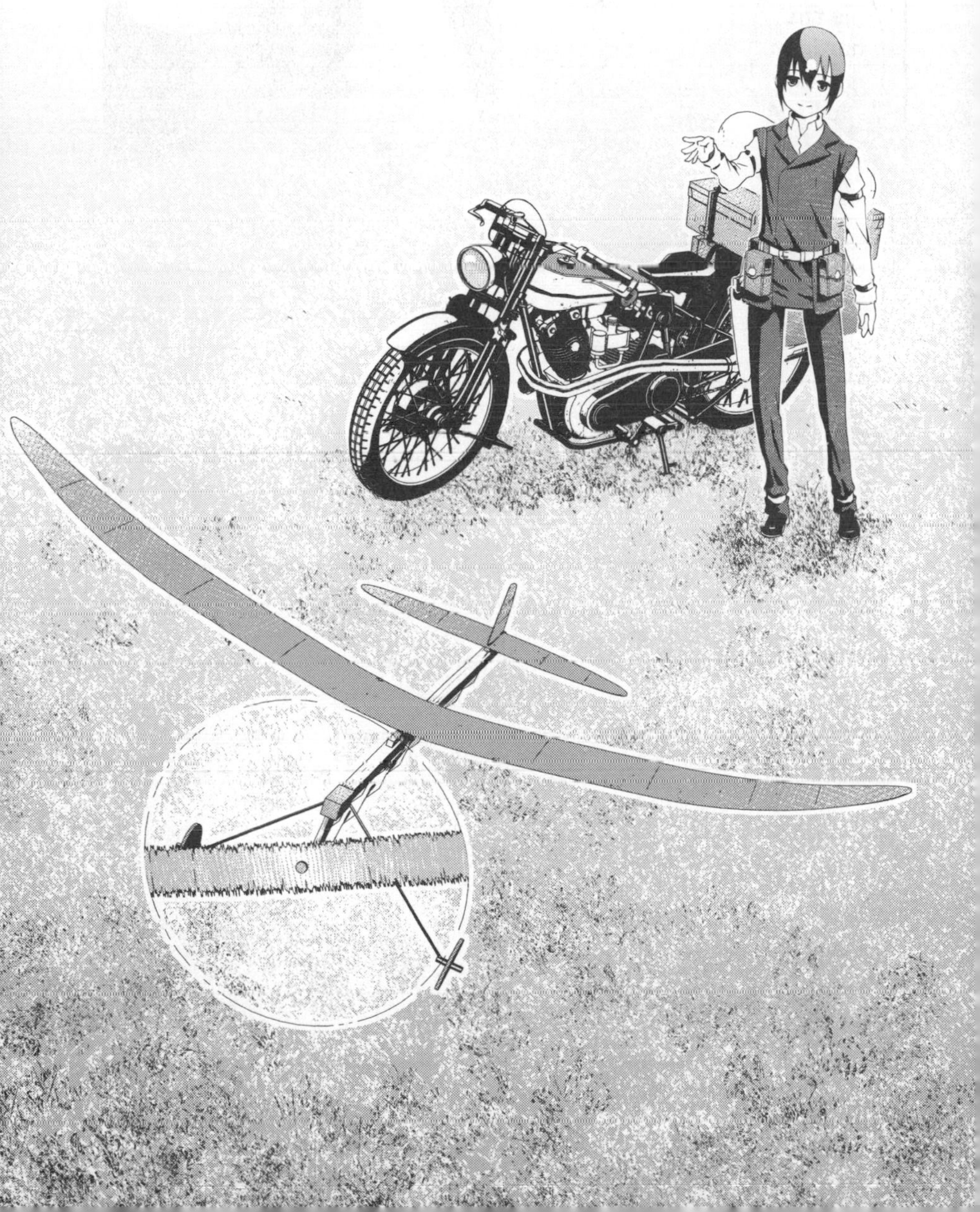

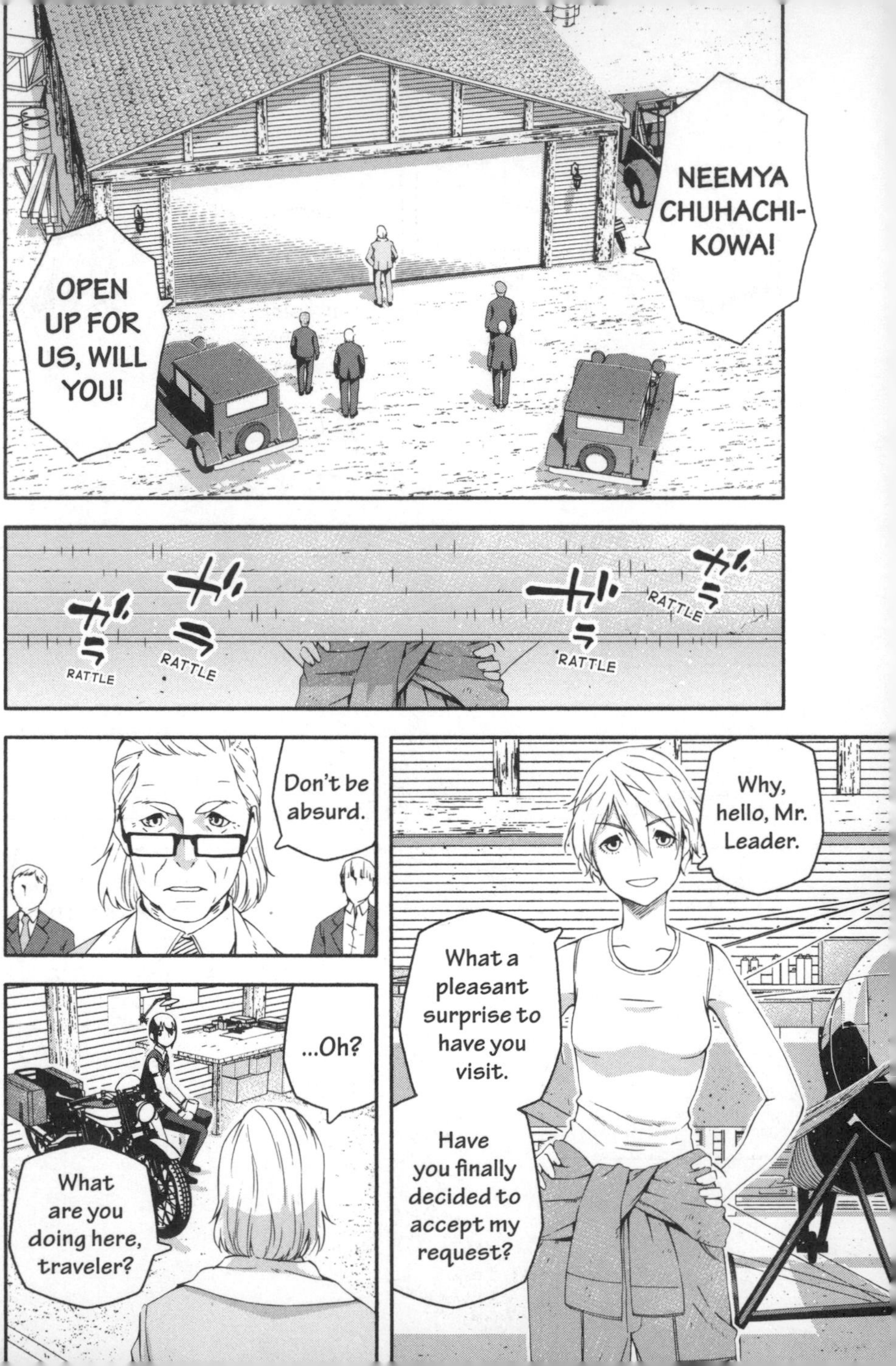
NEEMYA CHUHACHI-KOWA!
OPEN UP FOR US, WILL YOU!
RATTLE
RATTLE
RATTLE
RATTLE
Why, hello, Mr. Leader.
What a pleasant surprise to have you visit.
Have you finally decided to accept my request?
Don't be absurd.
...Oh?
What are you doing here, traveler?

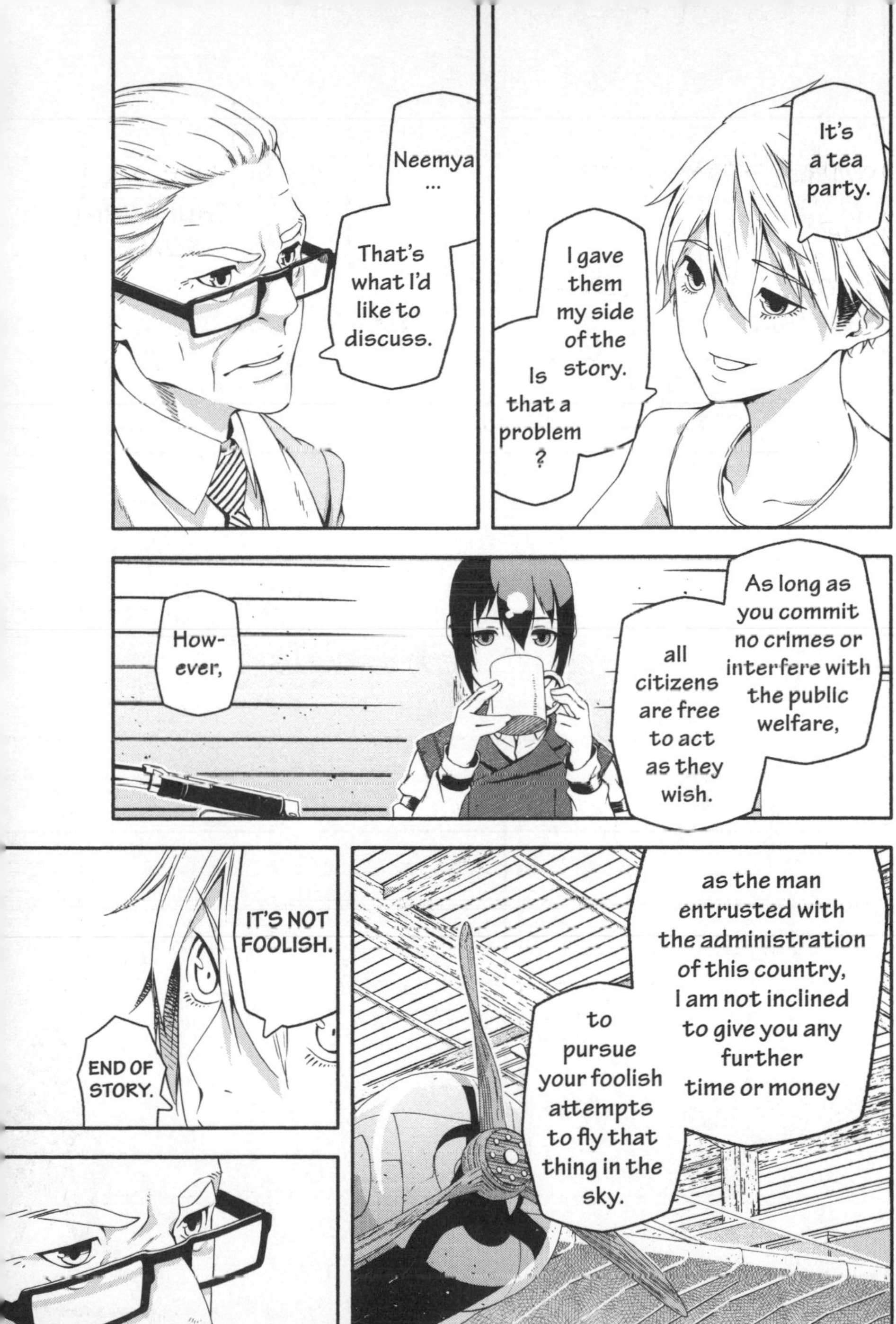
It's a tea party.
I gave them my side of the story.
Is that a problem?
Neemya...
That's what I'd like to discuss.
As long as you commit no crimes or interfere with the public welfare,
all citizens are free to act as they wish.
However,
as the man entrusted with the administration of this country, I am not inclined to give you any further time or money
to pursue your foolish attempts to fly that thing in the sky.
IT'S NOT FOOLISH.
END OF STORY.

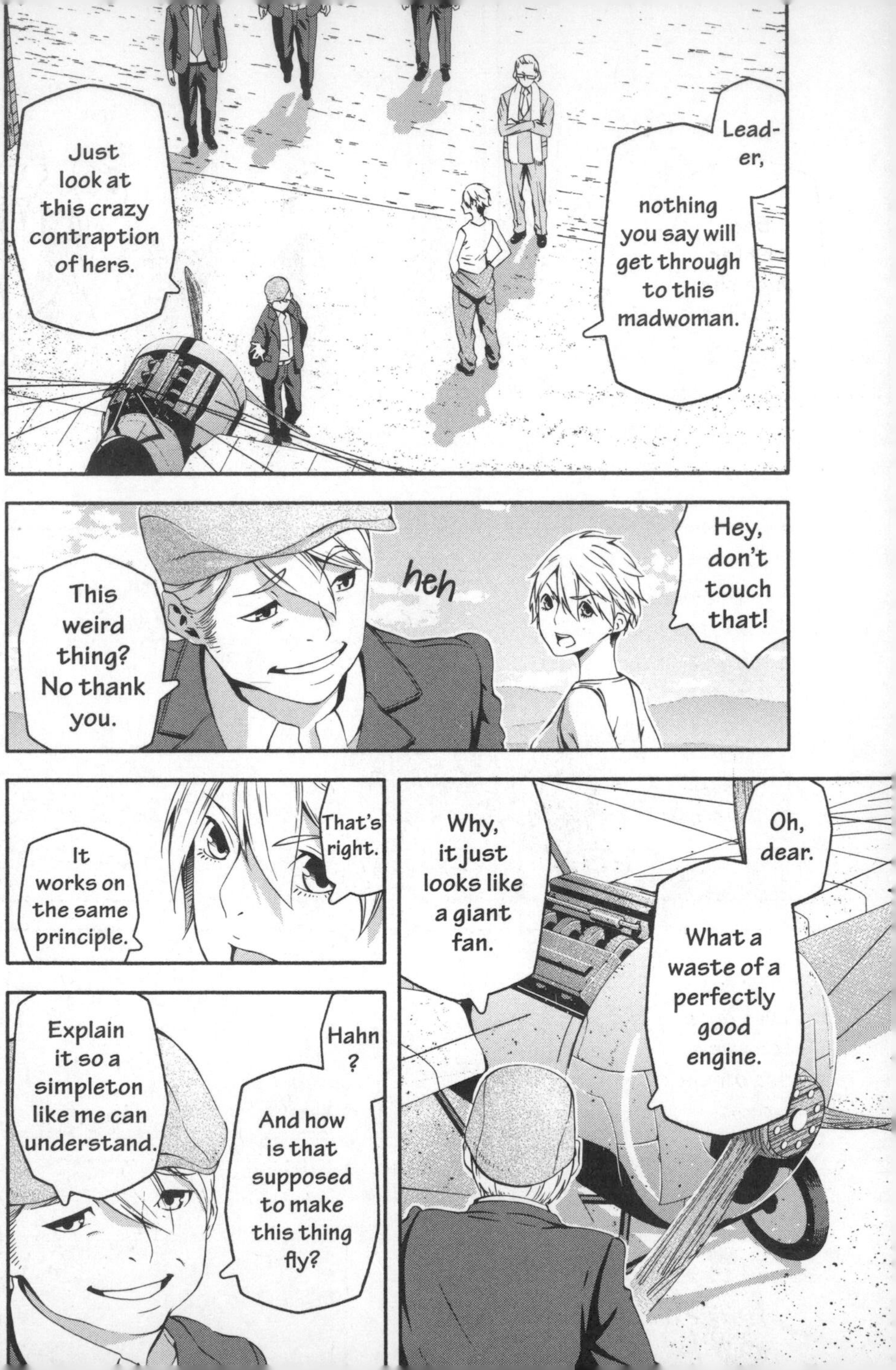
Leader, nothing you say will get through to this madwoman.
Just look at this crazy contraption of hers.
Hey, don't touch that!
heh
This weird thing? No thank you.
Oh, dear.
What a waste of a perfectly good engine.
Why, it just looks like a giant fan.
That's right.
It works on the same principle.
Hahn?
And how is that supposed to make this thing fly?
Explain it so a simpleton like me can understand.

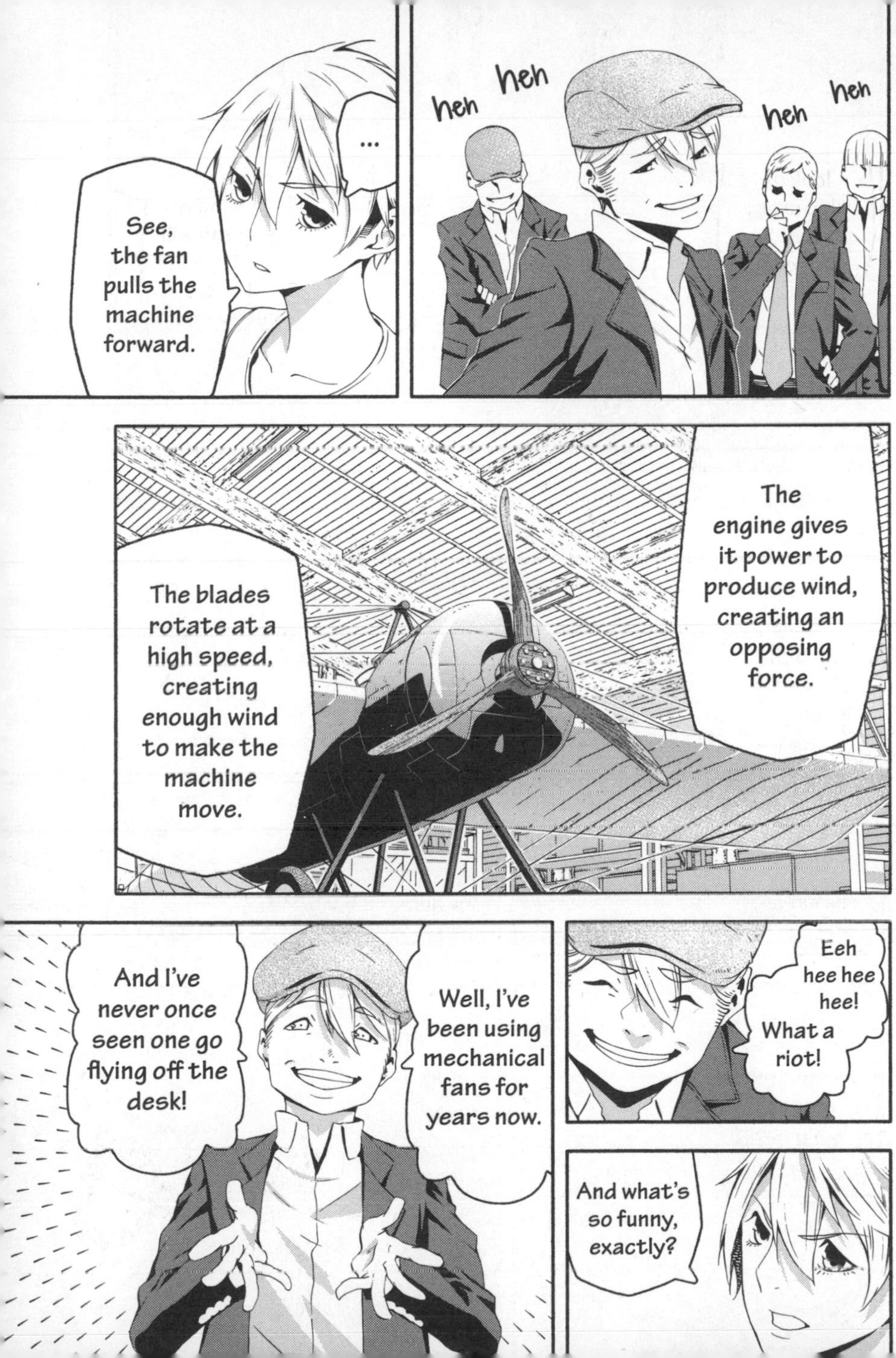
heh
heh
heh
heh
...
See, the fan pulls the machine forward.
The engine gives it power to produce wind, creating an opposing force.
The blades rotate at a high speed, creating enough wind to make the machine move.
Eeh hee hee hee! What a riot!
And what's so funny, exactly?
Well, I've been using mechanical fans for years now.
And I've never once seen one go flying off the desk!

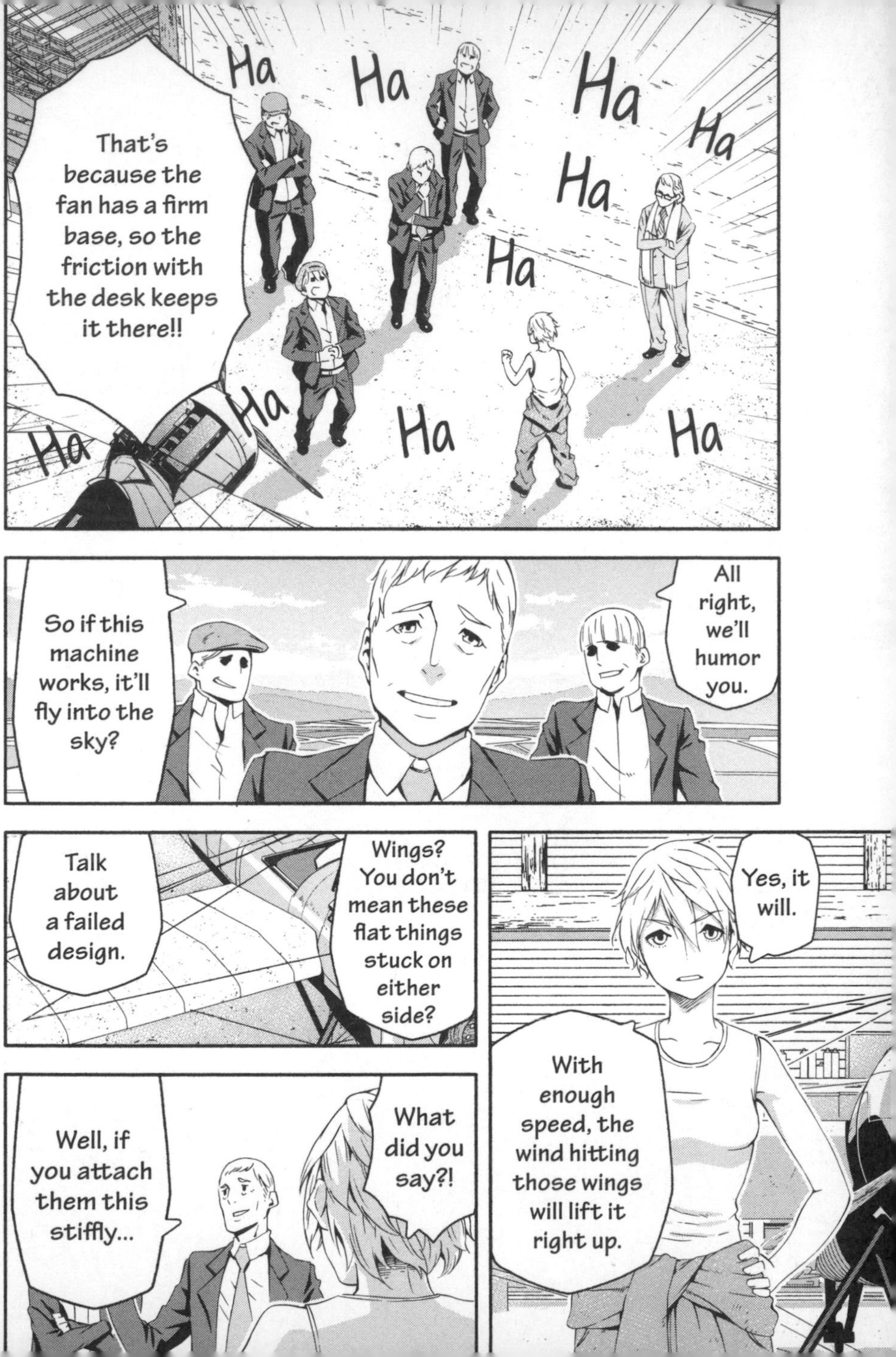
Ha
Ha
Ha
Ha
Ha
Ha
Ha
Ha
Ha
Ha
That's because the fan has a firm base, so the friction with the desk keeps it there!!
All right, we'll humor you.
So if this machine works, it'll fly into the sky?
Yes, it will.
With enough speed, the wind hitting those wings will lift it right up.
Wings? You don't mean these flat things stuck on either side?
Talk about a failed design.
What did you say?!
Well, if you attach them this stiffly...

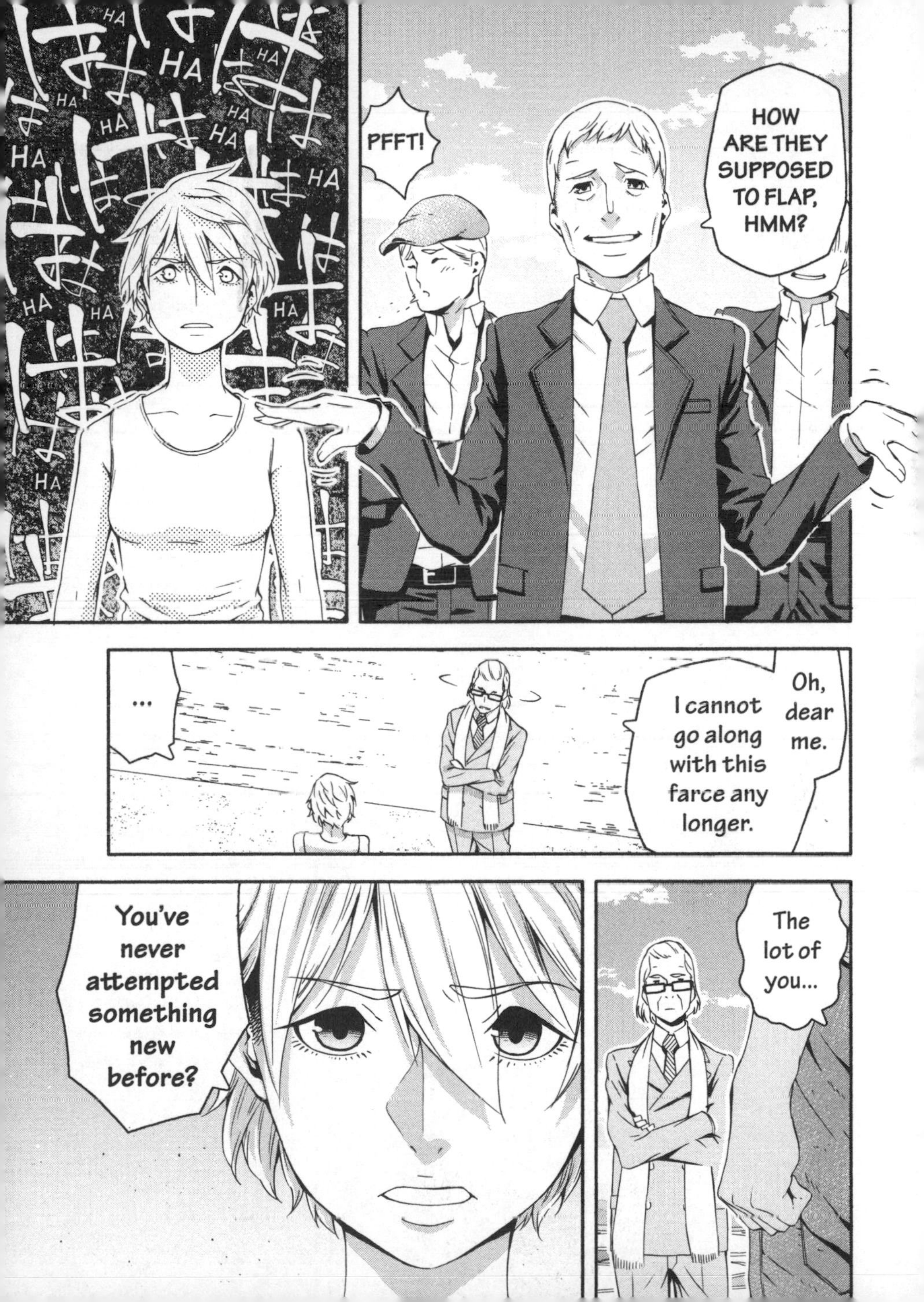
HOW ARE THEY SUPPOSED TO FLAP, HMM?
PFFT!
HA HA HA HA HA HA HA HA HA HA HA HA
Oh, dear me.
I cannot go along with this farce any longer.
...
The lot of you...
You've never attempted something new before?

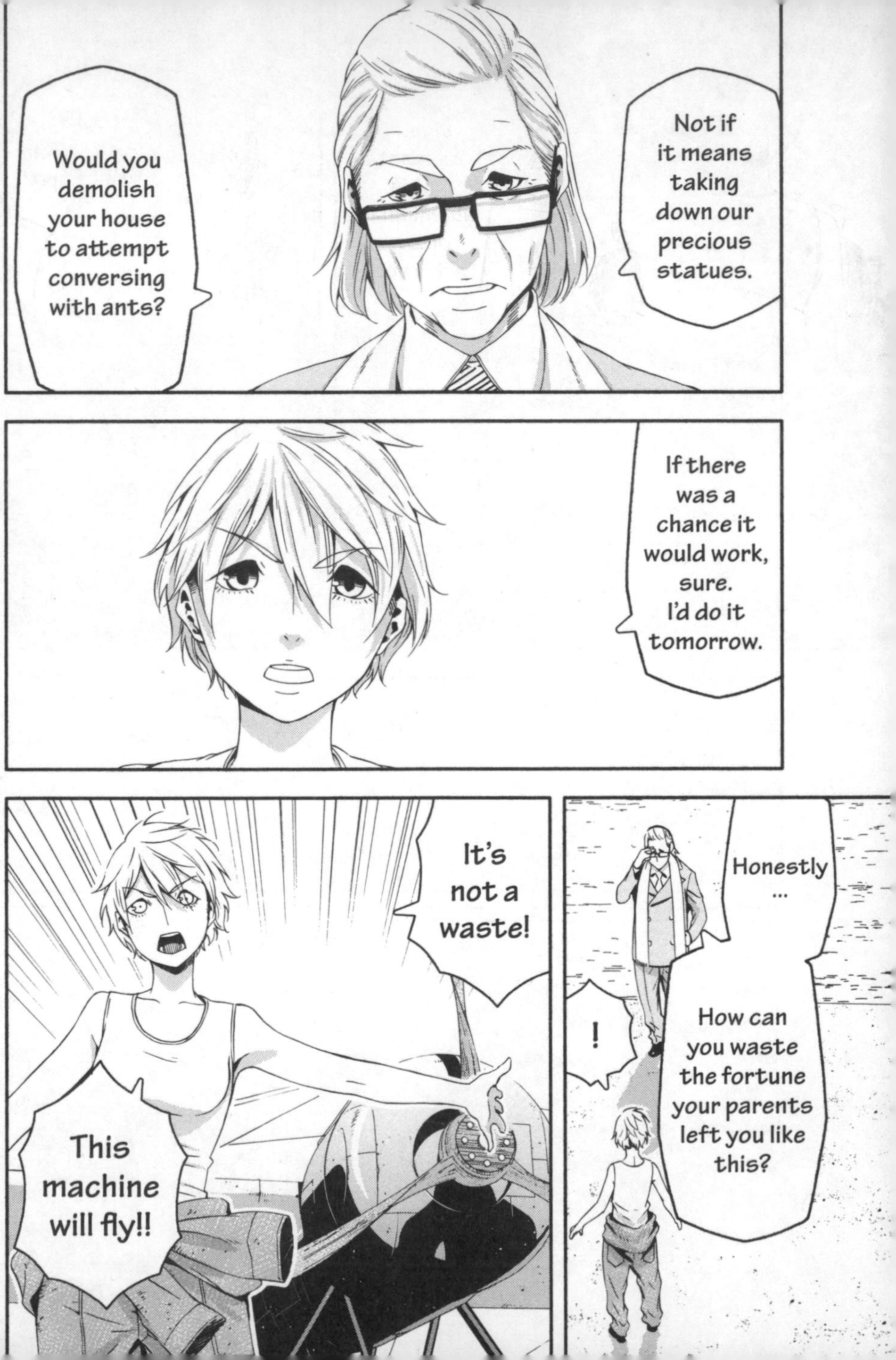
Not if it means taking down our precious statues.
Would you demolish your house to attempt conversing with ants?
If there was a chance it would work, sure. I'd do it tomorrow.
Honestly...
How can you waste the fortune your parents left you like this?
!
It's not a waste!
This machine will fly!!

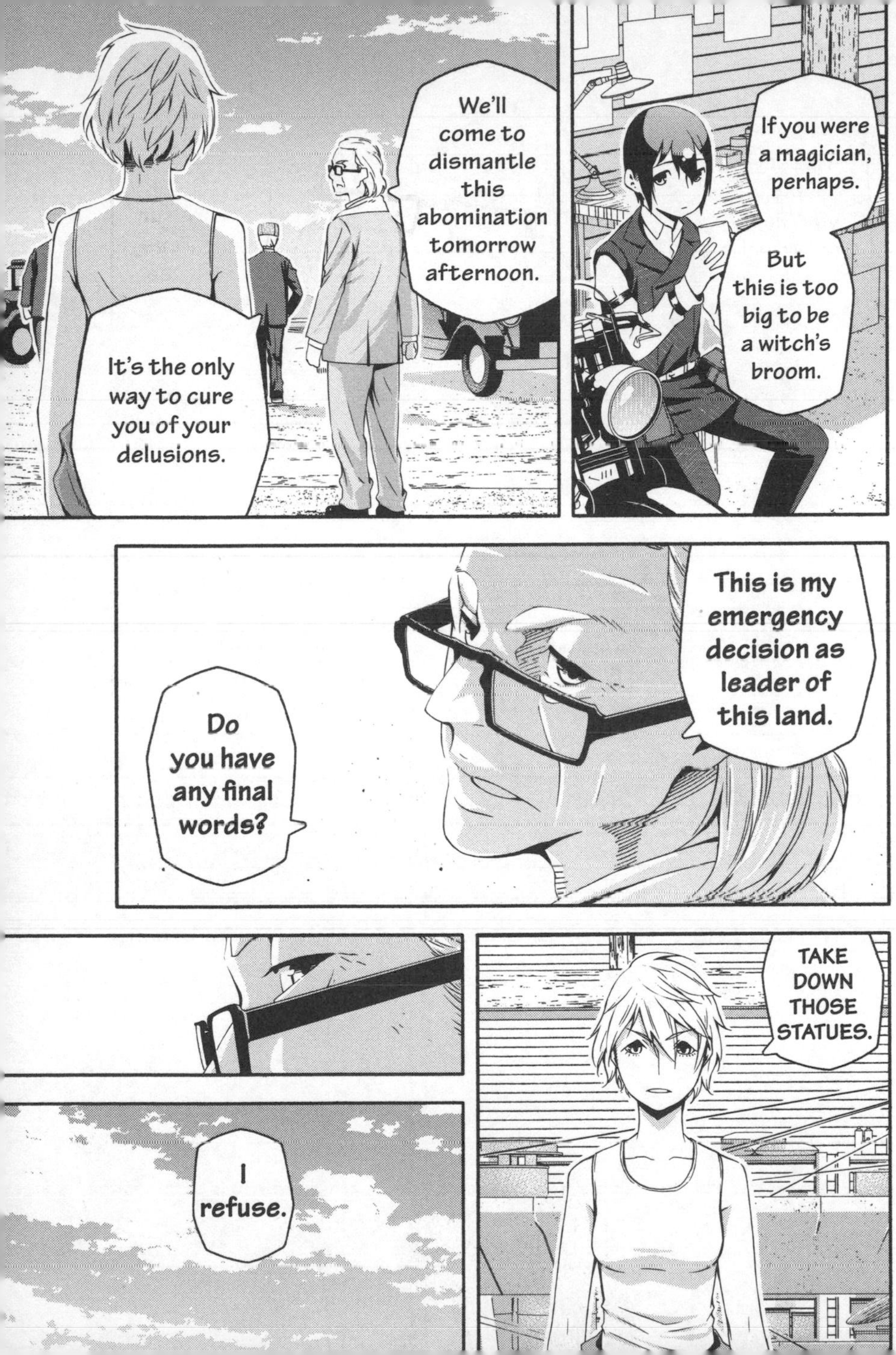
If you were a magician, perhaps.
But this is too big to be a witch's broom.
We'll come to dismantle this abomination tomorrow afternoon.
It's the only way to cure you of your delusions.
This is my emergency decision as leader of this land.
Do you have any final words?
TAKE DOWN THOSE STATUES.
I refuse.

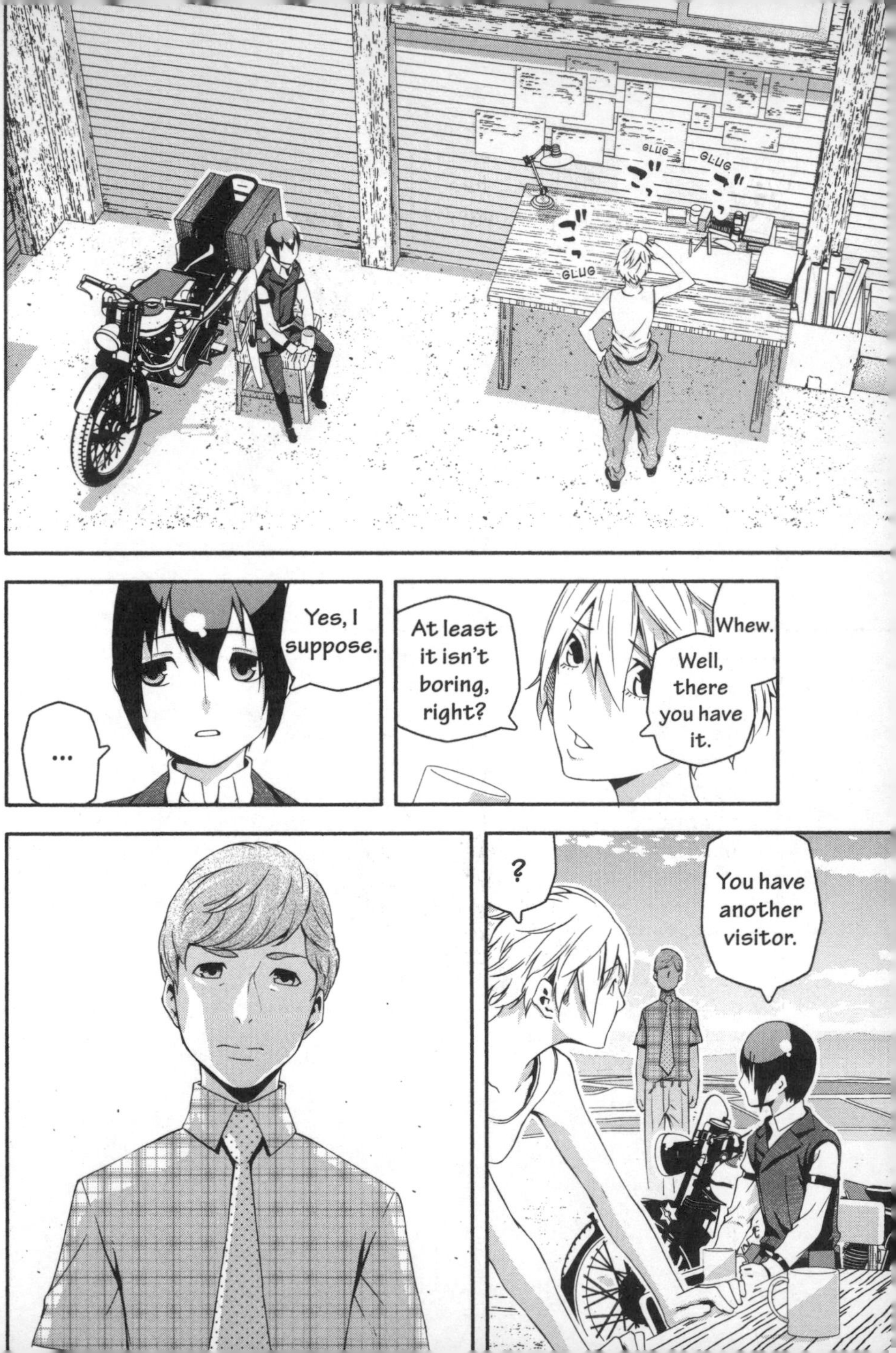
GLUG
GLUG
GLUG
Whew.
Well, there you have it.
At least it isn't boring, right?
Yes, I suppose.
...
You have another visitor.
?

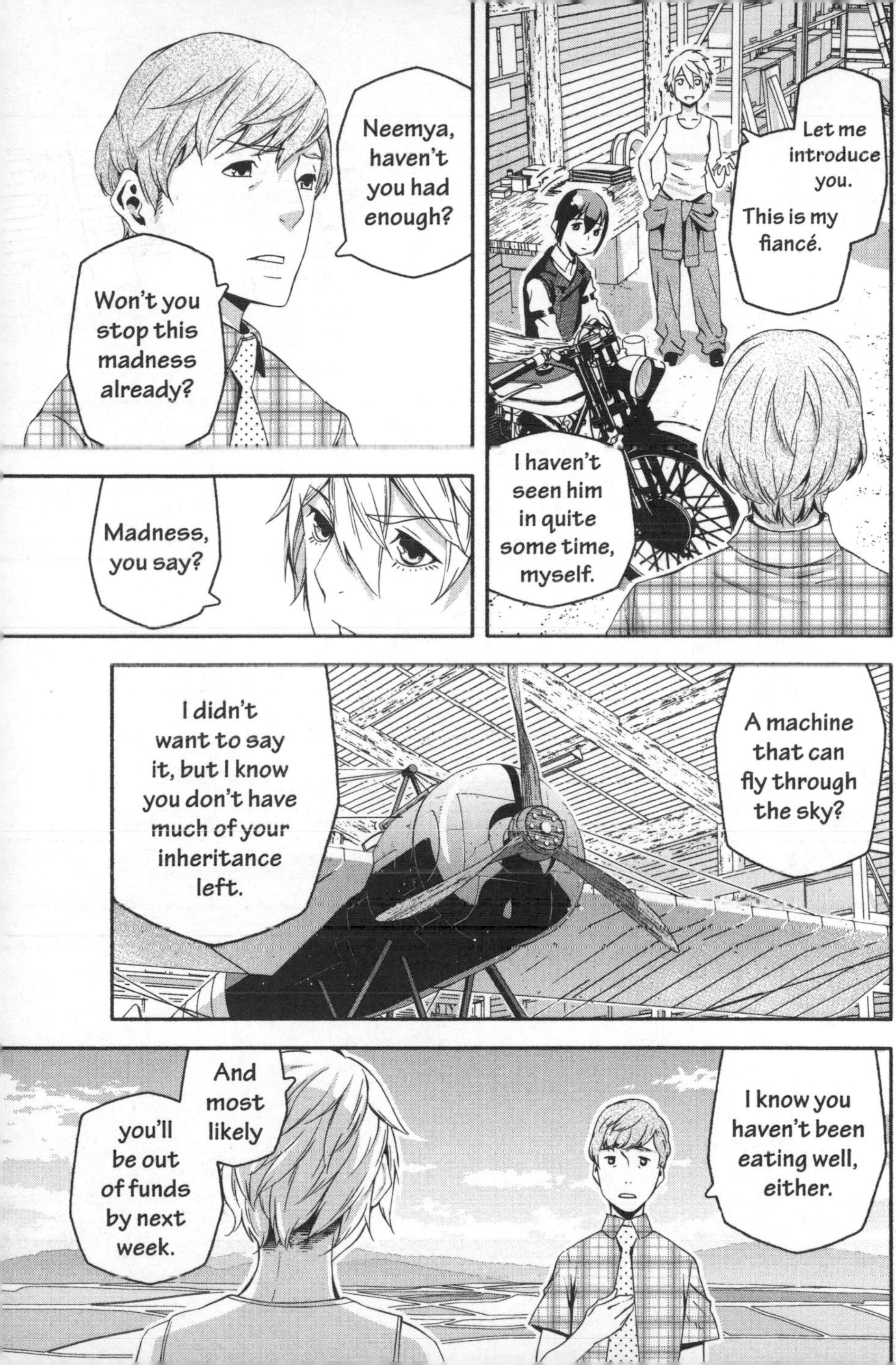
Let me introduce you.
This is my fiancé.
I haven't seen him in quite some time, myself.
Neemya, haven't you had enough?
Won't you stop this madness already?
Madness, you say?
A machine that can fly through the sky?
I didn't want to say it, but I know you don't have much of your inheritance left.
I know you haven't been eating well, either.
And most likely
you'll be out of funds by next week.

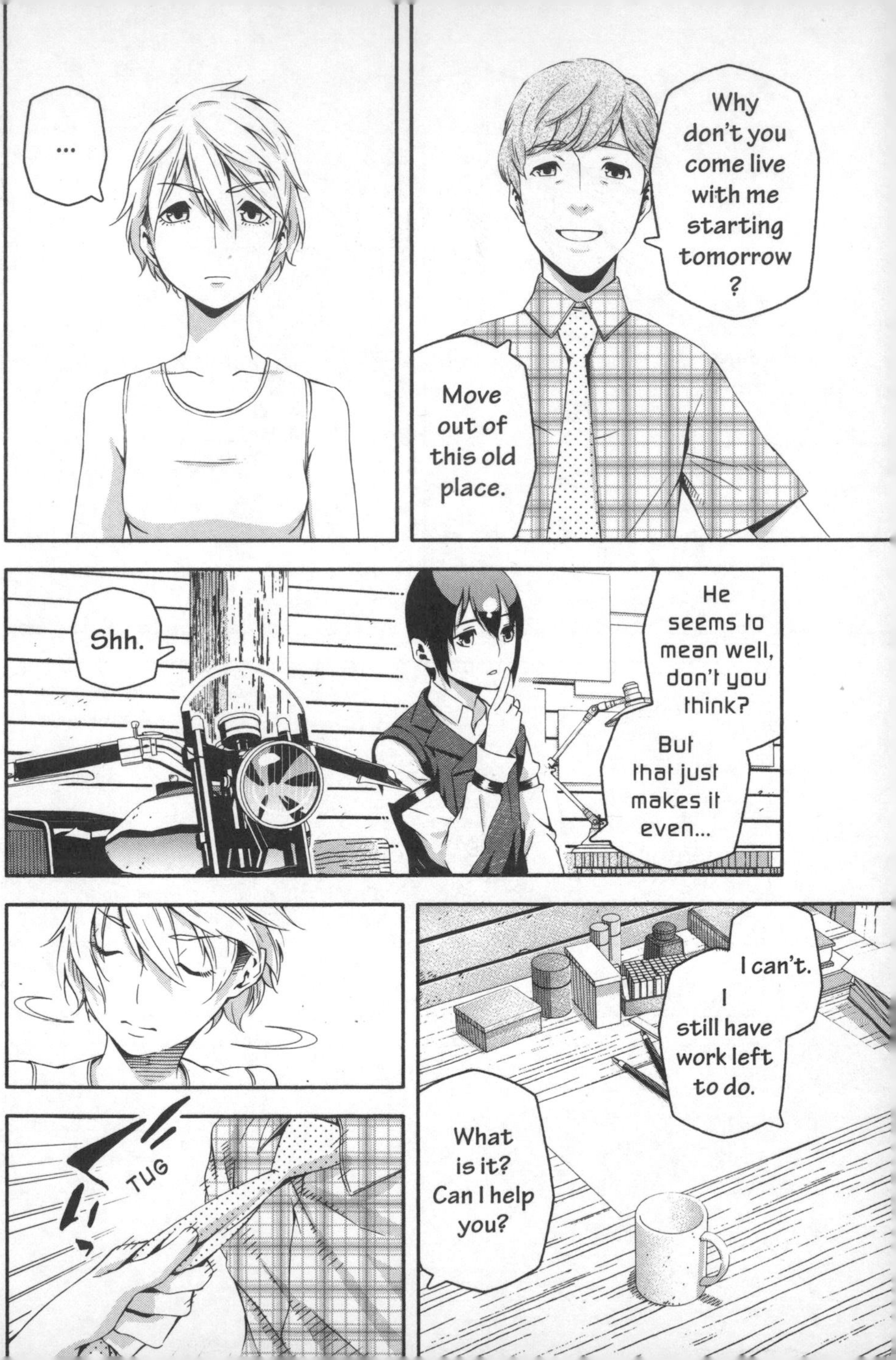

Why don't you come live with me starting tomorrow ?
Move out of this old place.
...
He seems to mean well, don't you think?
But that just makes it even...
Shh.
I can't.
I still have work left to do.
What is it? Can I help you?
TUG

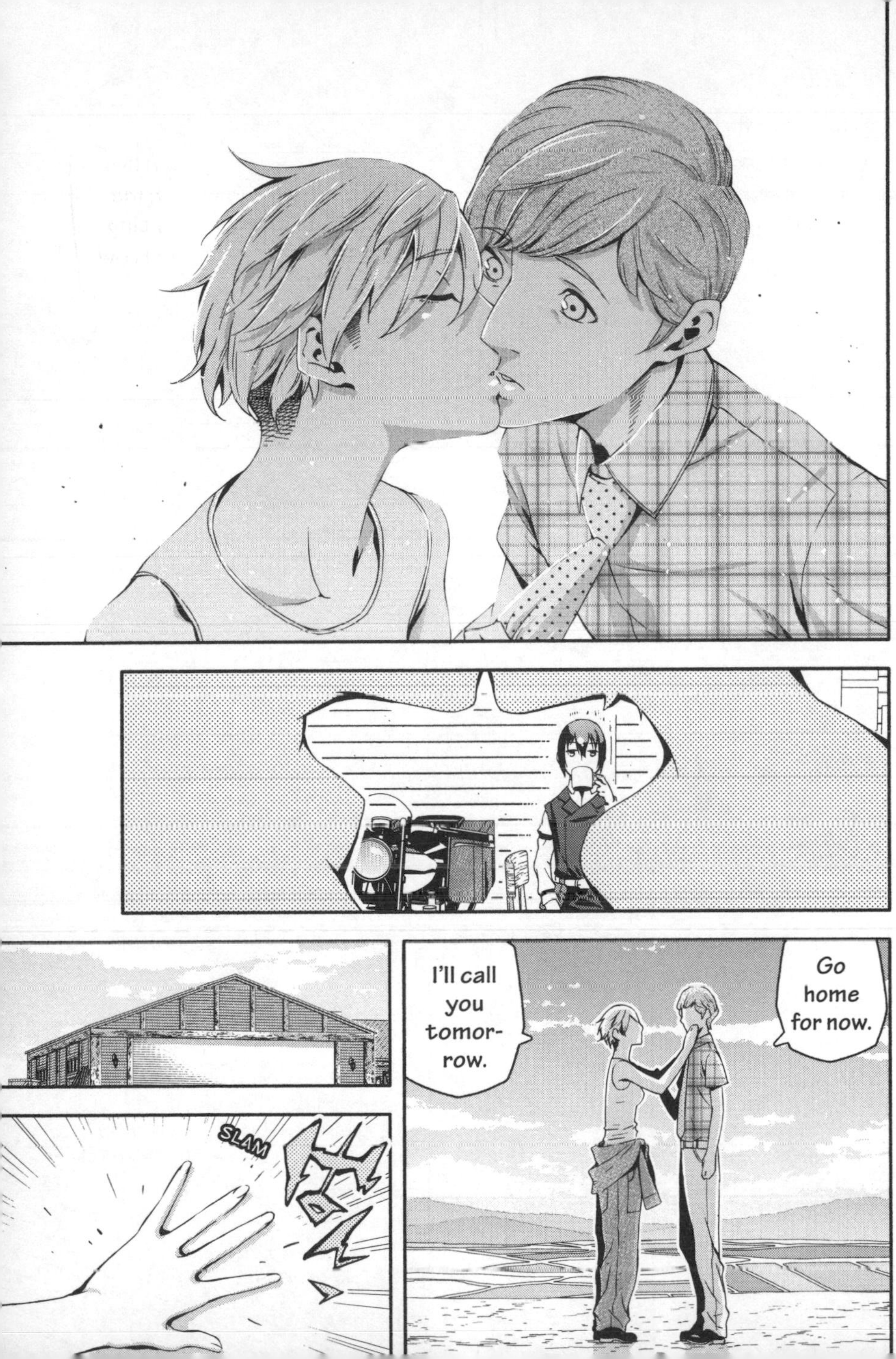
Go home for now.
I'll call you tomorrow.
SLAM

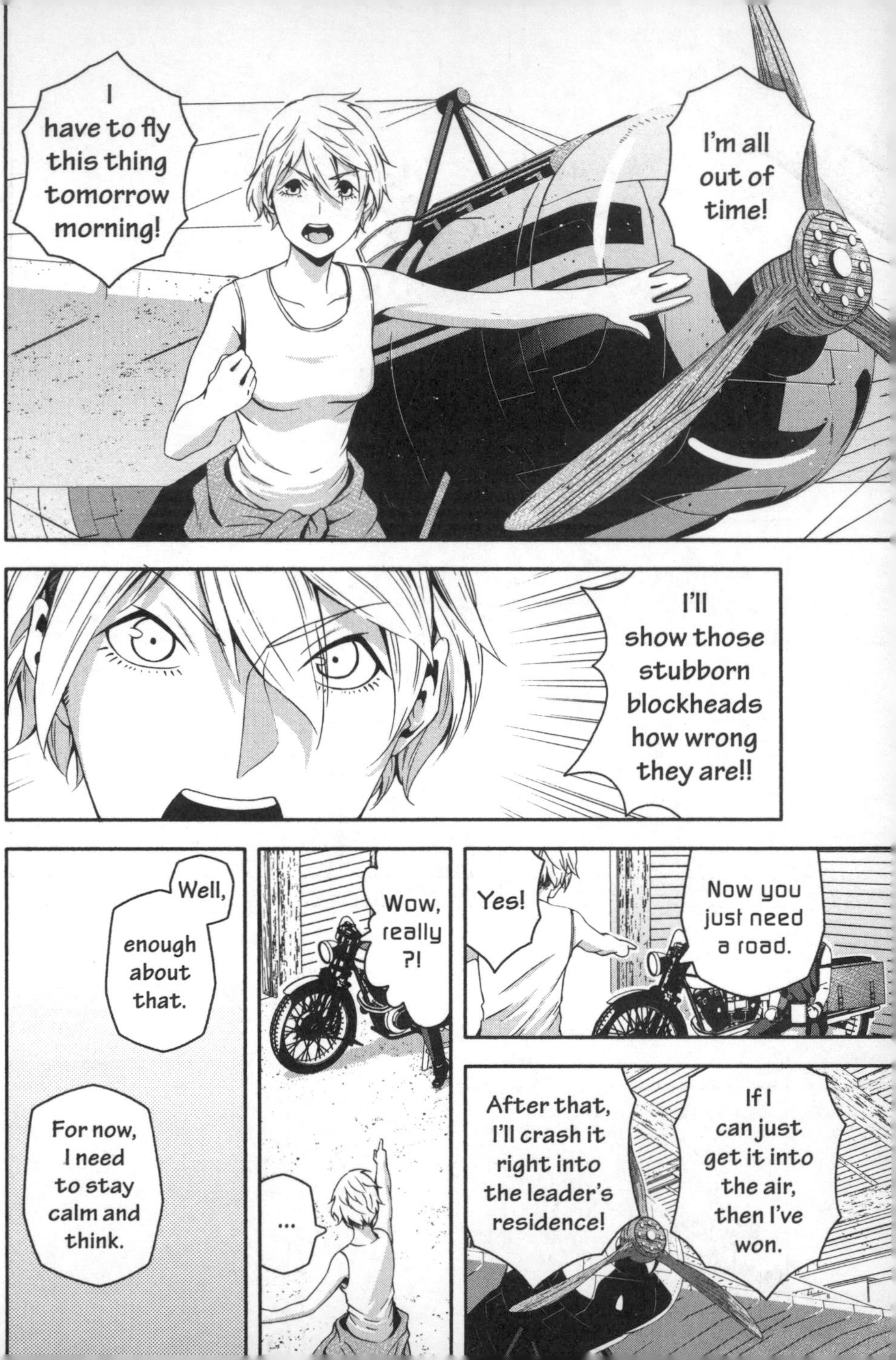
I'm all out of time!
I have to fly this thing tomorrow morning!
I'll show those stubborn blockheads how wrong they are!!
Now you just need a road.
Yes!
If I can just get it into the air, then I've won.
After that, I'll crash it right into the leader's residence!
Wow, really?!
...
Well,
enough about that.
For now, I need to stay calm and think.

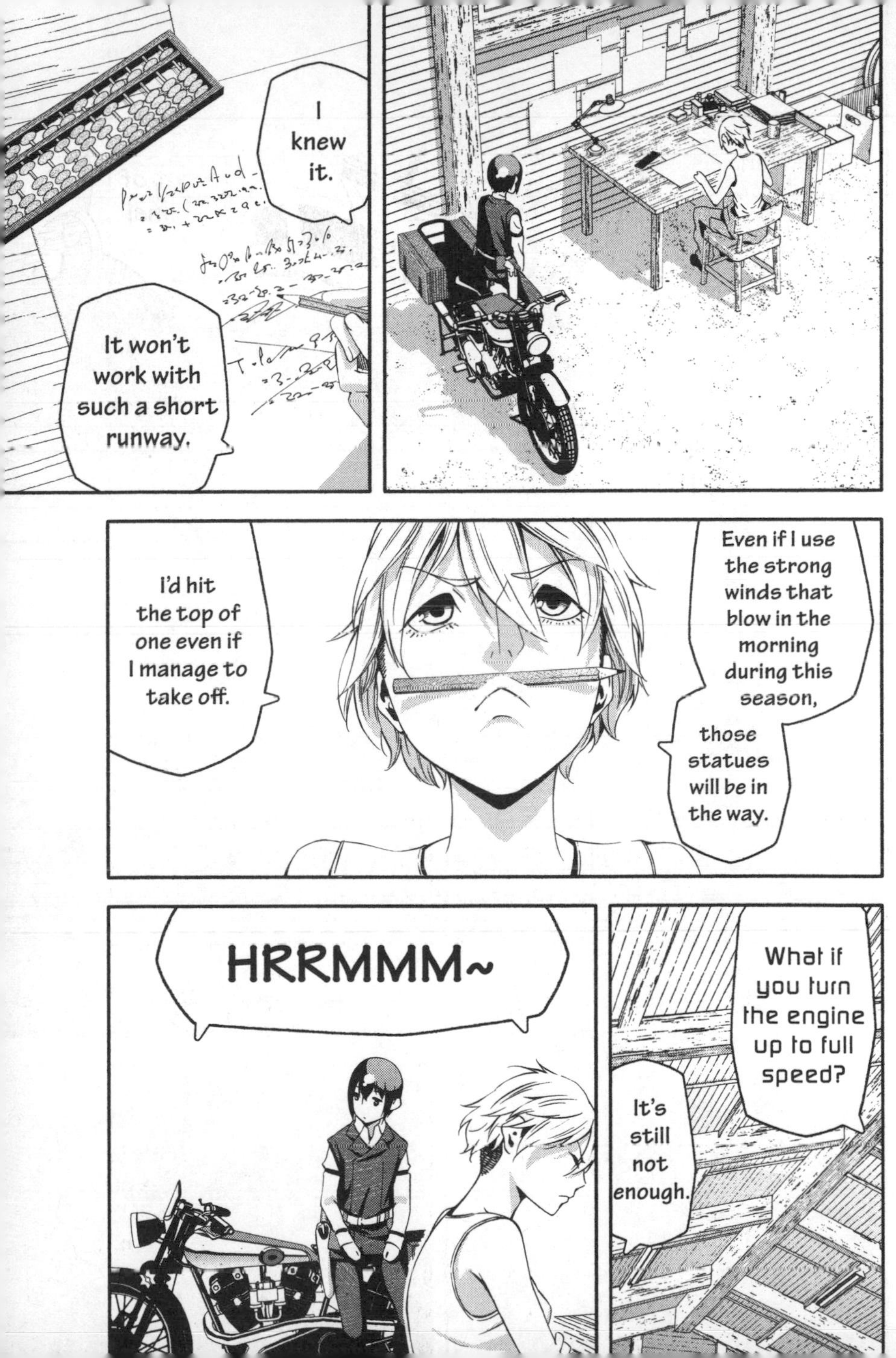
I knew it.
It won't work with such a short runway.
Even if I use the strong winds that blow in the morning during this season,
those statues will be in the way.
I'd hit the top of one even if I manage to take off.
What if you turn the engine up to full speed?
It's still not enough.
HRRMMM~

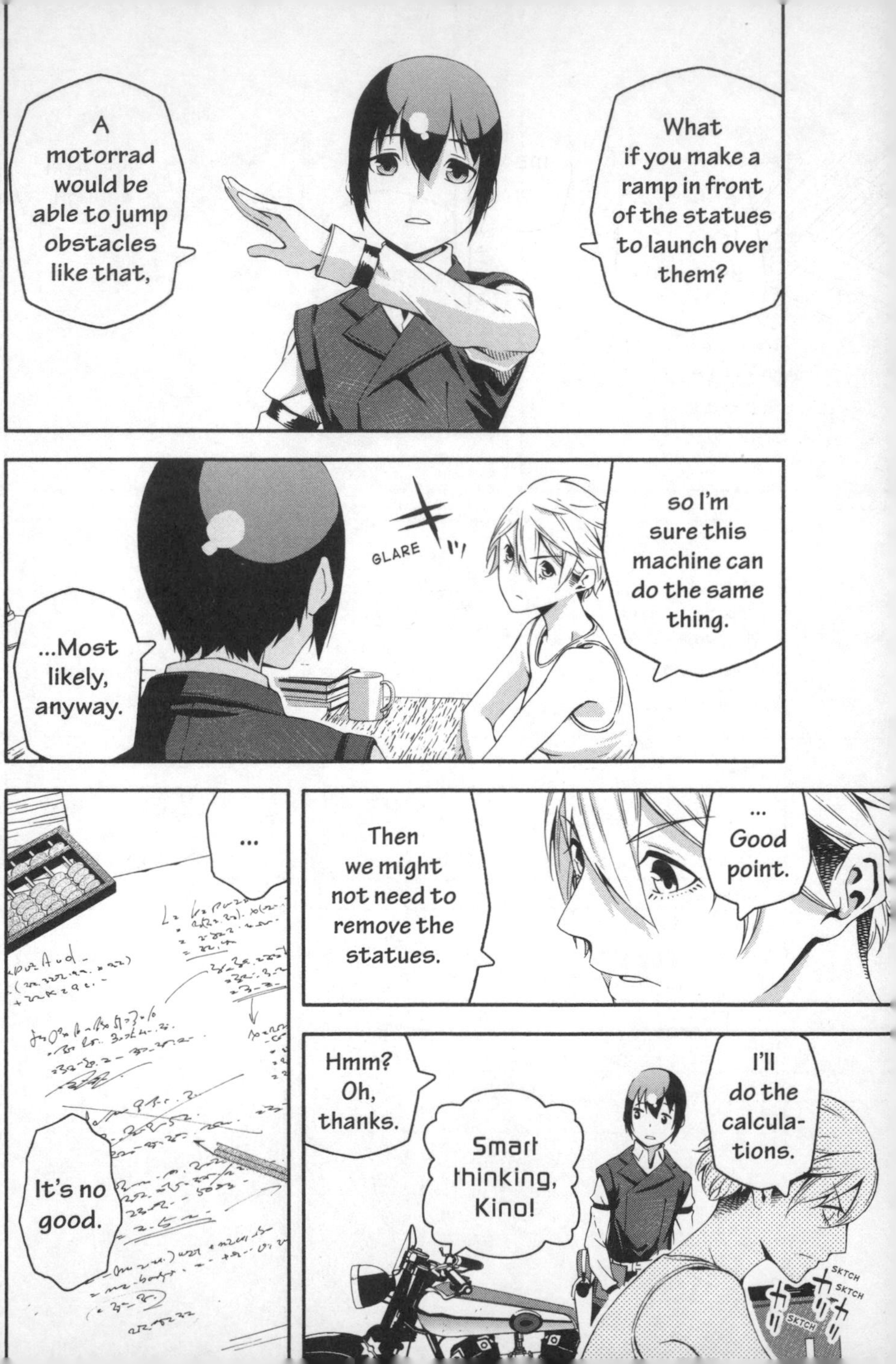
What if you make a ramp in front of the statues to launch over them?
A motorrad would be able to jump obstacles like that,
so I'm sure this machine can do the same thing.
GLARE
...Most likely, anyway.
... Good point.
Then we might not need to remove the statues.
I'll do the calculations.
Hmm? Oh, thanks.
Smart thinking, Kino!
SKTCH
SKTCH
SKTCH
...
It's no good.

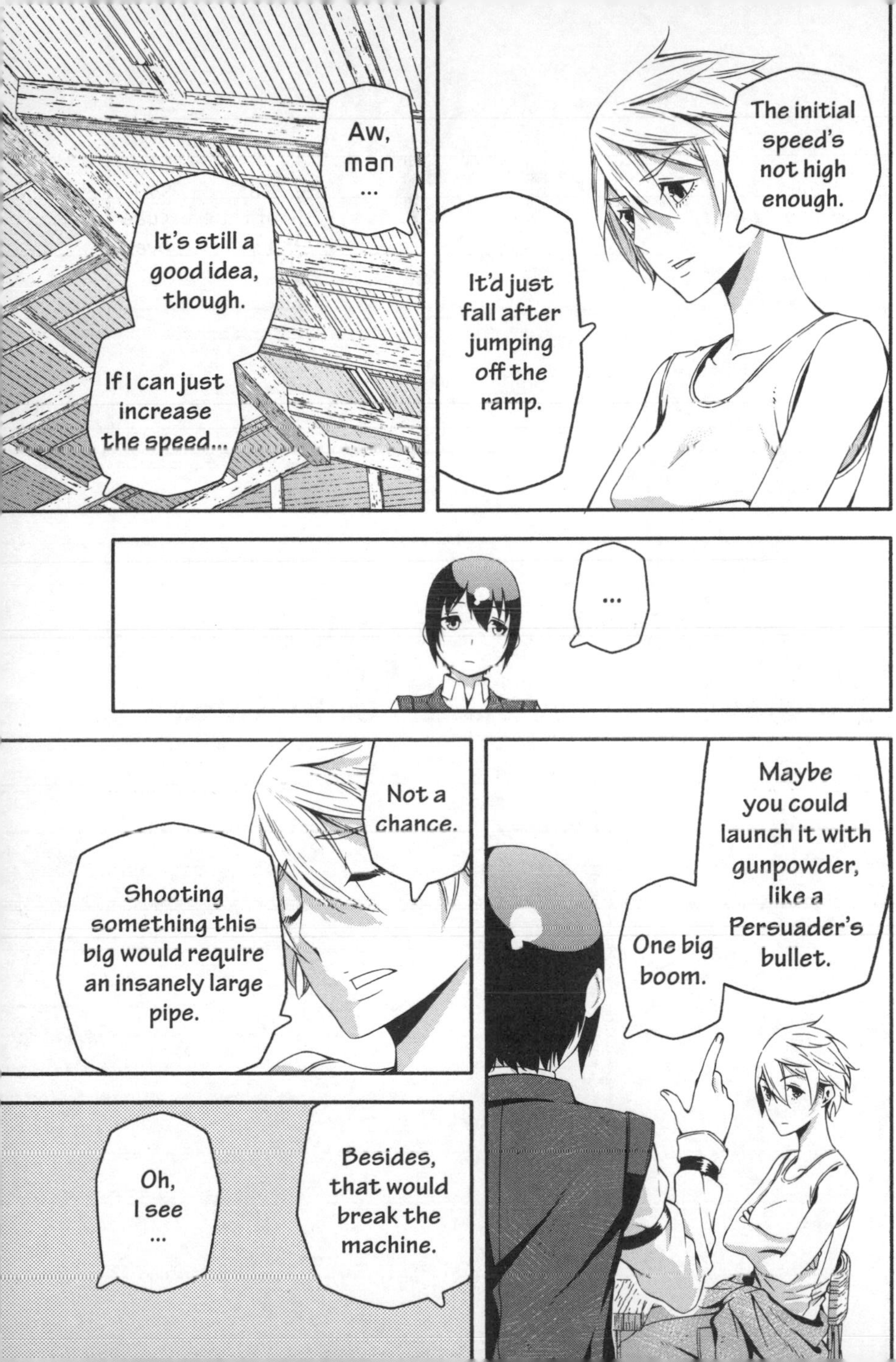
The initial speed's not high enough.
It'd just fall after jumping off the ramp.
Aw, man ...
It's still a good idea, though.
If I can just increase the speed...
...
Maybe you could launch it with gunpowder, like a Persuader's bullet.
One big boom.
Not a chance.
Shooting something this big would require an insanely large pipe.
Besides, that would break the machine.
Oh, I see ...

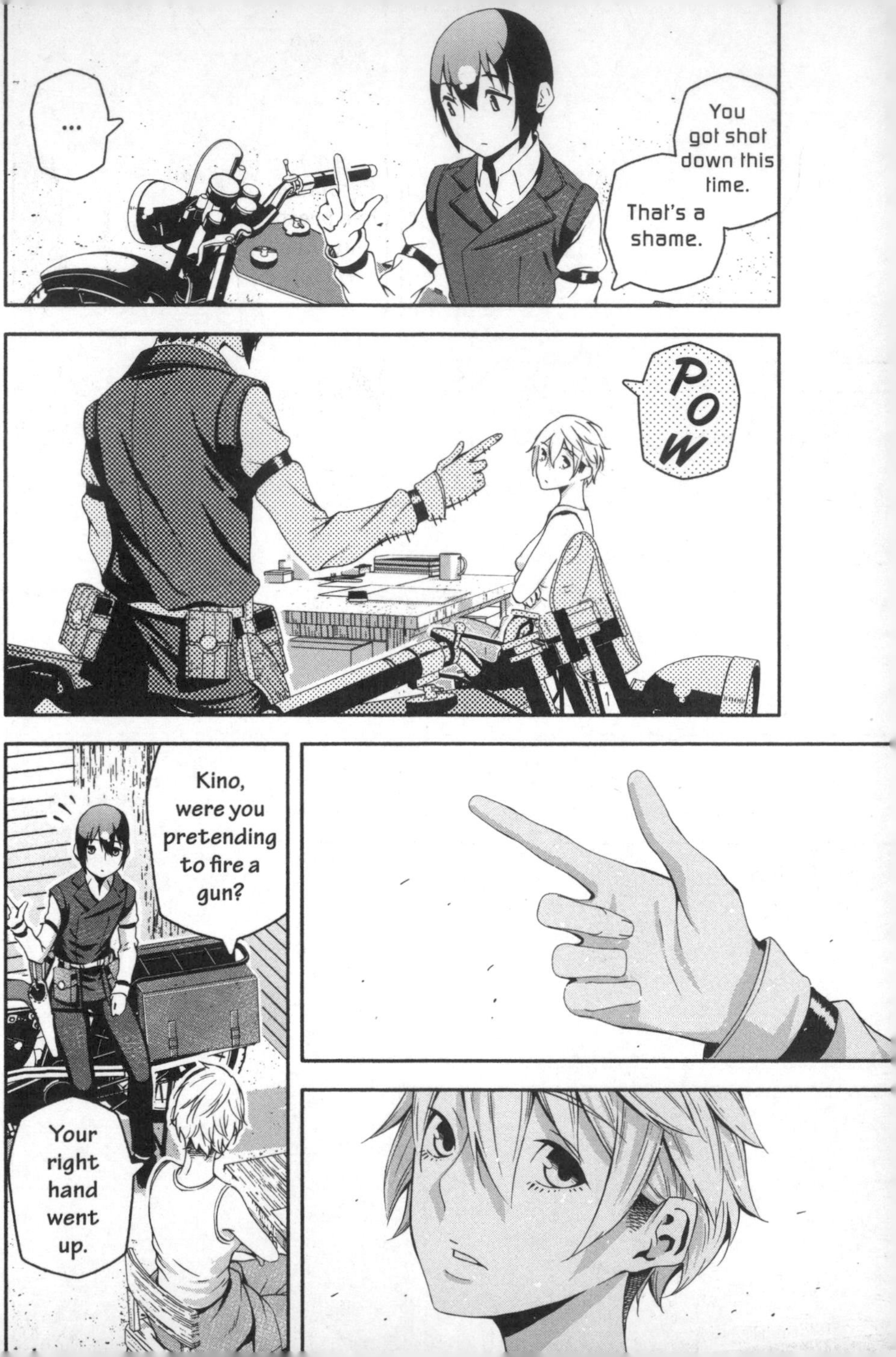
You got shot down this time.
That's a shame.
...
POW
Kino, were you pretending to fire a gun?
Your right hand went up.

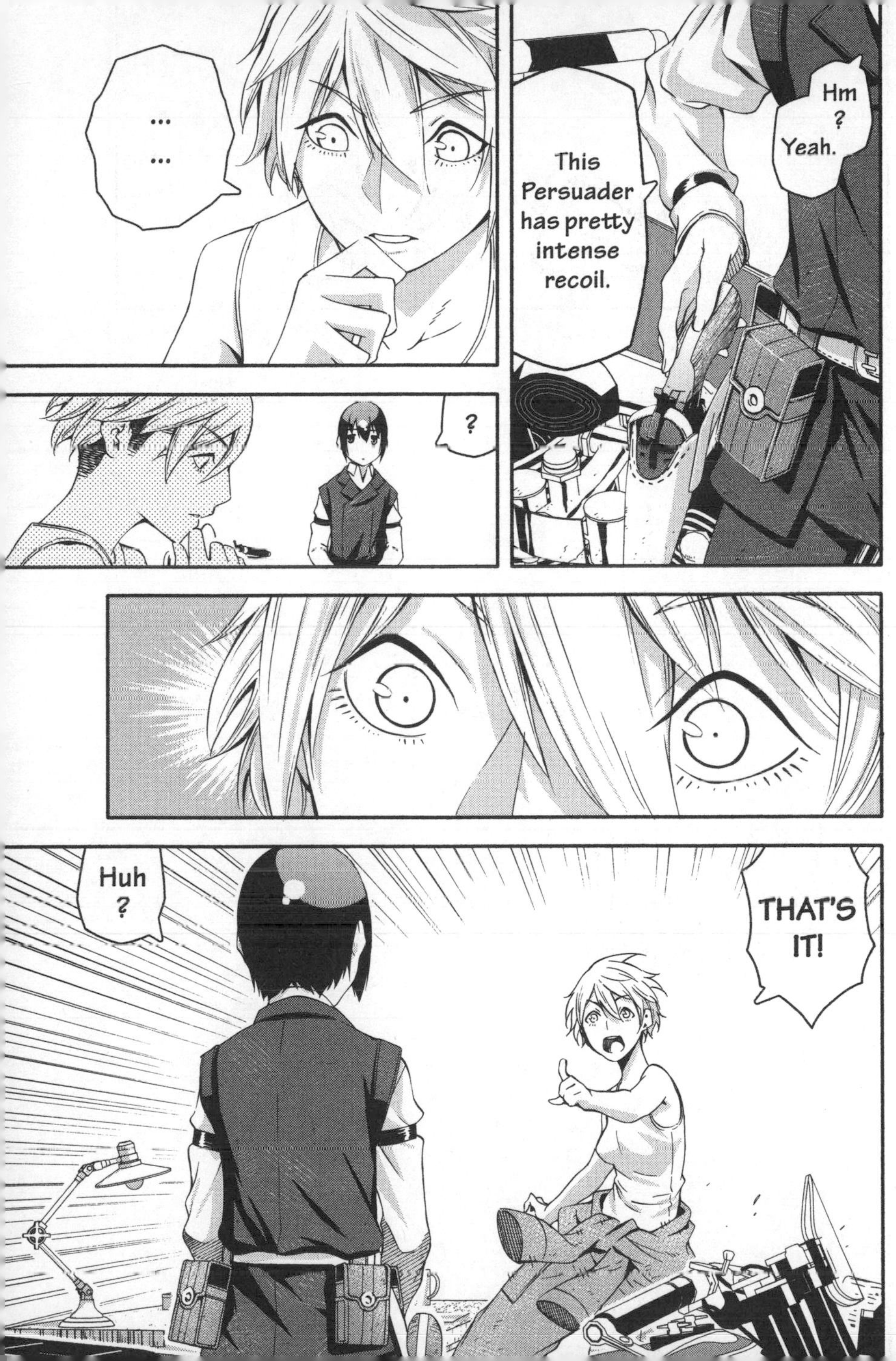
Hm? Yeah.
This Persuader has pretty intense recoil.
... ...
?
THAT'S IT!
Huh?

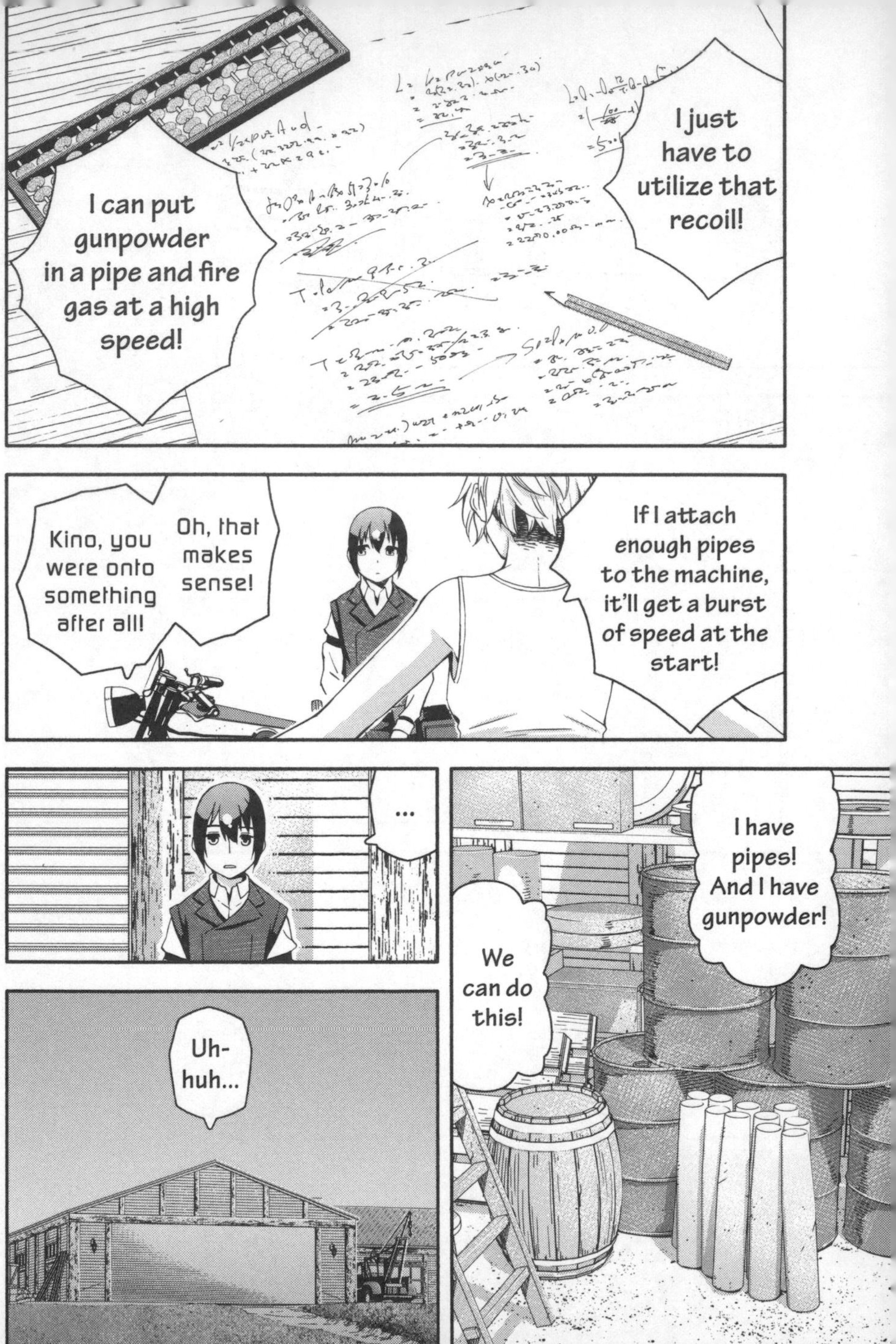
I just have to utilize that recoil!
I can put gunpowder in a pipe and fire gas at a high speed!
If I attach enough pipes to the machine, it'll get a burst of speed at the start!
Oh, that makes sense!
Kino, you were onto something after all!
I have pipes! And I have gunpowder!
We can do this!
...
Uh-huh...

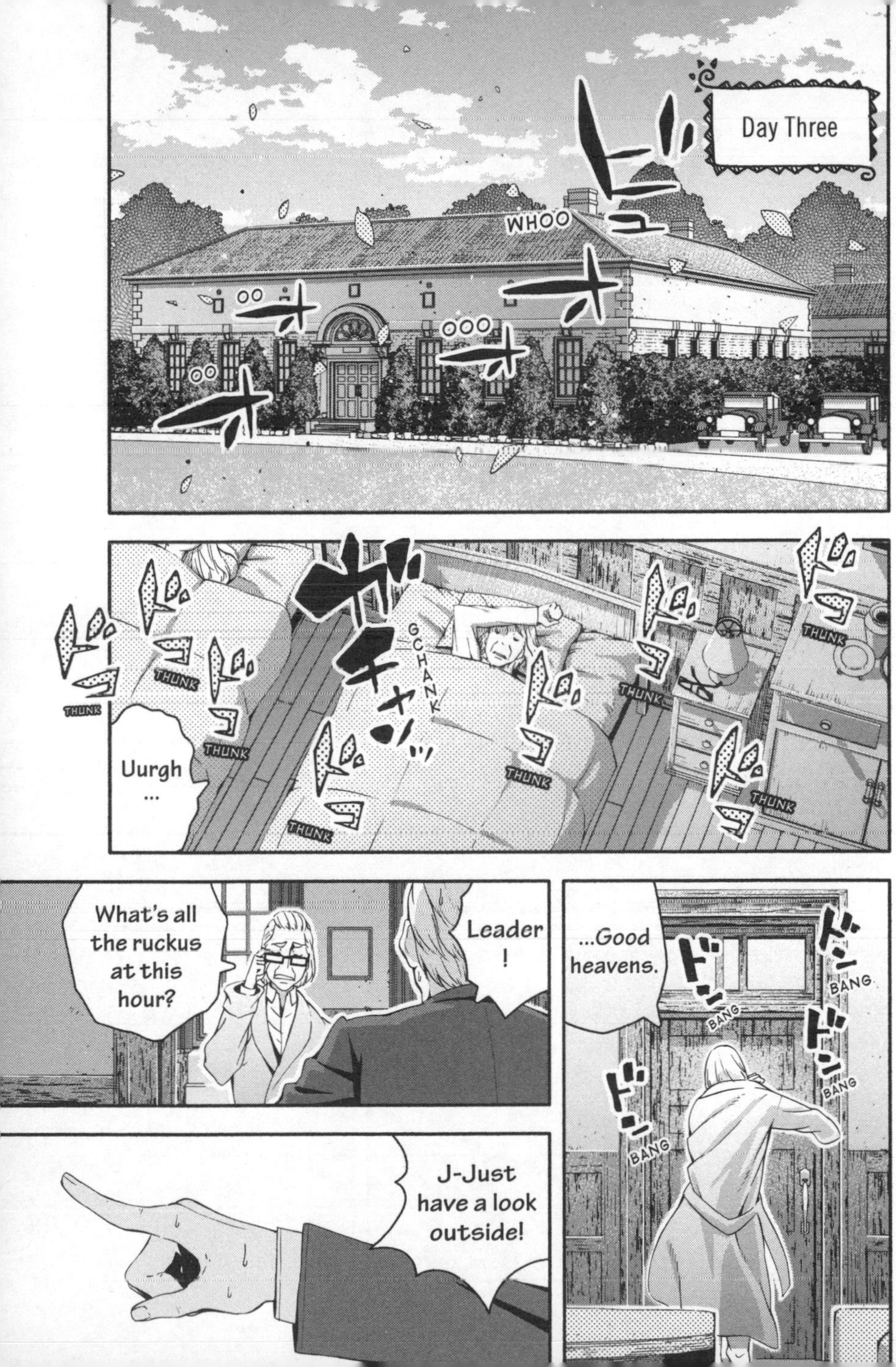

Day Three
WHOO
THUNK
THUNK
GCHANK
THUNK
THUNK
THUNK
THUNK
THUNK
THUNK
Uurgh ...
...Good heavens.
BANG
BANG
BANG
BANG
Leader!
What's all the ruckus at this hour?
J-Just have a look outside!

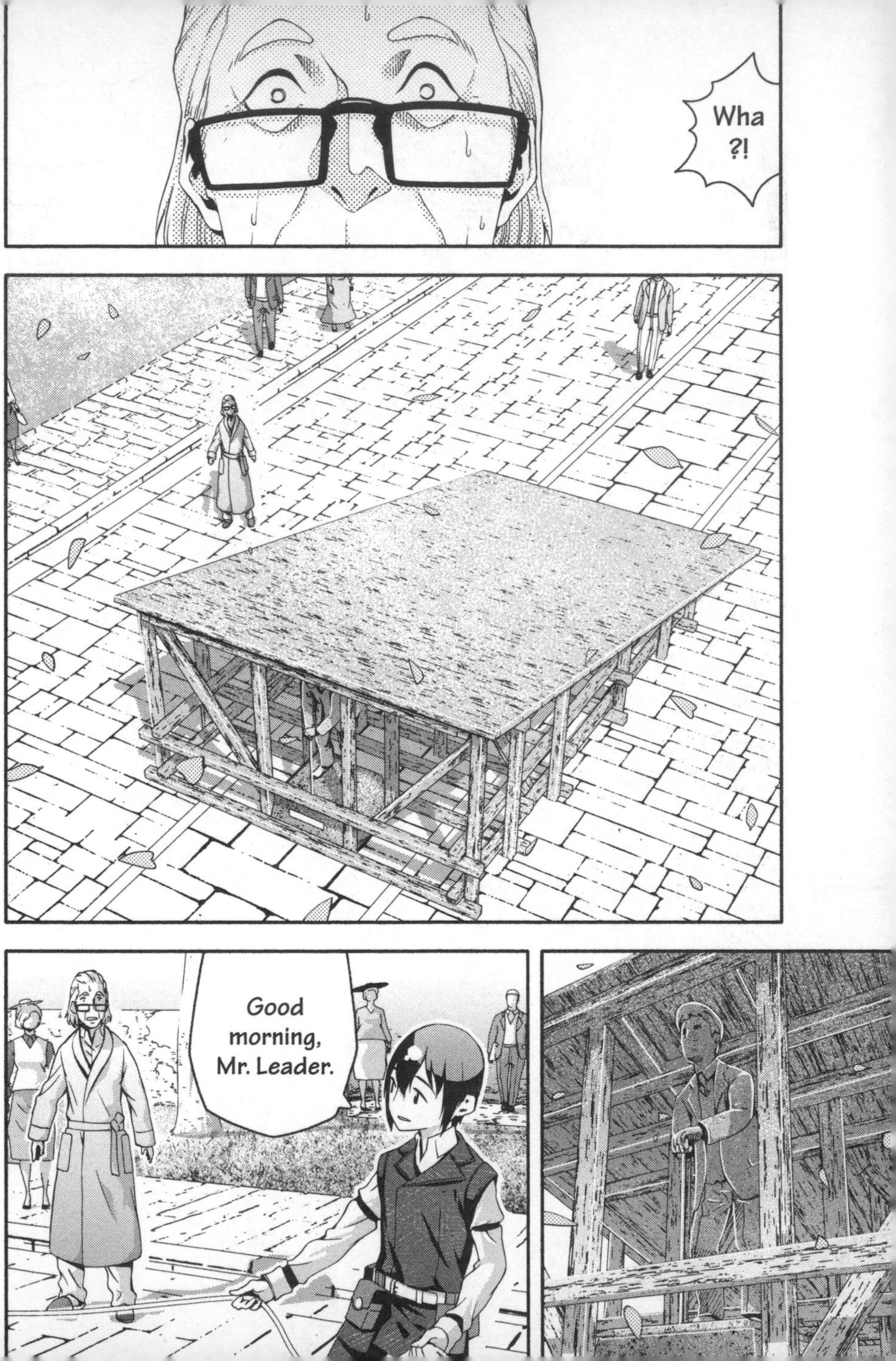
Wha ?!
Good morning, Mr. Leader.

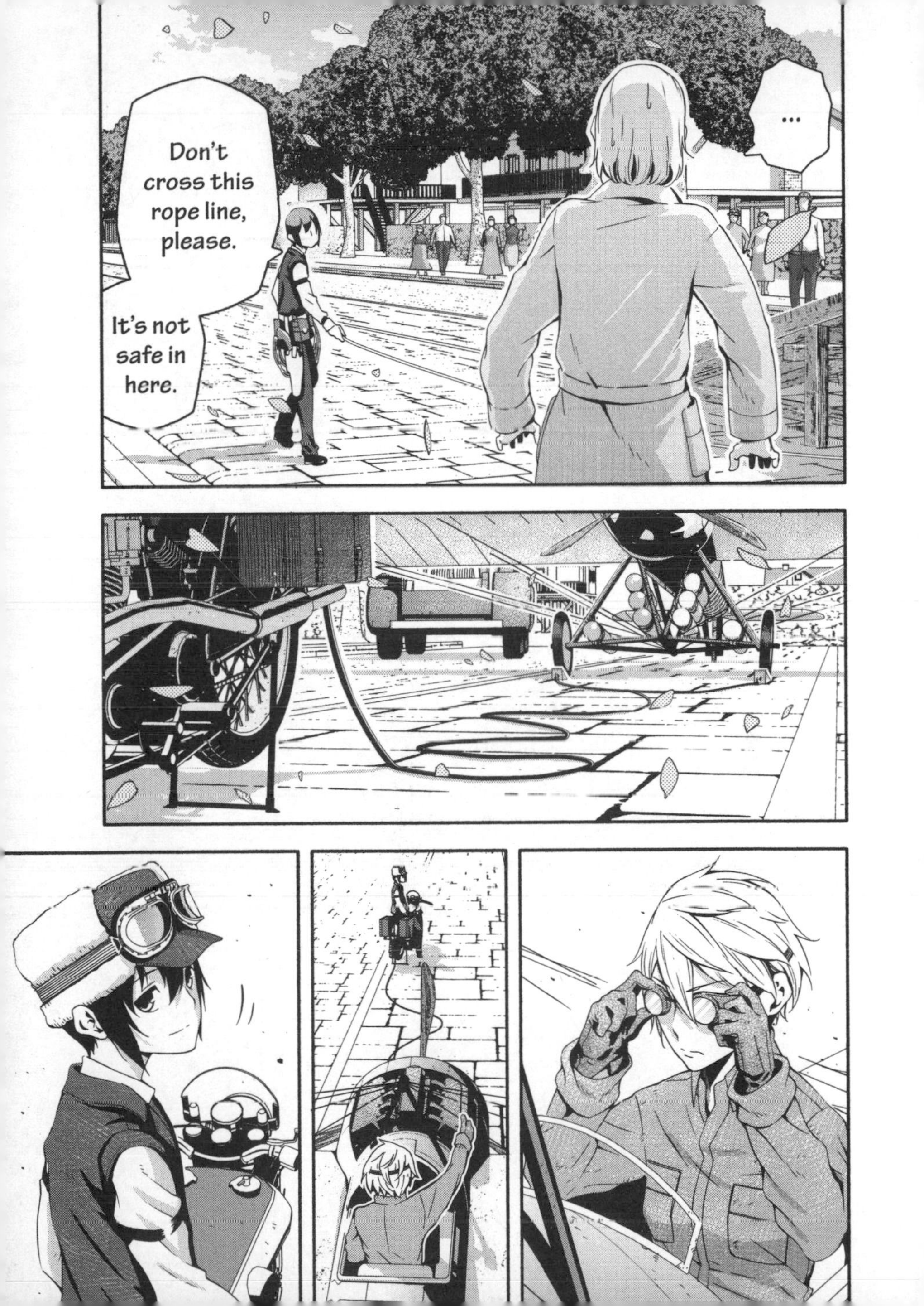
...
Don't cross this rope line, please.
It's not safe in here.

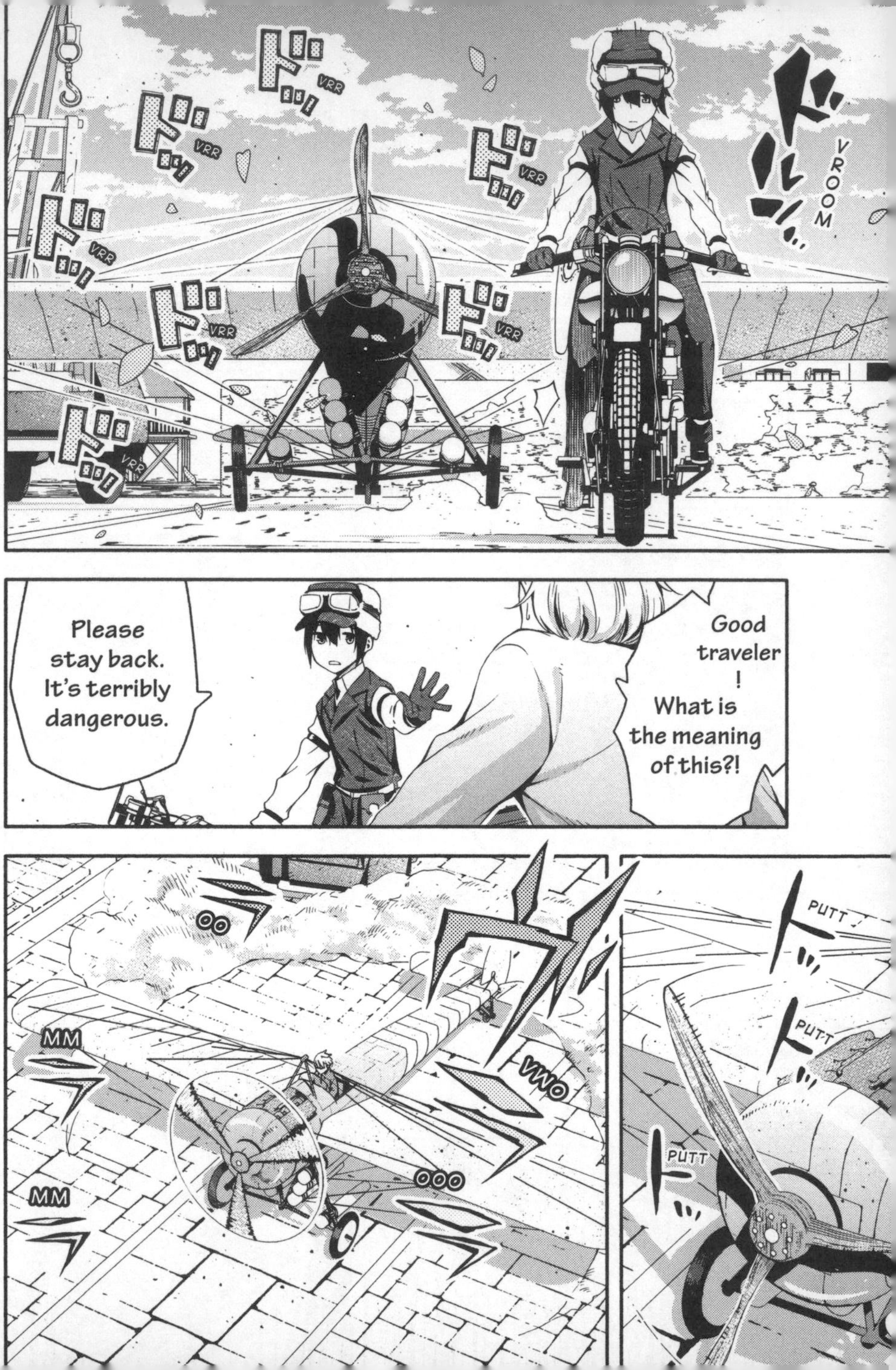
VROOM
VRR
VRR
VRR
VRR
VRR
VRR
Good traveler! What is the meaning of this?!
Please stay back. It's terribly dangerous.
PUTT
PUTT
PUTT
OO
VWO
MM
OOO
MM

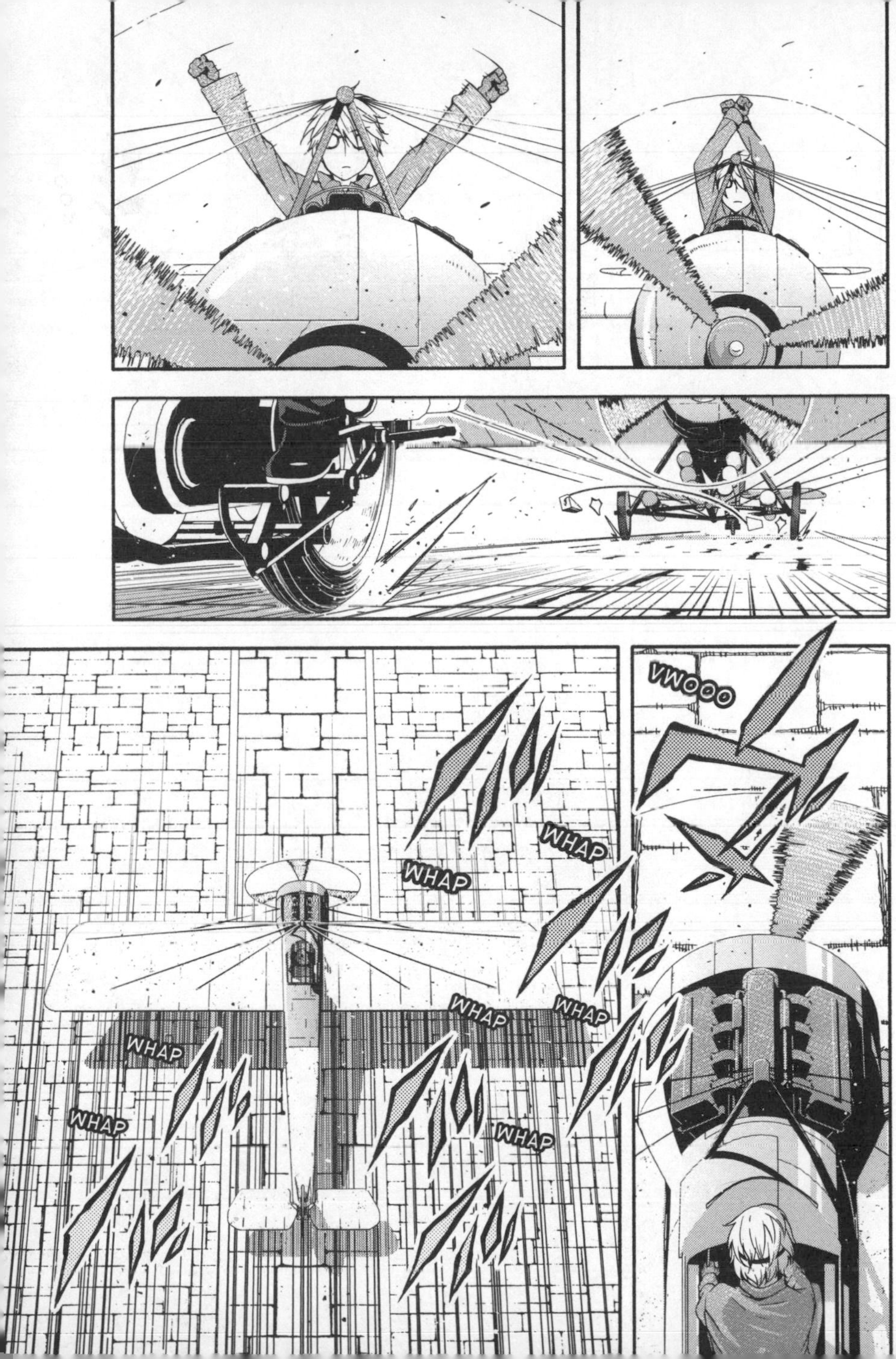
VWOOO
WHAP
WHAP
WHAP
WHAP
WHAP
WHAP
WHAP

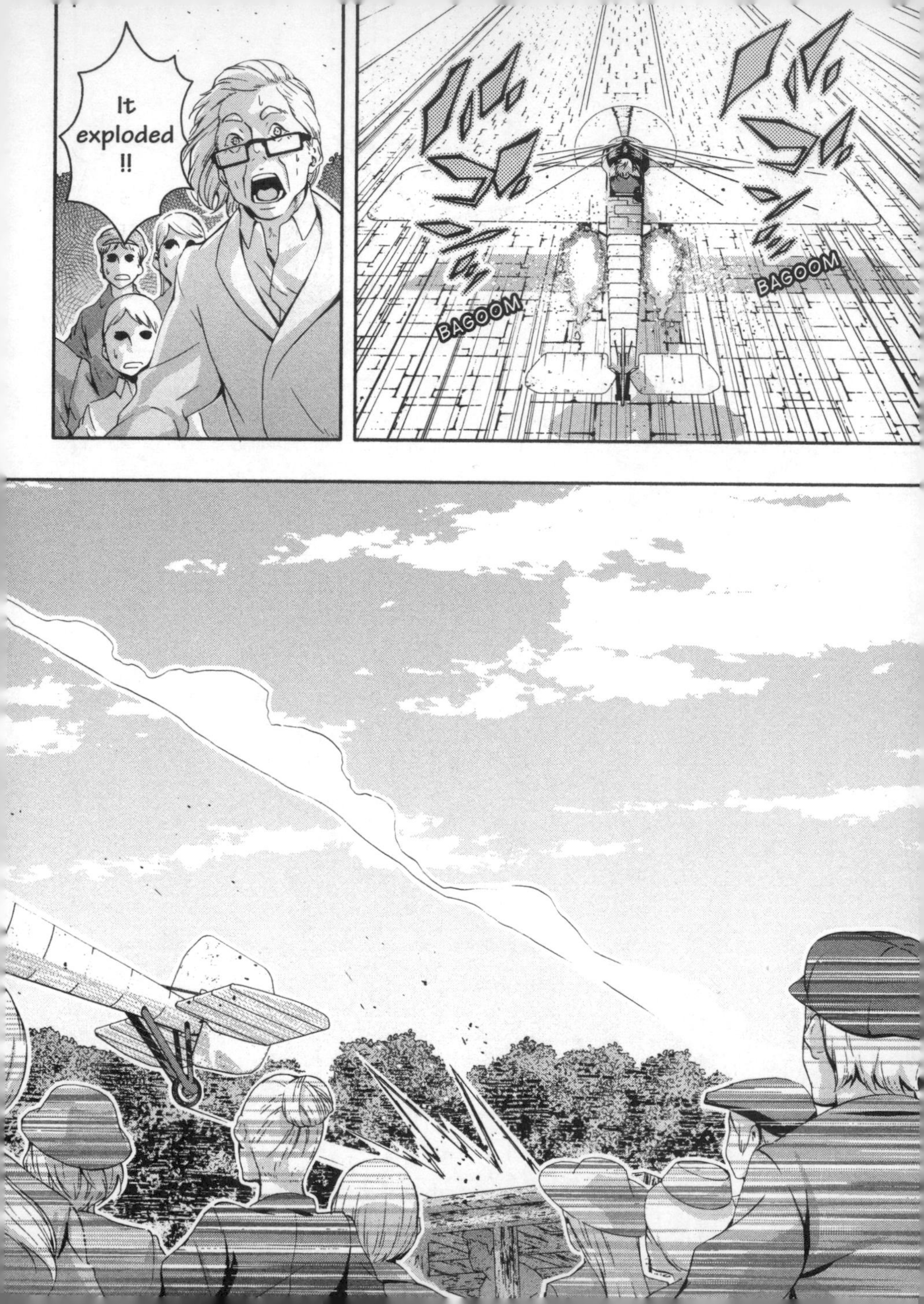
BAGOOM
BAGOOM
It exploded !!

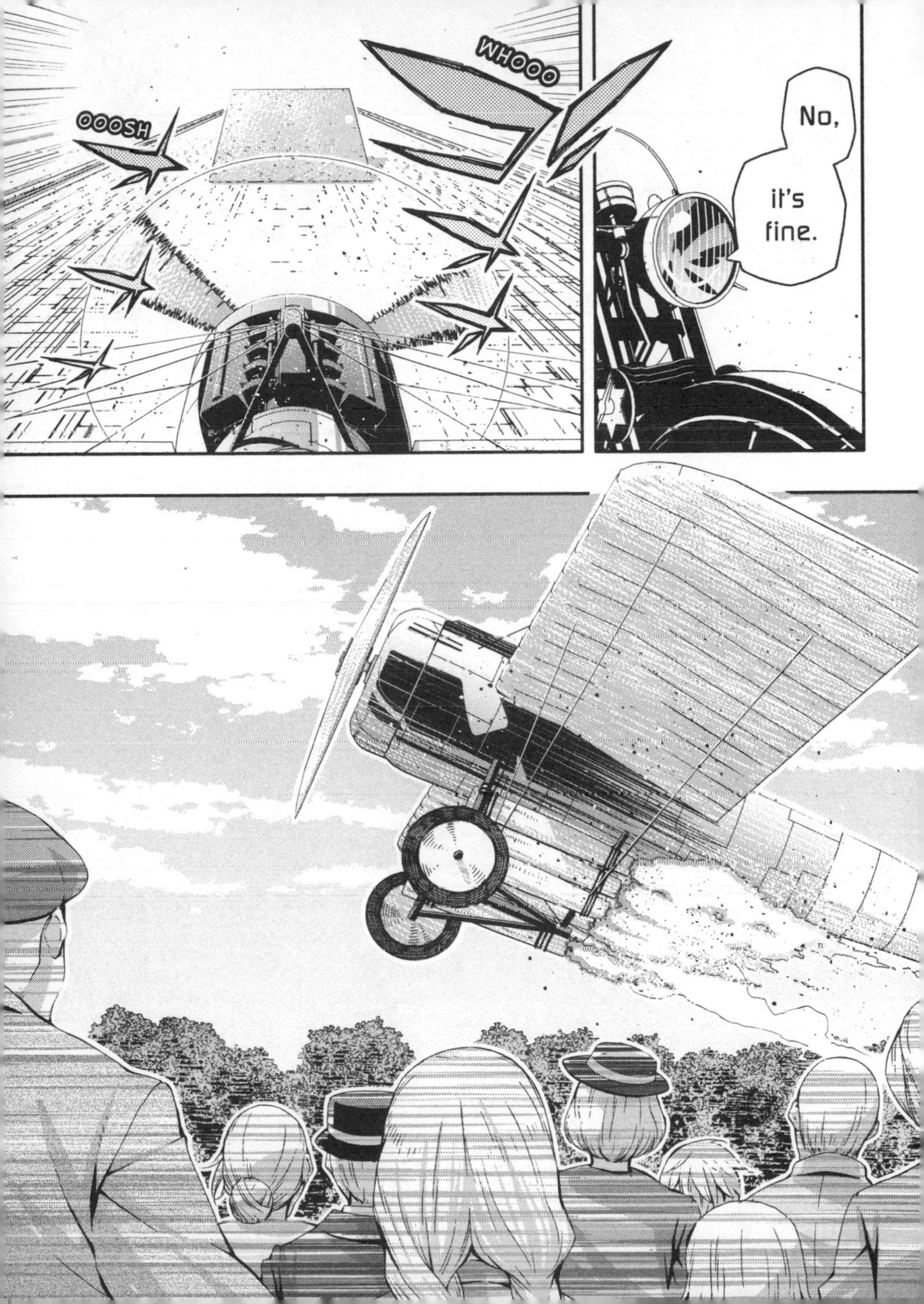
No, it's fine.
WHOOO
OOOSH

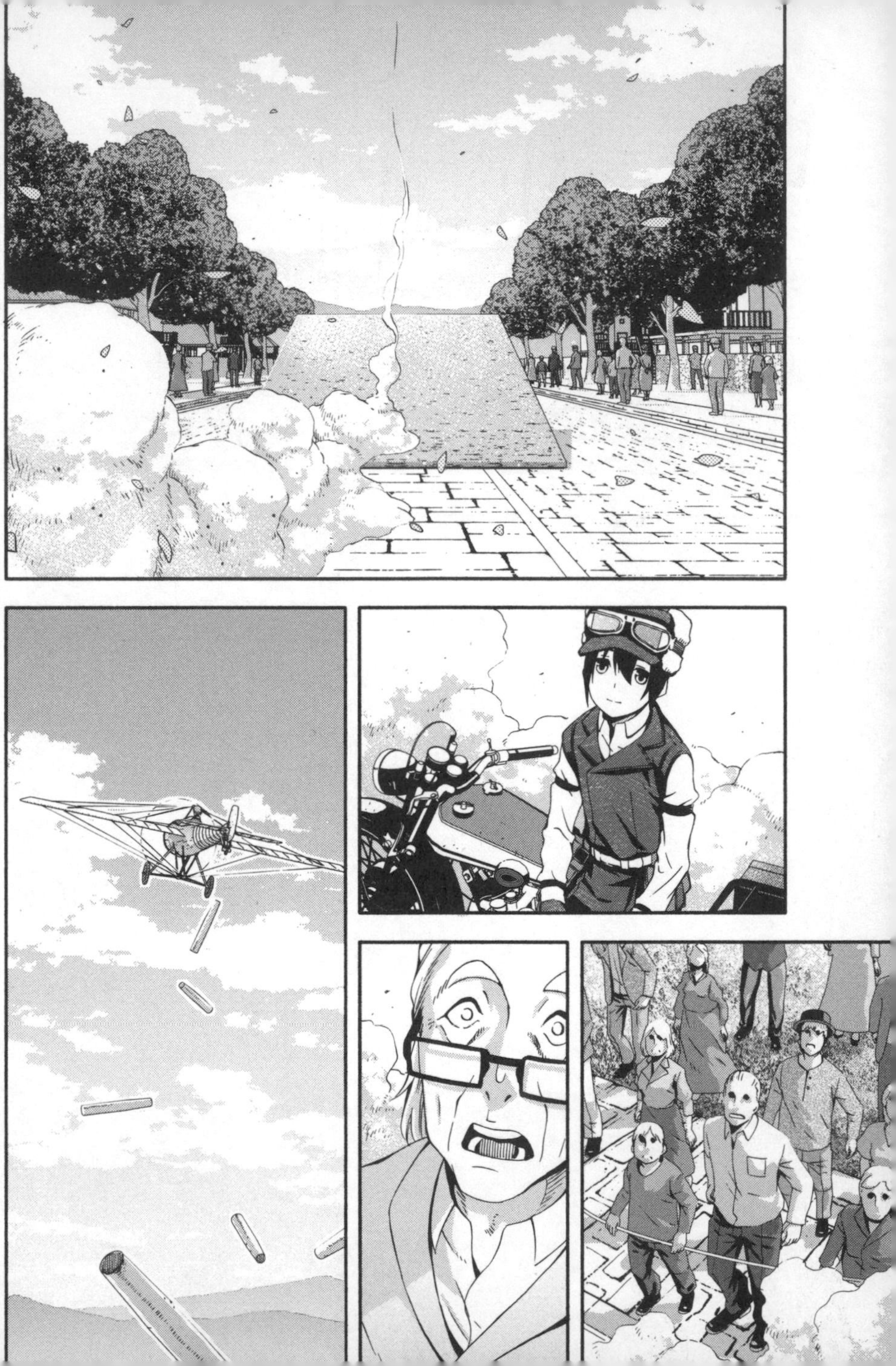

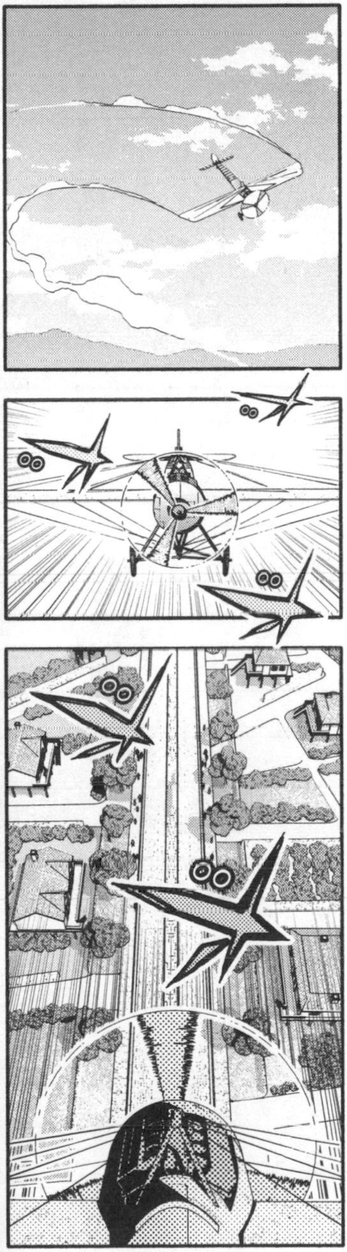
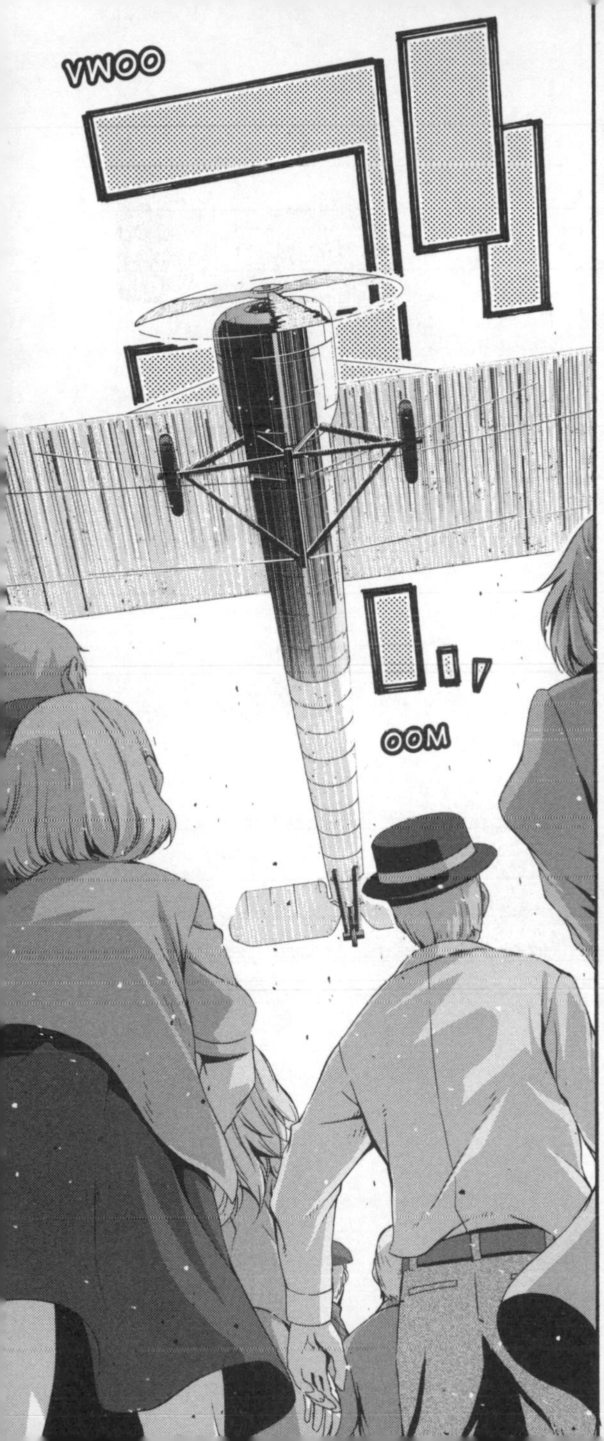
VWOO
OOM

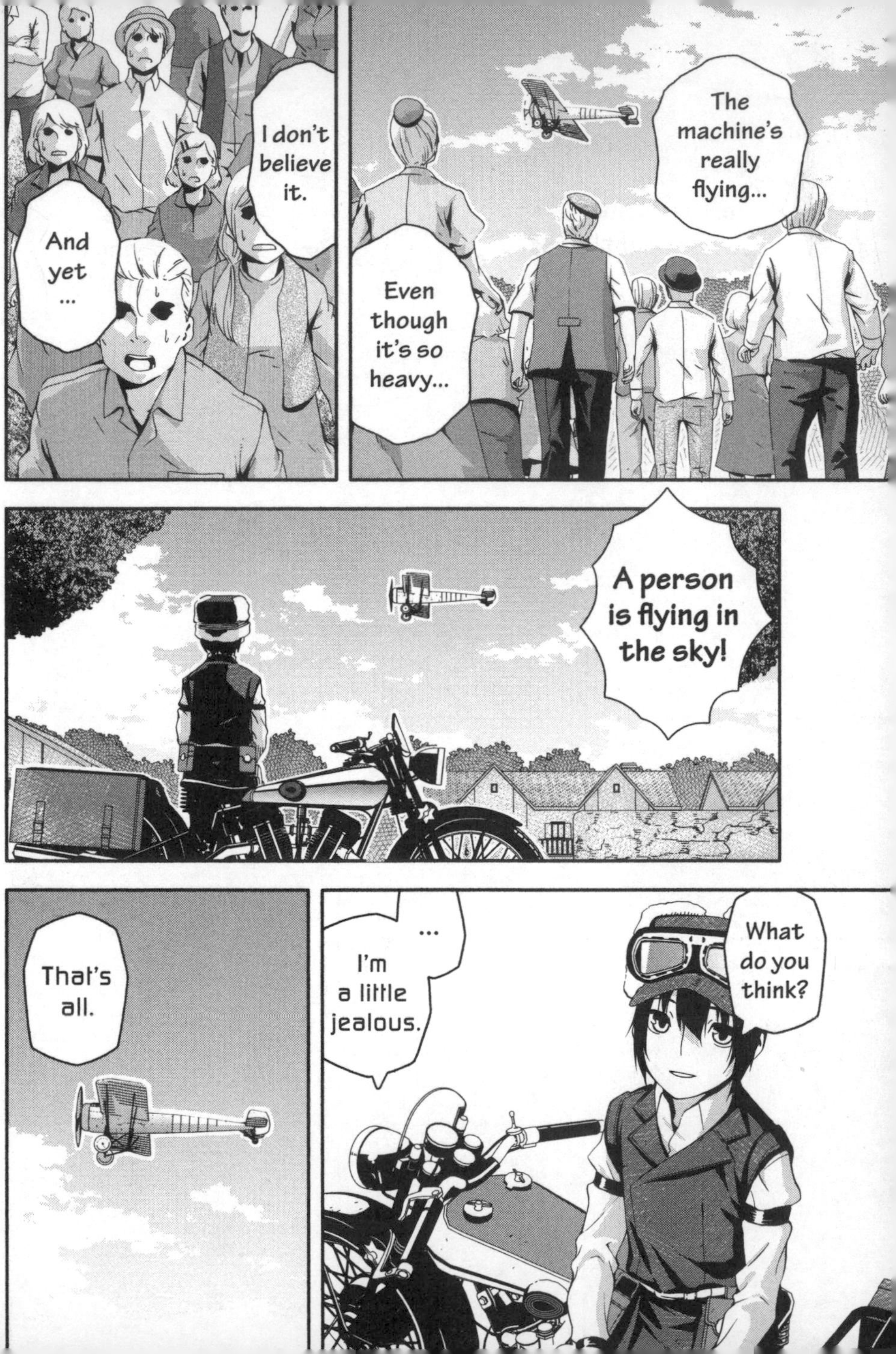
The machine's really flying...
Even though it's so heavy...
I don't believe it.
And yet ...
A person is flying in the sky!
What do you think?
... I'm a little jealous.
That's all.

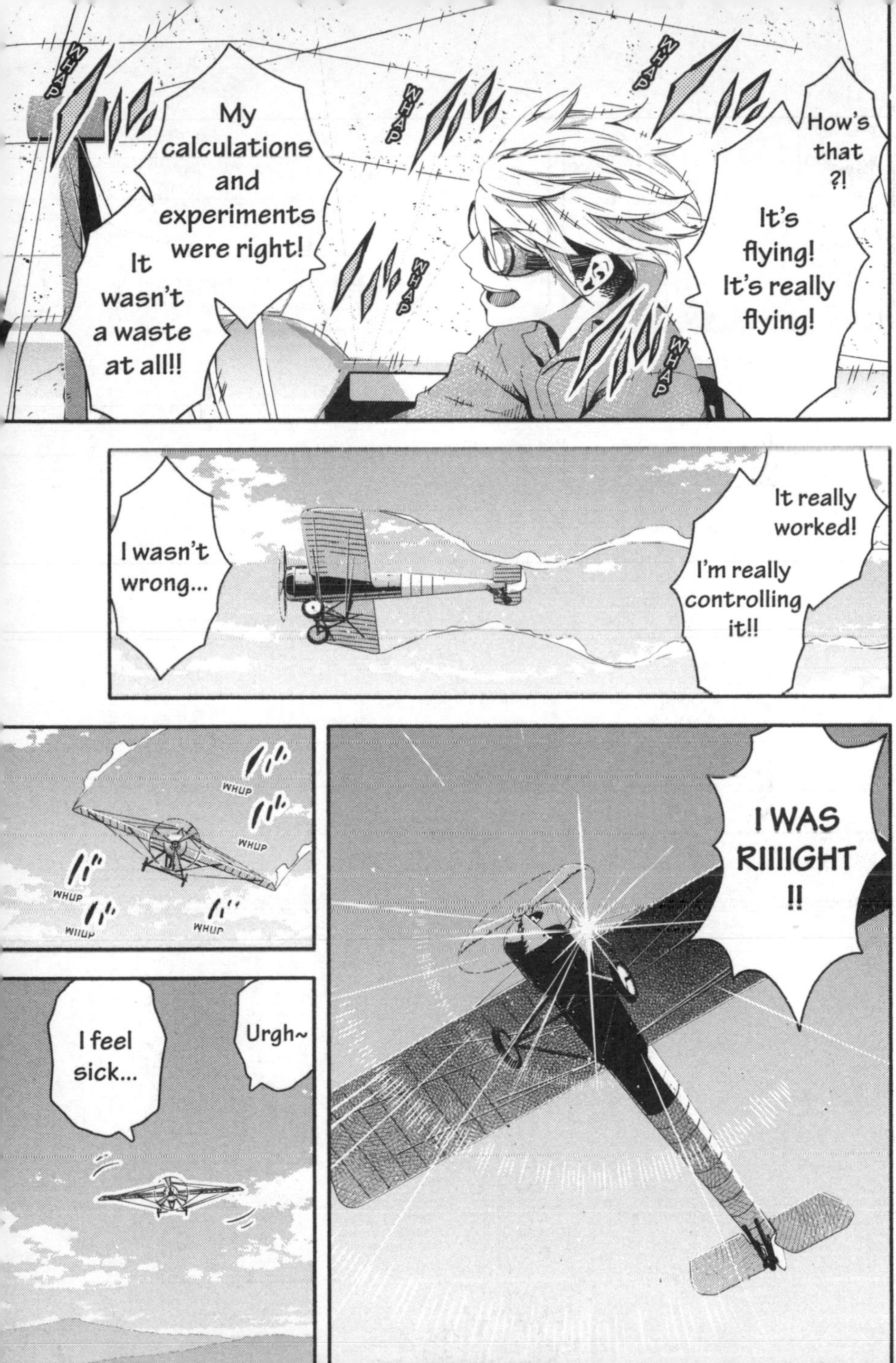
WHAP
WHAP
How's that?!
It's flying! It's really flying!
WHAP
WHAP
My calculations and experiments were right!
It wasn't a waste at all!!
WHAP
It really worked!
I'm really controlling it!!
I wasn't wrong...
I WAS RIIIIGHT!!
WHUP
WHUP
WHUP
WHUP
WHUP
Urgh~
I feel sick...

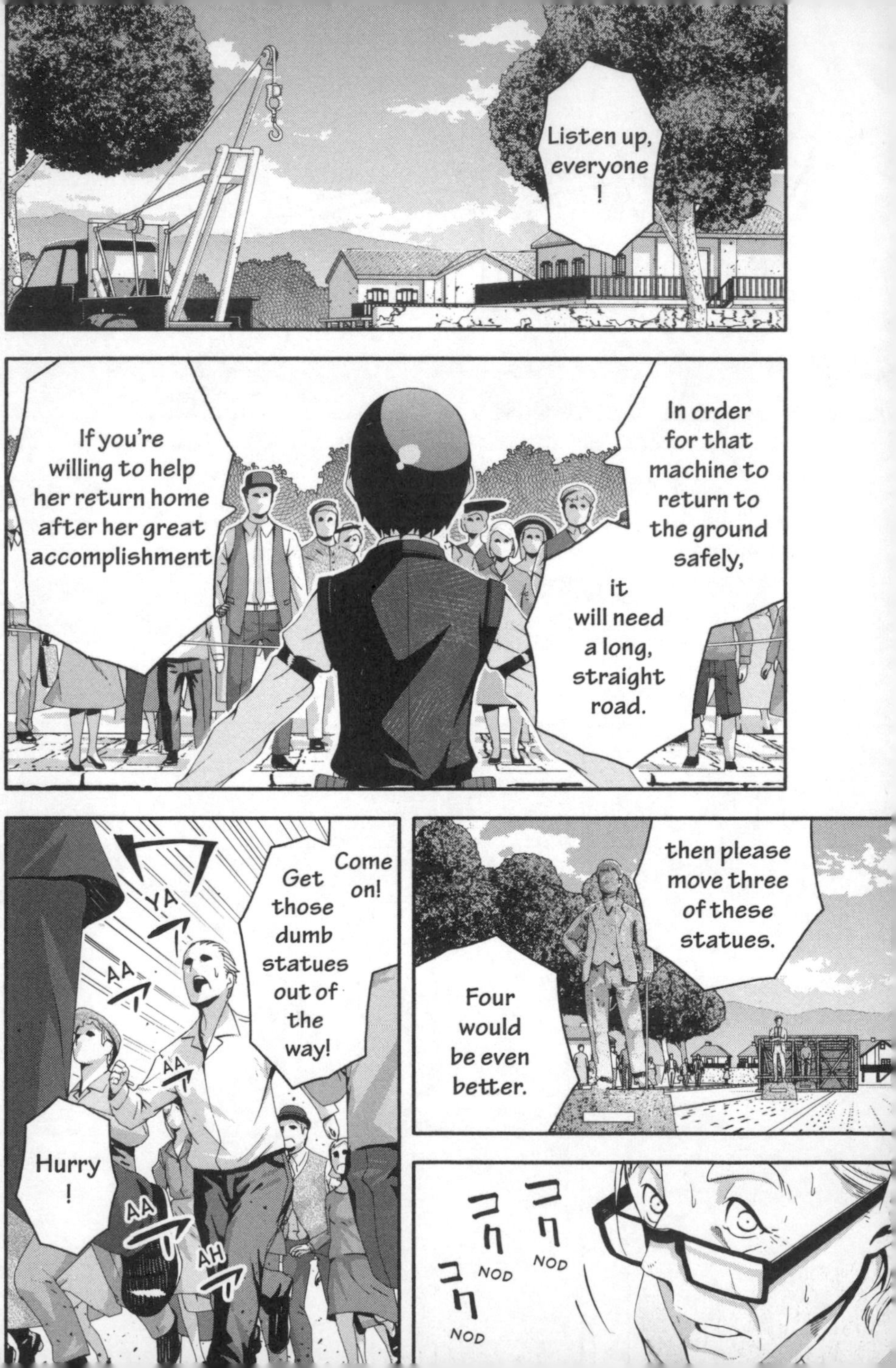
Listen up, everyone!
In order for that machine to return to the ground safely,
it will need a long, straight road.
If you're willing to help her return home after her great accomplishment
then please move three of these statues.
Four would be even better.
コク NOD
コク NOD
コク NOD
Come on!
Get those dumb statues out of the way!
YA
AA
AA
Hurry!
AA
AH

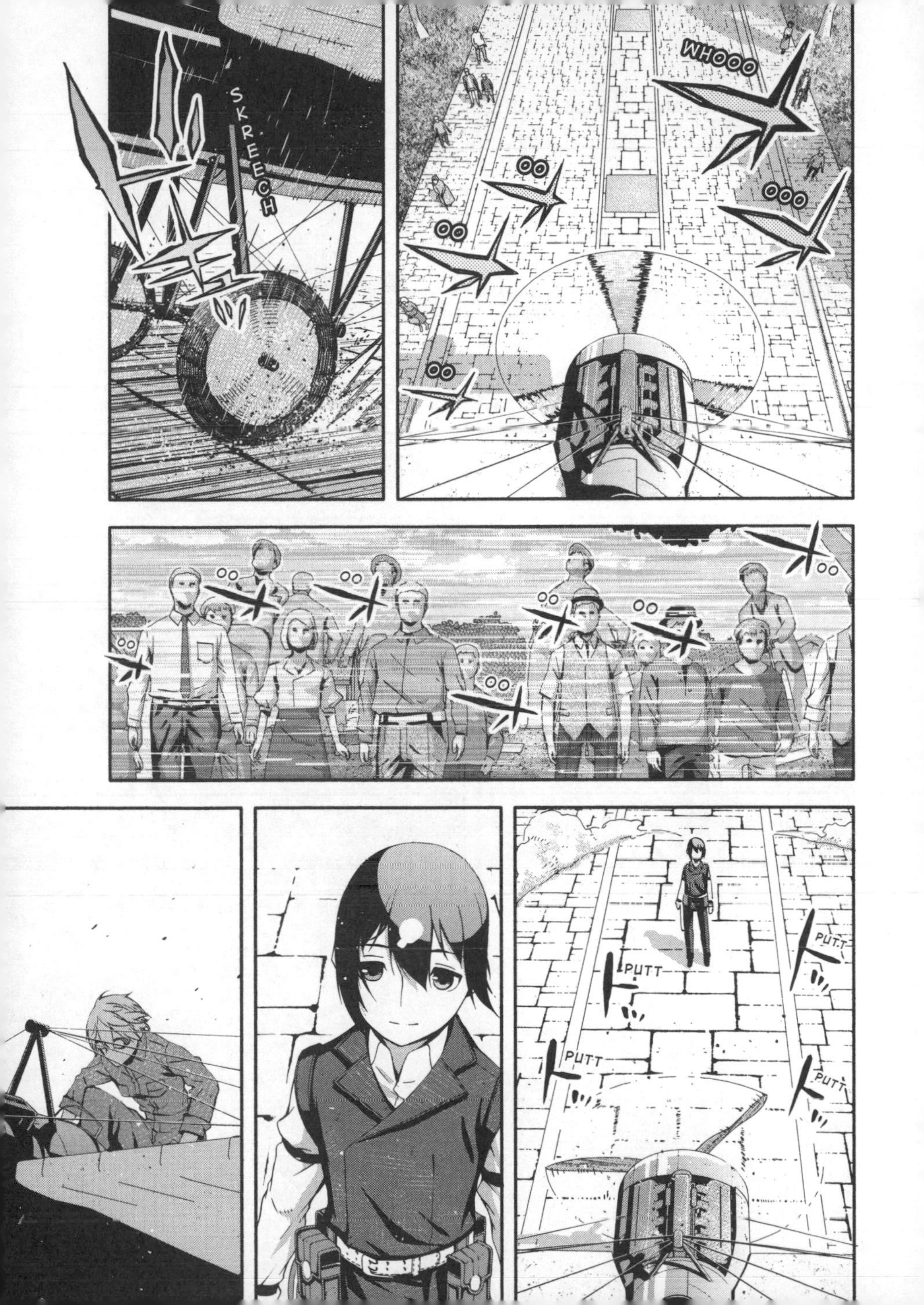
WHOOO
OO
OOO
OO
OO
SKREECH
OO
OO
OO
OO
OO
OO
OO
OO
PUTT
PUTT
PUTT
PUTT

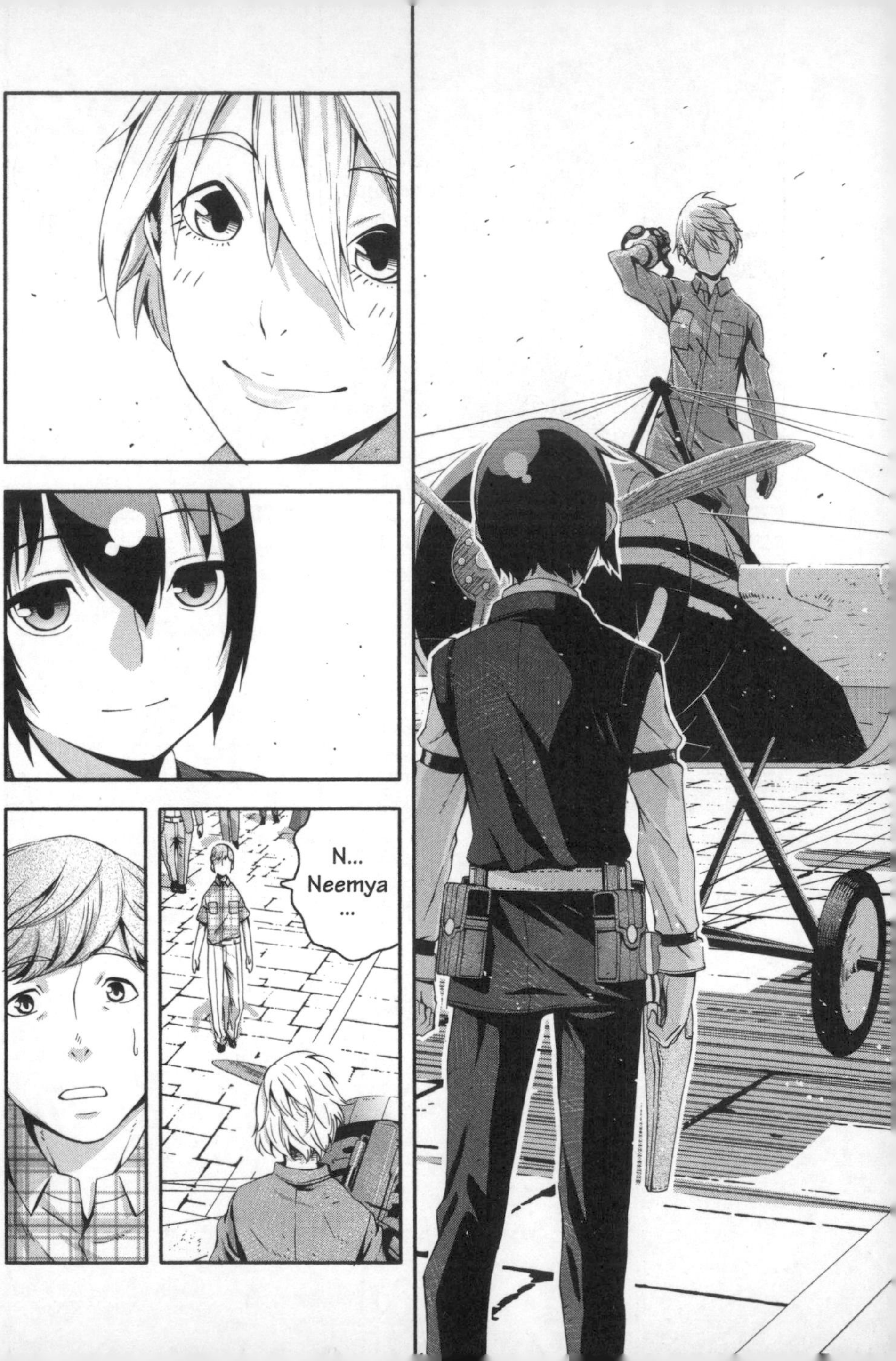
N... Neemya ...

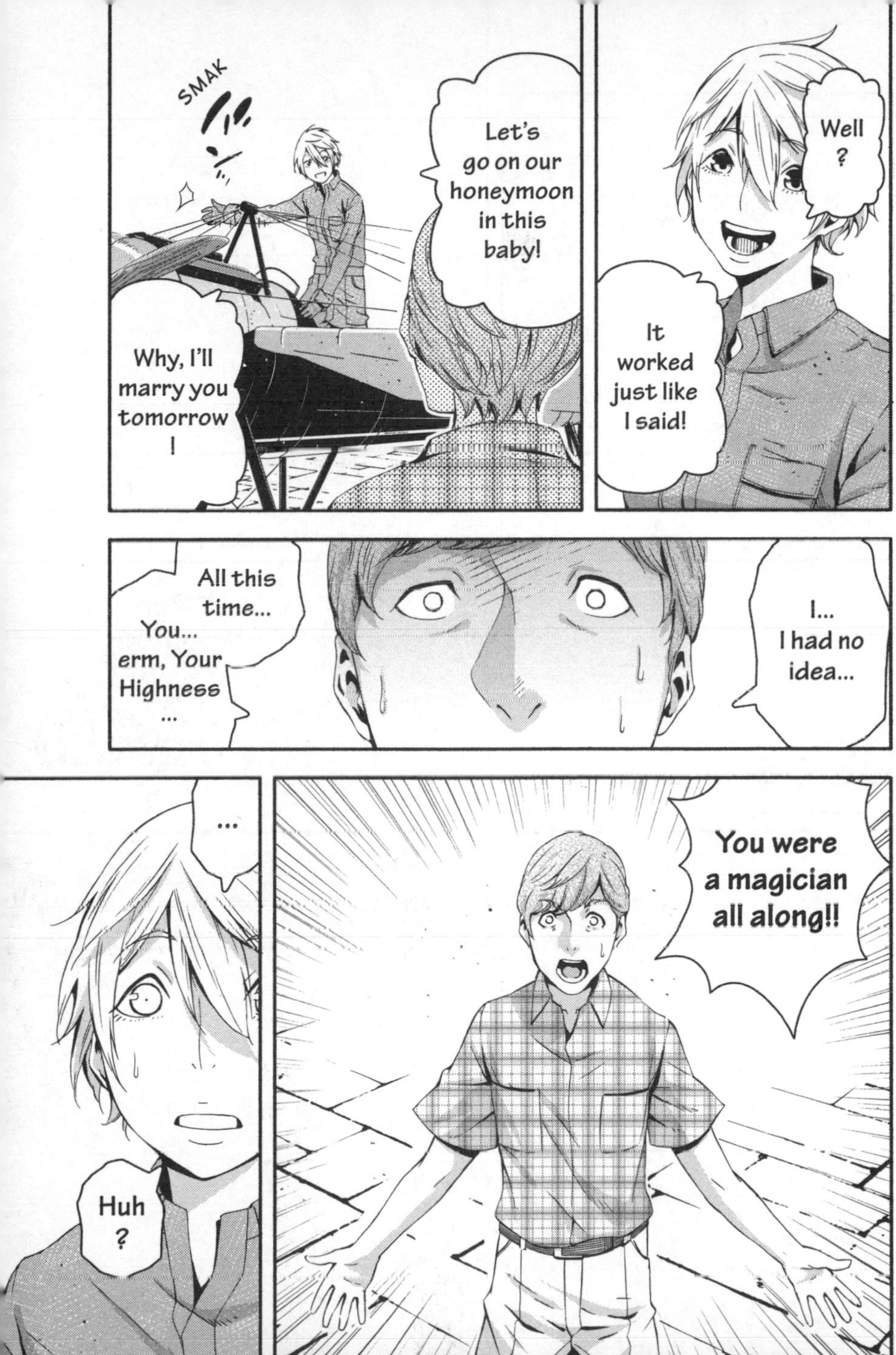
Well?
It worked just like I said!
Let's go on our honeymoon in this baby!
SMAK
Why, I'll marry you tomorrow!
I... I had no idea...
All this time... You... erm, Your Highness...
You were a magician all along!!
...
Huh?

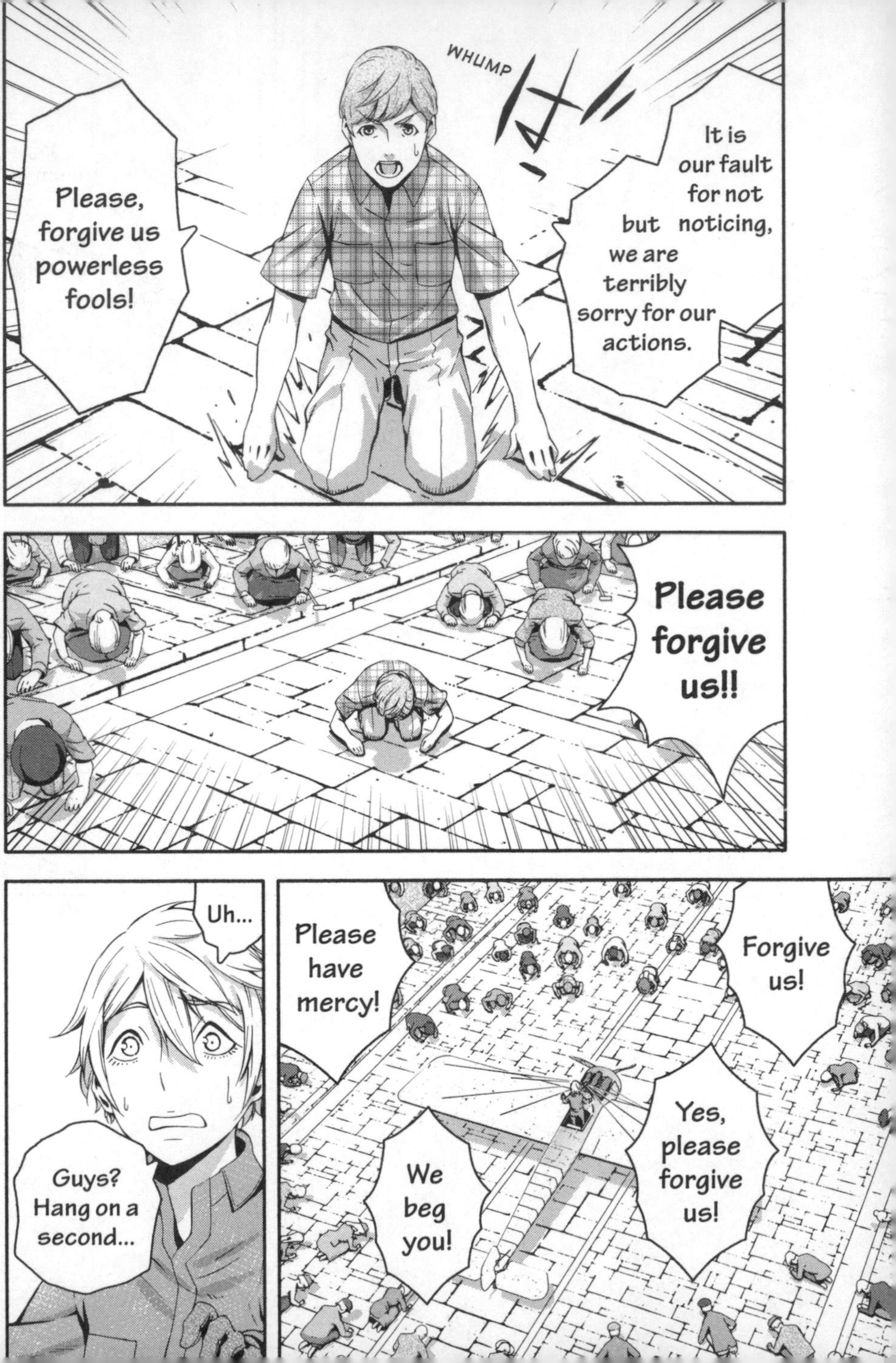
WHUMP
It is our fault for not noticing, but we are terribly sorry for our actions.
Please, forgive us powerless fools!
Please forgive us!!
Forgive us!
Please have mercy!
Yes, please forgive us!
We beg you!
Uh...
Guys? Hang on a second...

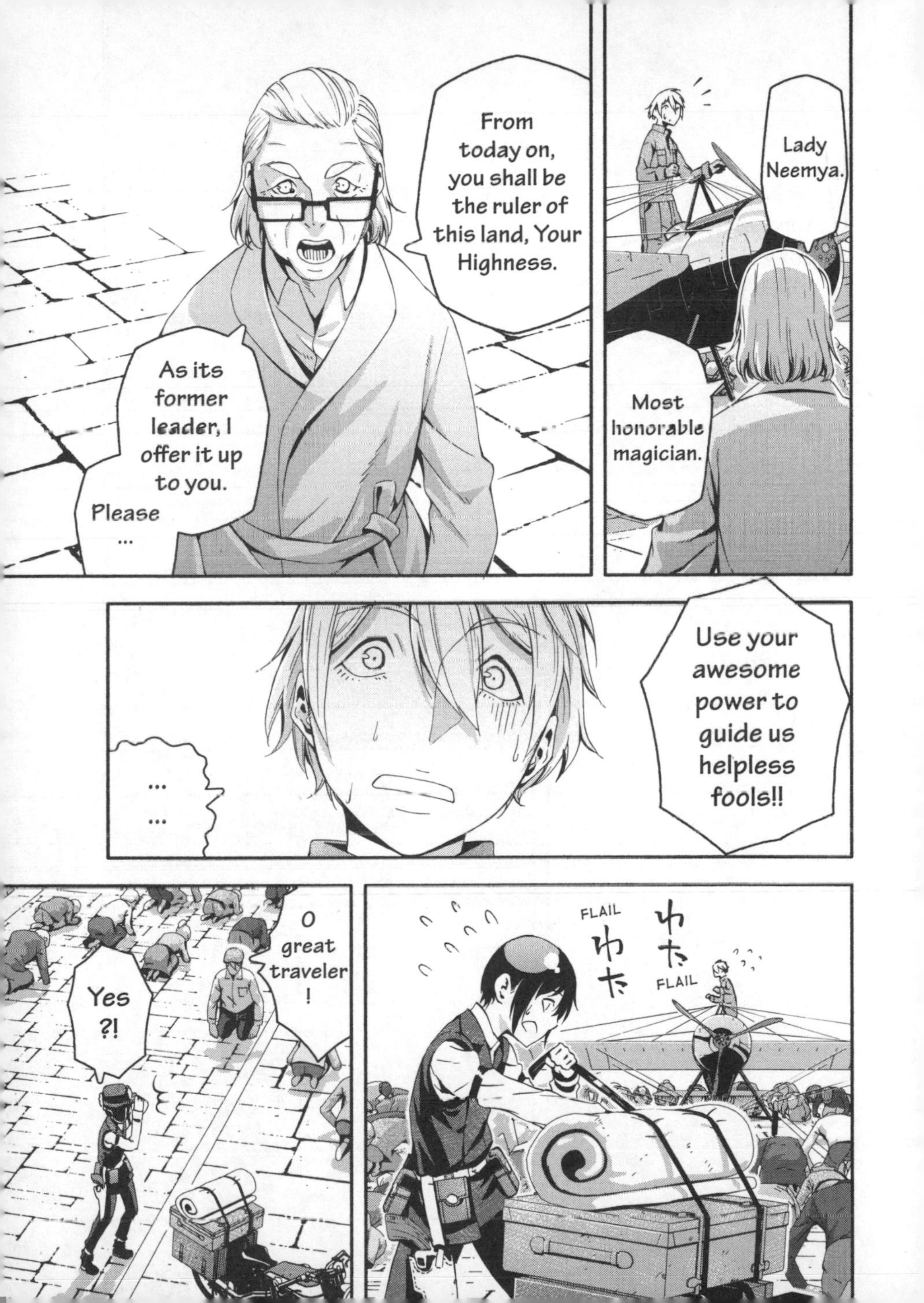
Lady Neemya.
Most honorable magician.
From today on, you shall be the ruler of this land, Your Highness.
As its former leader, I offer it up to you.
Please ...
Use your awesome power to guide us helpless fools!!
... ...
FLAIL
わた
FLAIL
わた
O great traveler!
Yes ?!

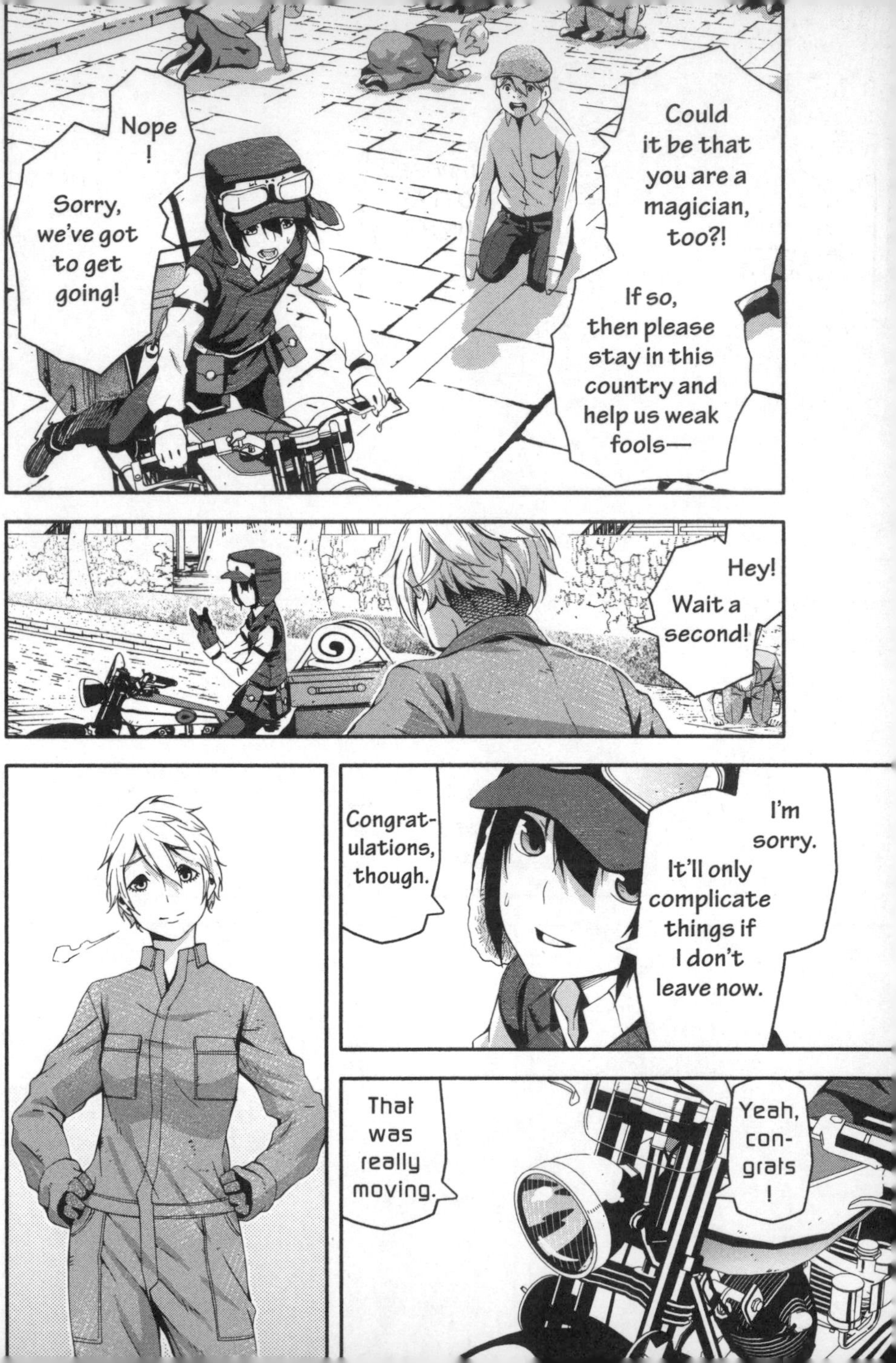
Could it be that you are a magician, too?!
If so, then please stay in this country and help us weak fools—
Nope!
Sorry, we've got to get going!
Hey!
Wait a second!
I'm sorry.
It'll only complicate things if I don't leave now.
Congratulations, though.
Yeah, congrats!
That was really moving.

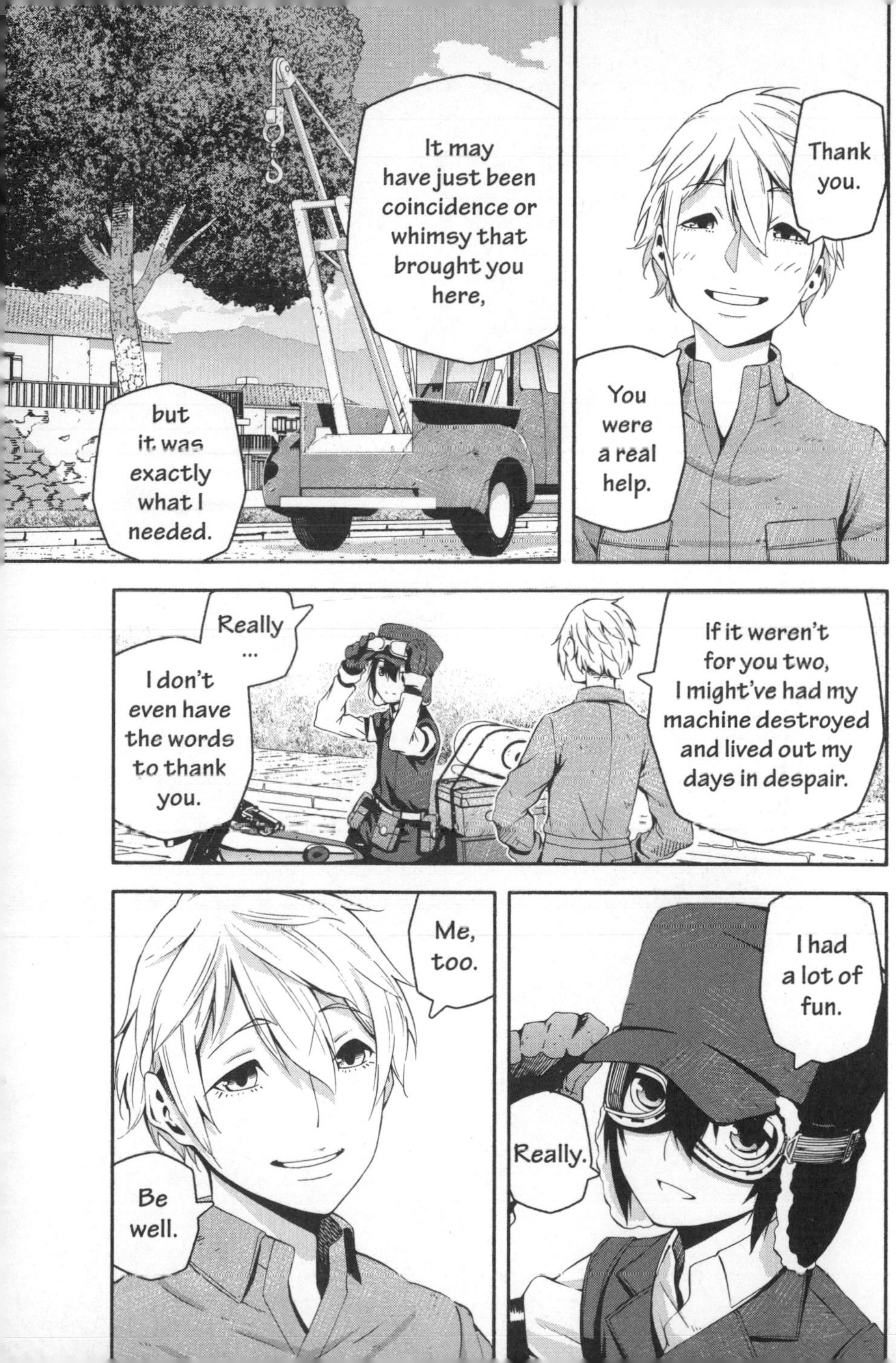
Thank you.
You were a real help.
It may have just been coincidence or whimsy that brought you here,
but it was exactly what I needed.
If it weren't for you two, I might've had my machine destroyed and lived out my days in despair.
Really ...
I don't even have the words to thank you.
I had a lot of fun.
Really.
Me, too.
Be well.

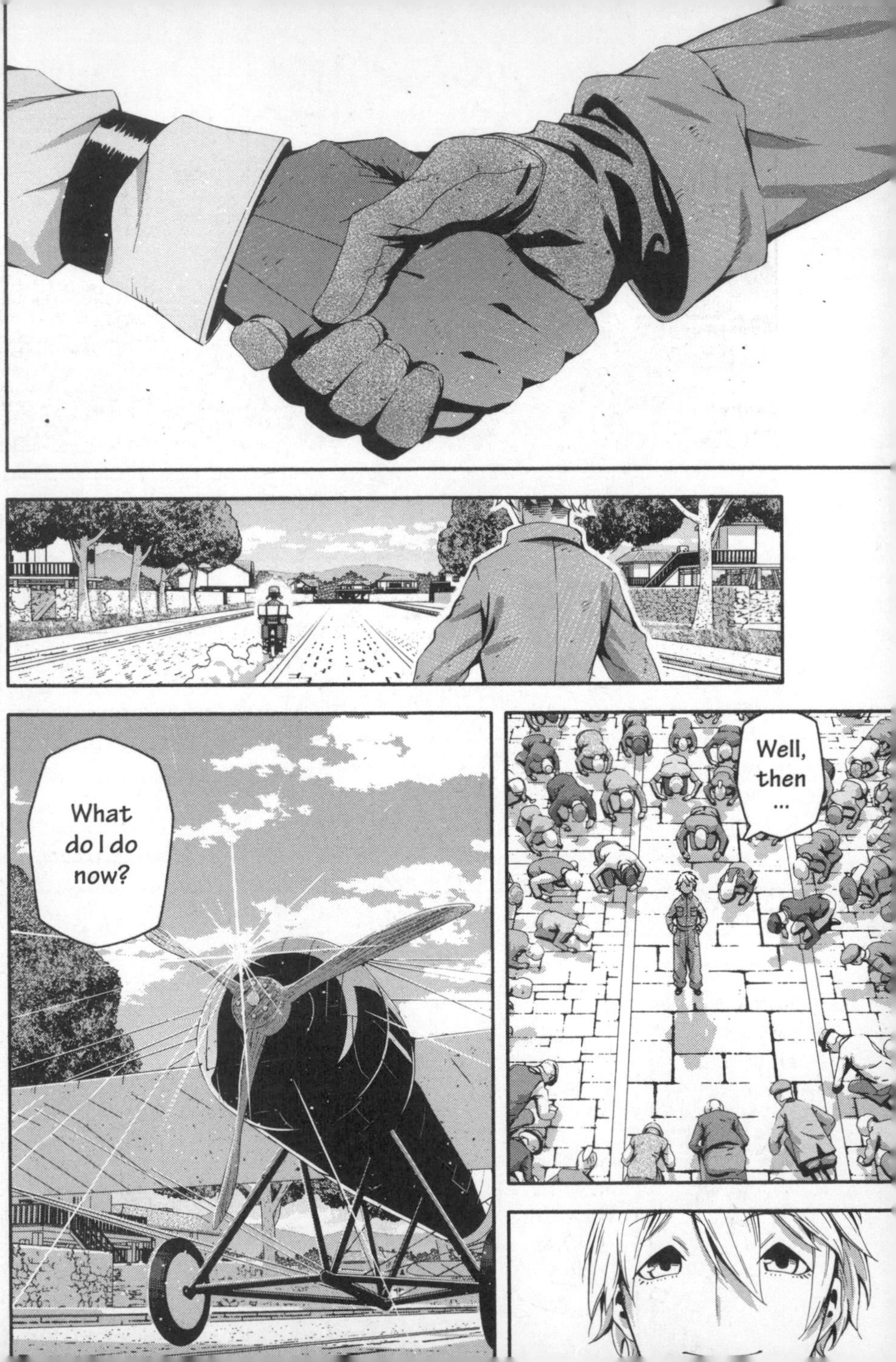
Well, then ...
What do I do now?

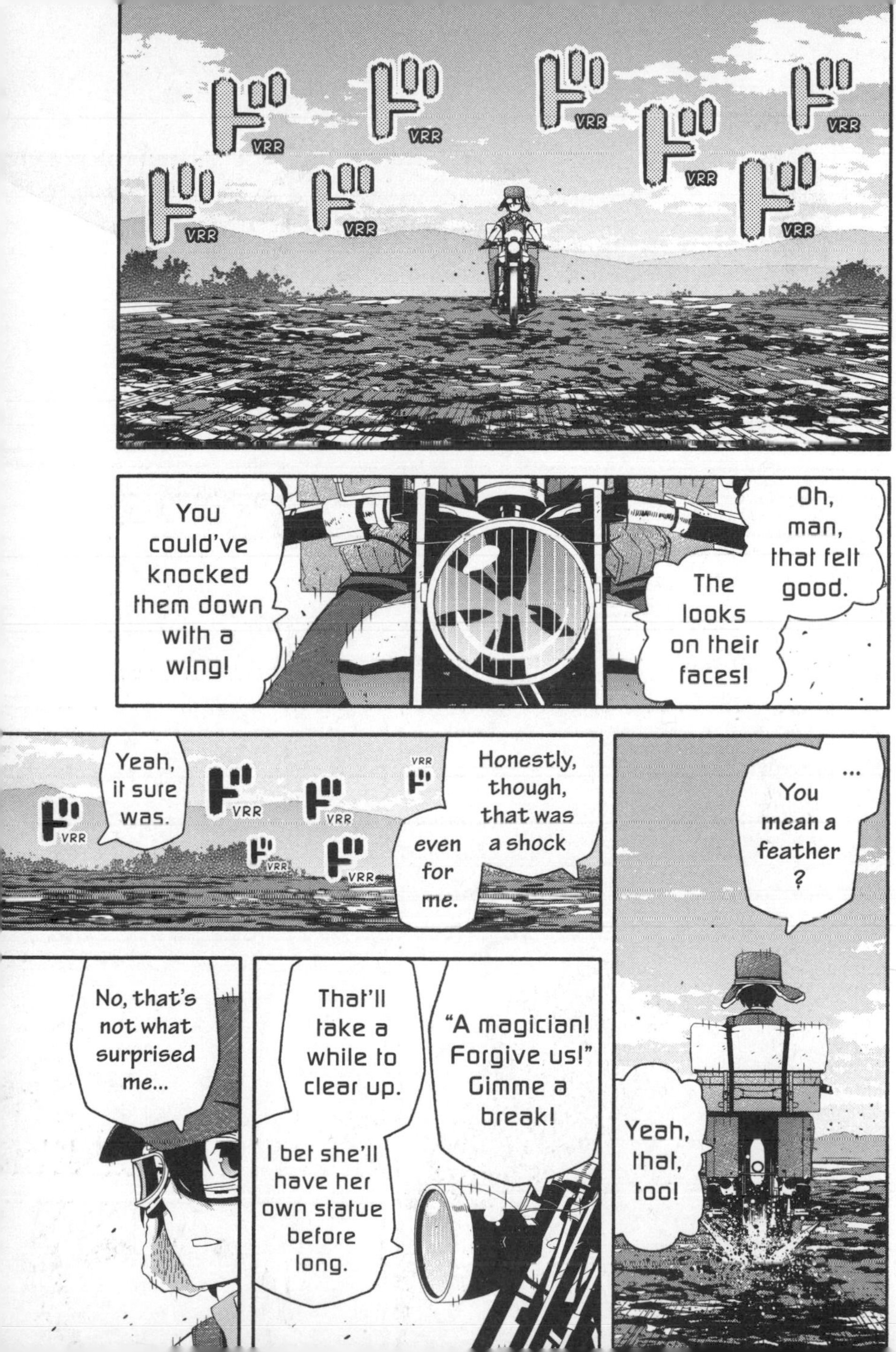

ドド VRR
ドド VRR
ドド VRR
ドド VRR
ドド VRR
ドド VRR
ドド VRR
ドド VRR
Oh, man, that felt good.
The looks on their faces!
You could've knocked them down with a wing!
... You mean a feather?
Yeah, that, too!
Honestly, though, that was a shock even for me.
ドド VRR
Yeah, it sure was.
“A magician! Forgive us!” Gimme a break!
That'll take a while to clear up.
I bet she'll have her own statue before long.
No, that's not what surprised me...

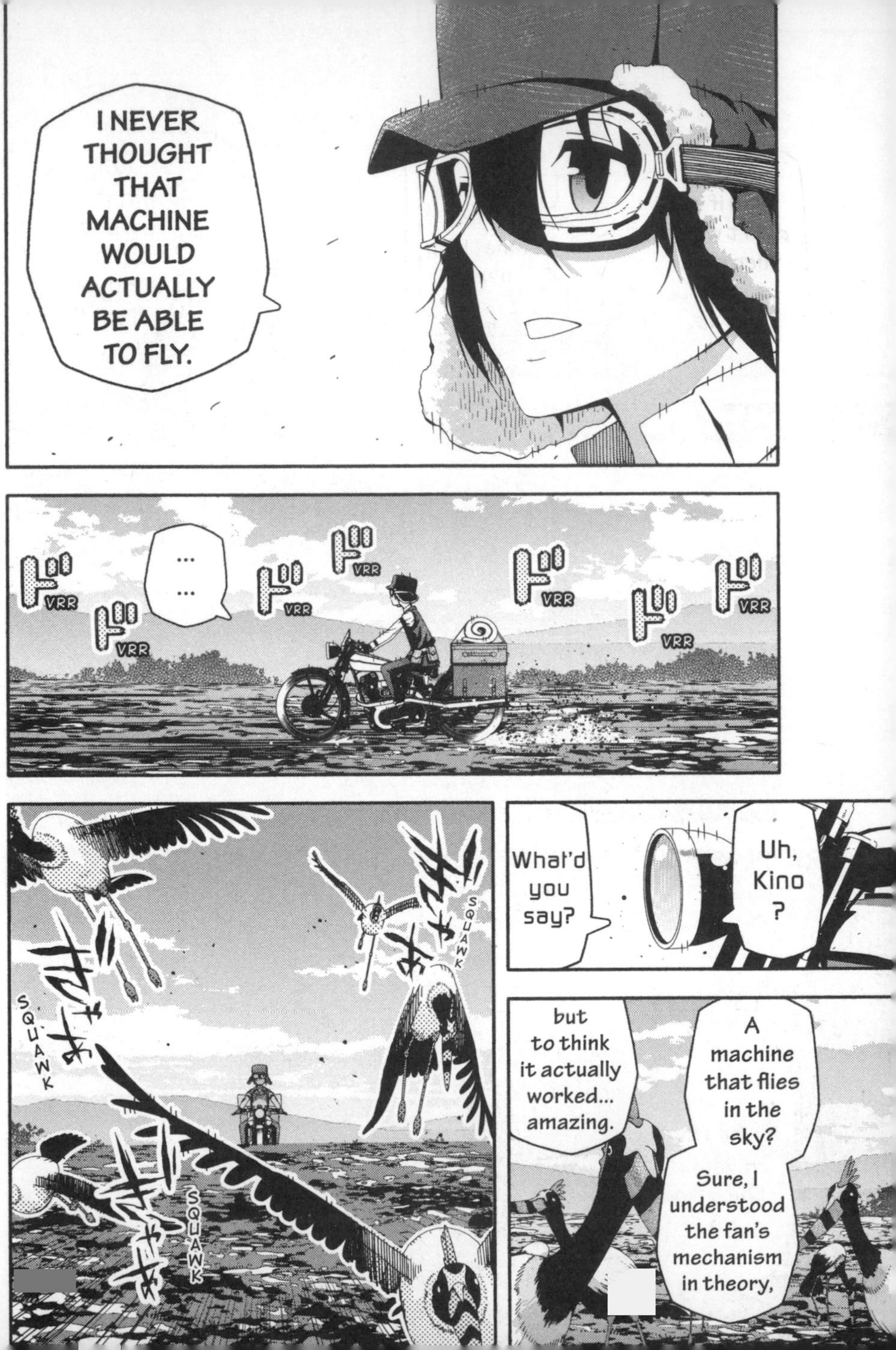
I NEVER THOUGHT THAT MACHINE WOULD ACTUALLY BE ABLE TO FLY.
ド VRR
ド VRR
ド VRR
ド VRR
… …
ド VRR
ド VRR
ド VRR
Uh, Kino?
What'd you say?
A machine that flies in the sky?
Sure, I understood the fan's mechanism in theory,
but to think it actually worked... amazing.
SQUAWK
SQUAWK
SQUAWK

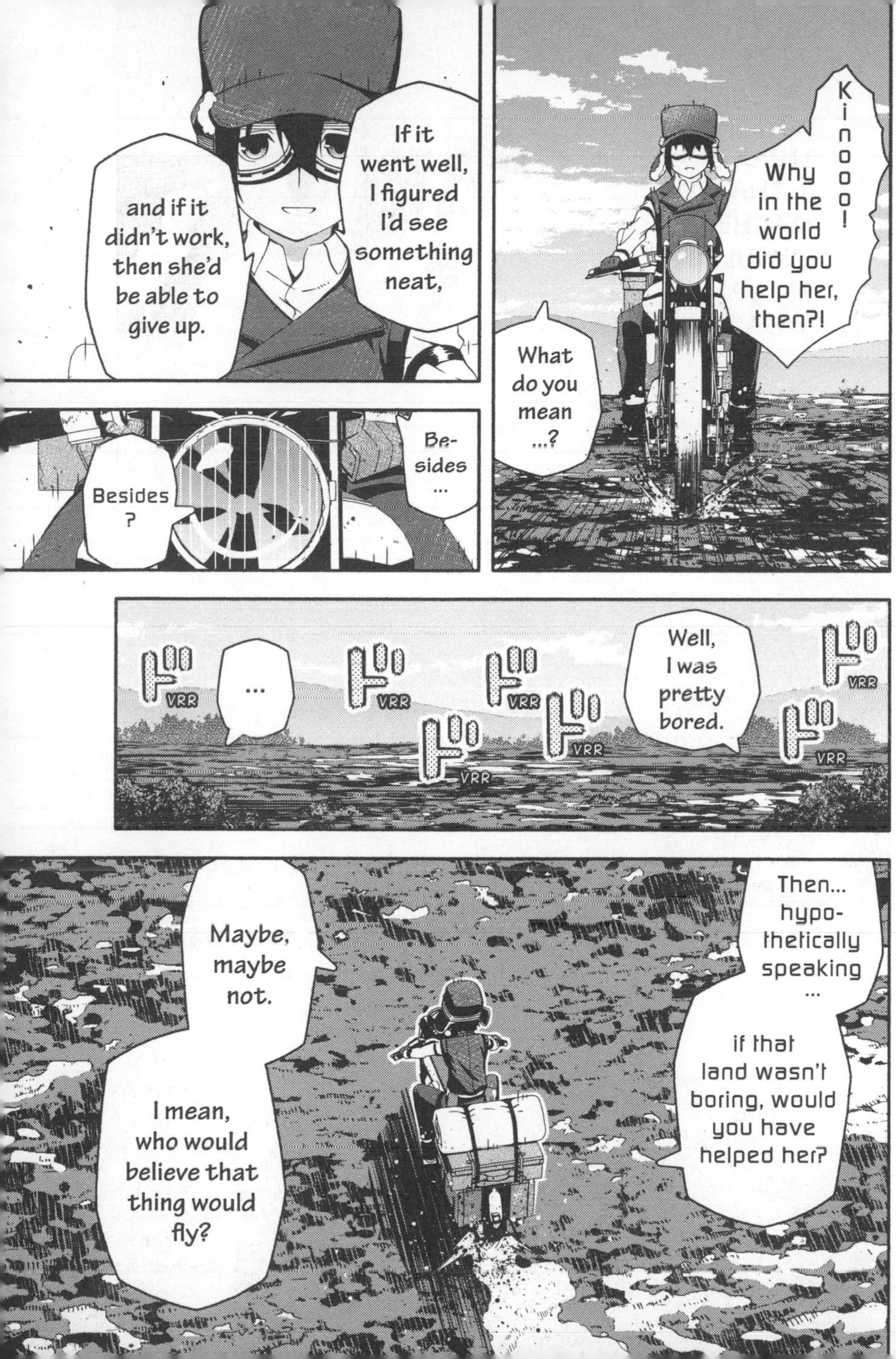
Kinoooo!
Why in the world did you help her, then?!
What do you mean ...?
If it went well, I figured I'd see something neat,
and if it didn't work, then she'd be able to give up.
Be-sides ...
Besides ?
VRR
Well, I was pretty bored.
VRR
VRR
VRR
VRR
...
VRR
Then... hypo-thetically speaking ...
if that land wasn't boring, would you have helped her?
Maybe, maybe not.
I mean, who would believe that thing would fly?

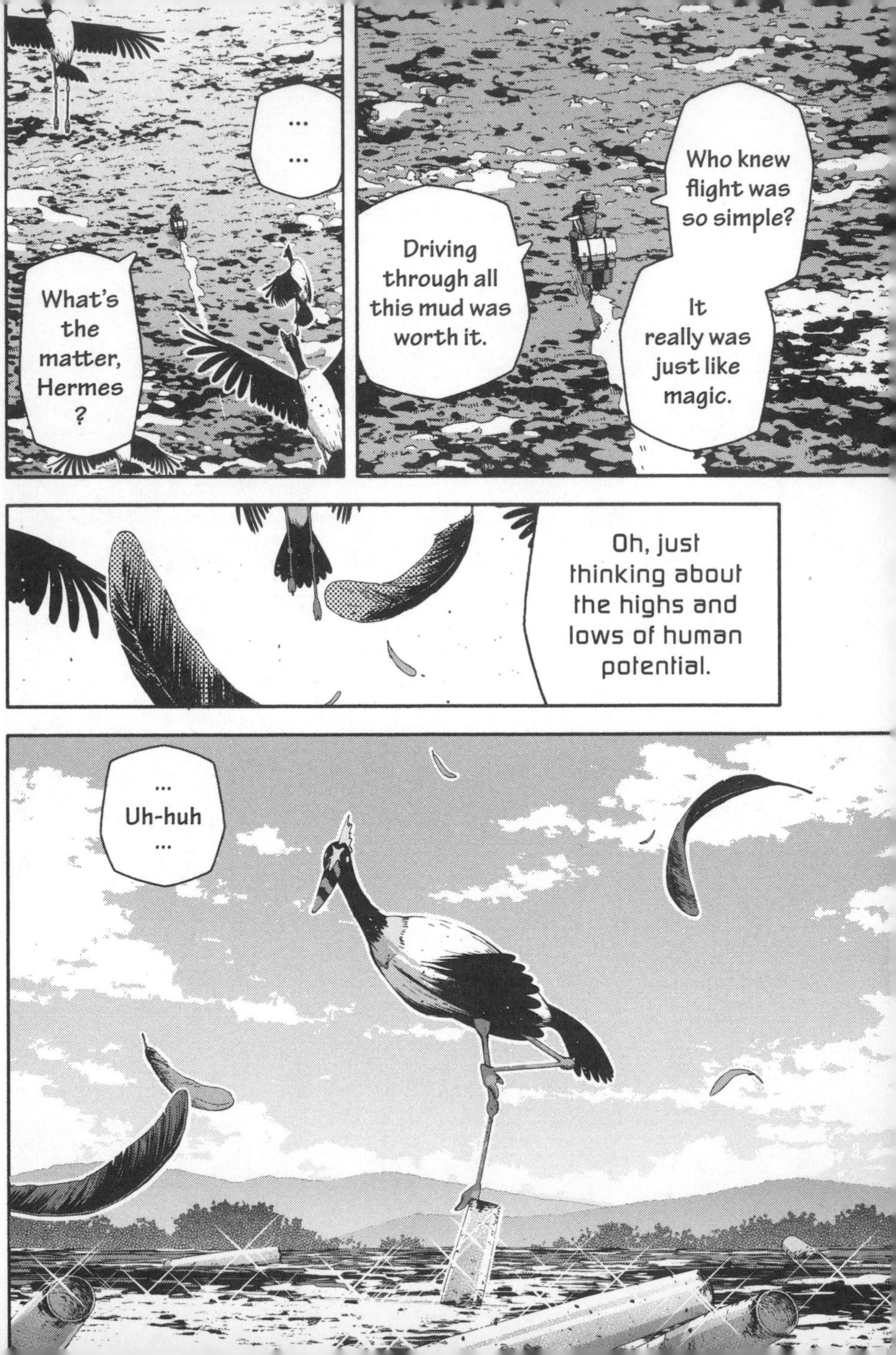
Who knew flight was so simple?
It really was just like magic.
Driving through all this mud was worth it.
...
...
What's the matter, Hermes?
Oh, just thinking about the highs and lows of human potential.
...
Uh-huh
...

Kino's Journey

————→ The Beautiful World ←————

Chapter 3
Overprotective
-Do You Need It?-

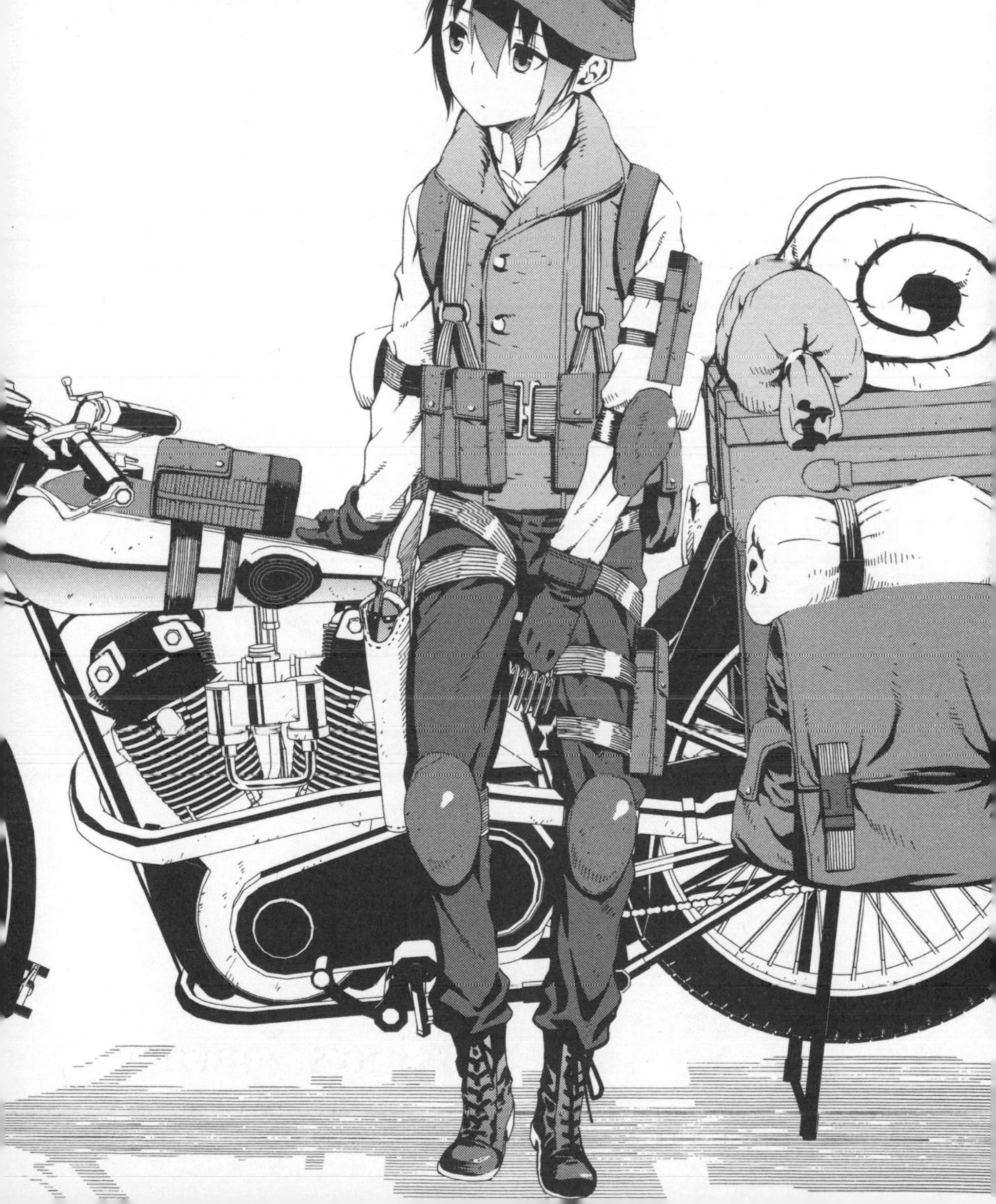

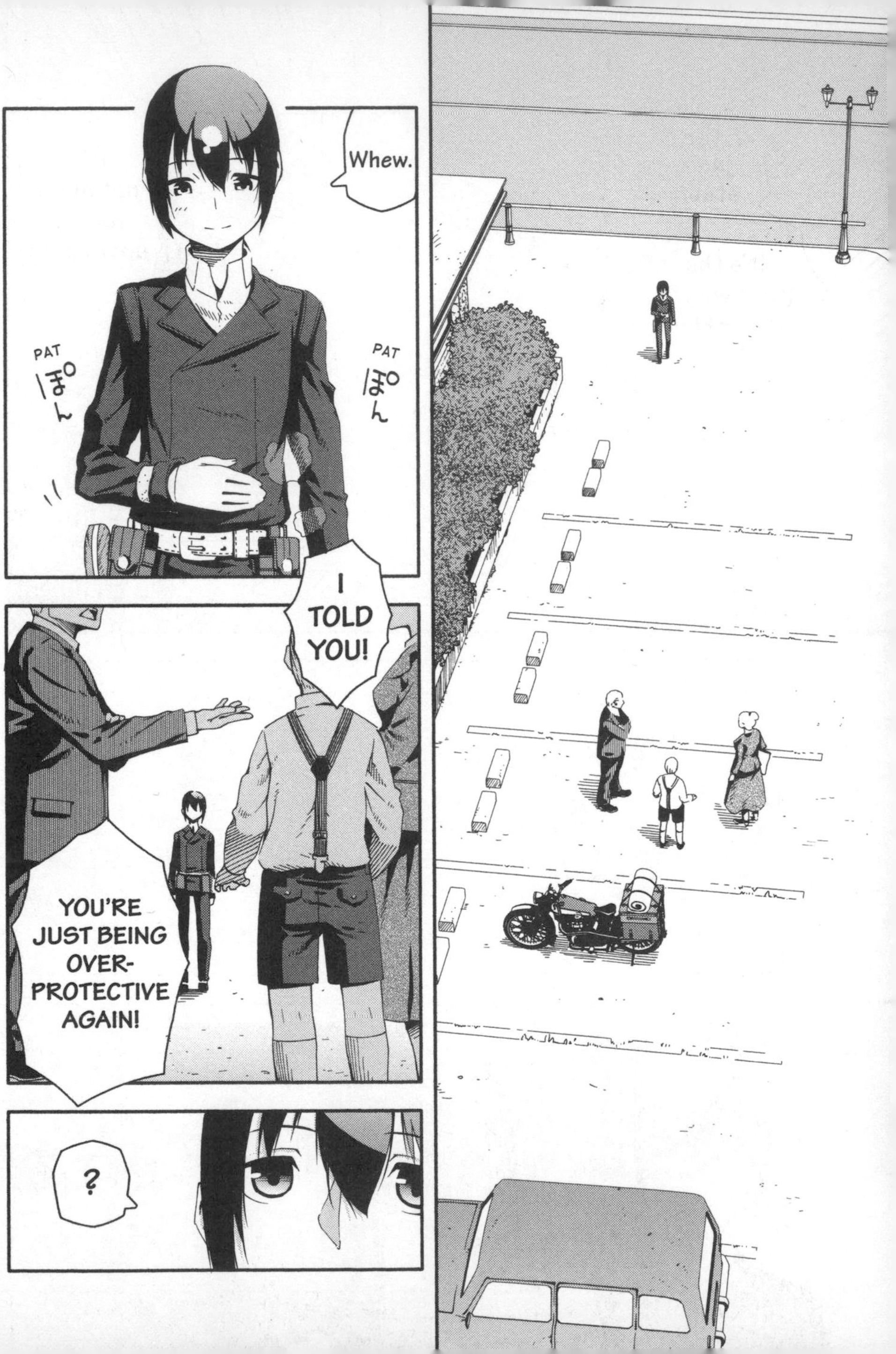
Whew.
PAT ぽん
PAT ぽん
I TOLD YOU!
YOU'RE JUST BEING OVER-PROTECTIVE AGAIN!
?

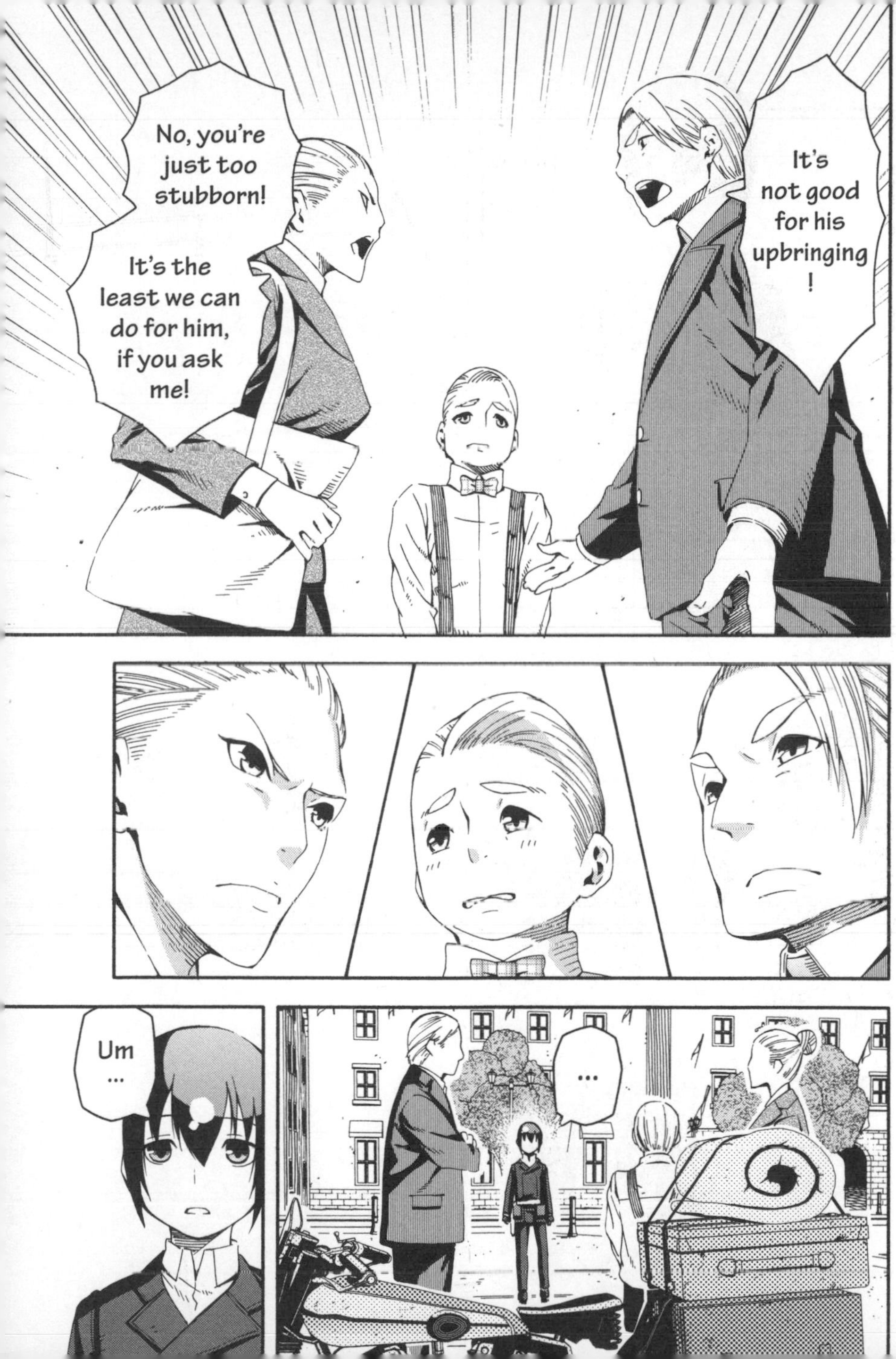
It's not good for his upbringing!
No, you're just too stubborn!
It's the least we can do for him, if you ask me!
...
Um ...

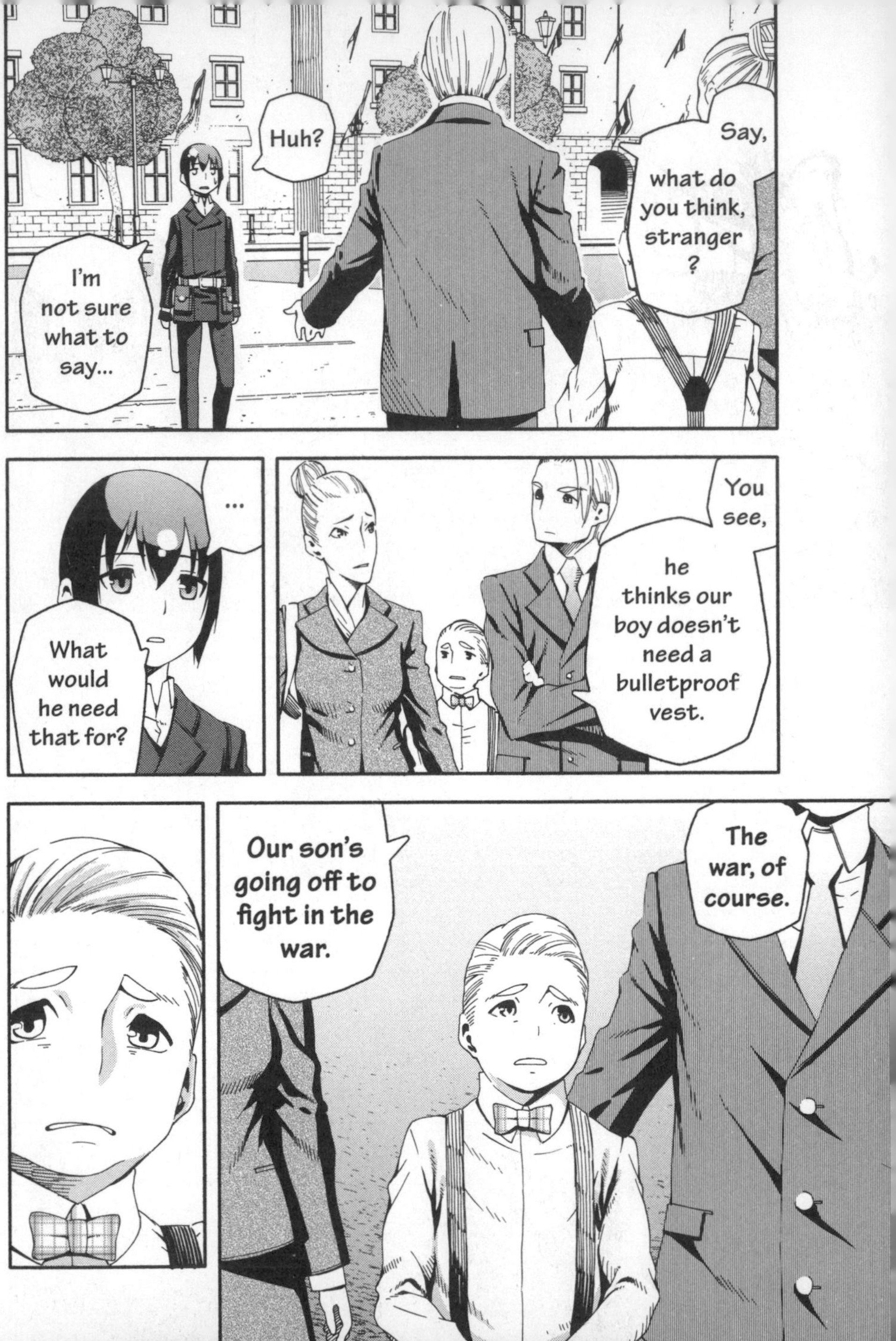
Say, what do you think, stranger?
Huh?
I'm not sure what to say...
You see, he thinks our boy doesn't need a bulletproof vest.
...
What would he need that for?
The war, of course.
Our son's going off to fight in the war.

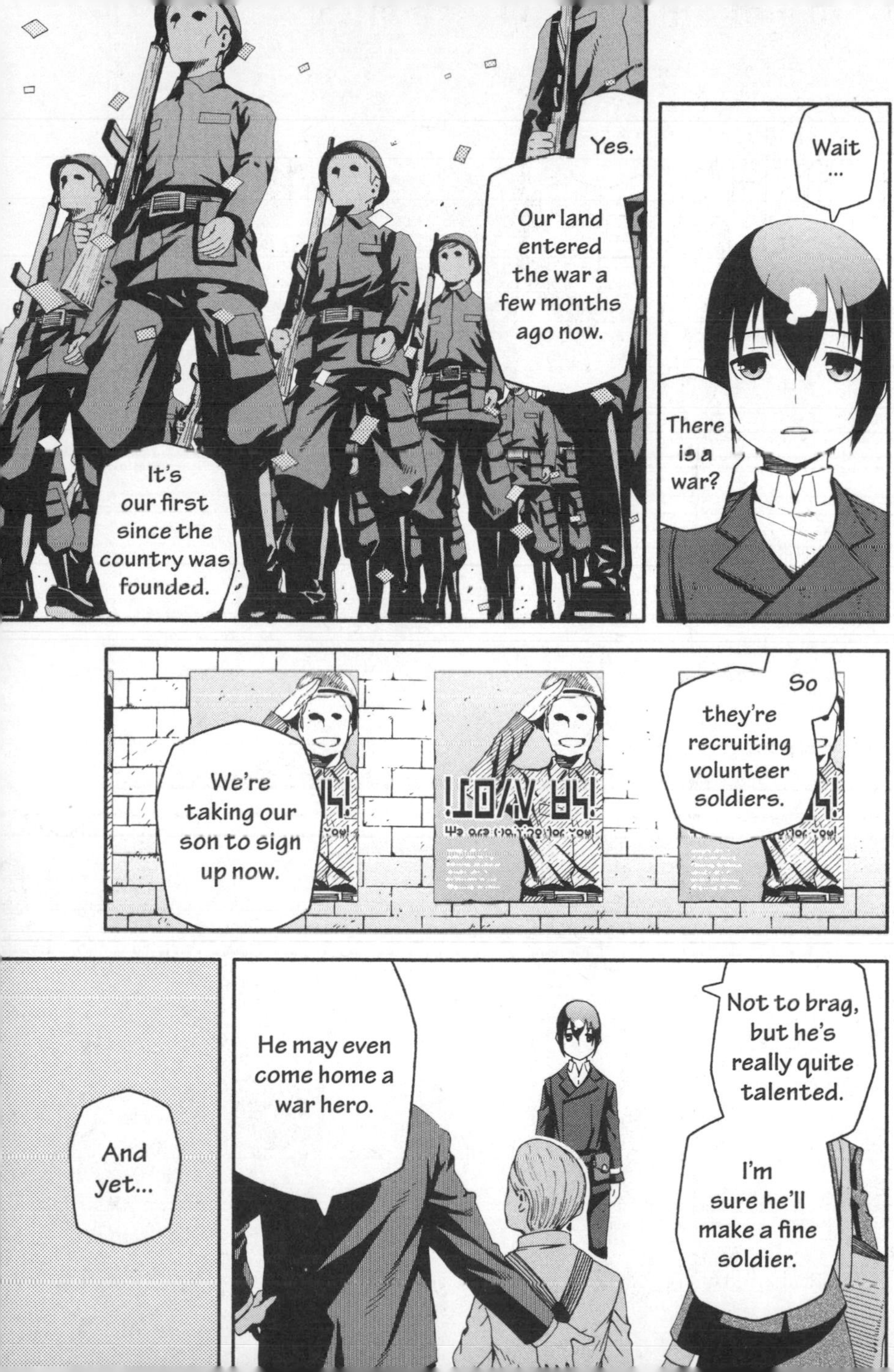
Wait ...
There is a war?
Yes.
Our land entered the war a few months ago now.
It's our first since the country was founded.
So they're recruiting volunteer soldiers.
We're taking our son to sign up now.
Not to brag, but he's really quite talented.
I'm sure he'll make a fine soldier.
He may even come home a war hero.
And yet...

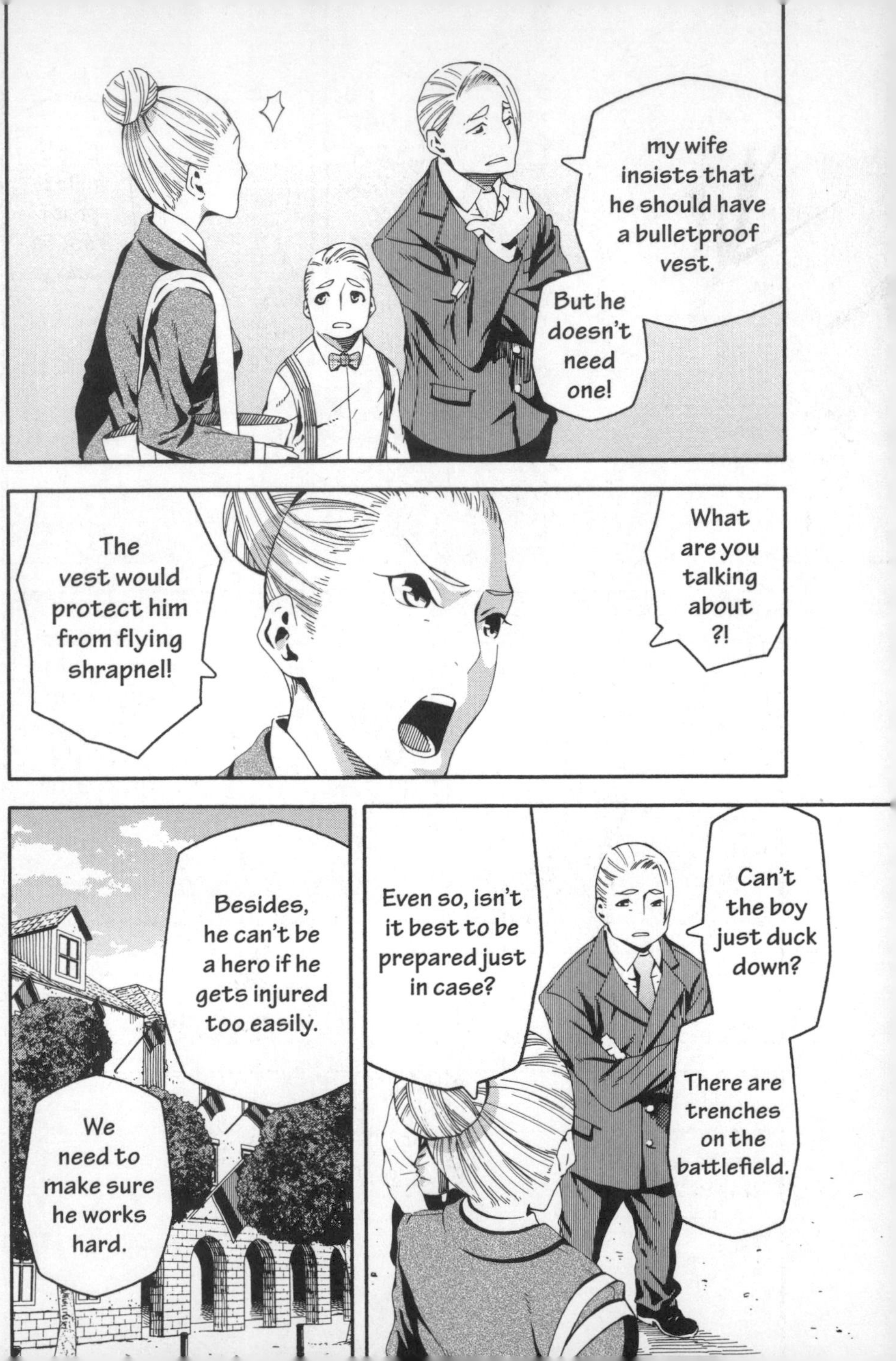
my wife insists that he should have a bulletproof vest.
But he doesn't need one!
What are you talking about?!
The vest would protect him from flying shrapnel!
Can't the boy just duck down?
There are trenches on the battlefield.
Even so, isn't it best to be prepared just in case?
Besides, he can't be a hero if he gets injured too easily.
We need to make sure he works hard.

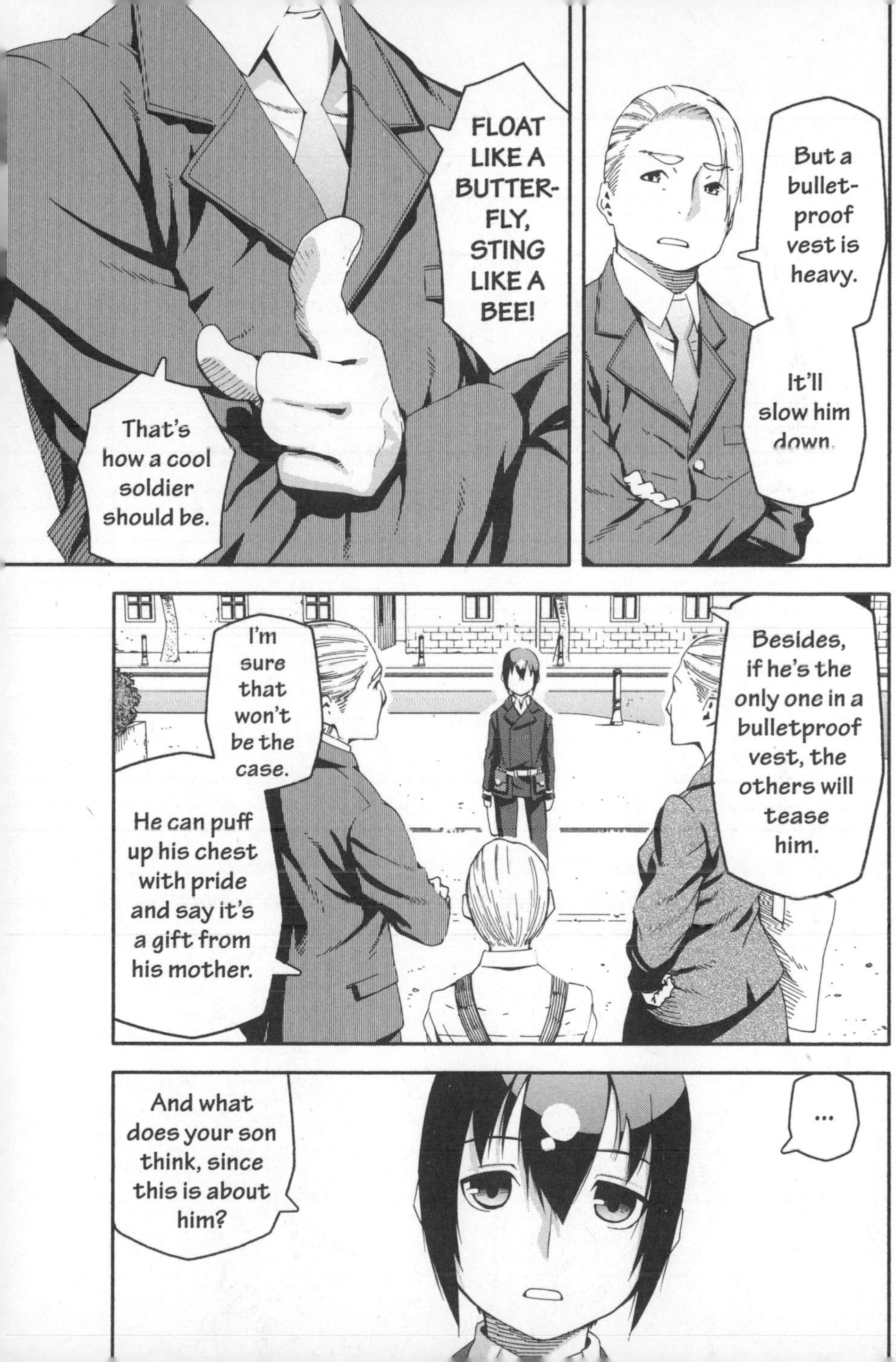
But a bullet-proof vest is heavy.
It'll slow him down.
FLOAT LIKE A BUTTER-FLY, STING LIKE A BEE!
That's how a cool soldier should be.
Besides, if he's the only one in a bulletproof vest, the others will tease him.
I'm sure that won't be the case.
He can puff up his chest with pride and say it's a gift from his mother.
...
And what does your son think, since this is about him?

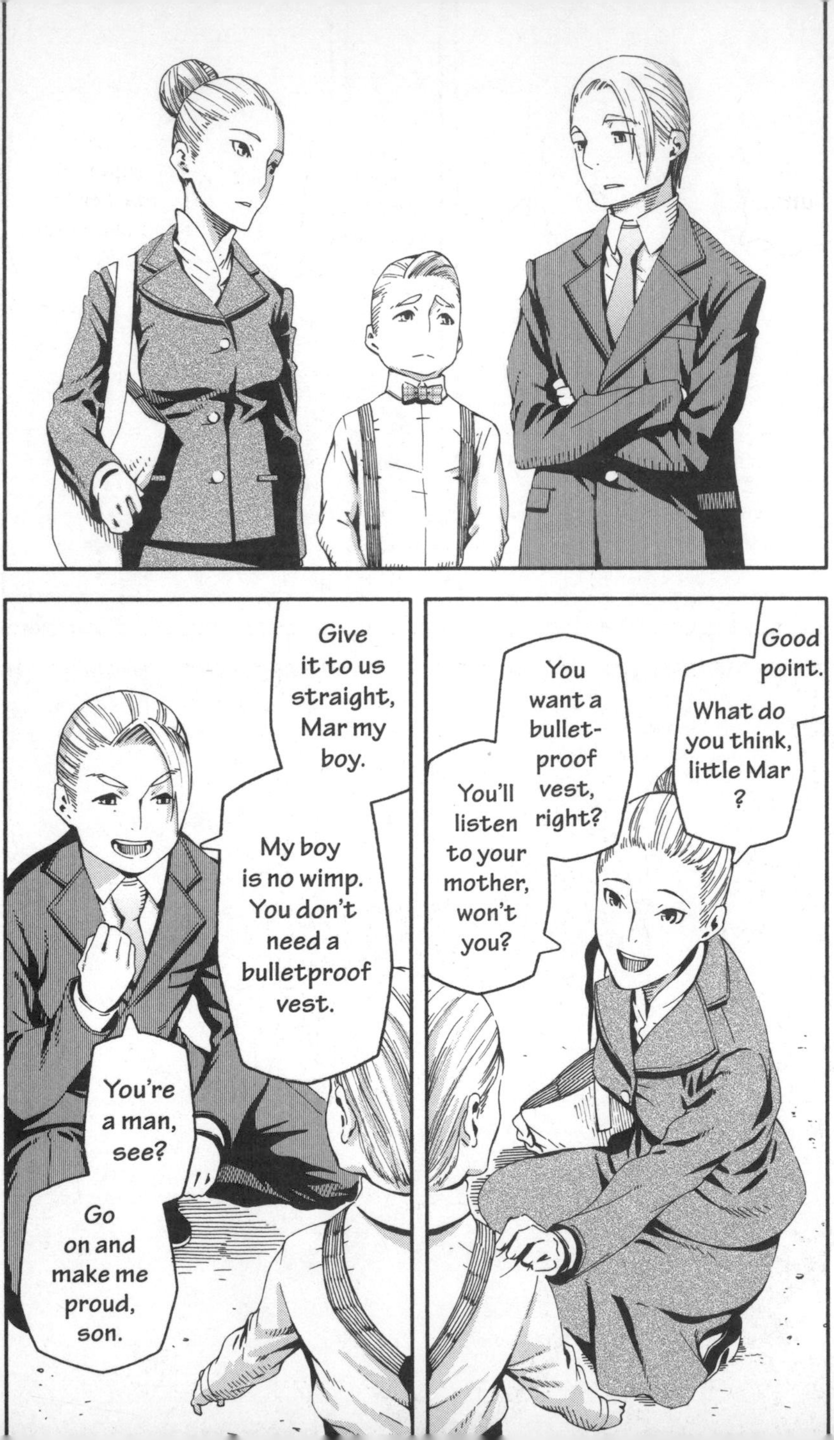
Good point.
What do you think, little Mar?
You want a bullet-proof vest, right?
You'll listen to your mother, won't you?
Give it to us straight, Mar my boy.
My boy is no wimp. You don't need a bulletproof vest.
You're a man, see?
Go on and make me proud, son.

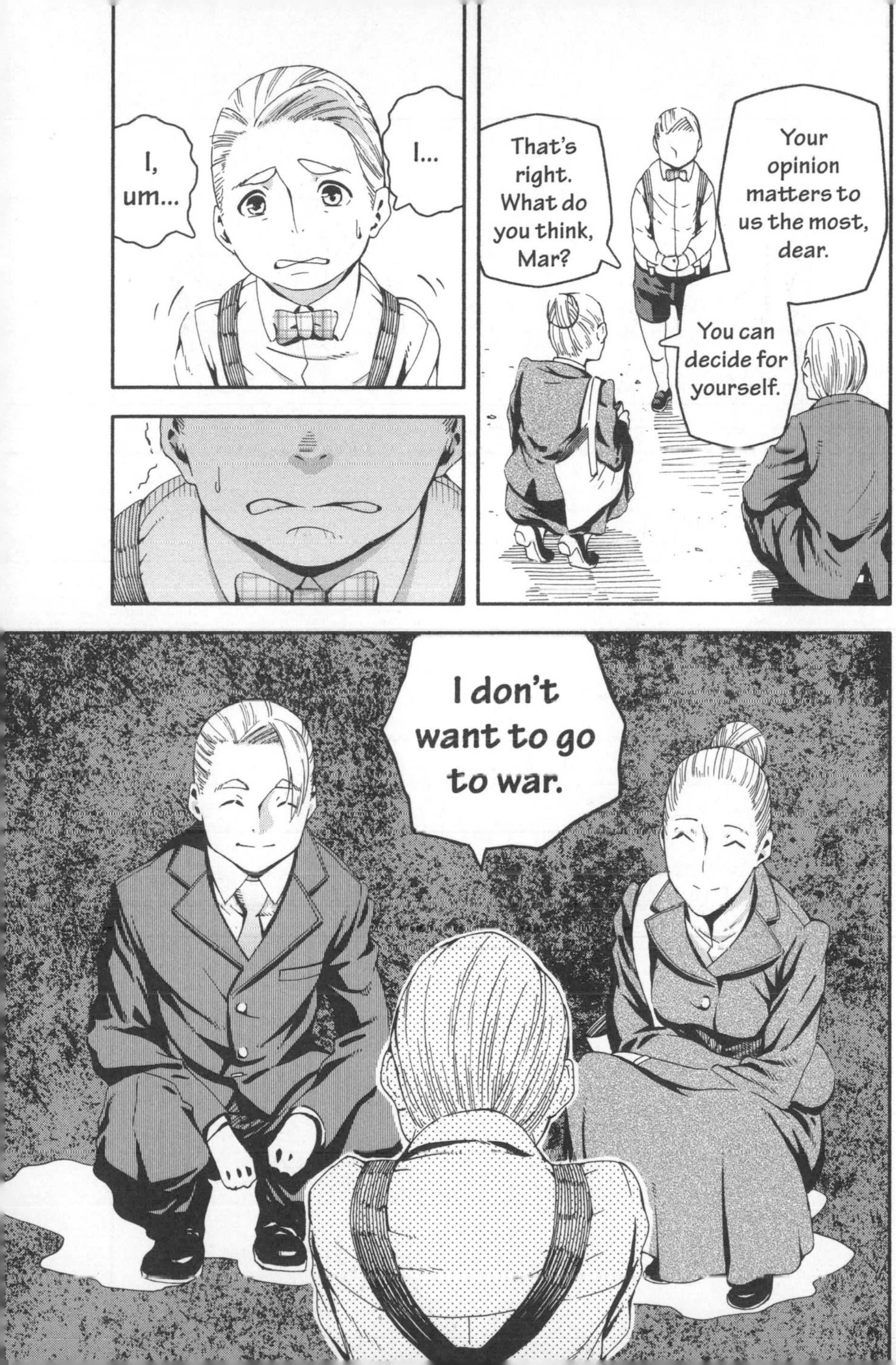
Your opinion matters to us the most, dear.
You can decide for yourself.
That's right. What do you think, Mar?
I...
I, um...
I don't want to go to war.

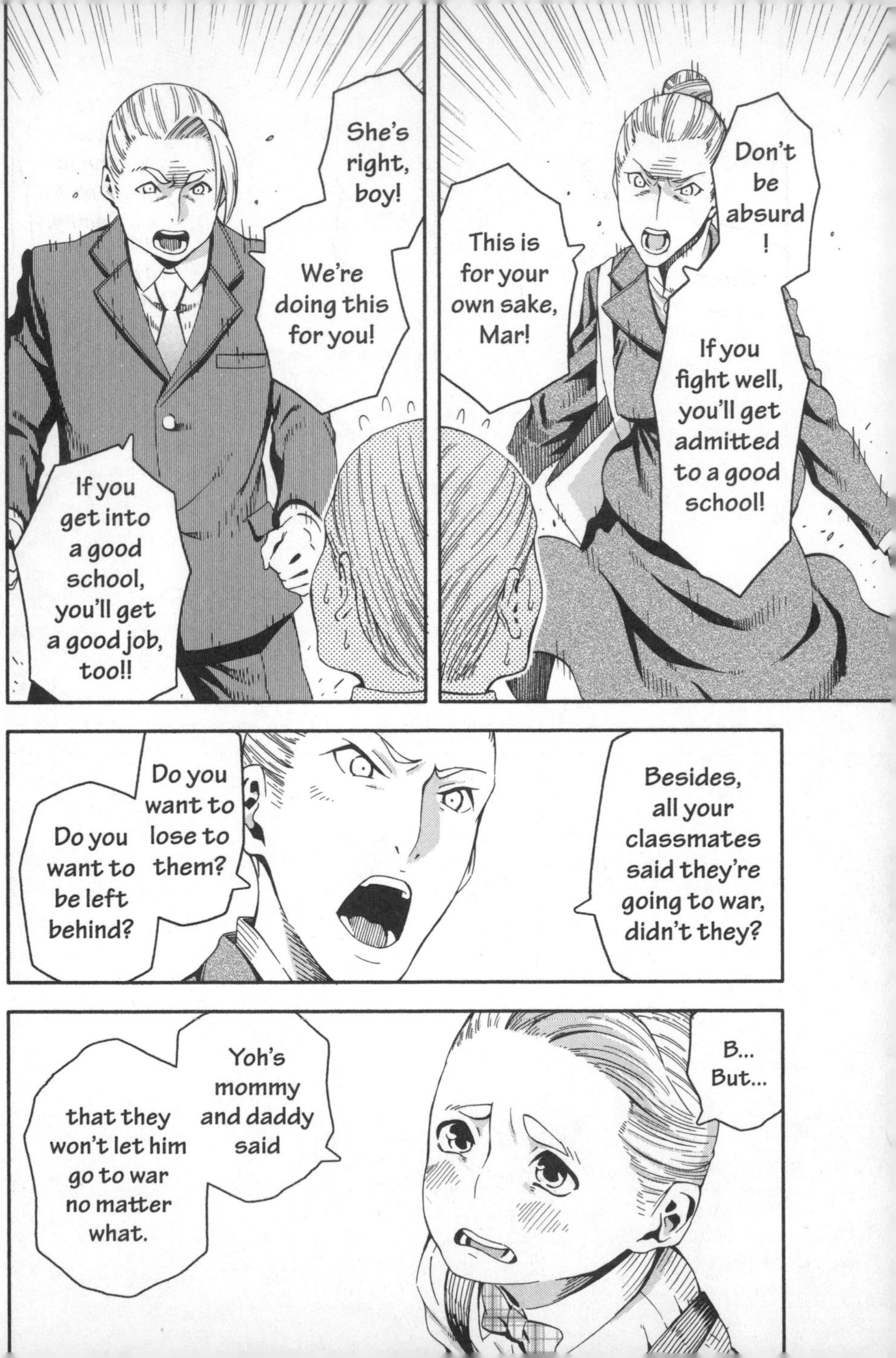
Don't be absurd!
This is for your own sake, Mar!
If you fight well, you'll get admitted to a good school!
She's right, boy!
We're doing this for you!
If you get into a good school, you'll get a good job, too!!
Besides, all your classmates said they're going to war, didn't they?
Do you want to lose to them?
Do you want to be left behind?
B... But...
Yoh's mommy and daddy said
that they won't let him go to war no matter what.

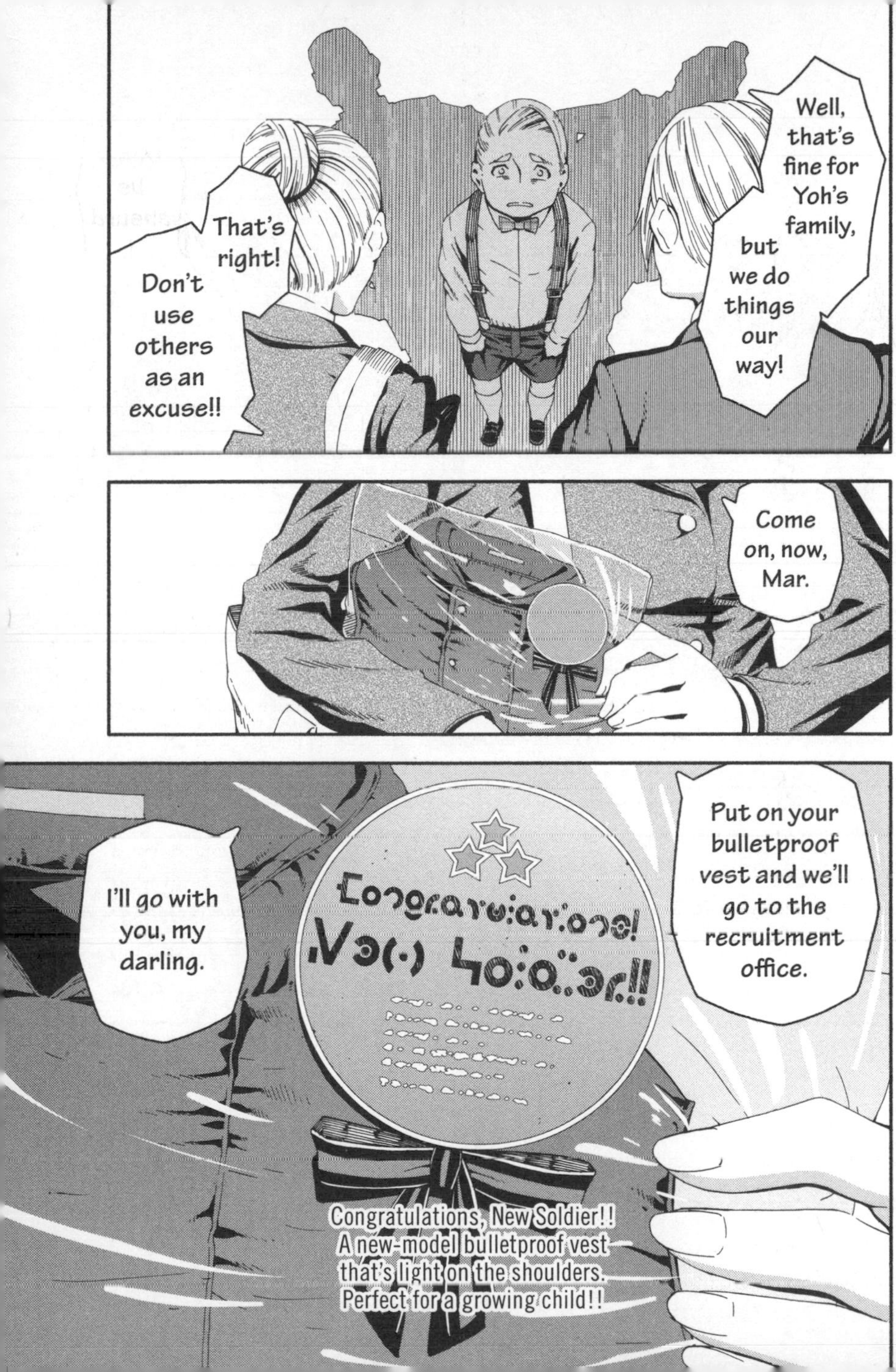
Well, that's fine for Yoh's family, but we do things our way!
That's right!
Don't use others as an excuse!!
Come on, now, Mar.
Put on your bulletproof vest and we'll go to the recruitment office.
I'll go with you, my darling.
Congratulations, New Soldier!! A new-model bulletproof vest that's light on the shoulders. Perfect for a growing child!!

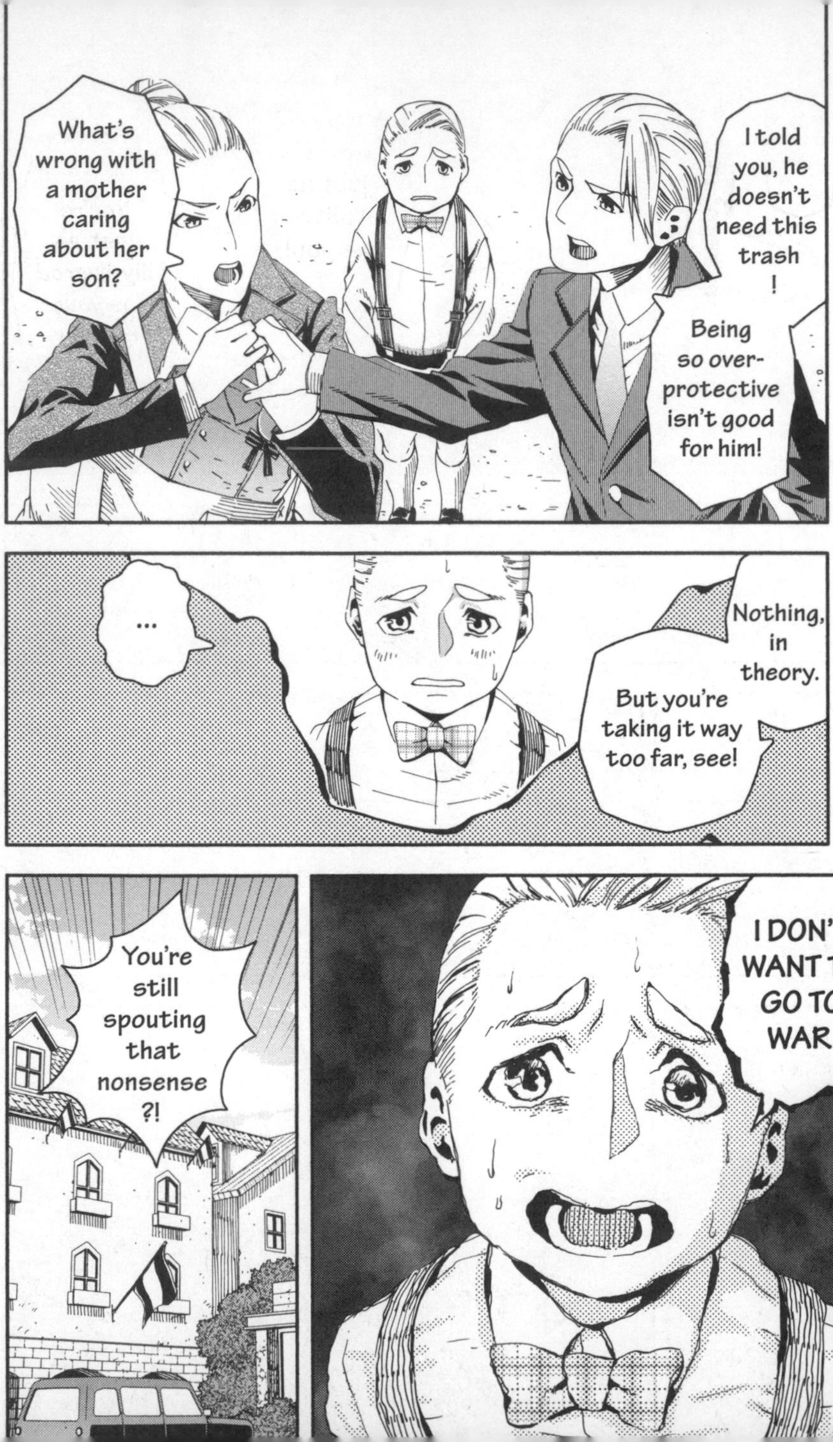
I told you, he doesn't need this trash!
Being so over-protective isn't good for him!
What's wrong with a mother caring about her son?
Nothing, in theory.
But you're taking it way too far, see!
...
I DON'T WANT TO GO TO WAR.
You're still spouting that nonsense?!

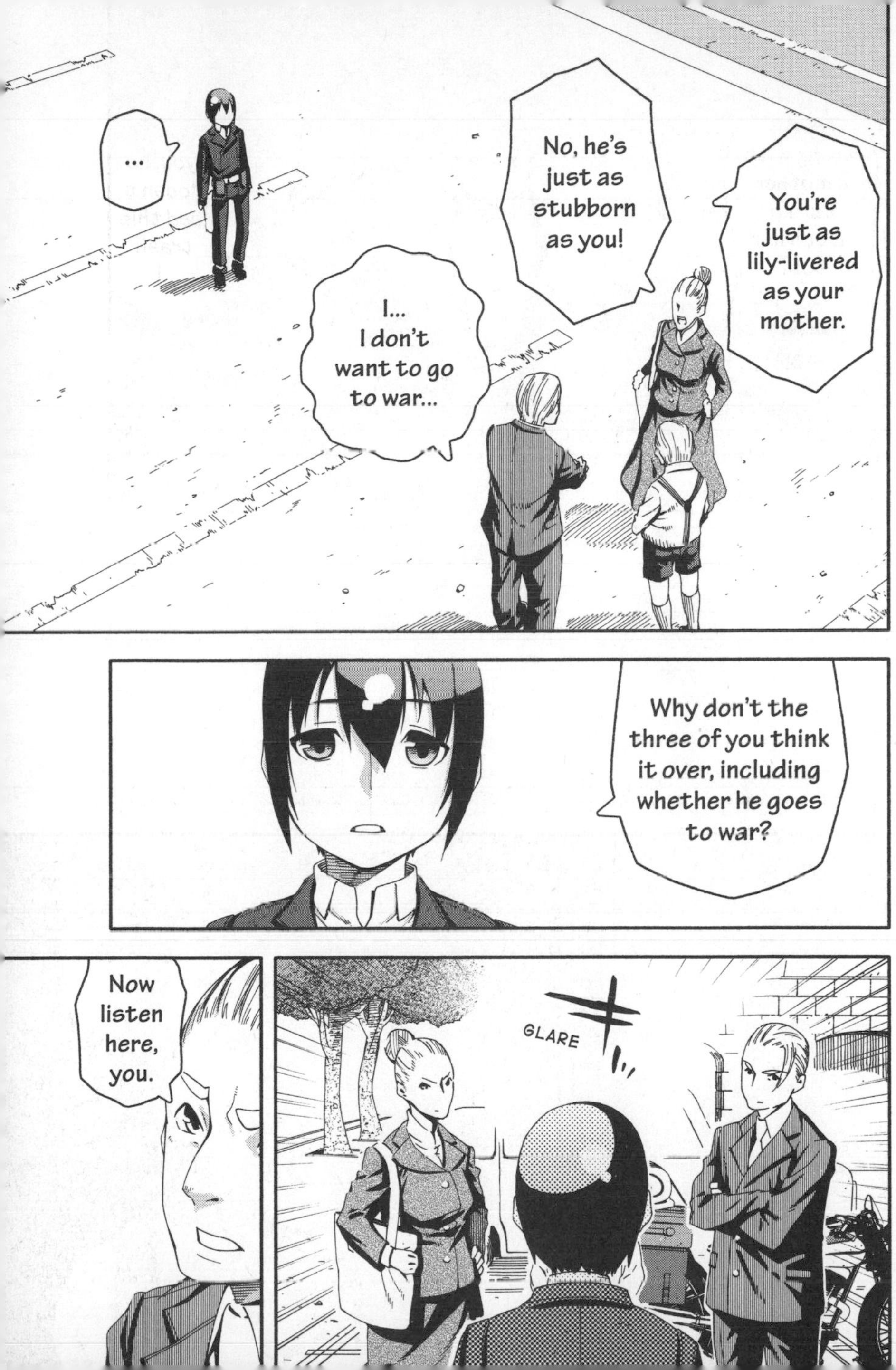
You're just as lily-livered as your mother.
No, he's just as stubborn as you!
I... I don't want to go to war...
...
Why don't the three of you think it over, including whether he goes to war?
GLARE
Now listen here, you.

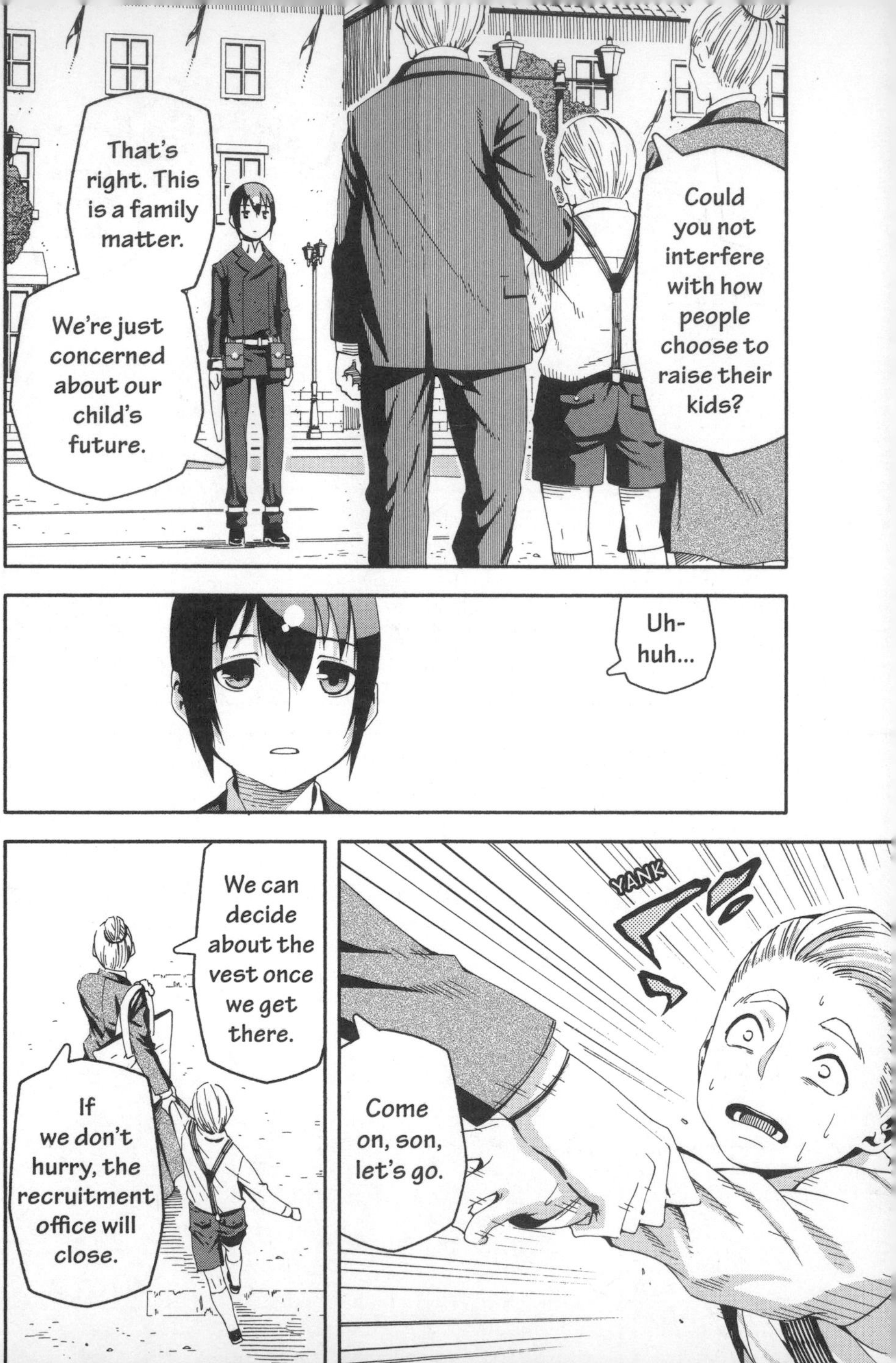
Could you not interfere with how people choose to raise their kids?
That's right. This is a family matter.
We're just concerned about our child's future.
Uh-huh...
YANK
Come on, son, let's go.
We can decide about the vest once we get there.
If we don't hurry, the recruitment office will close.

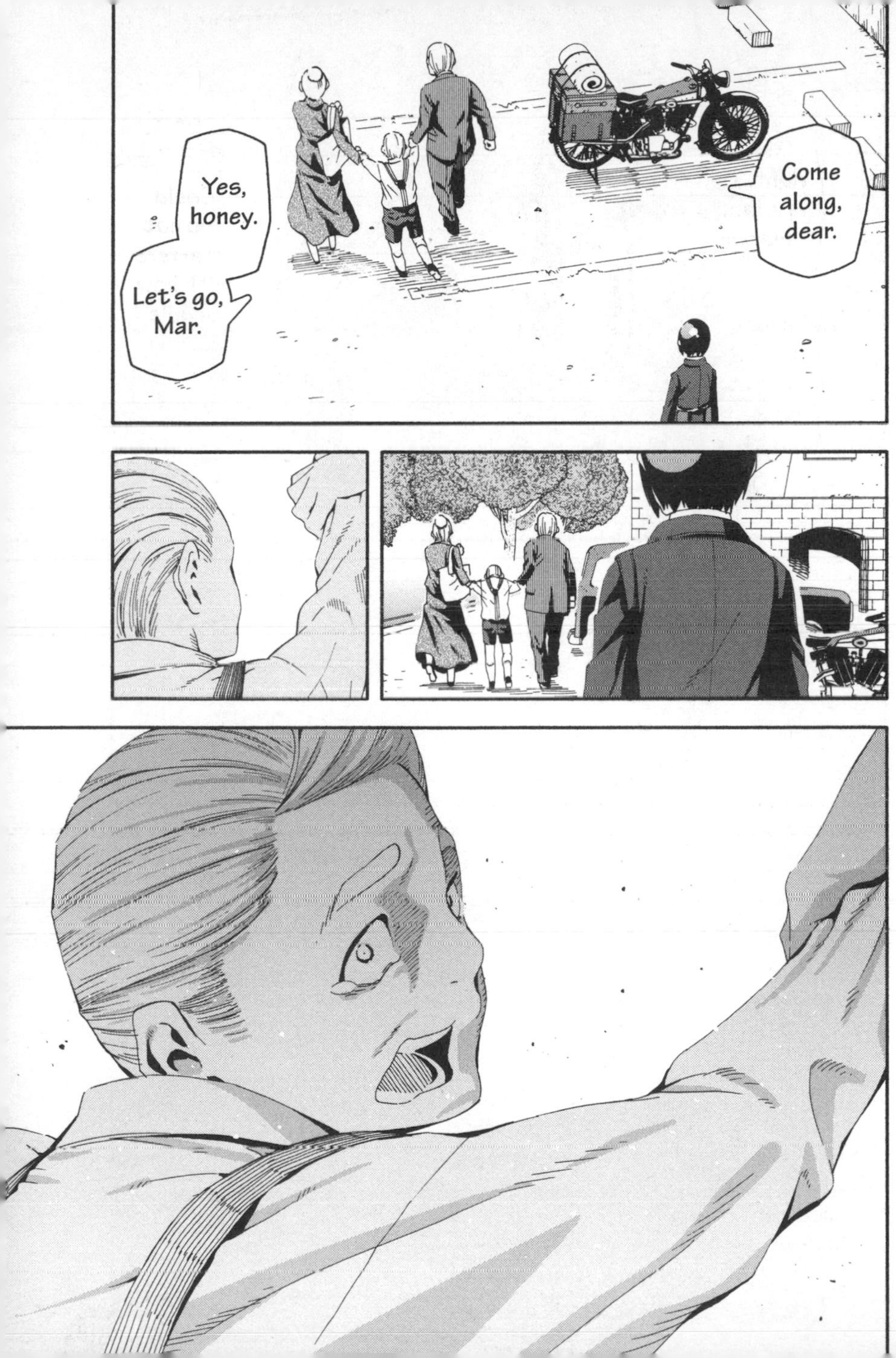
Come along, dear.
Yes, honey.
Let's go, Mar.

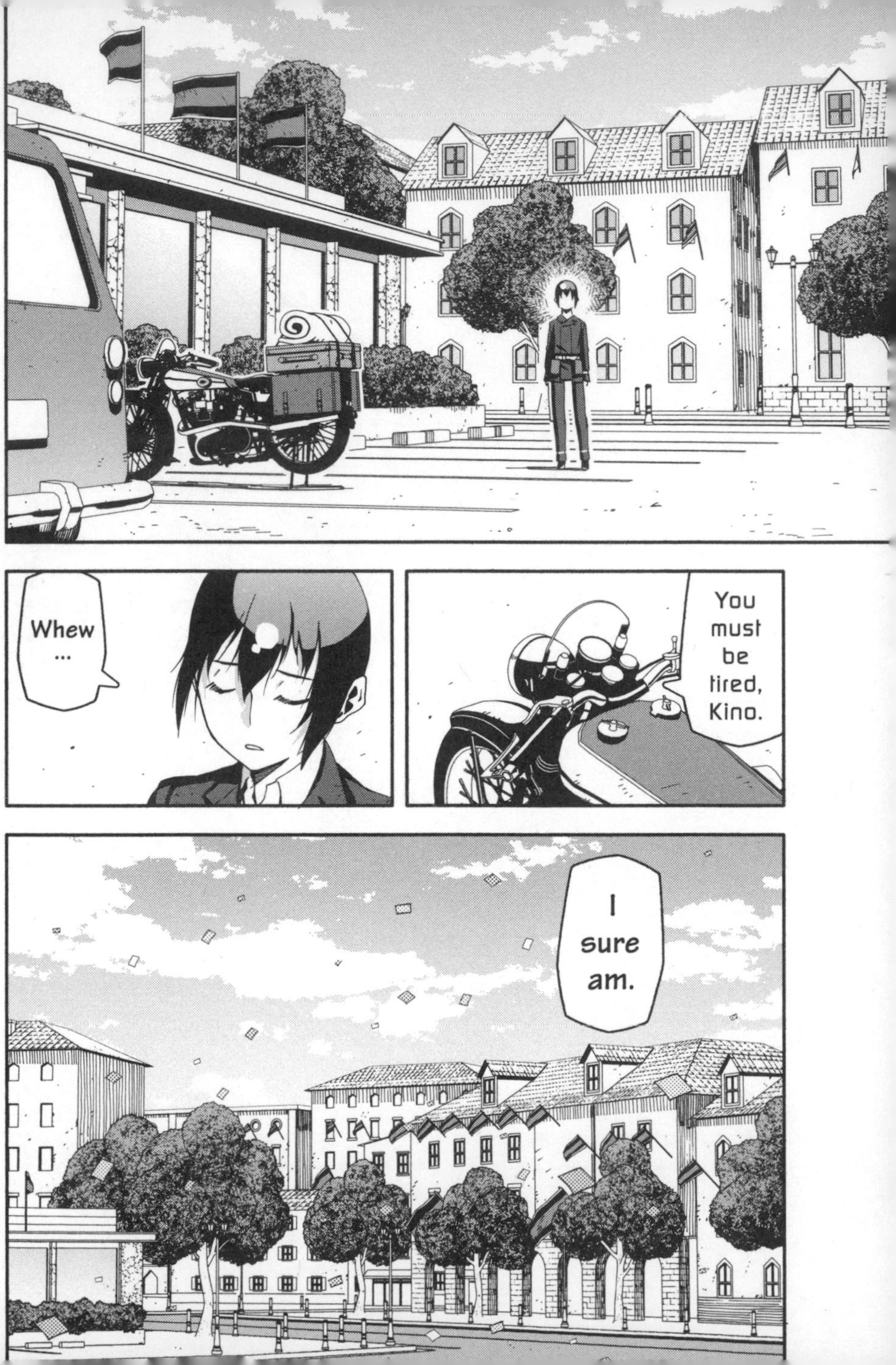
You must be tired, Kino.
Whew ...
I sure am.

Kino's Journey

— The Beautiful World —

Chapter 4
The Story of the Paintings
-Happiness-

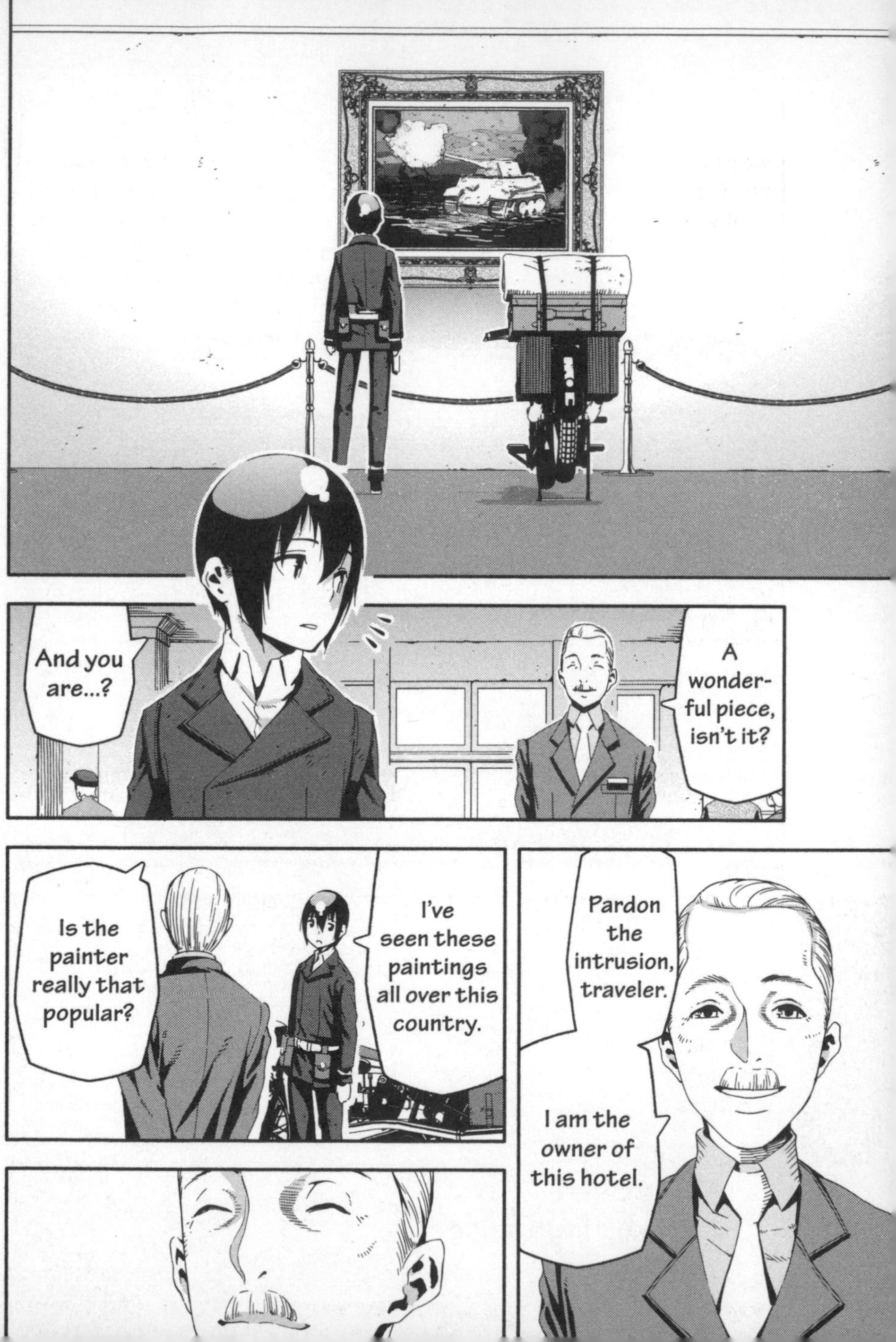
A wonderful piece, isn't it?
And you are...?
Pardon the intrusion, traveler.
I am the owner of this hotel.
I've seen these paintings all over this country.
Is the painter really that popular?

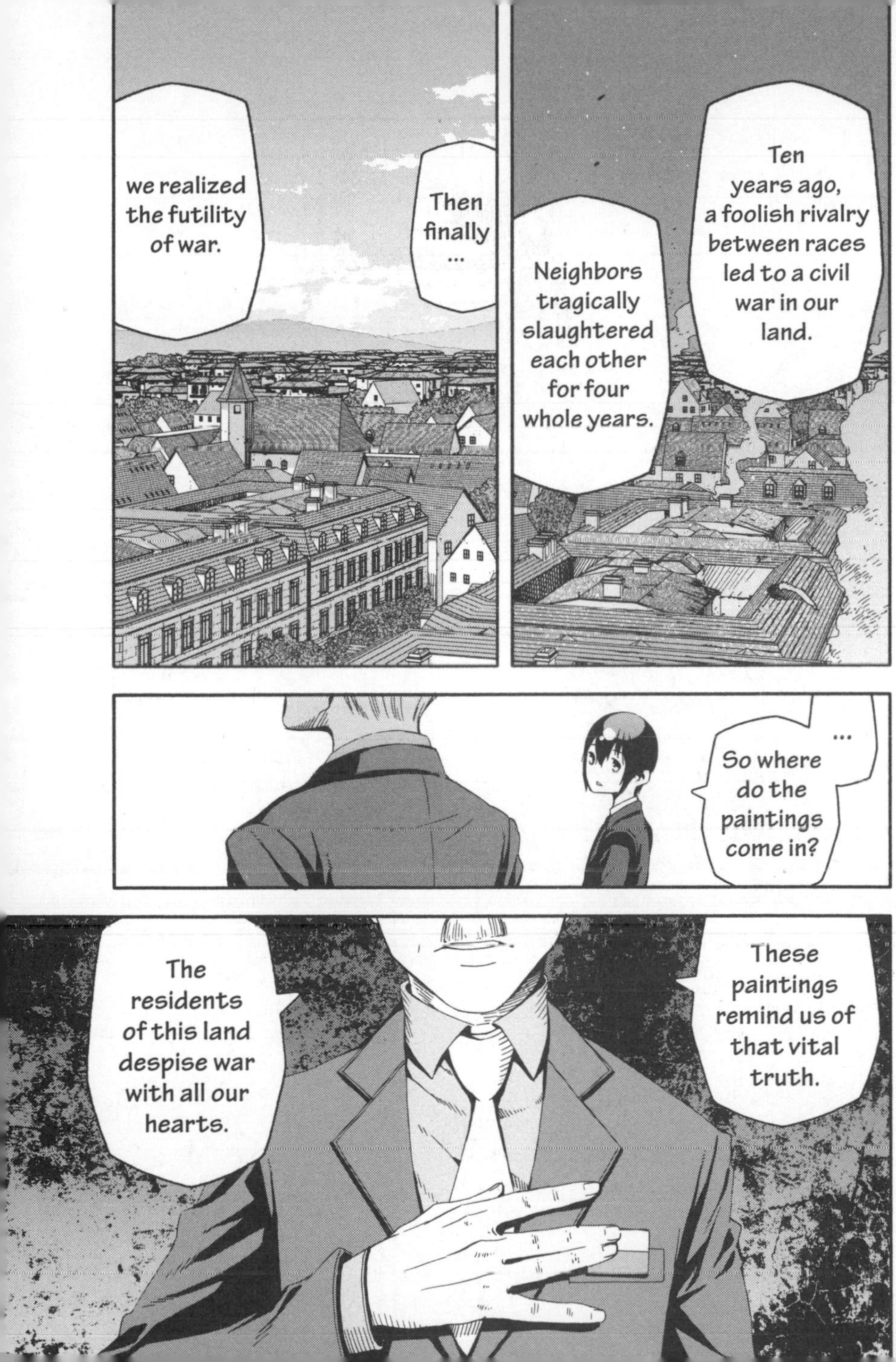
Ten years ago, a foolish rivalry between races led to a civil war in our land.
Neighbors tragically slaughtered each other for four whole years.
Then finally ...
we realized the futility of war.
... So where do the paintings come in?
These paintings remind us of that vital truth.
The residents of this land despise war with all our hearts.

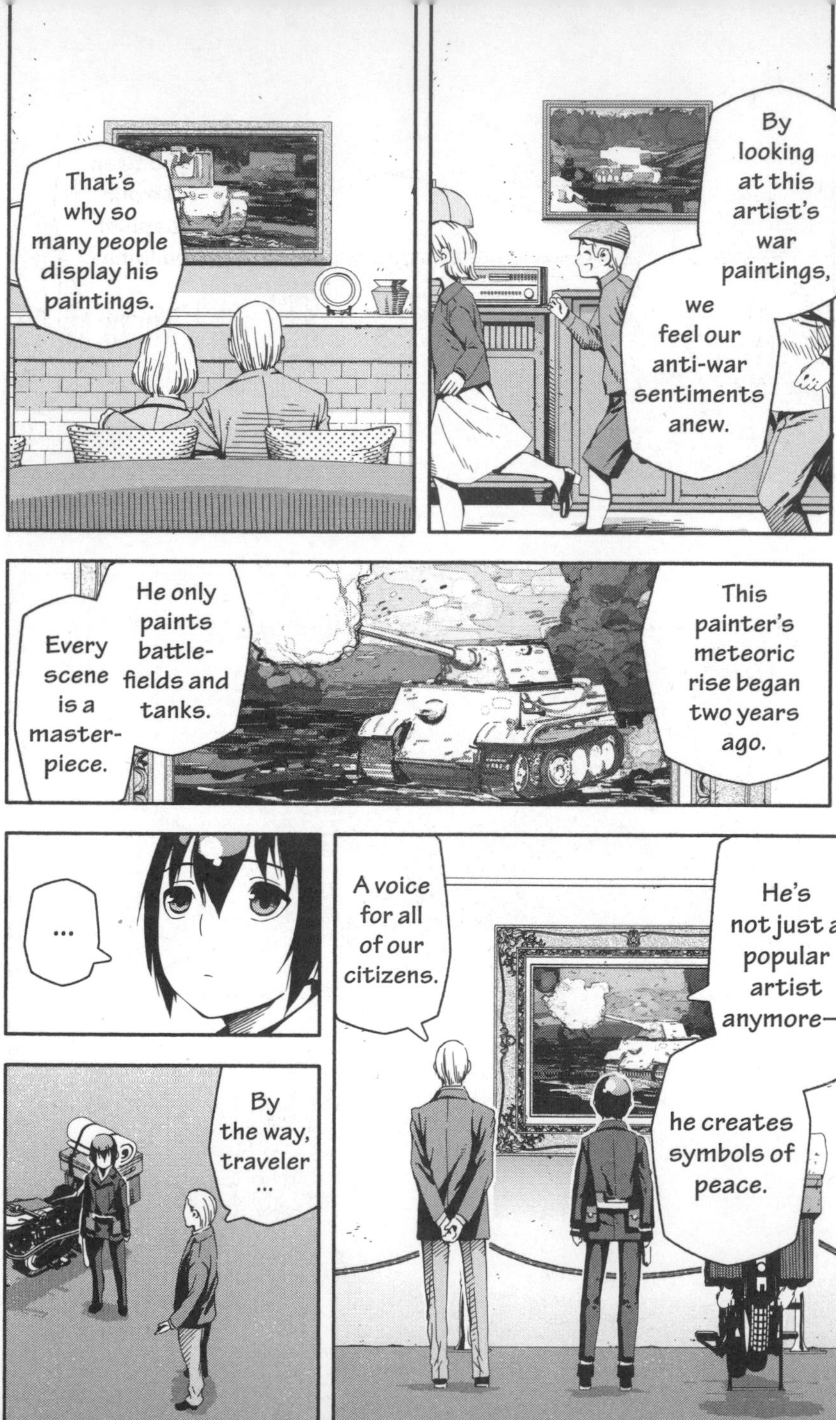

By looking at this artist's war paintings,
we feel our anti-war sentiments anew.
That's why so many people display his paintings.
This painter's meteoric rise began two years ago.
He only paints battle-fields and tanks.
Every scene is a master-piece.
He's not just a popular artist anymore—
he creates symbols of peace.
A voice for all of our citizens.
...
By the way, traveler ...

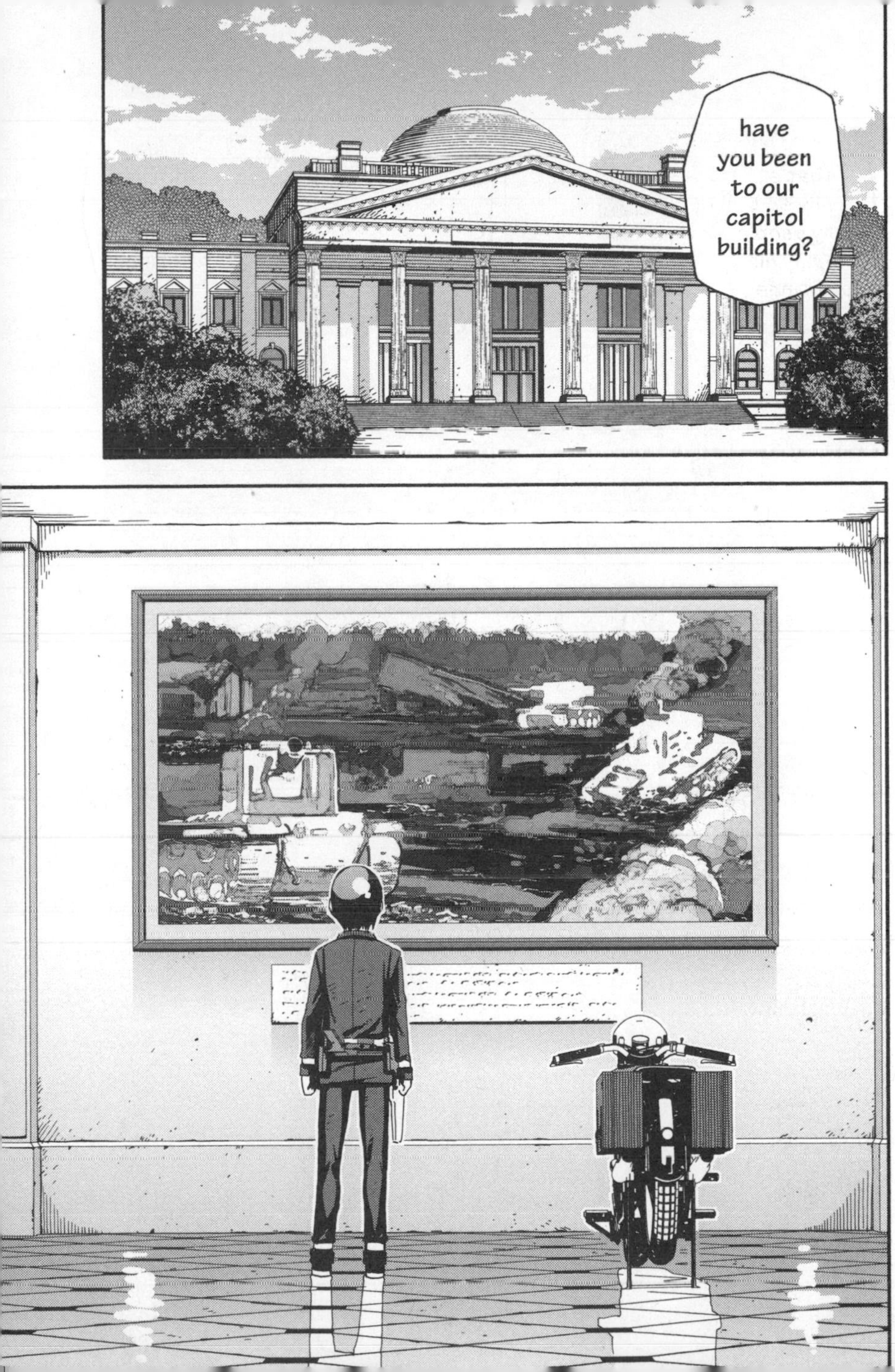
have you been to our capitol building?

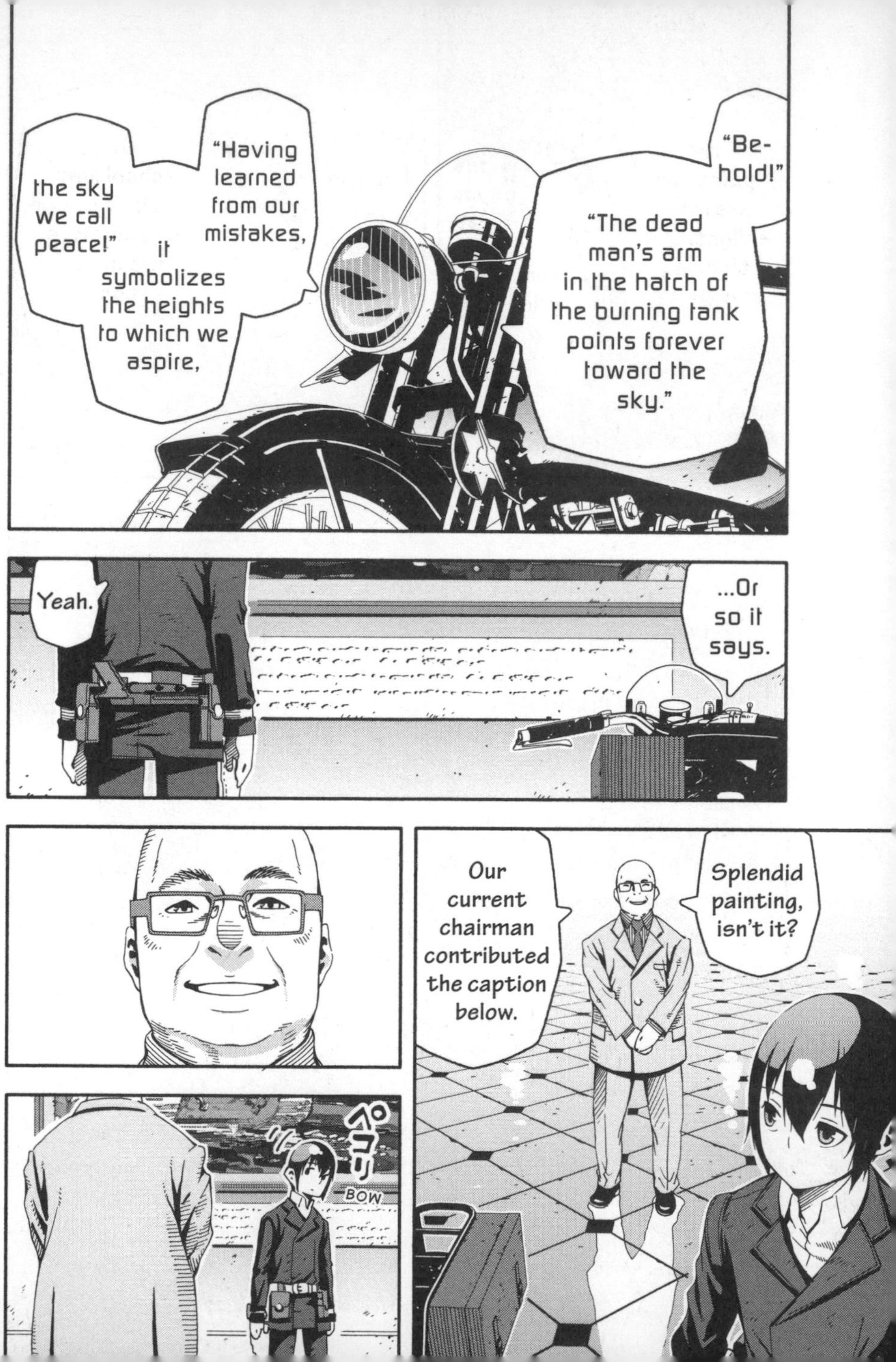
"Be-hold!"
"The dead man's arm in the hatch of the burning tank points forever toward the sky."
"Having learned from our mistakes, it symbolizes the heights to which we aspire, the sky we call peace!"
...Or so it says.
Yeah.
Splendid painting, isn't it?
Our current chairman contributed the caption below.
BOW

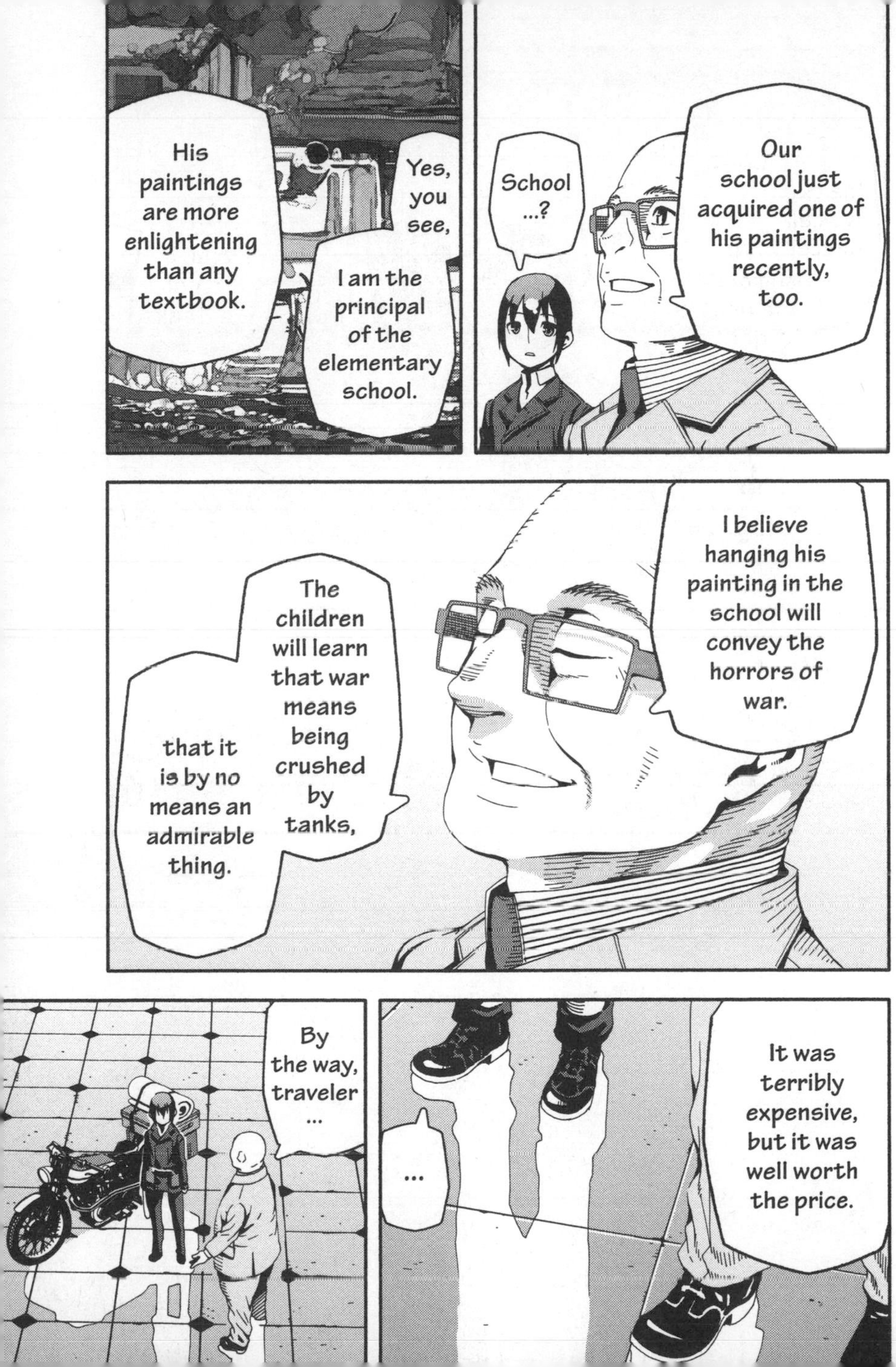
Our school just acquired one of his paintings recently, too.
School ...?
Yes, you see,
I am the principal of the elementary school.
His paintings are more enlightening than any textbook.
I believe hanging his painting in the school will convey the horrors of war.
The children will learn that war means being crushed by tanks,
that it is by no means an admirable thing.
It was terribly expensive, but it was well worth the price.
...
By the way, traveler ...

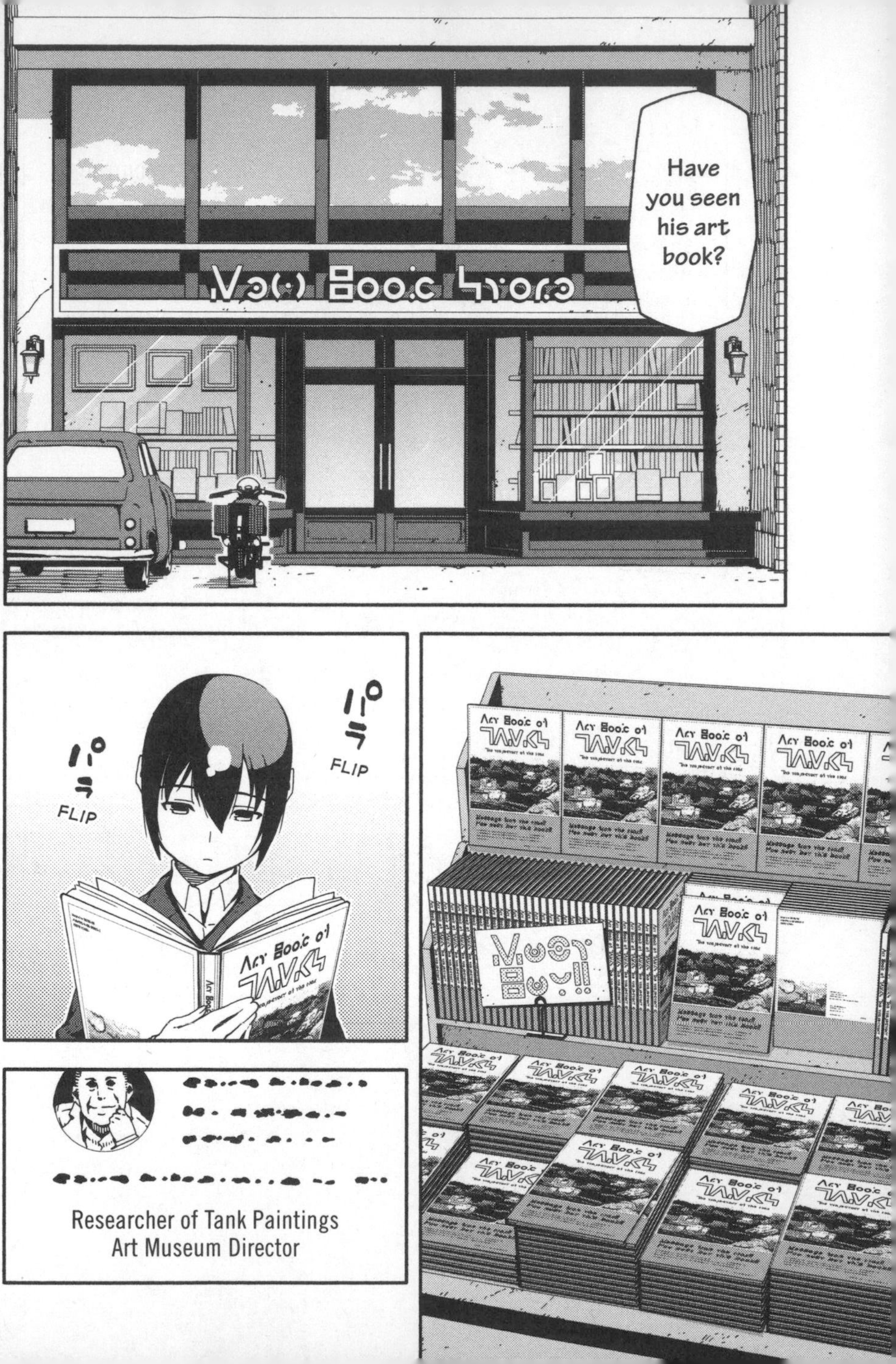
Have you seen his art book?
パラ
FLIP
パラ
FLIP
Researcher of Tank Paintings
Art Museum Director

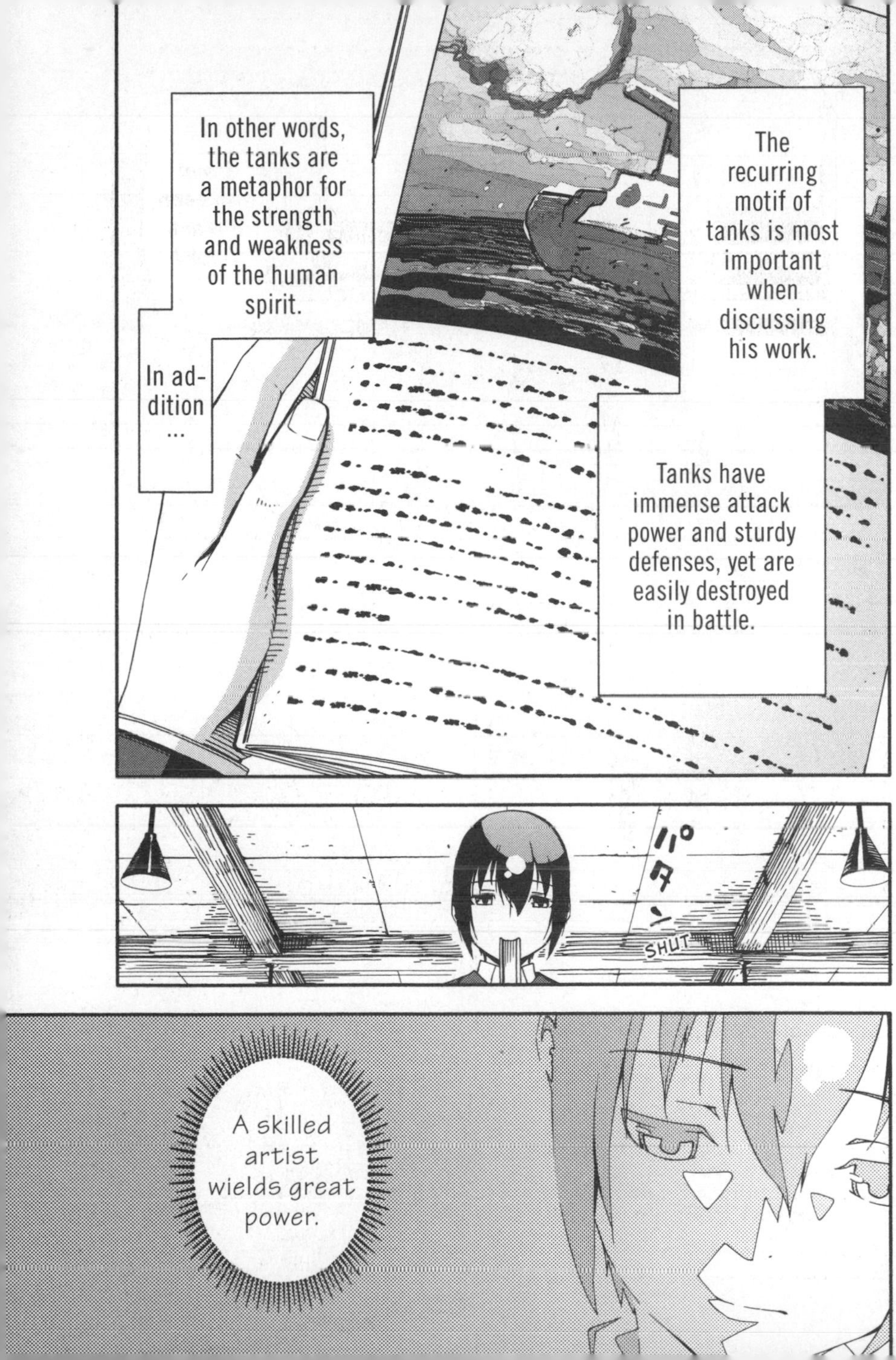
The recurring motif of tanks is most important when discussing his work.
Tanks have immense attack power and sturdy defenses, yet are easily destroyed in battle.
In other words, the tanks are a metaphor for the strength and weakness of the human spirit.
In ad-dition ...
パタン
SHUT
A skilled artist wields great power.

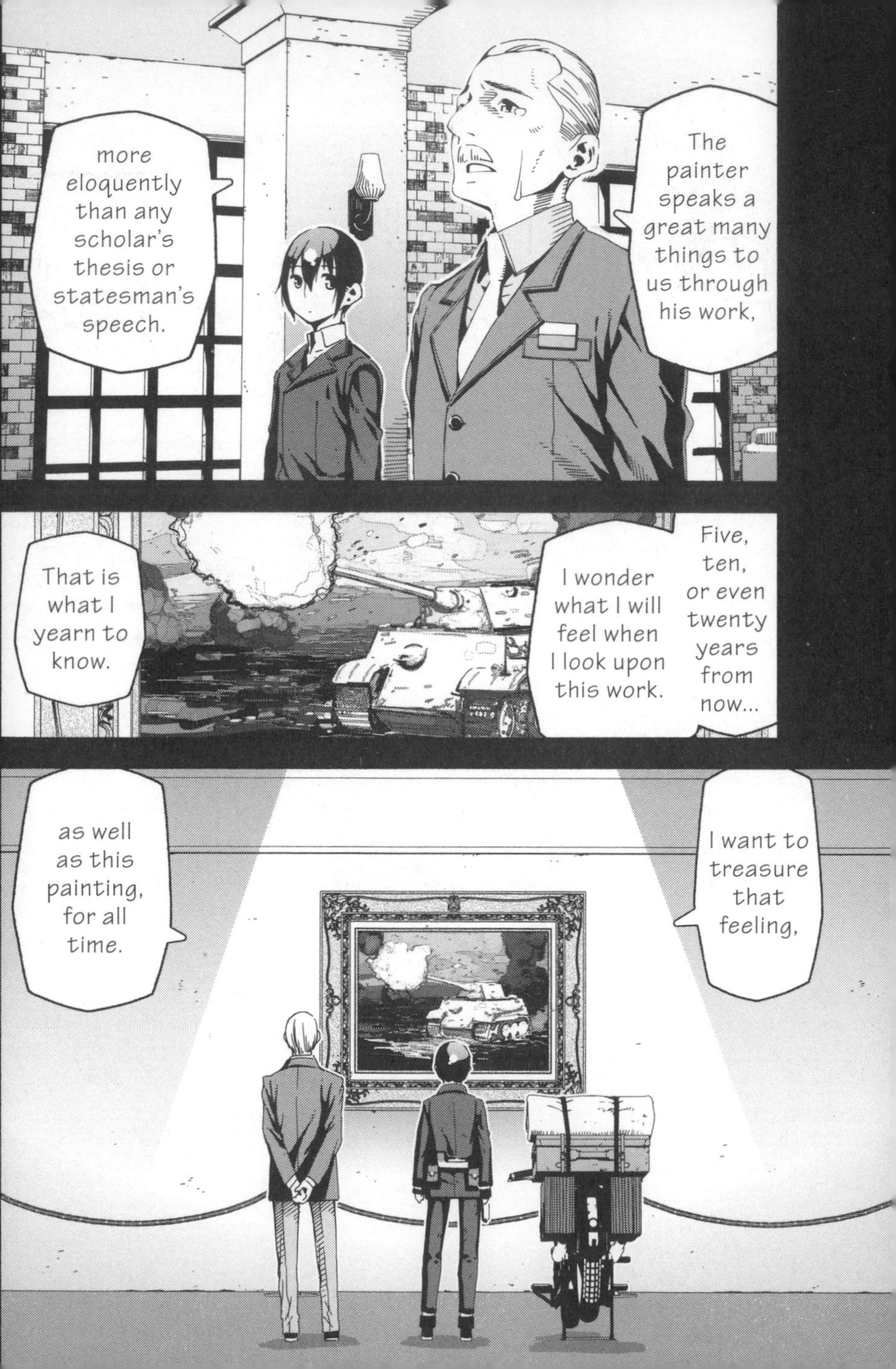
The painter speaks a great many things to us through his work,
more eloquently than any scholar's thesis or statesman's speech.
Five, ten, or even twenty years from now...
I wonder what I will feel when I look upon this work.
That is what I yearn to know.
I want to treasure that feeling,
as well as this painting, for all time.

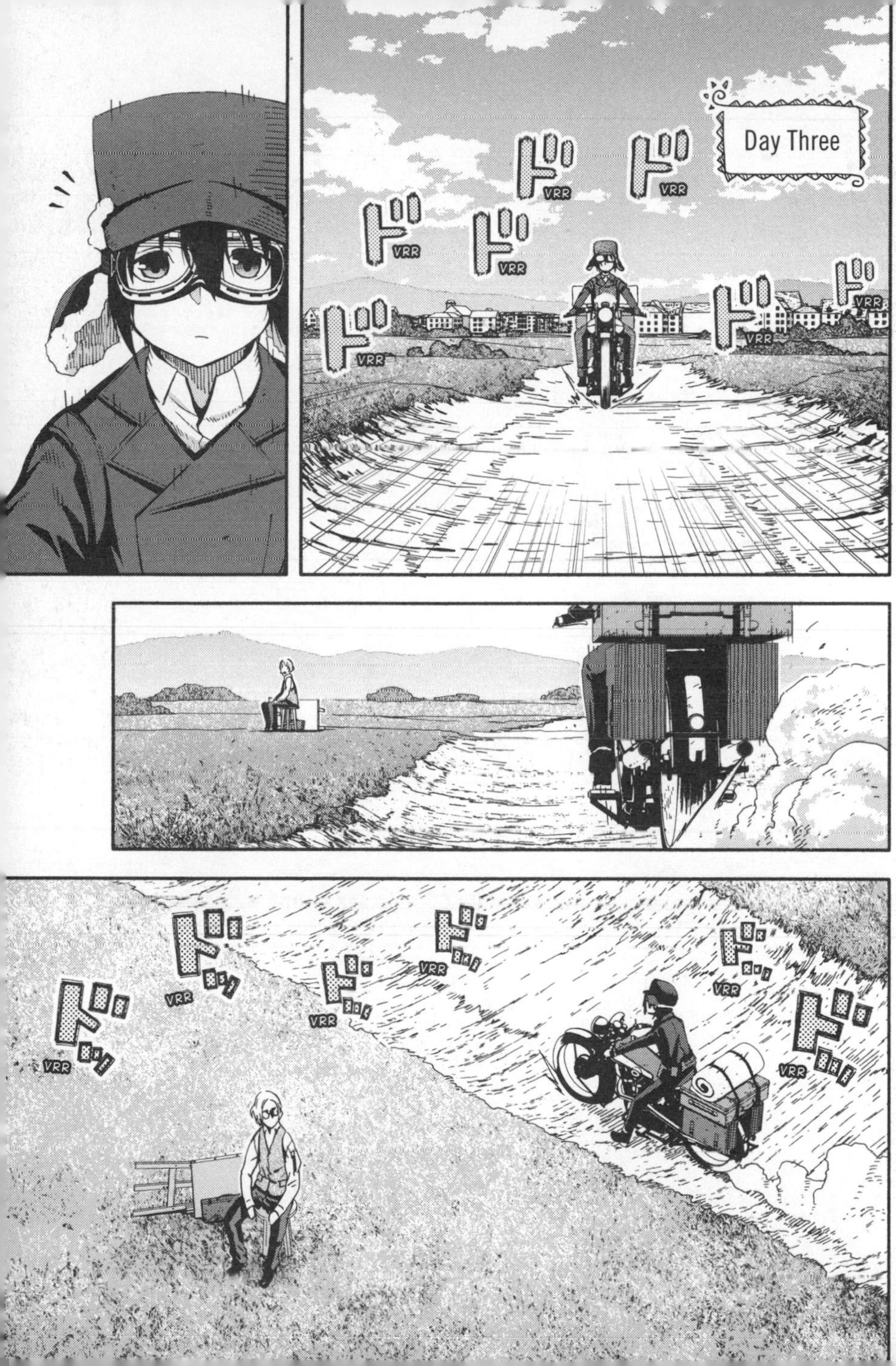
Day Three
ド VRR
ド VRR
ド VRR
ド VRR
ド VRR
ド VRR
ド VRR
ド VRR
ド VRR
ド VRR
ド VRR
ド VRR
ド VRR
ド VRR

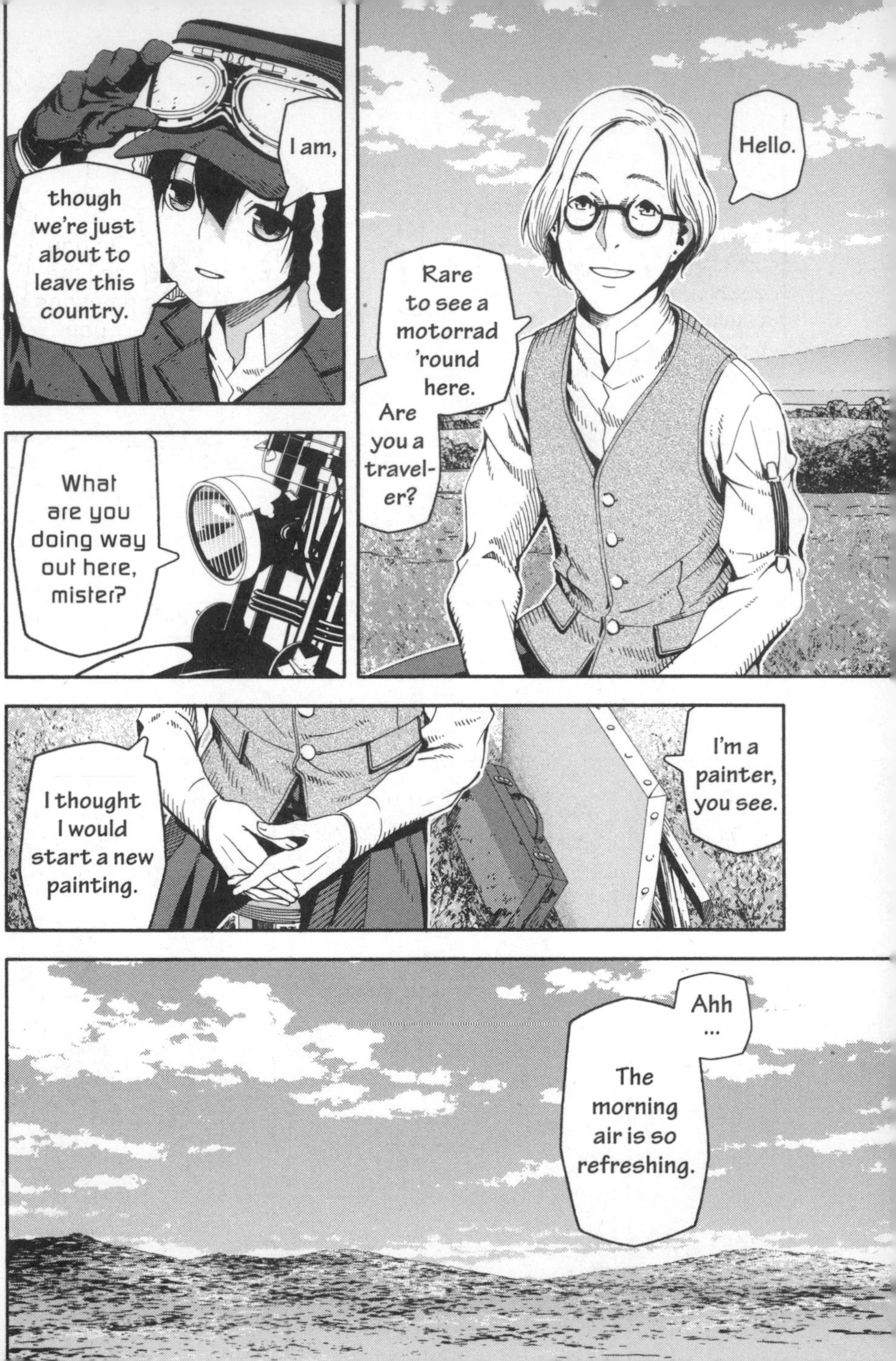
Hello.
Rare to see a motorrad 'round here.
Are you a travel-er?
I am,
though we're just about to leave this country.
What are you doing way out here, mister?
I'm a painter, you see.
I thought I would start a new painting.
Ahh ...
The morning air is so refreshing.

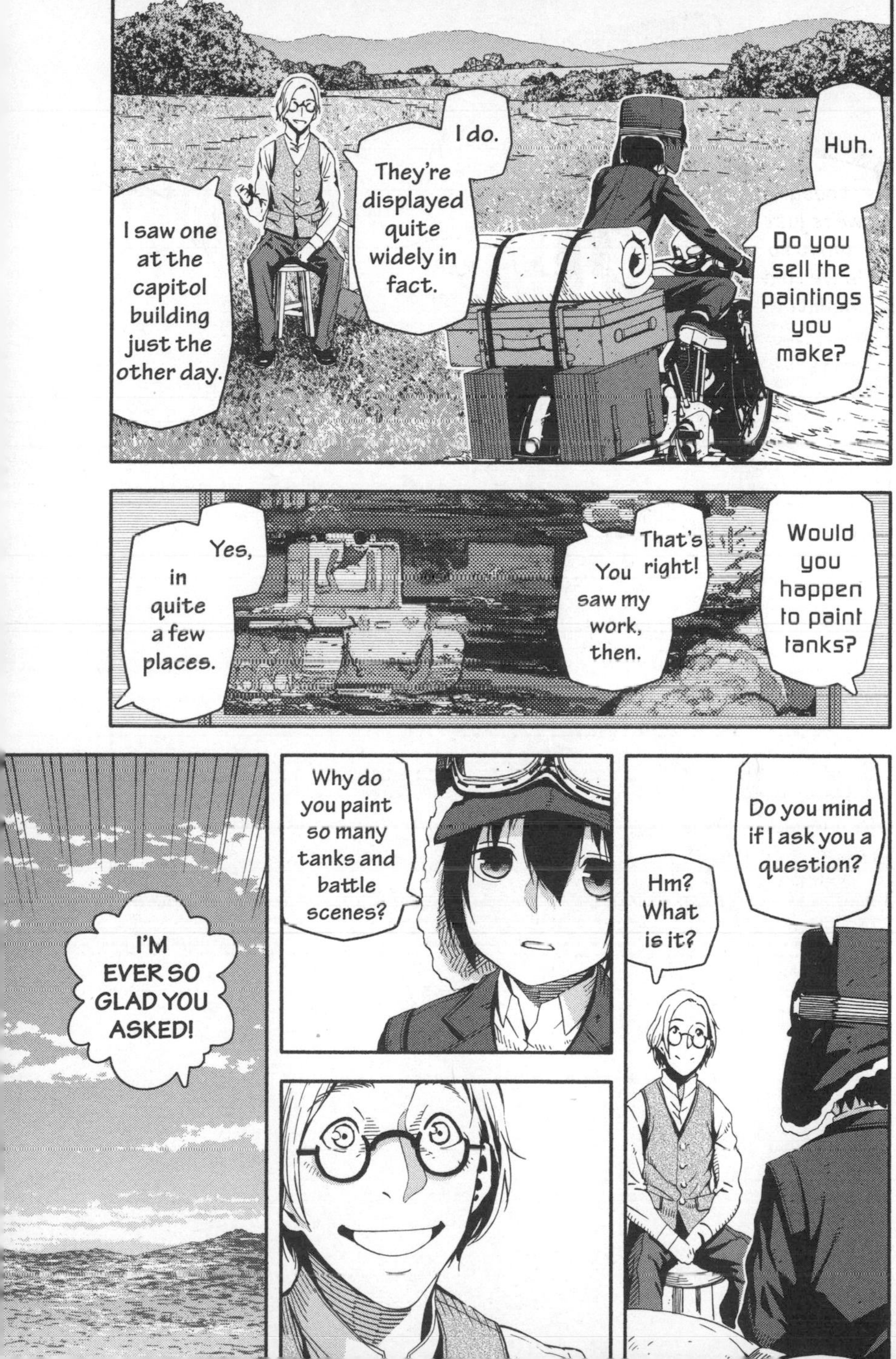
Huh.
Do you sell the paintings you make?
I do.
They're displayed quite widely in fact.
I saw one at the capitol building just the other day.
Would you happen to paint tanks?
That's right!
You saw my work, then.
Yes, in quite a few places.
Do you mind if I ask you a question?
Hm? What is it?
Why do you paint so many tanks and battle scenes?
I'M EVER SO GLAD YOU ASKED!

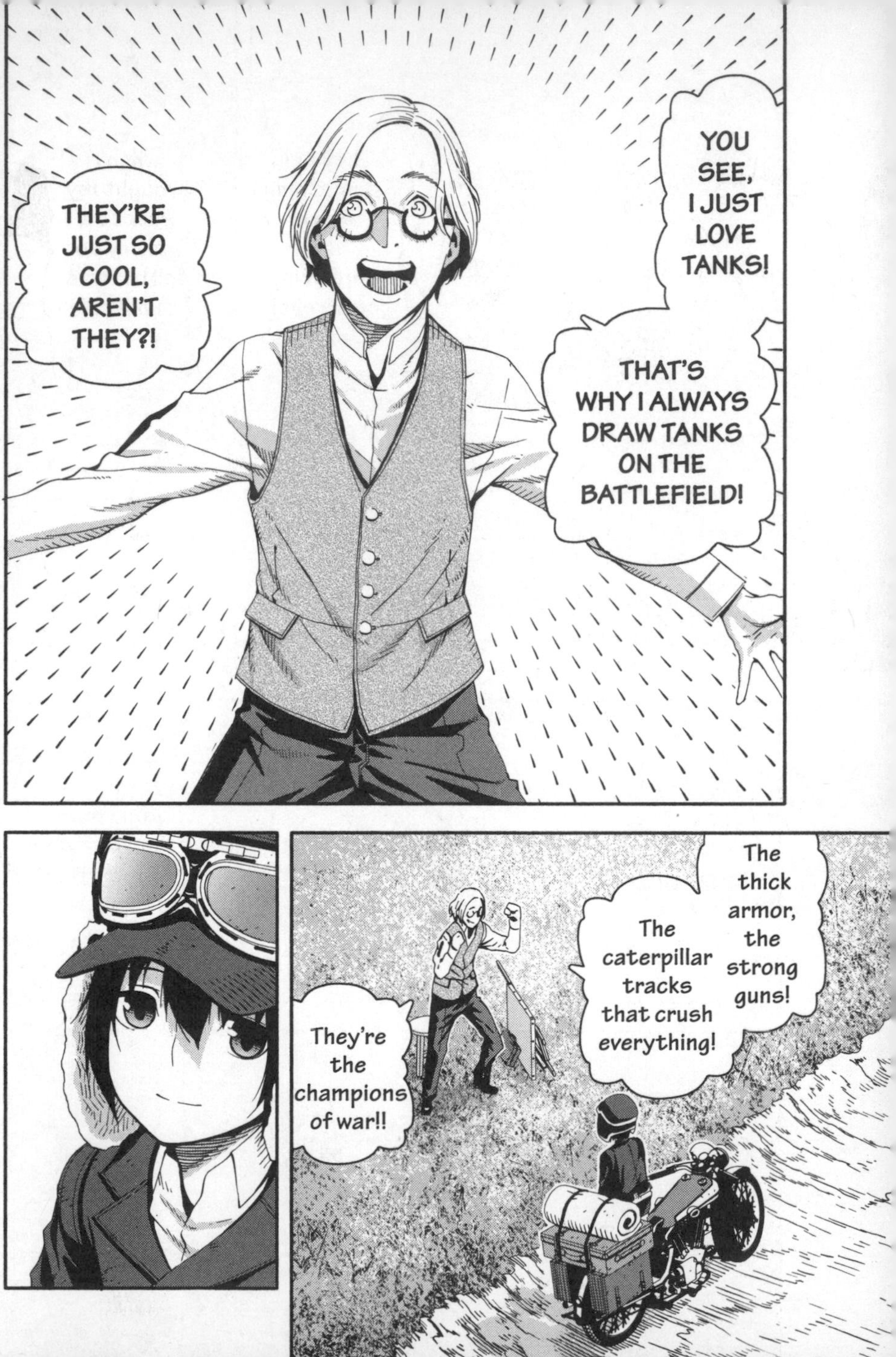
YOU SEE, I JUST LOVE TANKS!
THEY'RE JUST SO COOL, AREN'T THEY?!
THAT'S WHY I ALWAYS DRAW TANKS ON THE BATTLEFIELD!
The thick armor, the strong guns!
The caterpillar tracks that crush everything!
They're the champions of war!!

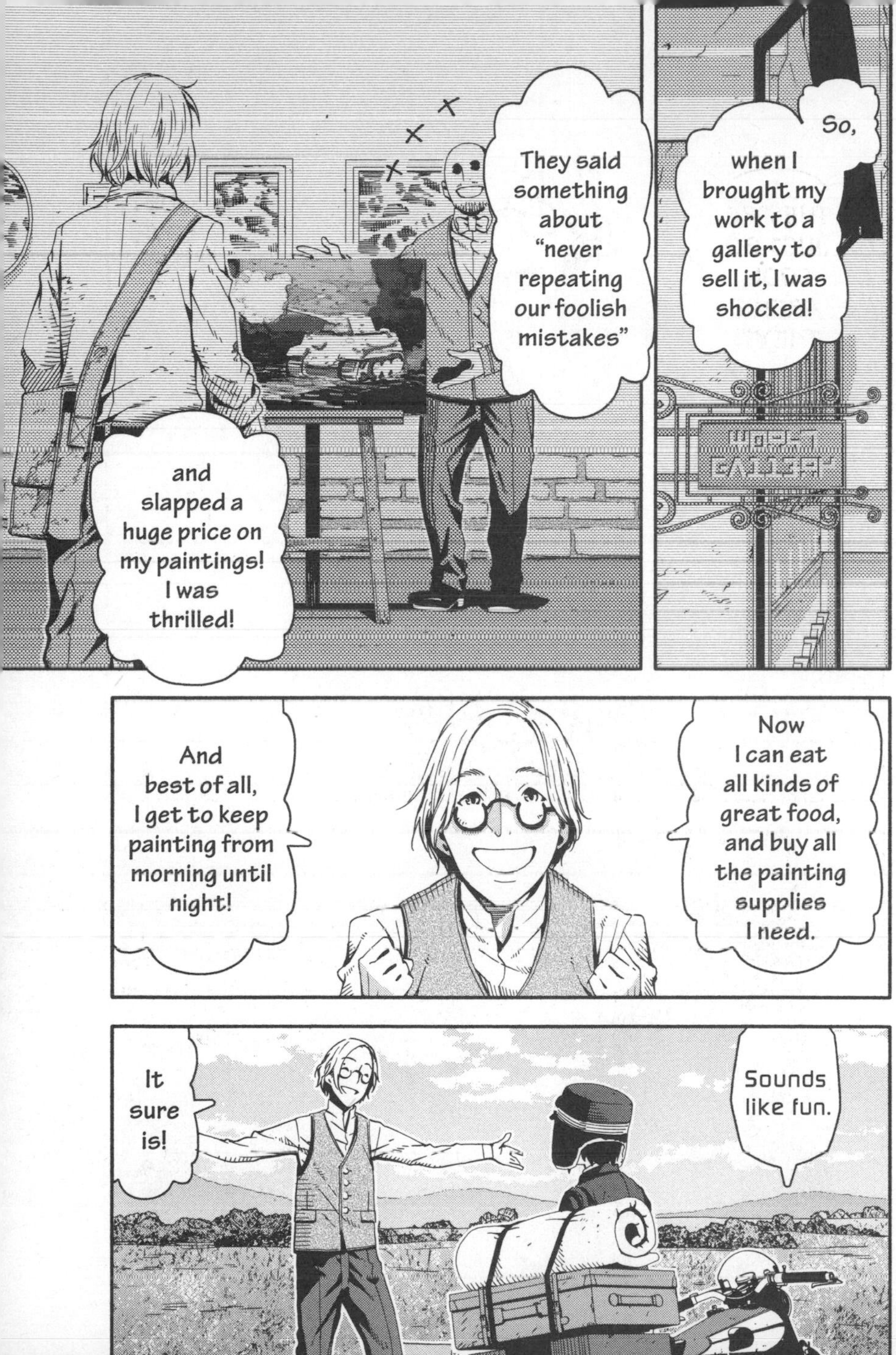
So, when I brought my work to a gallery to sell it, I was shocked!
They sald something about “never repeating our foolish mistakes”
and slapped a huge price on my paintings! I was thrilled!
Now I can eat all kinds of great food, and buy all the painting supplies I need.
And best of all, I get to keep painting from morning until night!
Sounds like fun.
It sure is!

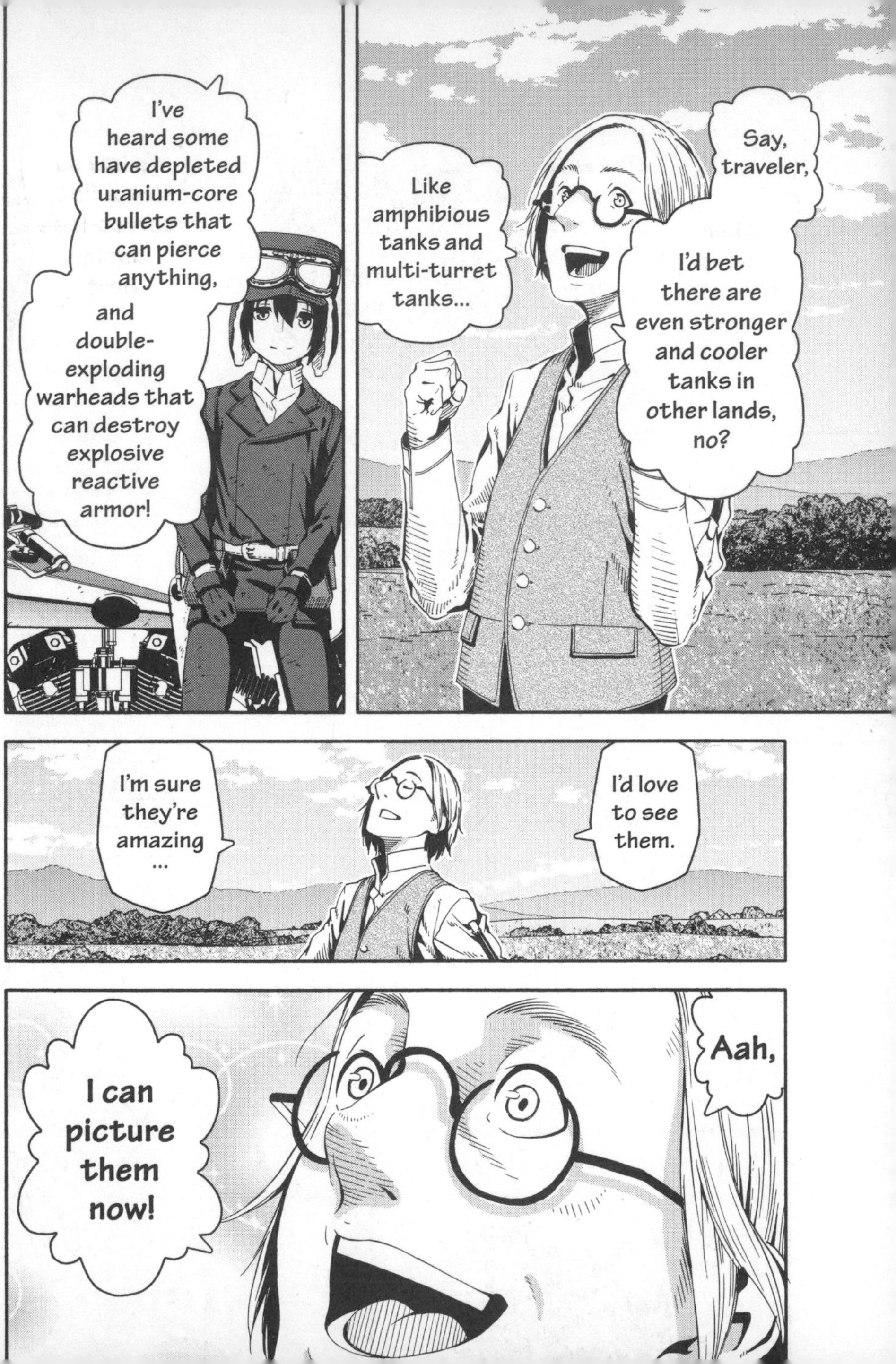
Say, traveler,
I'd bet there are even stronger and cooler tanks in other lands, no?
Like amphibious tanks and multi-turret tanks...
I've heard some have depleted uranium-core bullets that can pierce anything,
and double-exploding warheads that can destroy explosive reactive armor!
I'd love to see them.
I'm sure they're amazing ...
Aah,
I can picture them now!

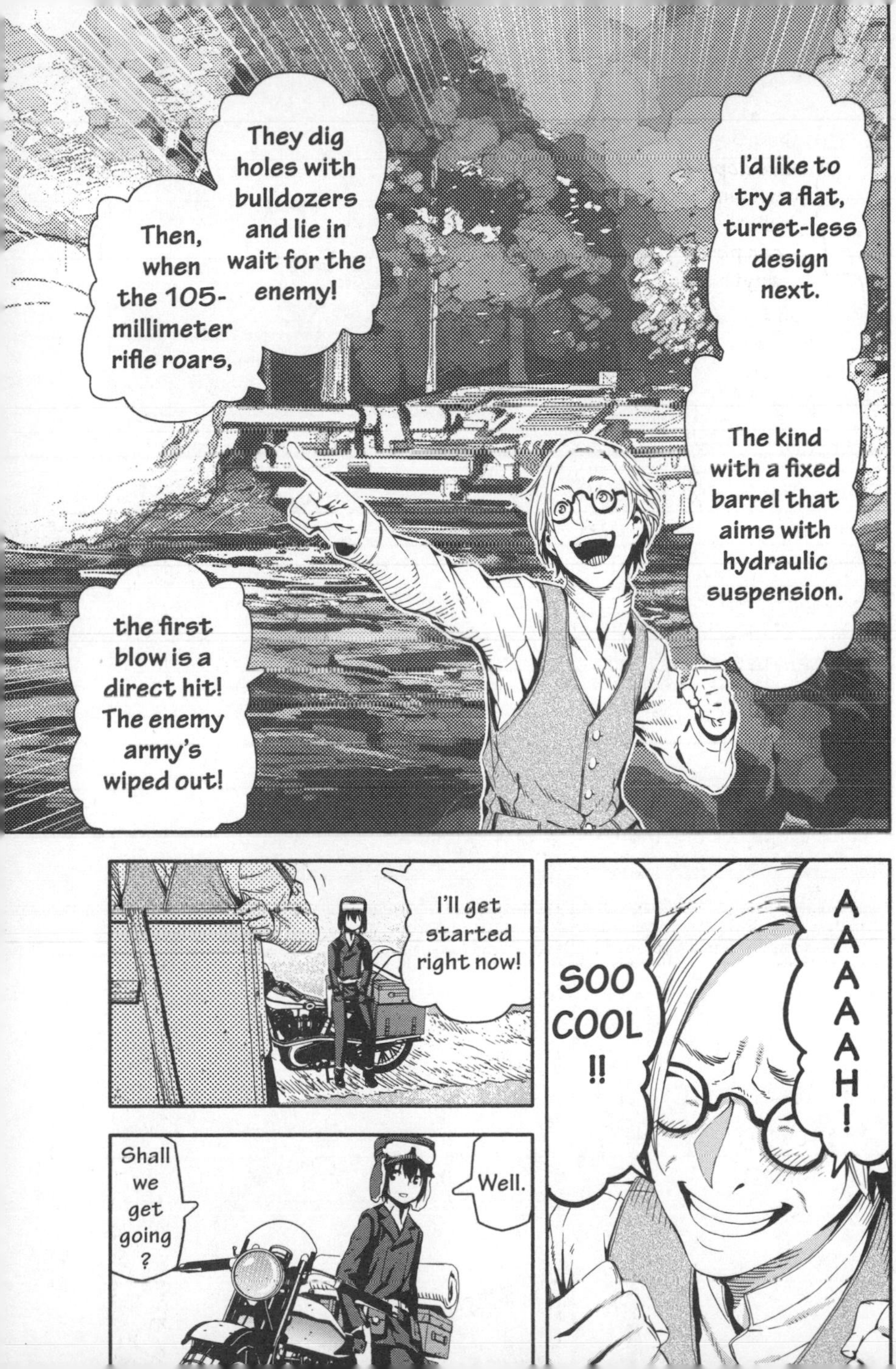
I'd like to try a flat, turret-less design next.
The kind with a fixed barrel that aims with hydraulic suspension.
They dig holes with bulldozers and lie in wait for the enemy!
Then, when the 105-millimeter rifle roars,
the first blow is a direct hit! The enemy army's wiped out!
AAAAAH!
SOO COOL !!
I'll get started right now!
Well.
Shall we get going ?

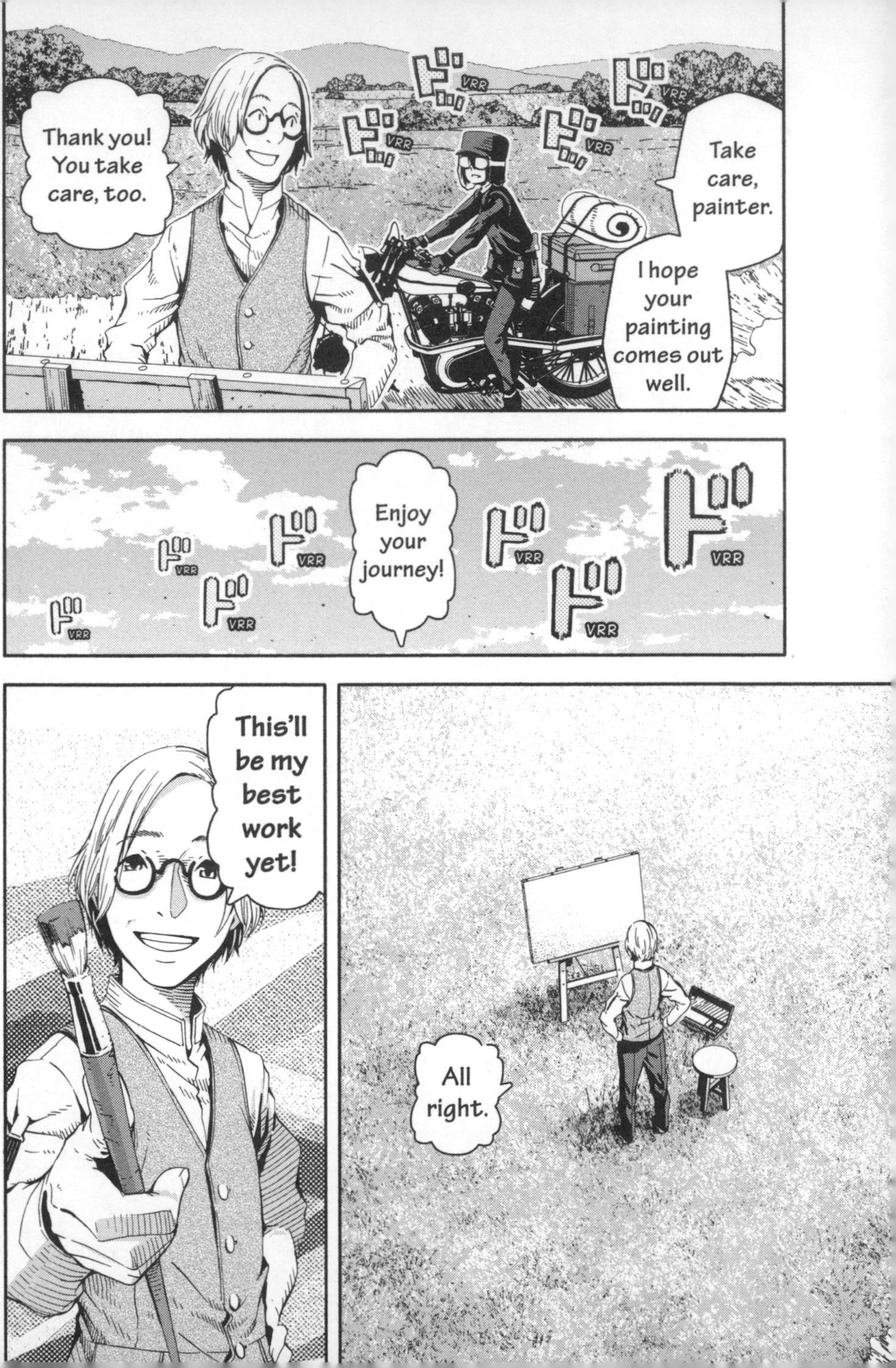
VRR
VRR
VRR
VRR
Take care, painter.
I hope your painting comes out well.
Thank you! You take care, too.
VRR
VRR
VRR
Enjoy your journey!
VRR
VRR
VRR
VRR
All right.
This'll be my best work yet!

Kino's Journey

The Beautiful World

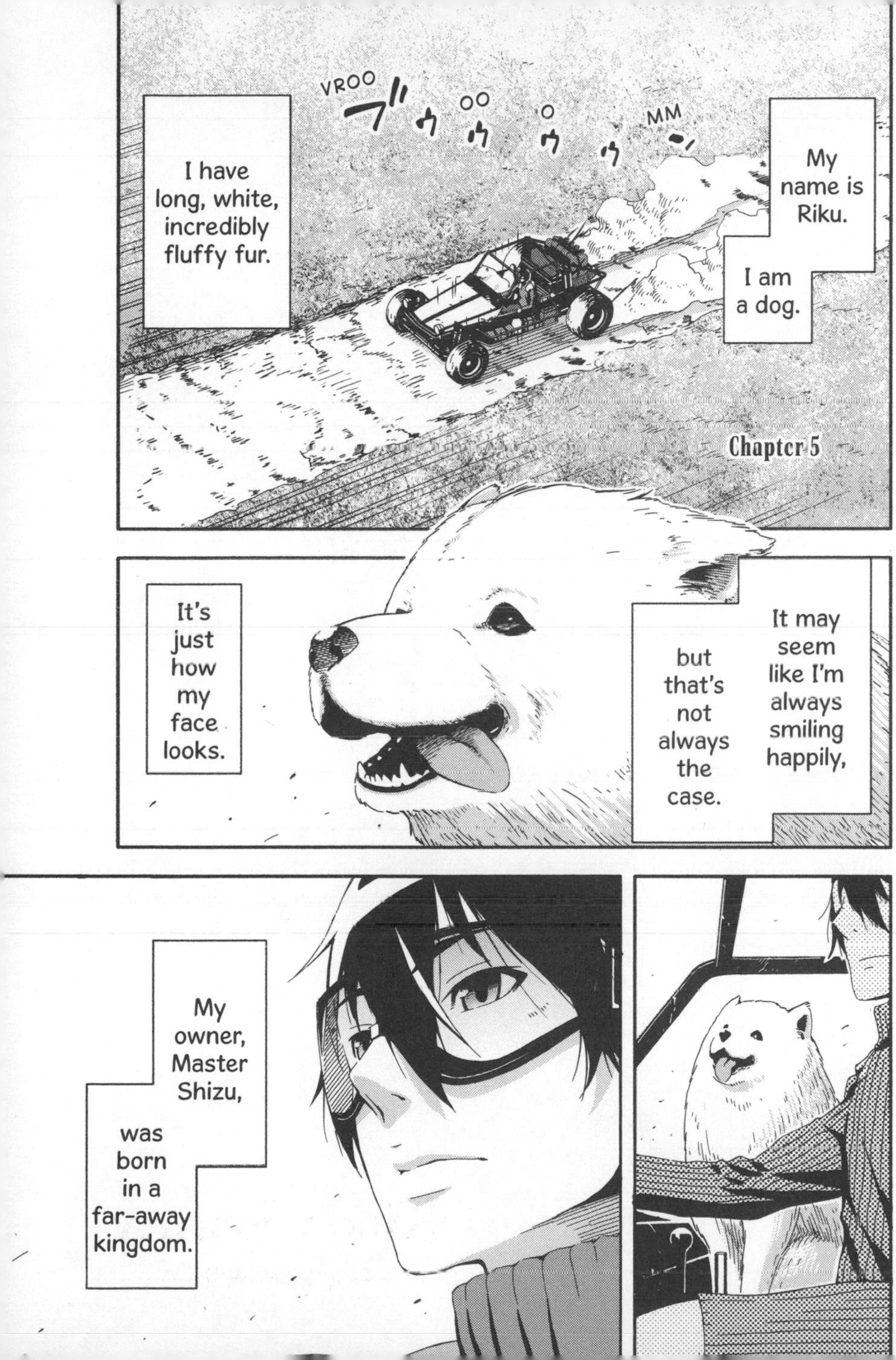
My name is Riku.
I am a dog.
VROO OO O MM
I have long, white, incredibly fluffy fur.
Chapter 5
It may seem like I'm always smiling happily,
but that's not always the case.
It's just how my face looks.
My owner, Master Shizu,
was born in a far-away kingdom.

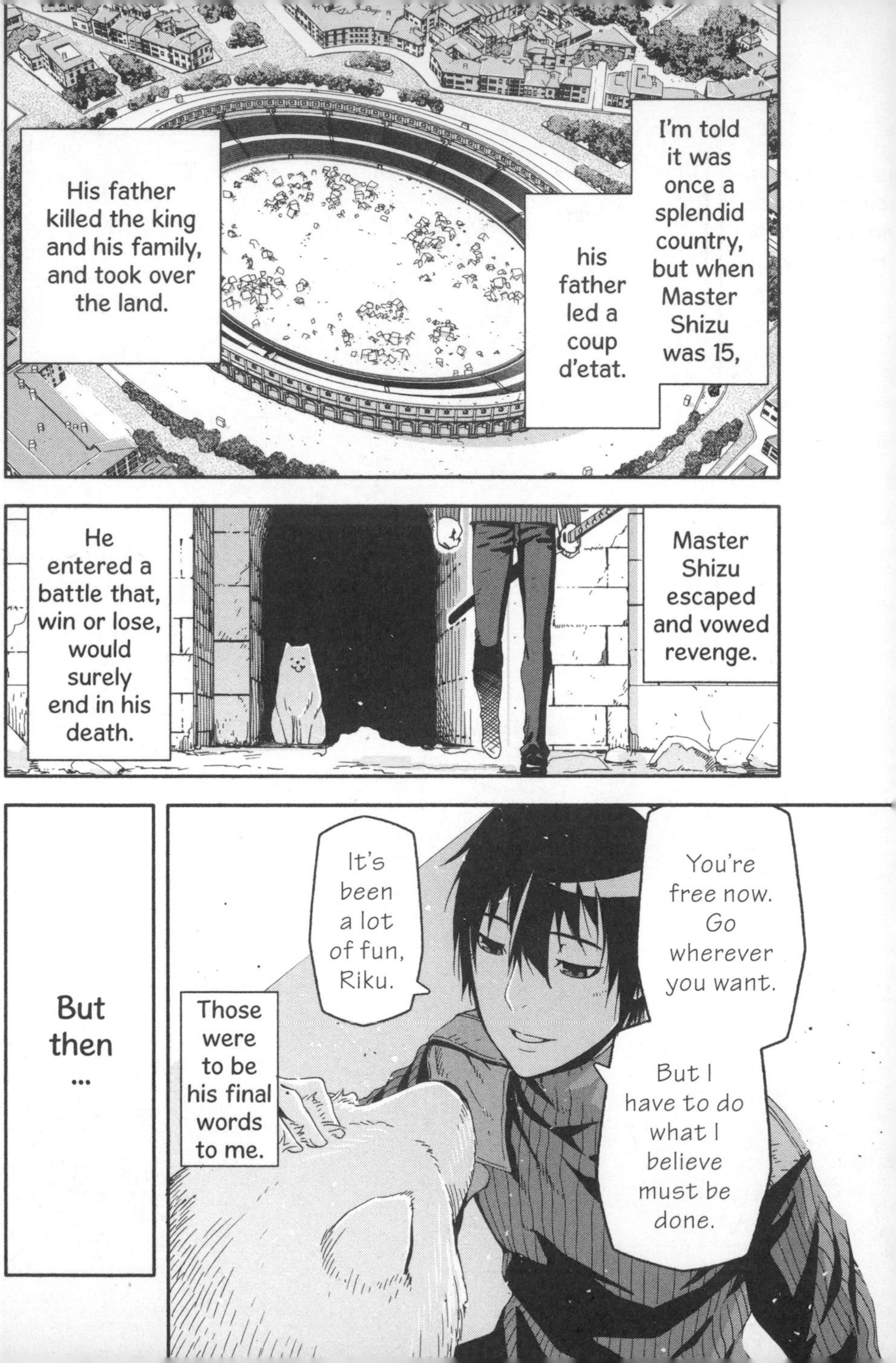

I'm told it was once a splendid country, but when Master Shizu was 15,
his father led a coup d'etat.
His father killed the king and his family, and took over the land.
Master Shizu escaped and vowed revenge.
He entered a battle that, win or lose, would surely end in his death.
You're free now. Go wherever you want.
It's been a lot of fun, Riku.
But I have to do what I believe must be done.
Those were to be his final words to me.
But then ...

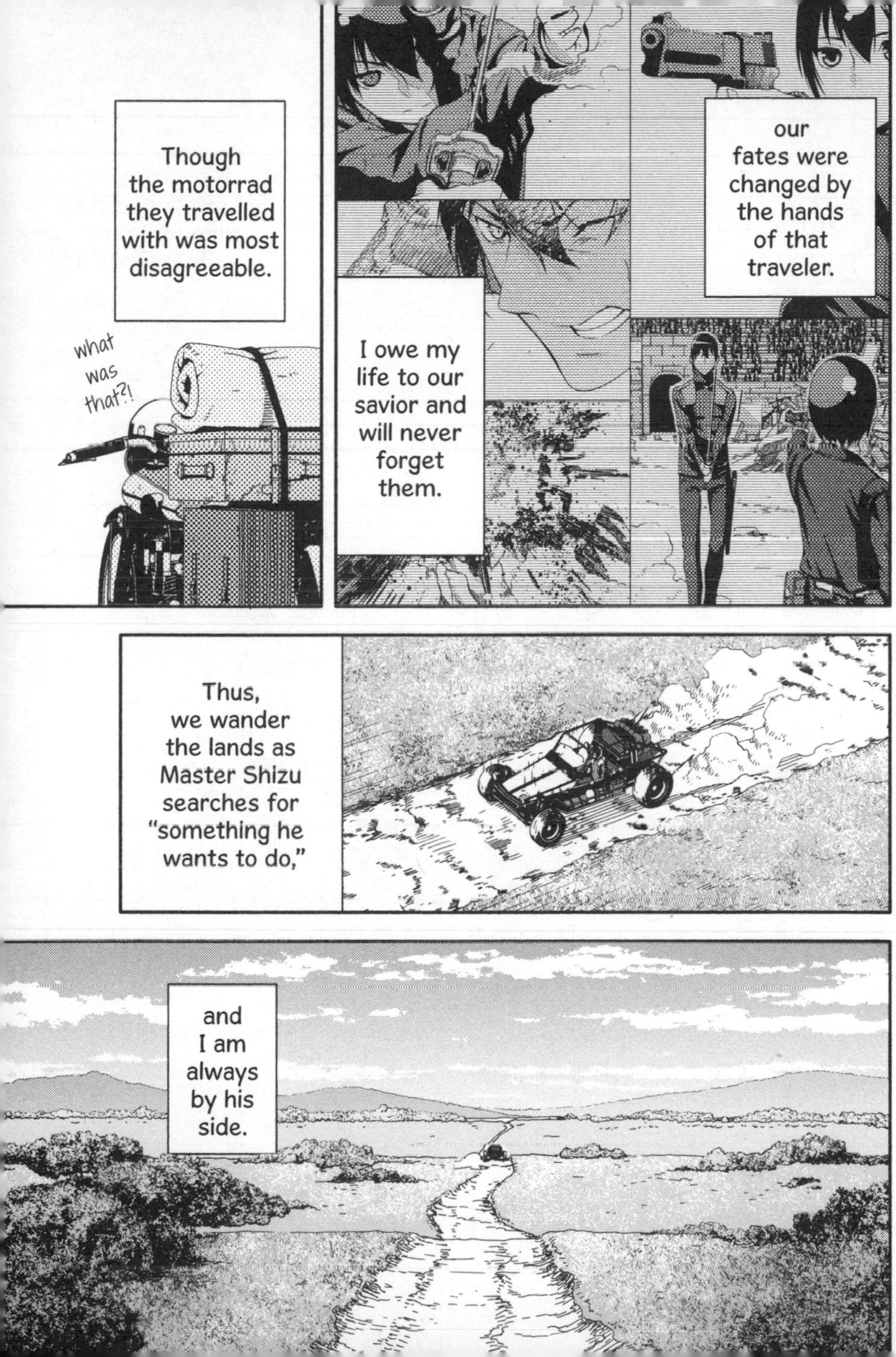
our fates were changed by the hands of that traveler.
I owe my life to our savior and will never forget them.
Though the motorrad they travelled with was most disagreeable.
what was that?!
Thus, we wander the lands as Master Shizu searches for "something he wants to do,"
and I am always by his side.

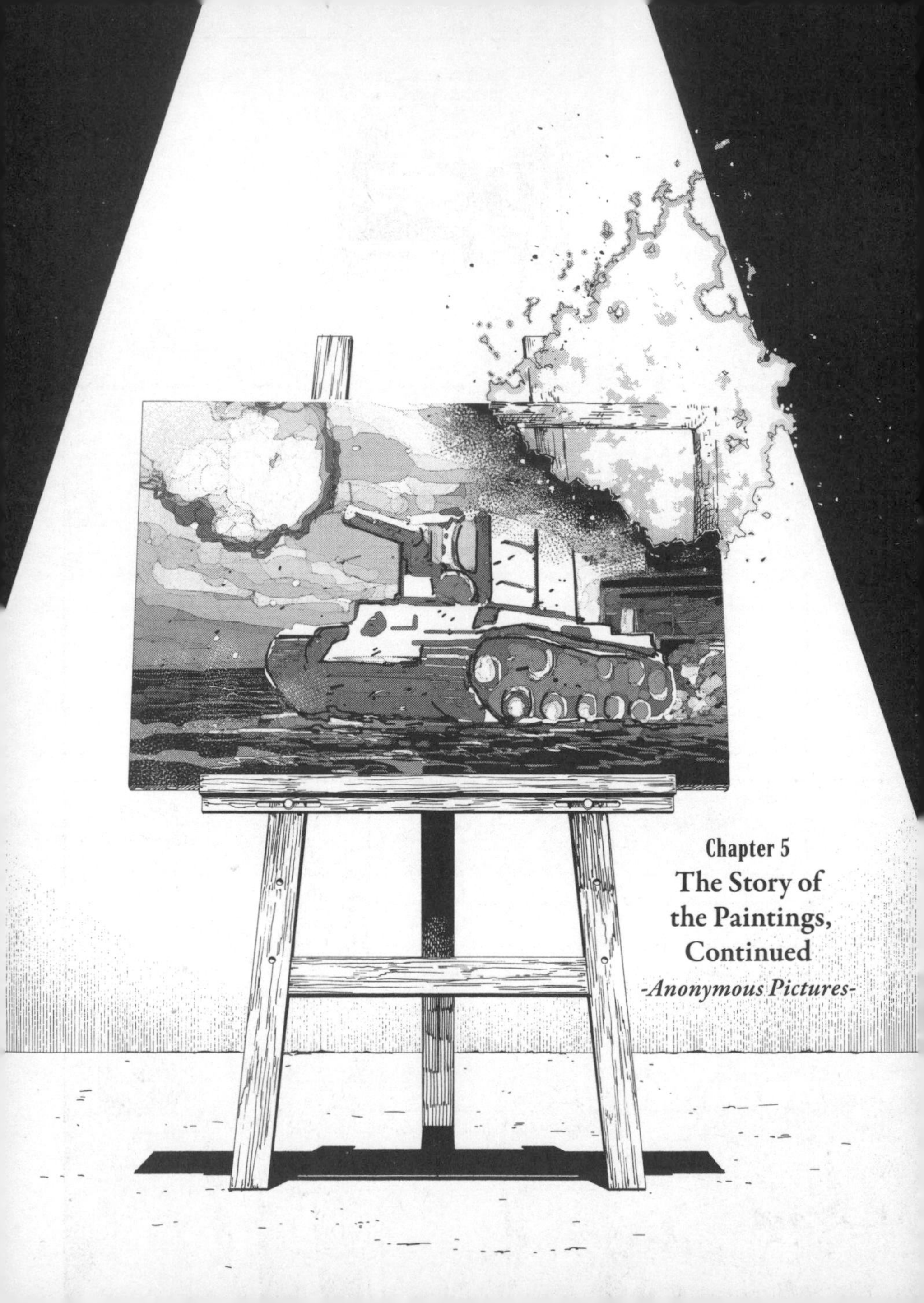

Chapter 5
The Story of the Paintings, Continued
-Anonymous Pictures-

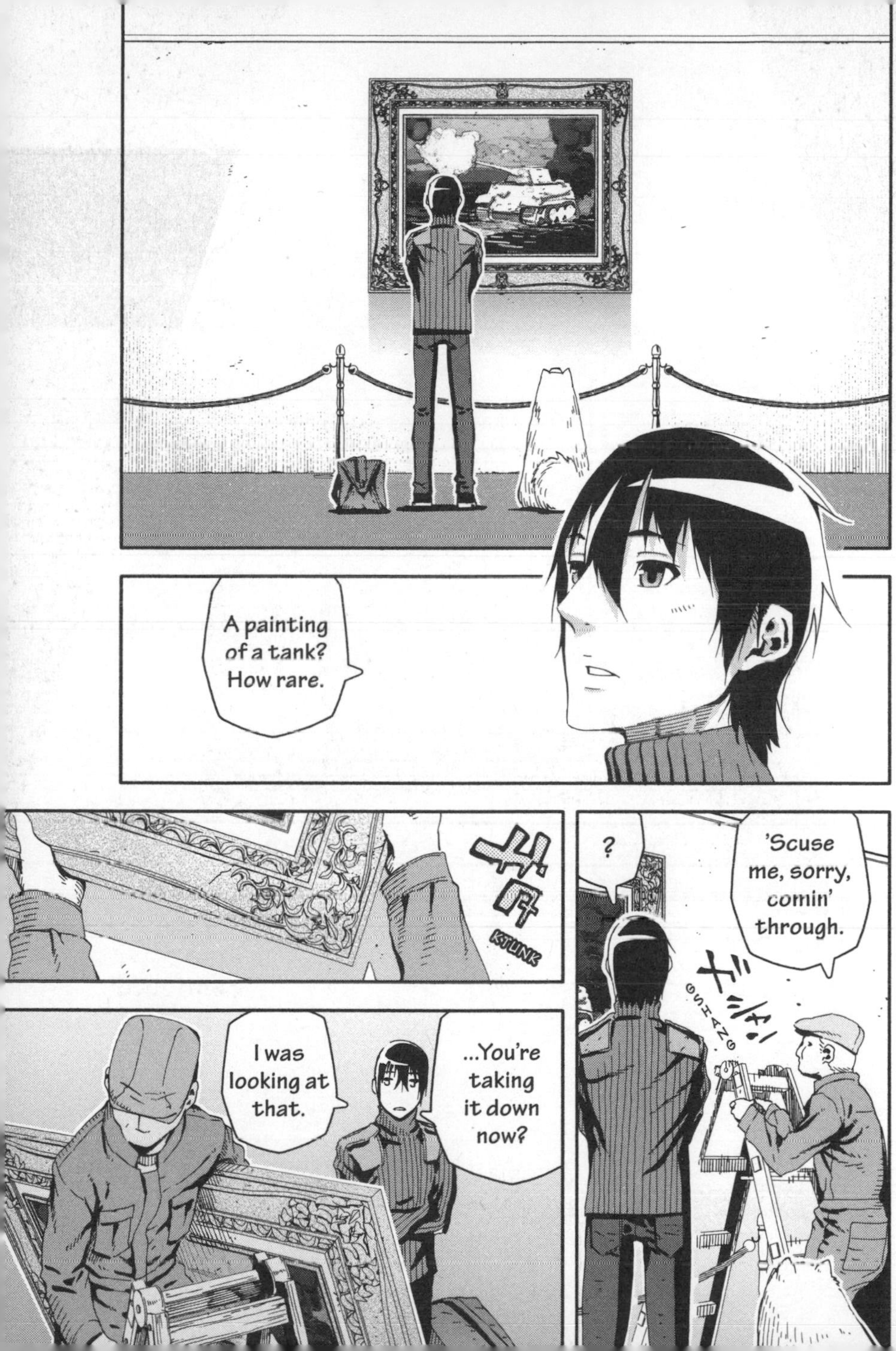
A painting of a tank? How rare.
'Scuse me, sorry, comin' through.
?
GSHANG
KTUNK
...You're taking it down now?
I was looking at that.

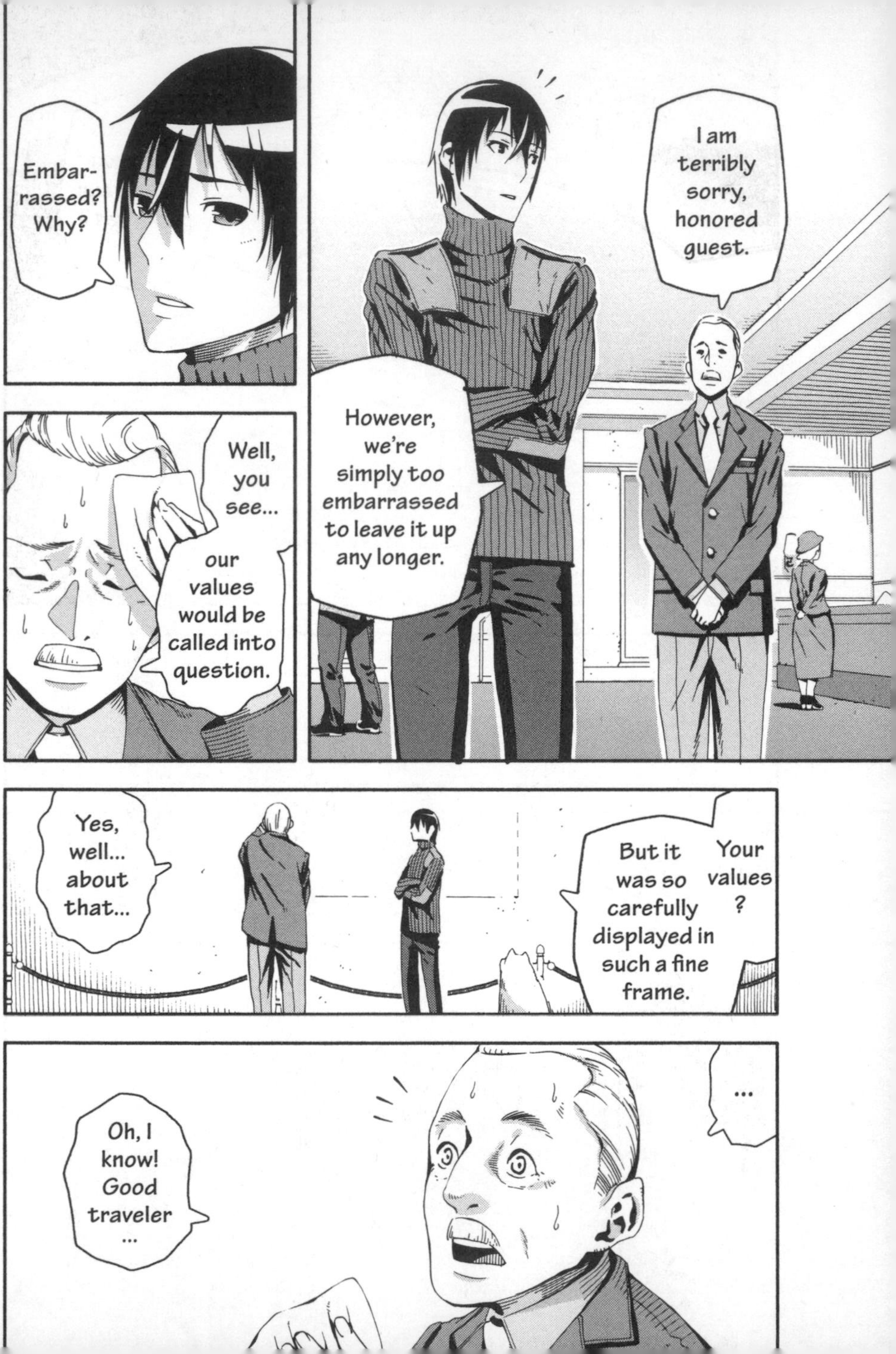
I am terribly sorry, honored guest.
However, we're simply too embarrassed to leave it up any longer.
Embar-rassed? Why?
Well, you see...
our values would be called into question.
Your values?
But it was so carefully displayed in such a fine frame.
Yes, well... about that...
...
Oh, I know! Good traveler...

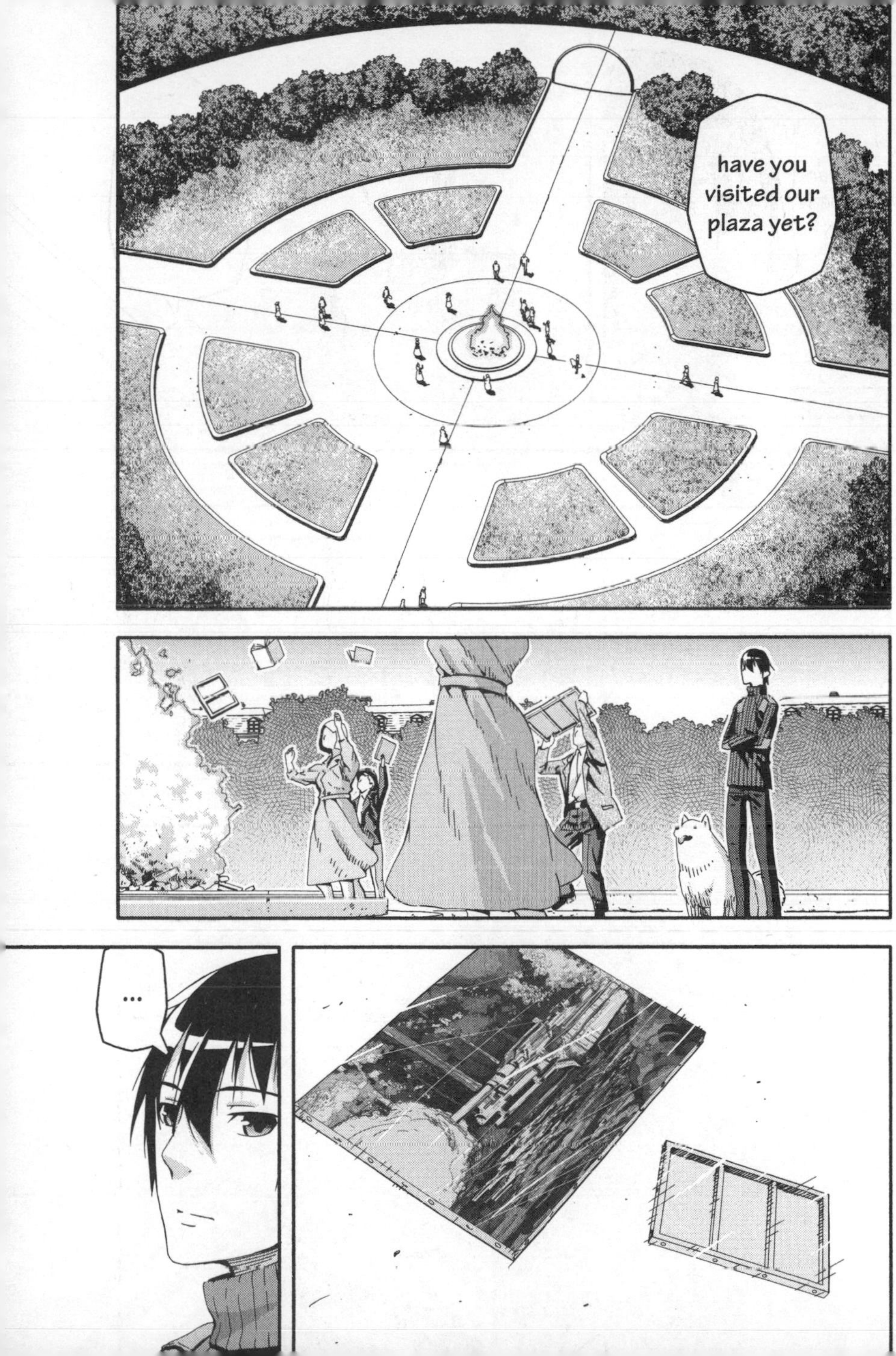

have you visited our plaza yet?
...

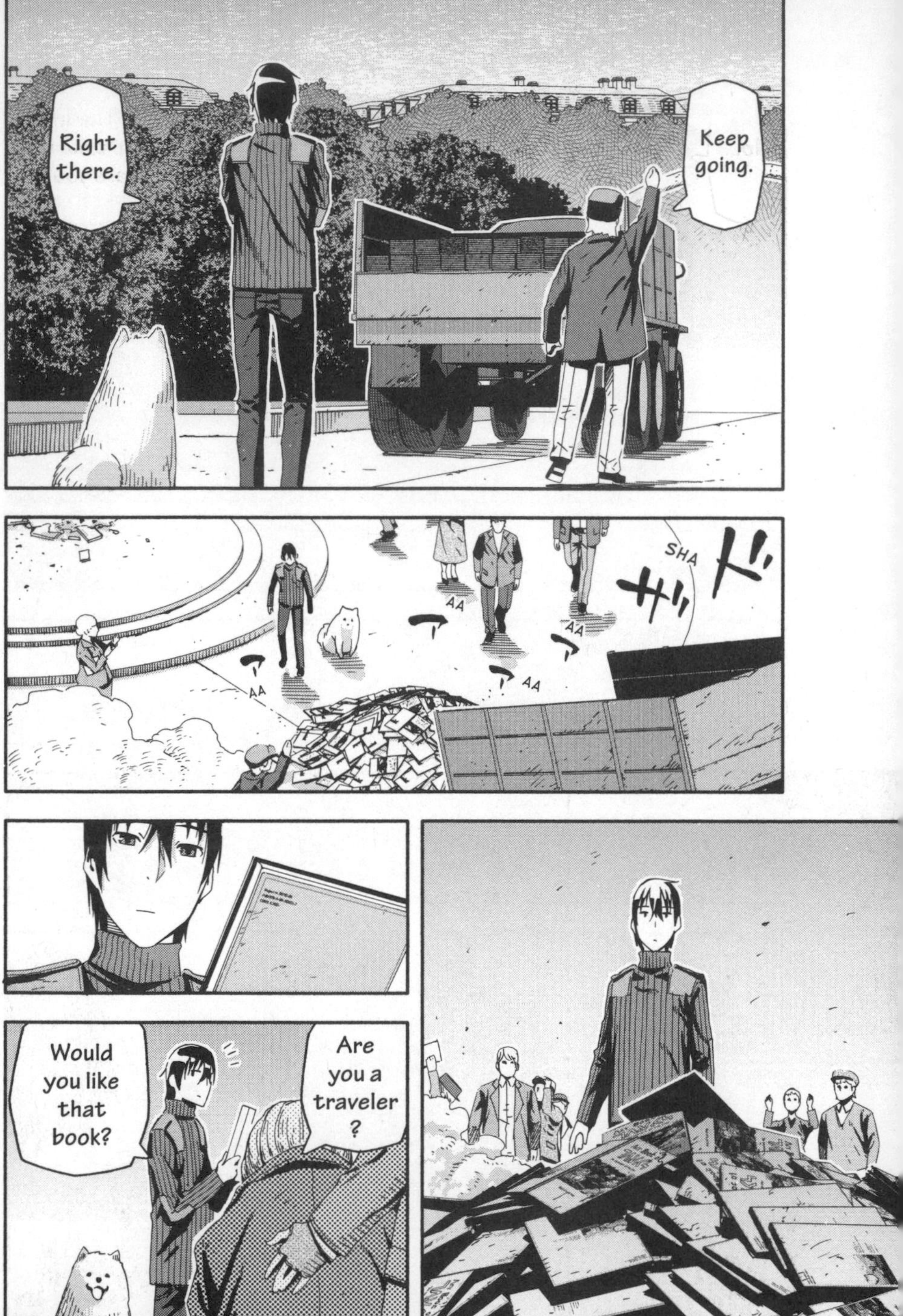
Keep going.
Right there.
SHA
AA
AA
AA
AA
Are you a traveler?
Would you like that book?

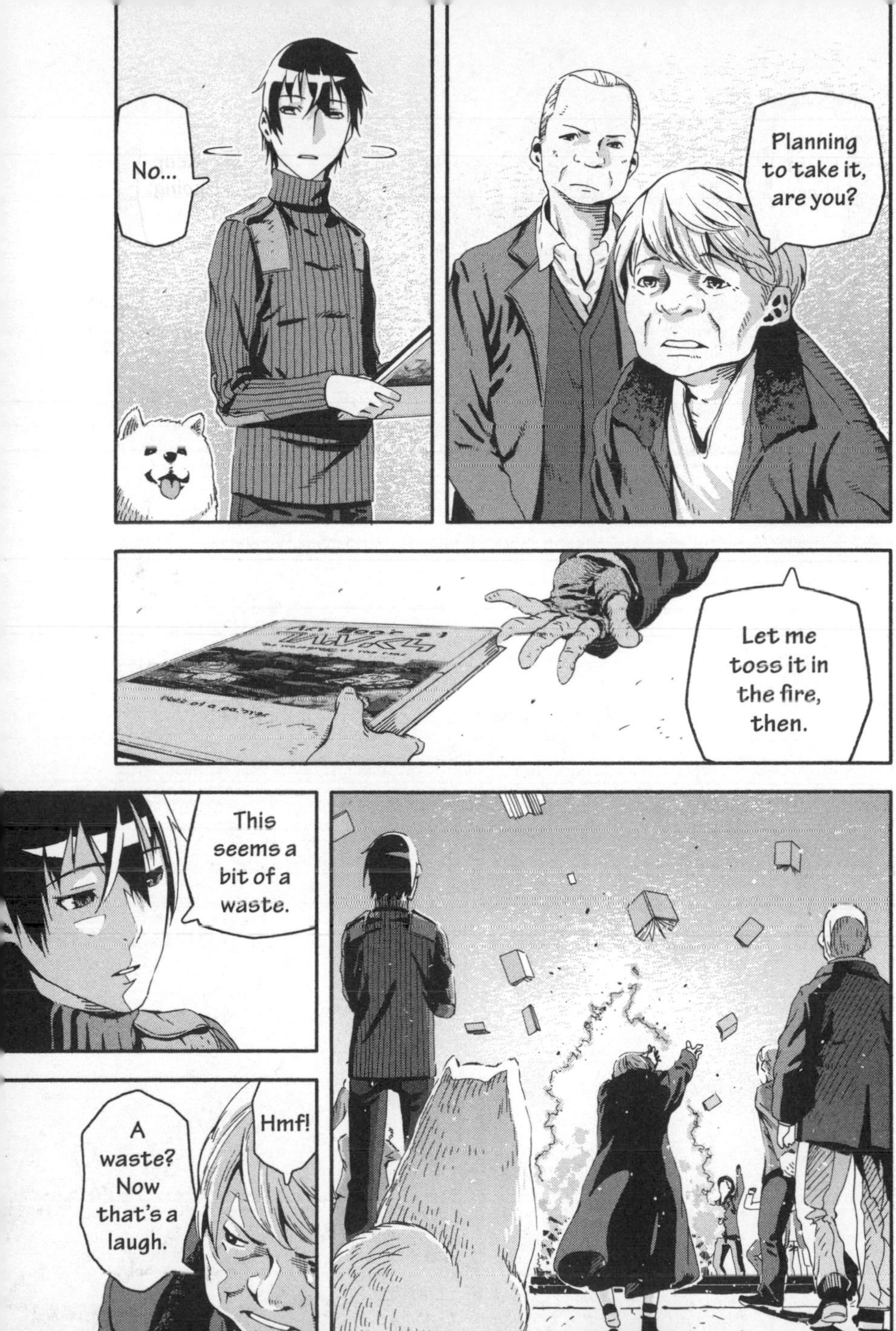
Planning to take it, are you?
No...
Let me toss it in the fire, then.
This seems a bit of a waste.
Hmf!
A waste? Now that's a laugh.

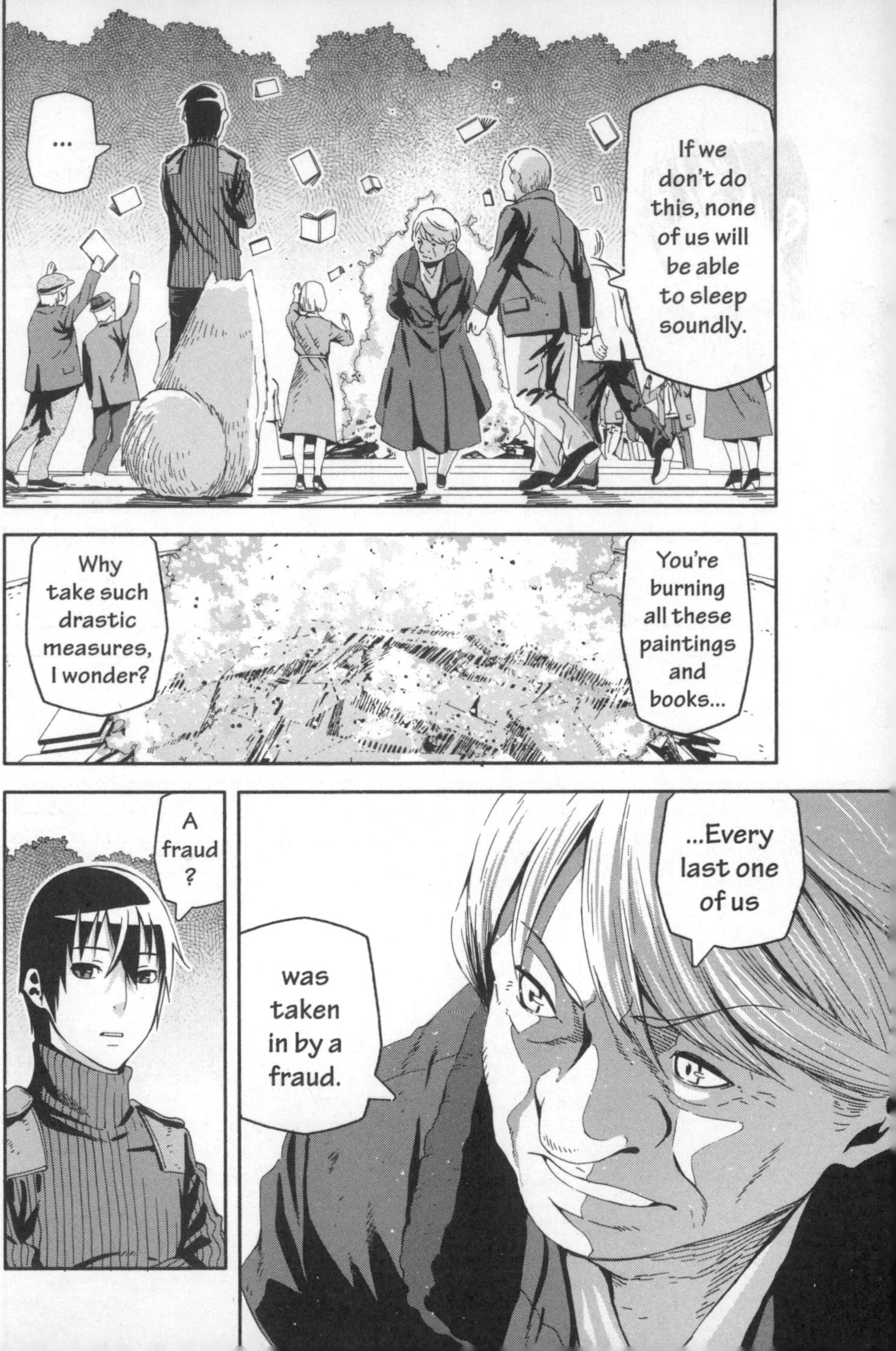
If we don't do this, none of us will be able to sleep soundly.
...
You're burning all these paintings and books...
Why take such drastic measures, I wonder?
...Every last one of us
was taken in by a fraud.
A fraud?

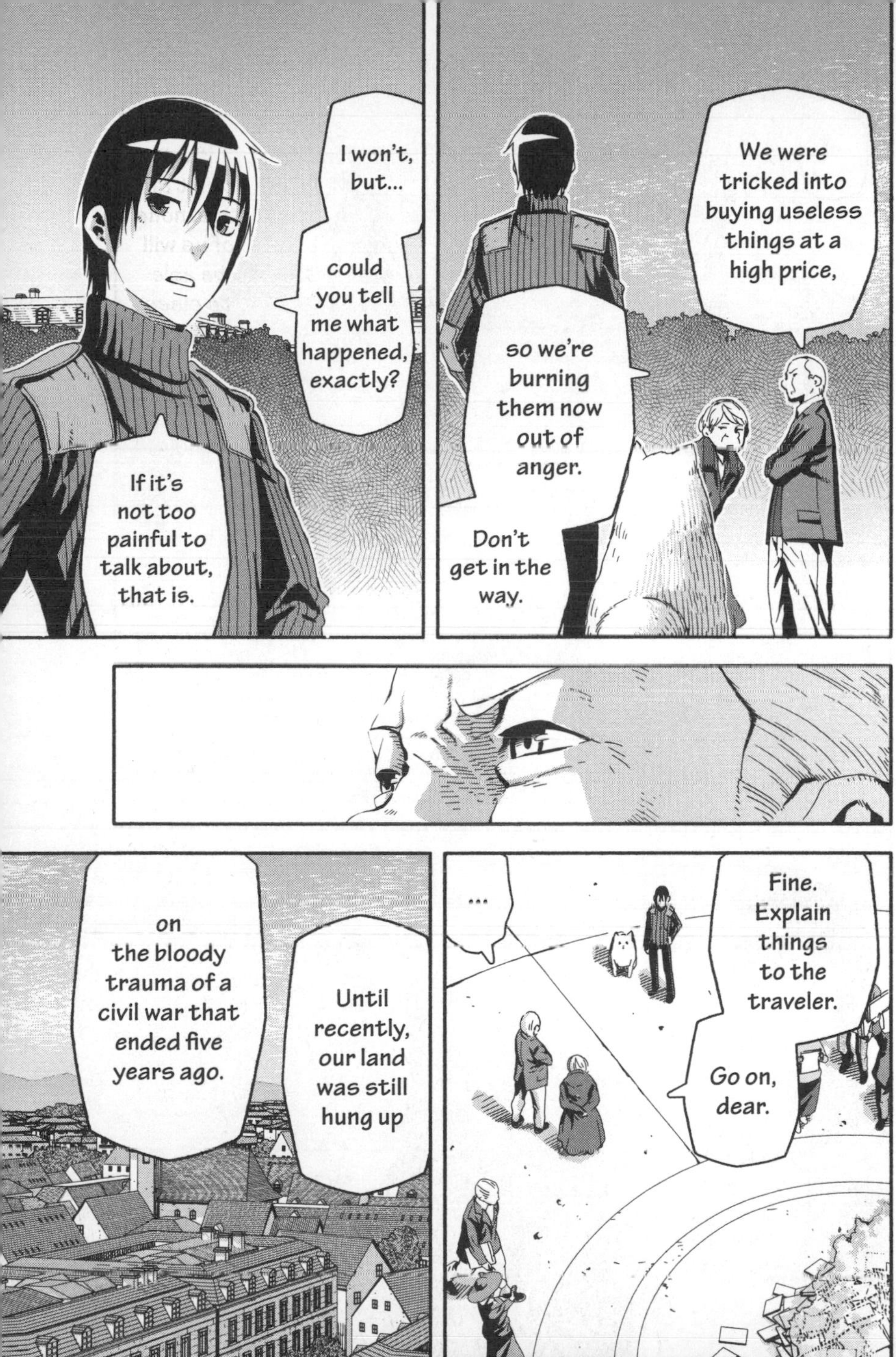
We were tricked into buying useless things at a high price,
so we're burning them now out of anger.
Don't get in the way.
I won't, but...
could you tell me what happened, exactly?
If it's not too painful to talk about, that is.
Fine. Explain things to the traveler.
Go on, dear.
...
Until recently, our land was still hung up
on the bloody trauma of a civil war that ended five years ago.

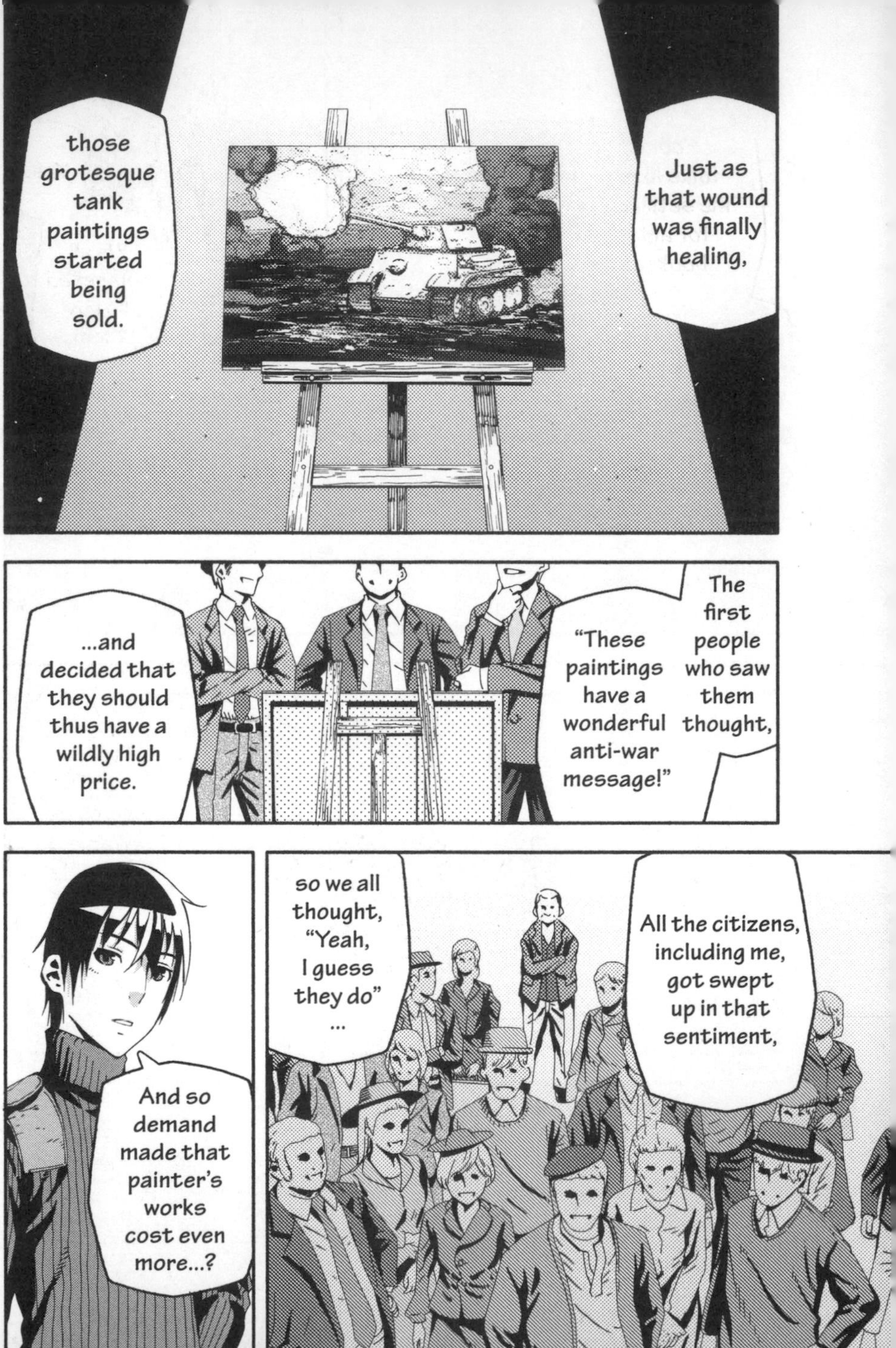
Just as that wound was finally healing,
those grotesque tank paintings started being sold.
The first people who saw them thought,
"These paintings have a wonderful anti-war message!"
...and decided that they should thus have a wildly high price.
All the citizens, including me, got swept up in that sentiment,
so we all thought, "Yeah, I guess they do" ...
And so demand made that painter's works cost even more...?

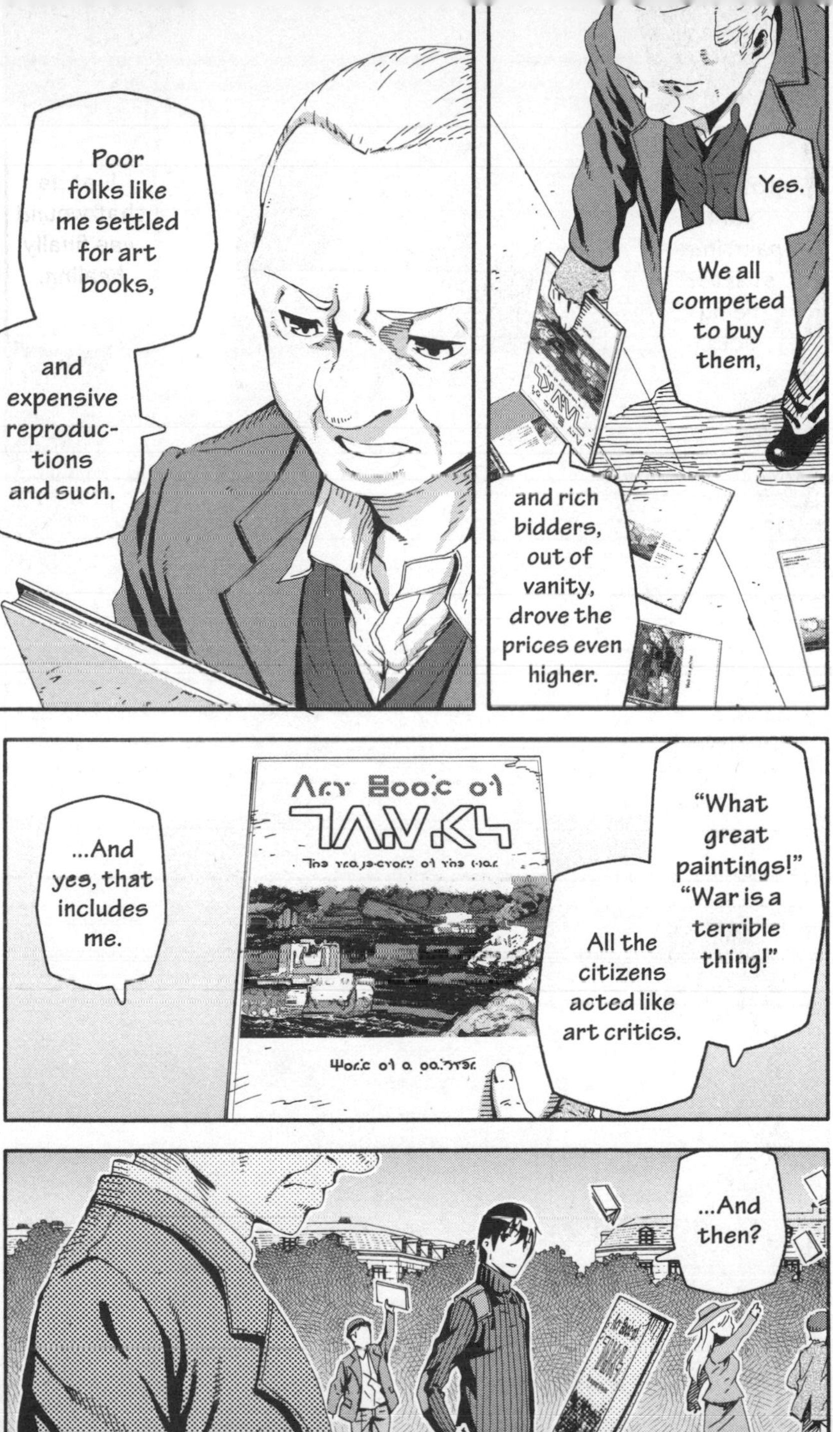
Yes.
We all competed to buy them,
and rich bidders, out of vanity, drove the prices even higher.
Poor folks like me settled for art books,
and expensive reproductions and such.
"What great paintings!" "War is a terrible thing!"
All the citizens acted like art critics.
...And yes, that includes me.
...And then?

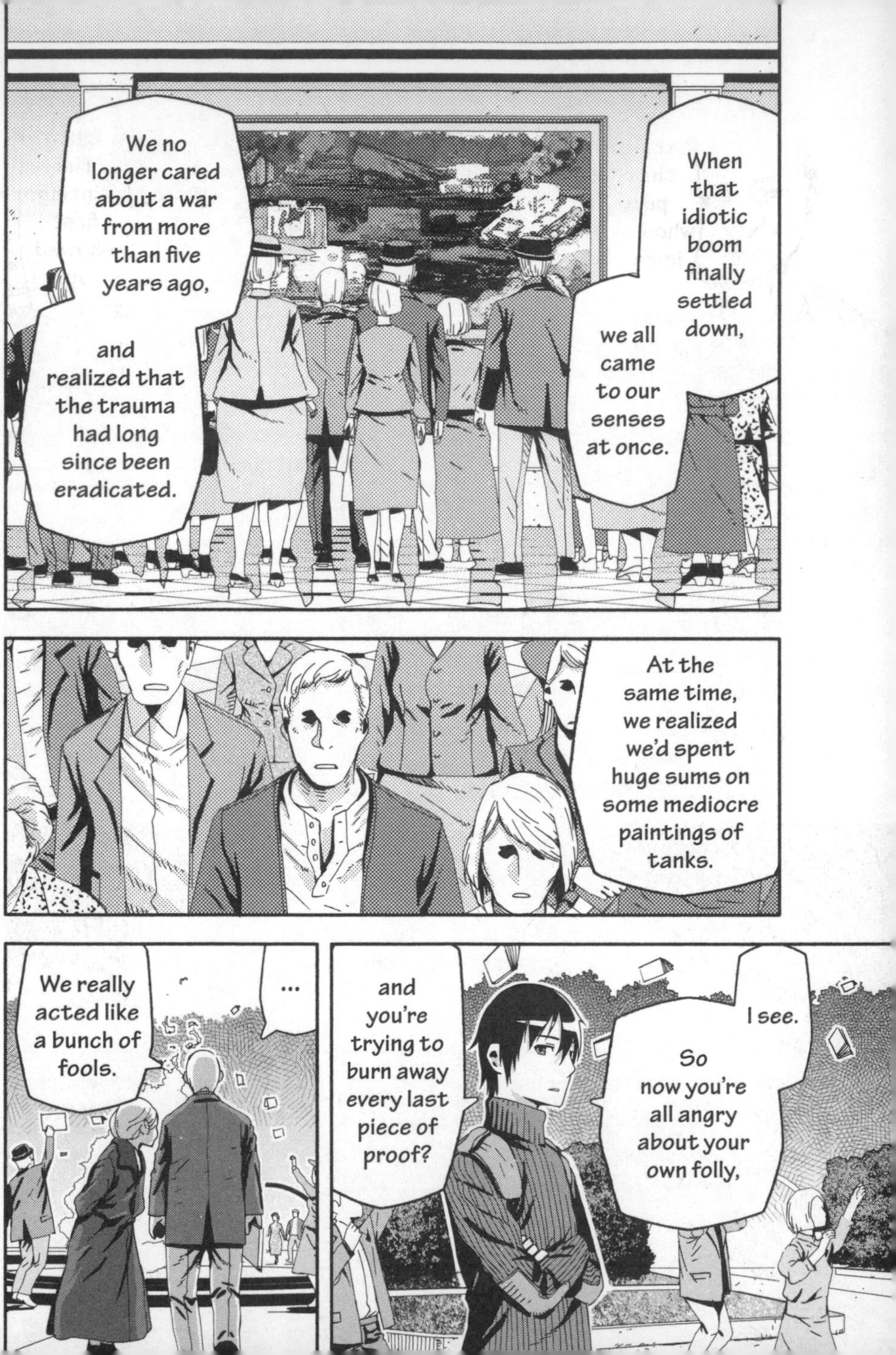
When that idiotic boom finally settled down,
we all came to our senses at once.
We no longer cared about a war from more than five years ago,
and realized that the trauma had long since been eradicated.
At the same time, we realized we'd spent huge sums on some mediocre paintings of tanks.
I see.
So now you're all angry about your own folly,
and you're trying to burn away every last piece of proof?
...
We really acted like a bunch of fools.

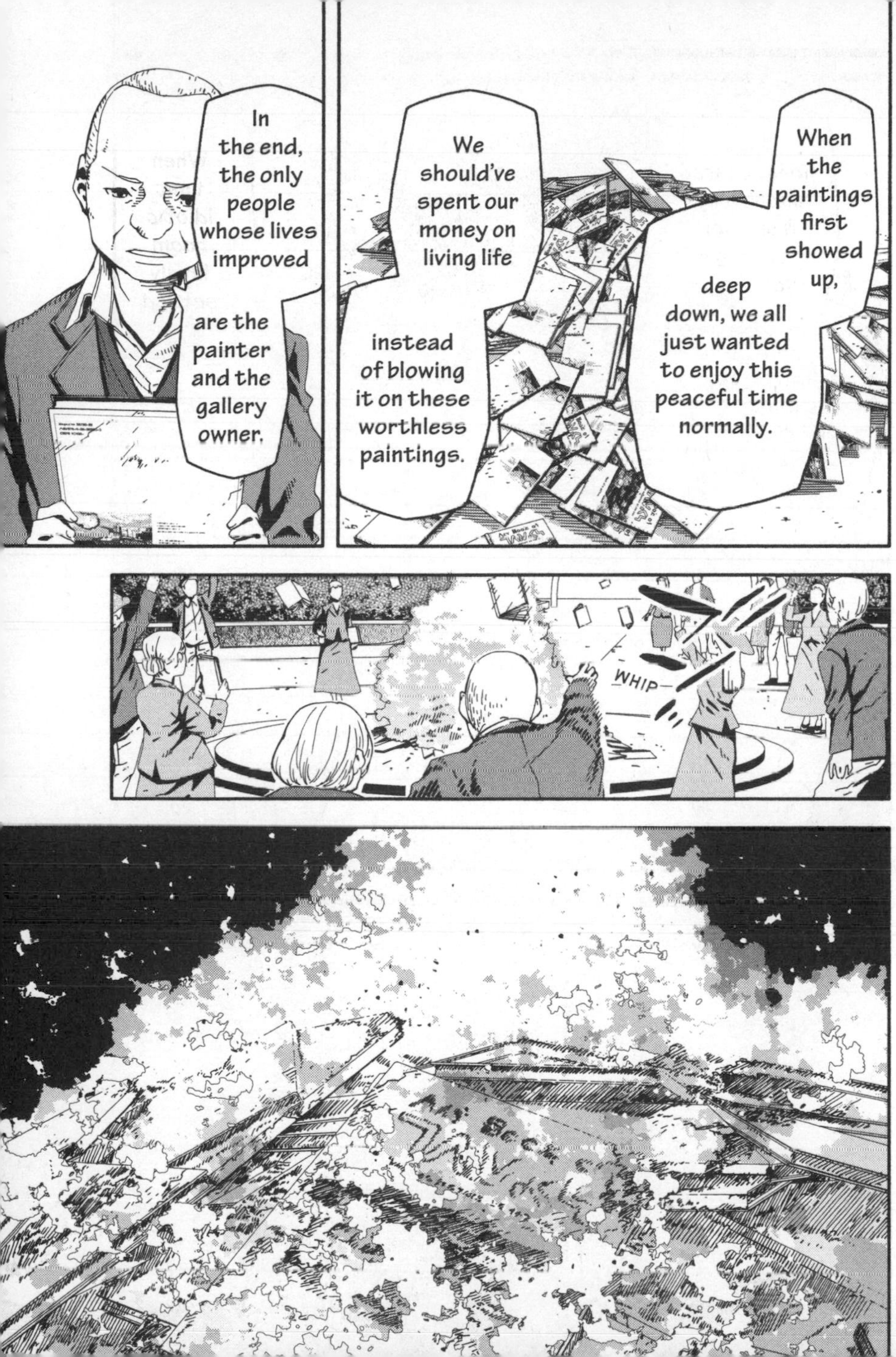
When the paintings first showed up,
deep down, we all just wanted to enjoy this peaceful time normally.
We should've spent our money on living life
instead of blowing it on these worthless paintings.
In the end, the only people whose lives improved
are the painter and the gallery owner.
WHIP

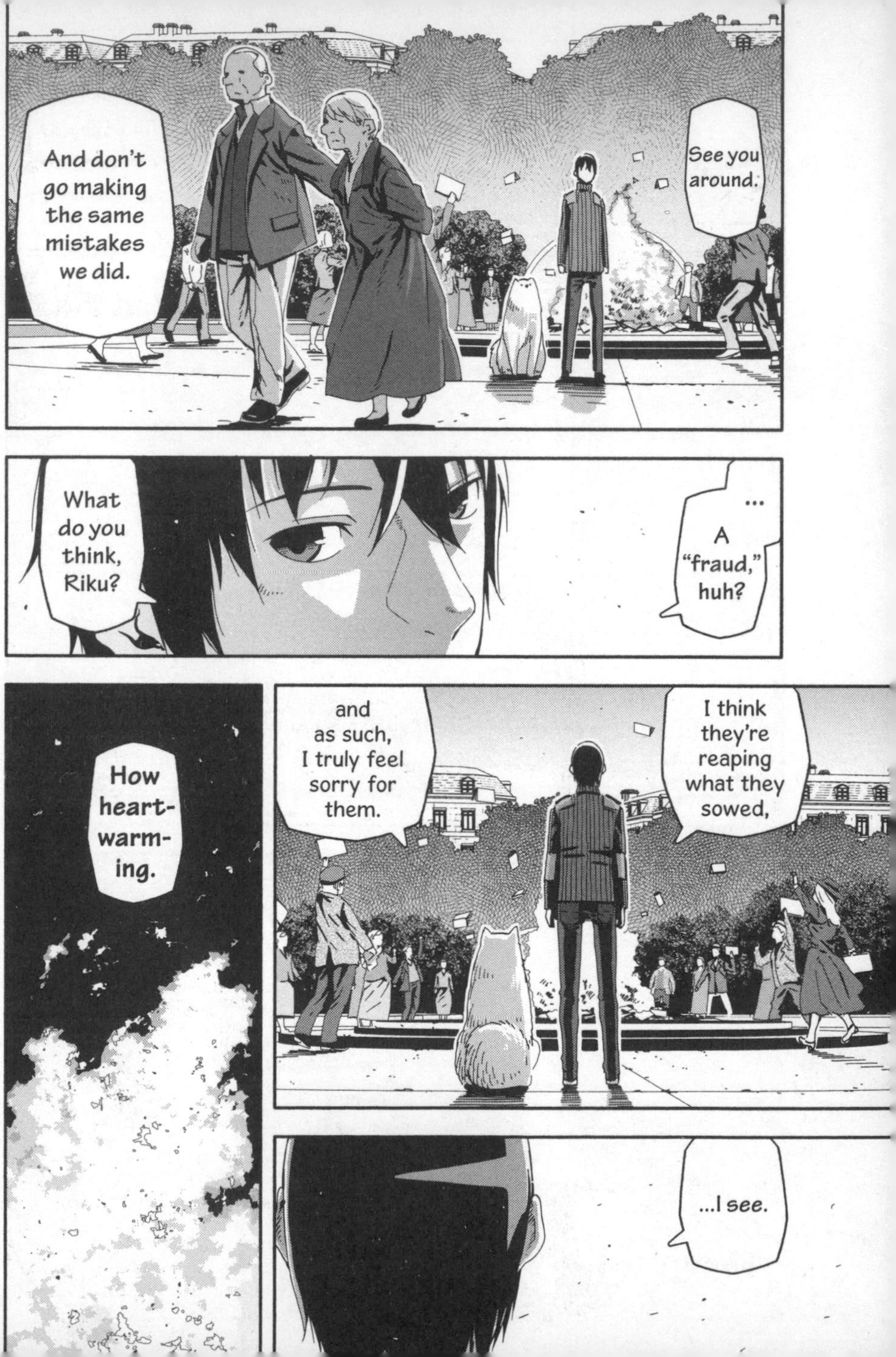
See you around.
And don't go making the same mistakes we did.
... A "fraud," huh?
What do you think, Riku?
I think they're reaping what they sowed,
and as such, I truly feel sorry for them.
...I see.
How heart-warming.

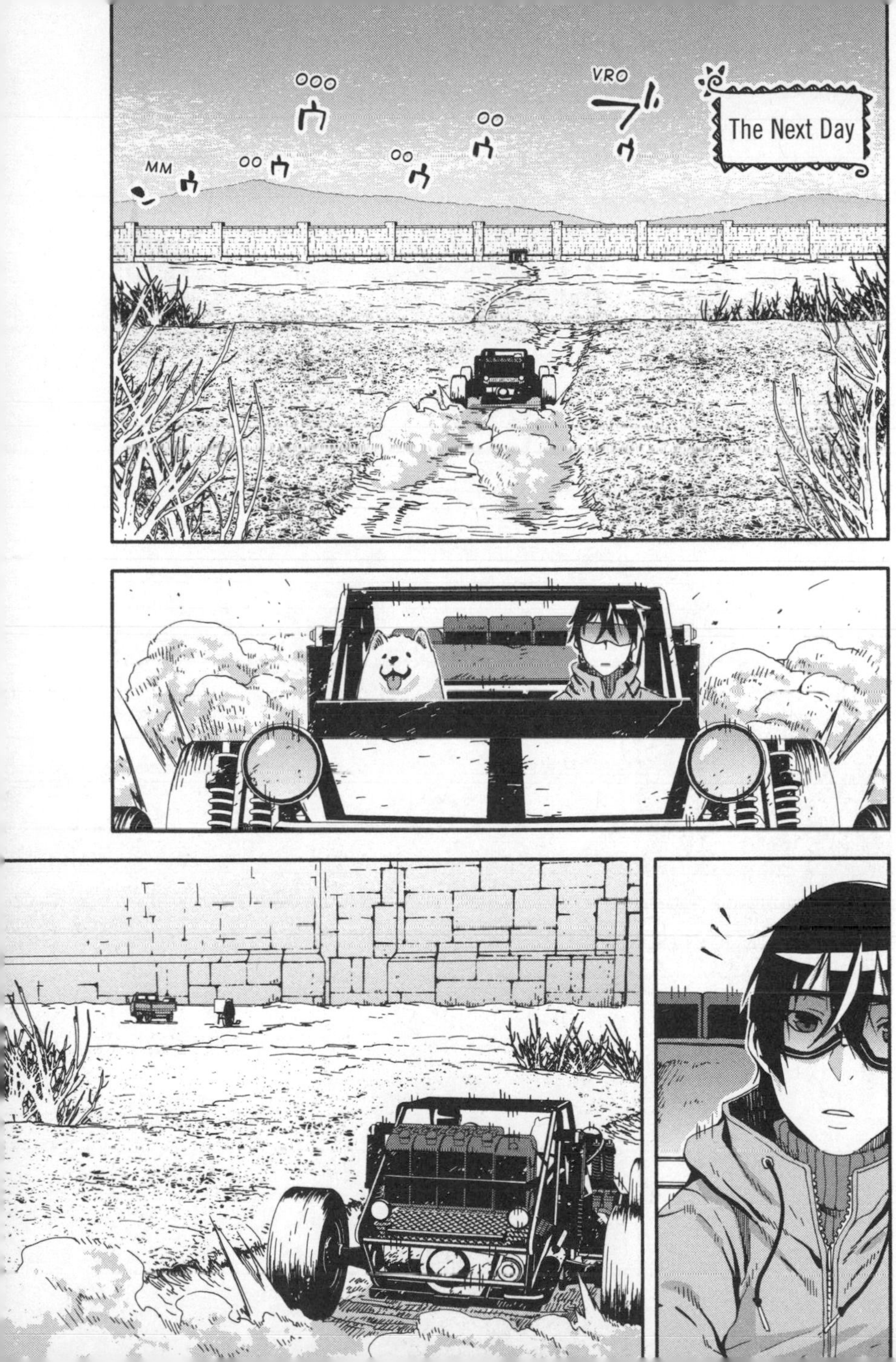
The Next Day
VRO
OOO
OO
OO
OO
MM

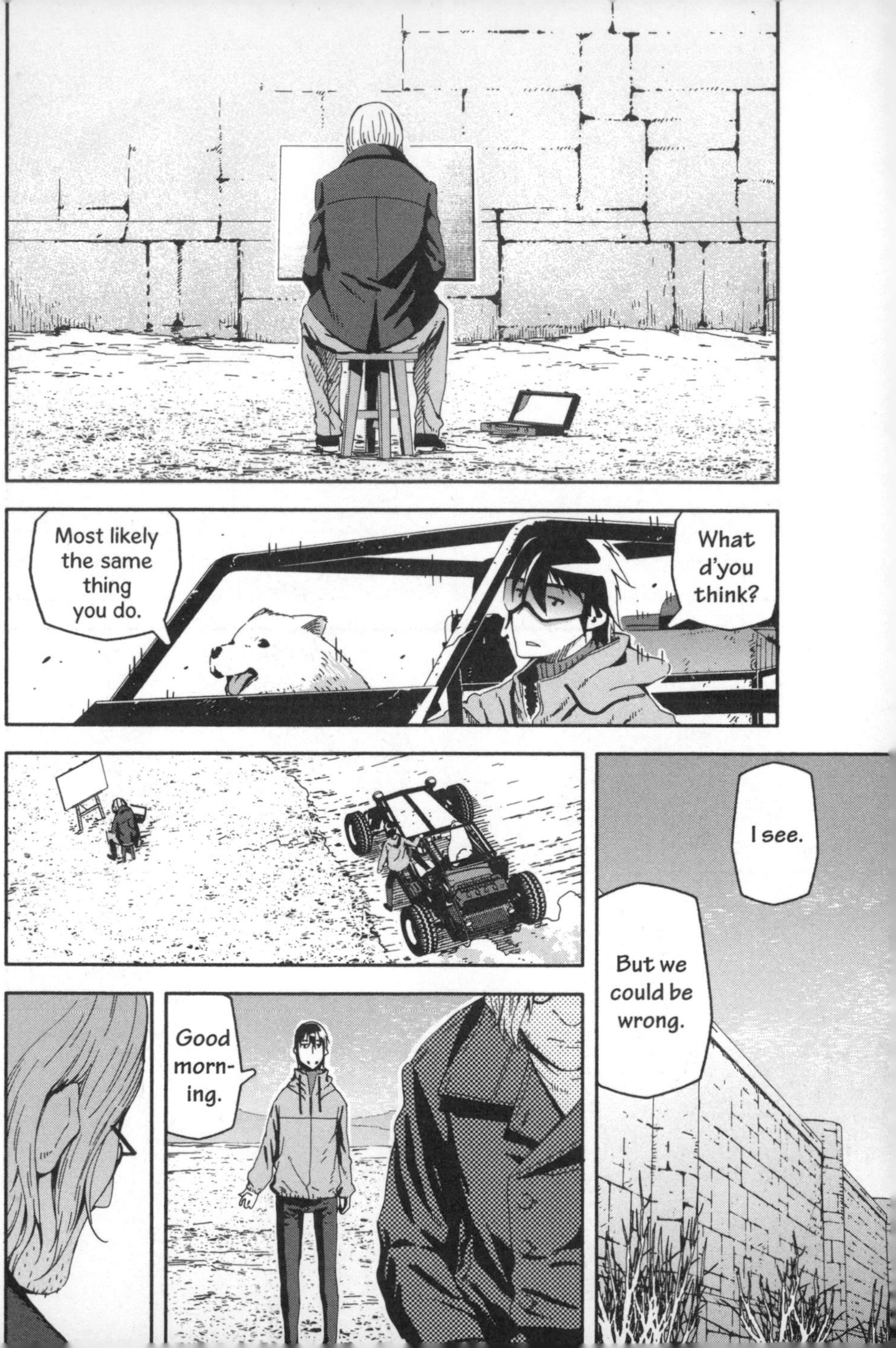
What d'you think?
Most likely the same thing you do.
I see.
But we could be wrong.
Good morning.

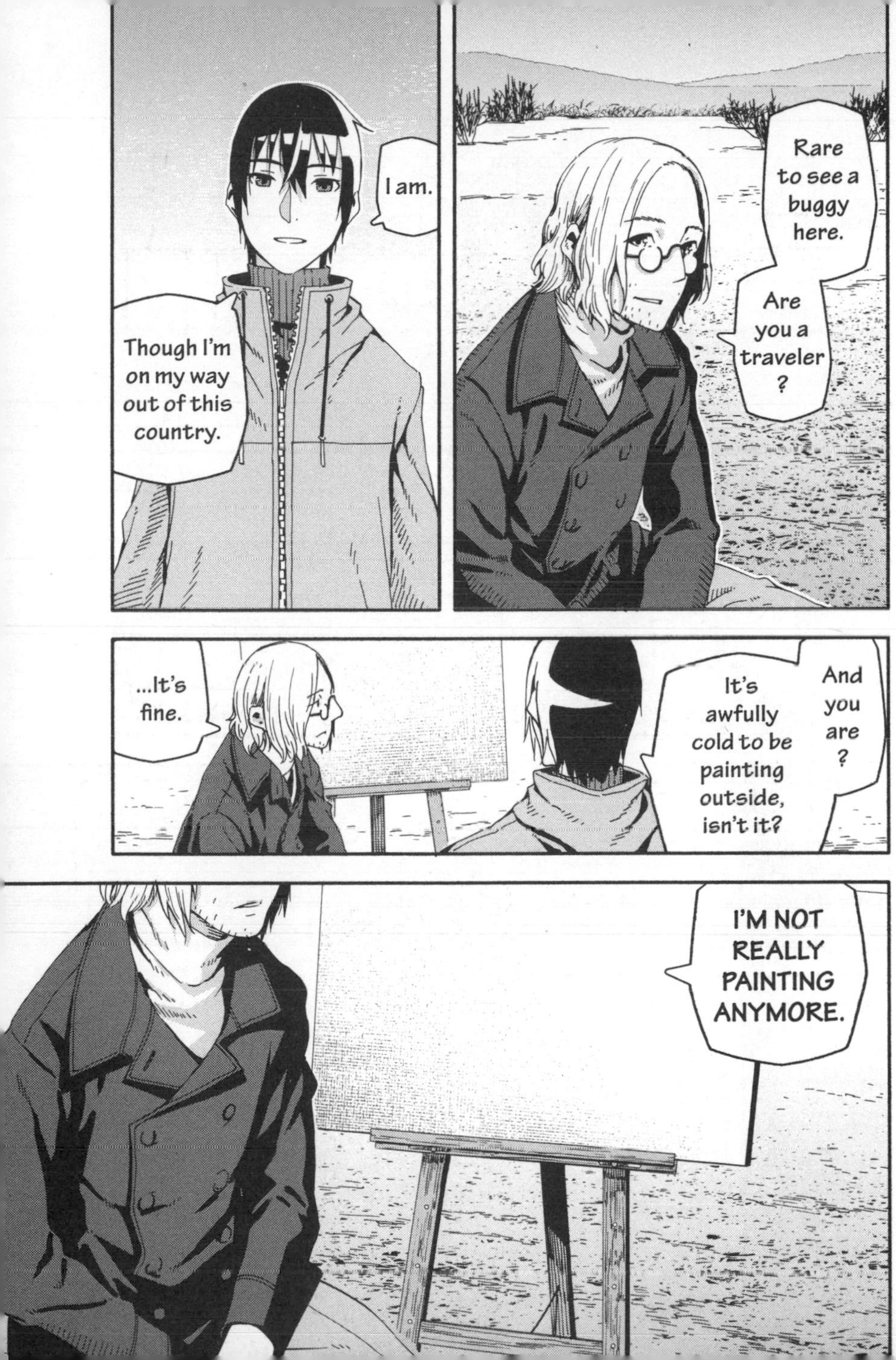
Rare to see a buggy here.
Are you a traveler?
I am.
Though I'm on my way out of this country.
And you are?
It's awfully cold to be painting outside, isn't it?
...It's fine.
I'M NOT REALLY PAINTING ANYMORE.

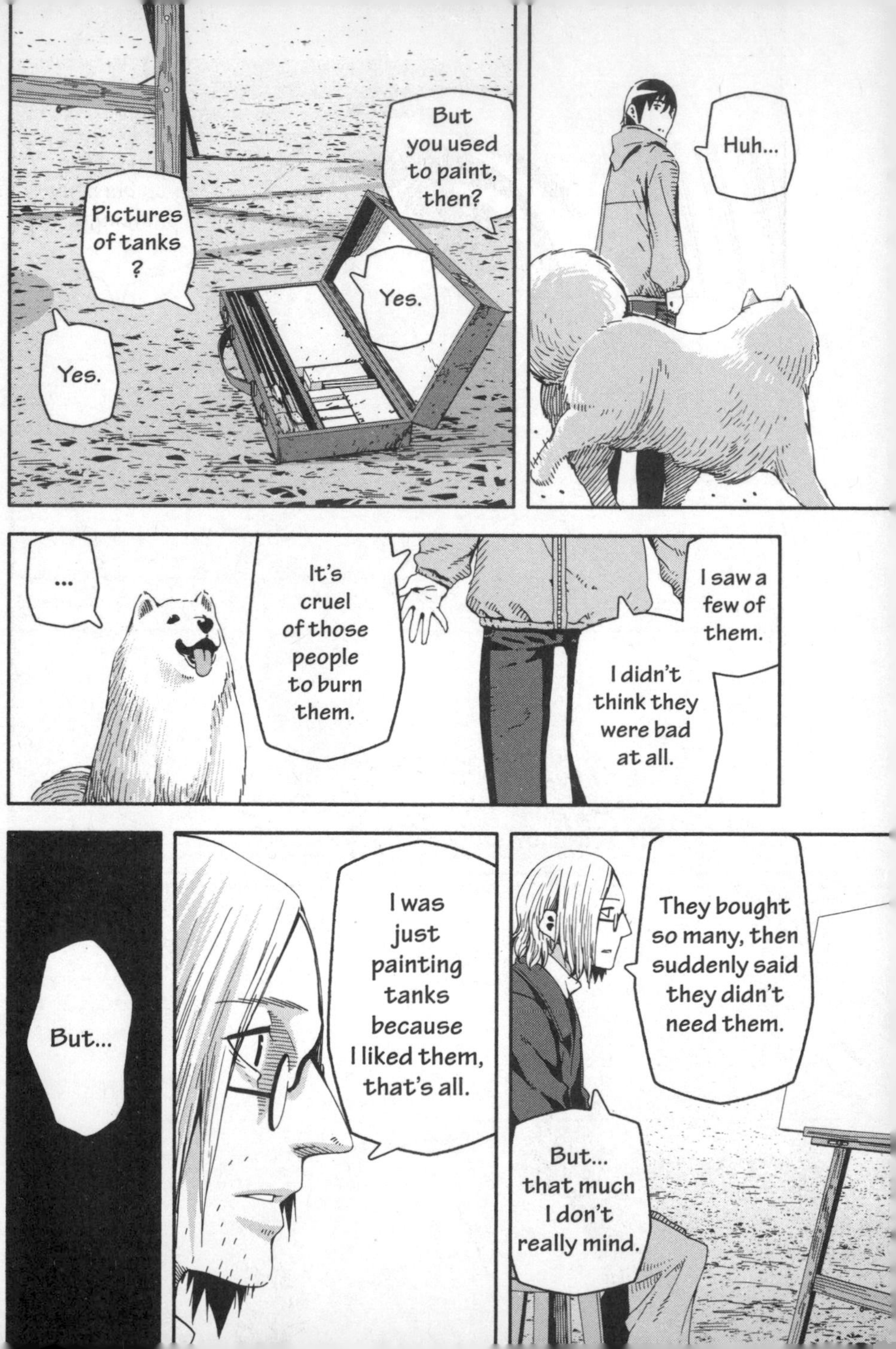
Huh...
But you used to paint, then?
Yes.
Pictures of tanks ?
Yes.
I saw a few of them.
I didn't think they were bad at all.
It's cruel of those people to burn them.
...
They bought so many, then suddenly said they didn't need them.
But... that much I don't really mind.
I was just painting tanks because I liked them, that's all.
But...

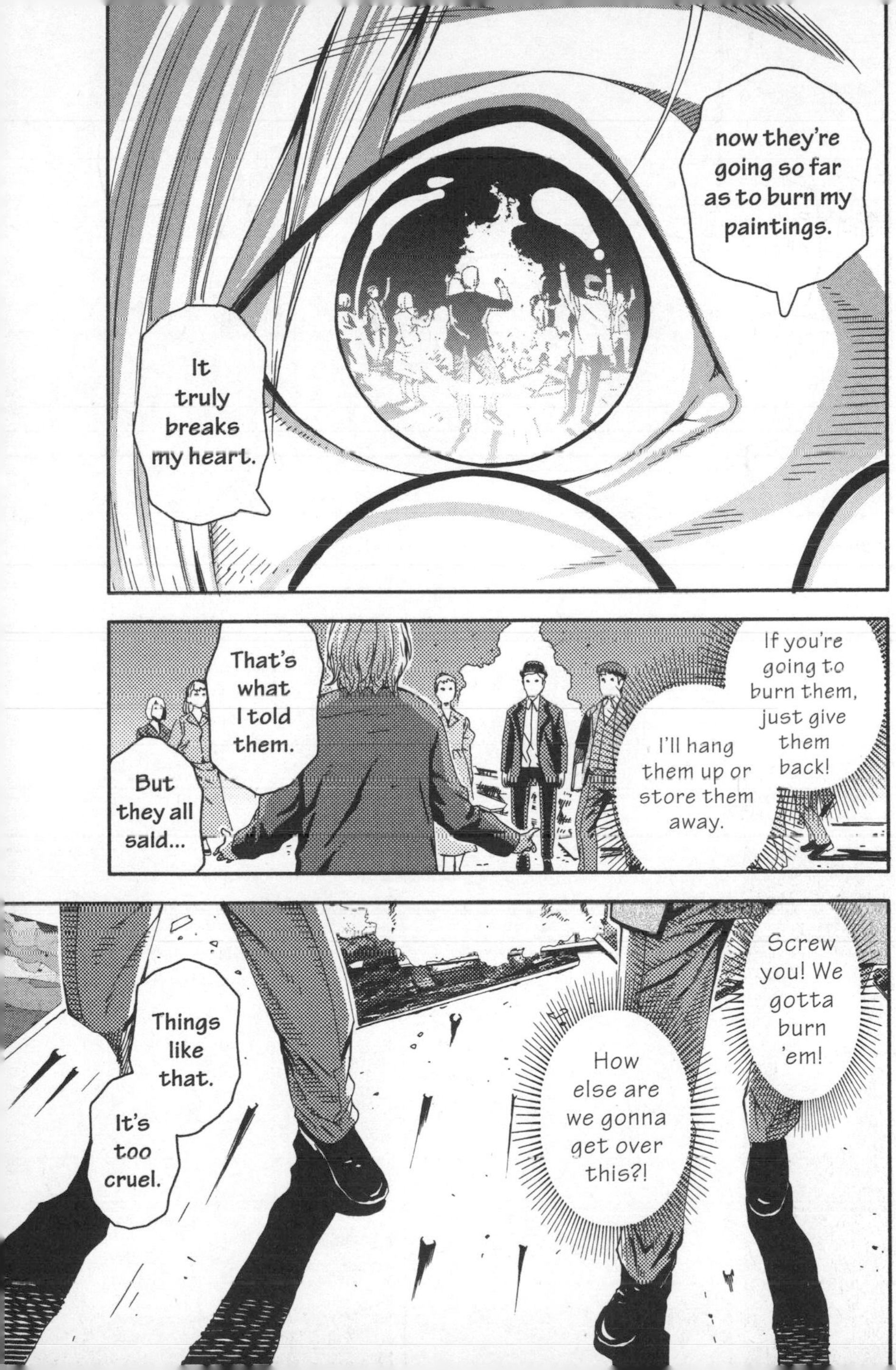
now they're going so far as to burn my paintings.
It truly breaks my heart.
If you're going to burn them, just give them back!
I'll hang them up or store them away.
That's what I told them.
But they all said...
Screw you! We gotta burn 'em!
How else are we gonna get over this?!
Things like that.
It's too cruel.

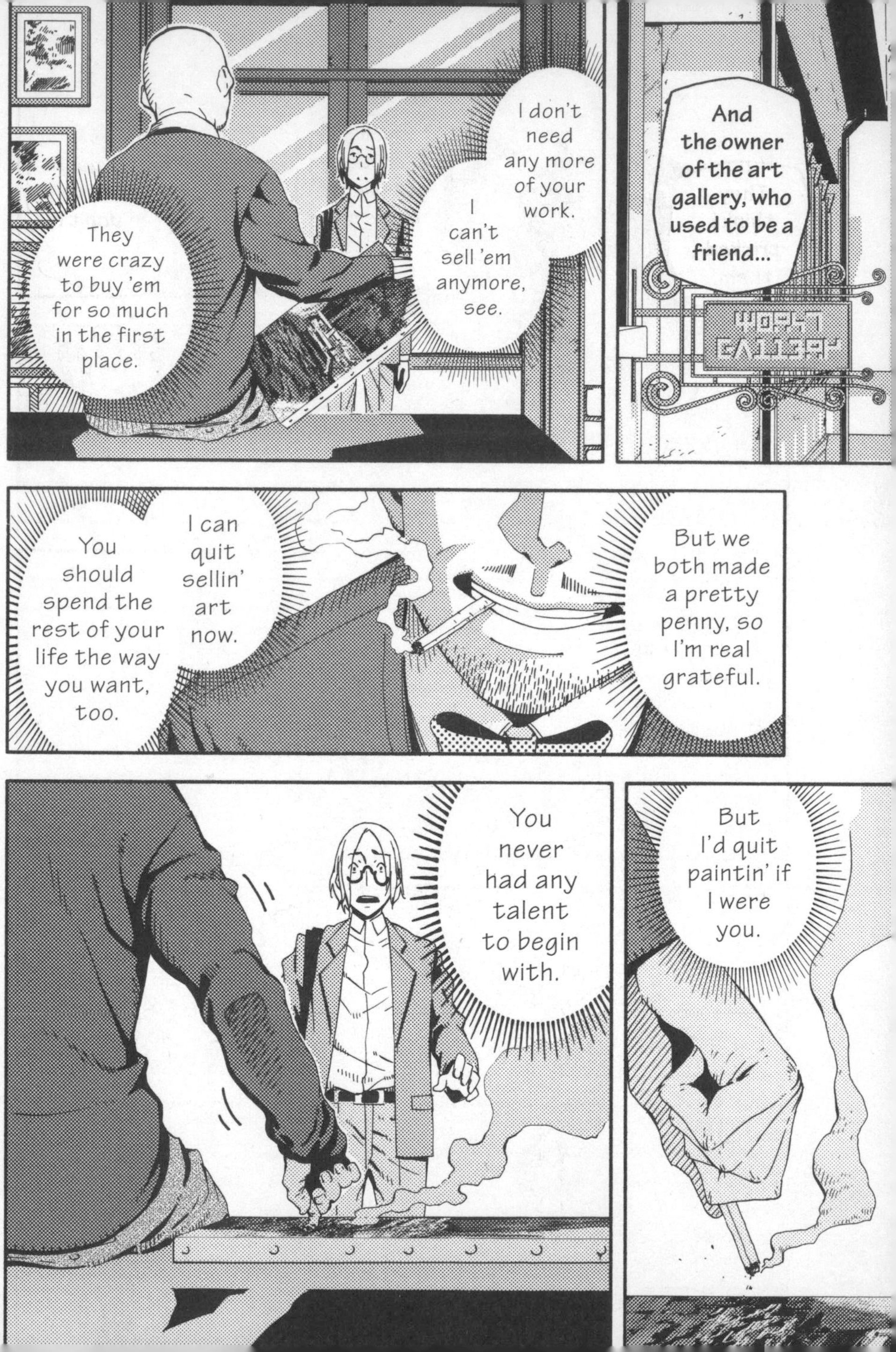
And the owner of the art gallery, who used to be a friend...
I don't need any more of your work.
I can't sell 'em anymore, see.
They were crazy to buy 'em for so much in the first place.
But we both made a pretty penny, so I'm real grateful.
I can quit sellin' art now.
You should spend the rest of your life the way you want, too.
But I'd quit paintin' if I were you.
You never had any talent to begin with.

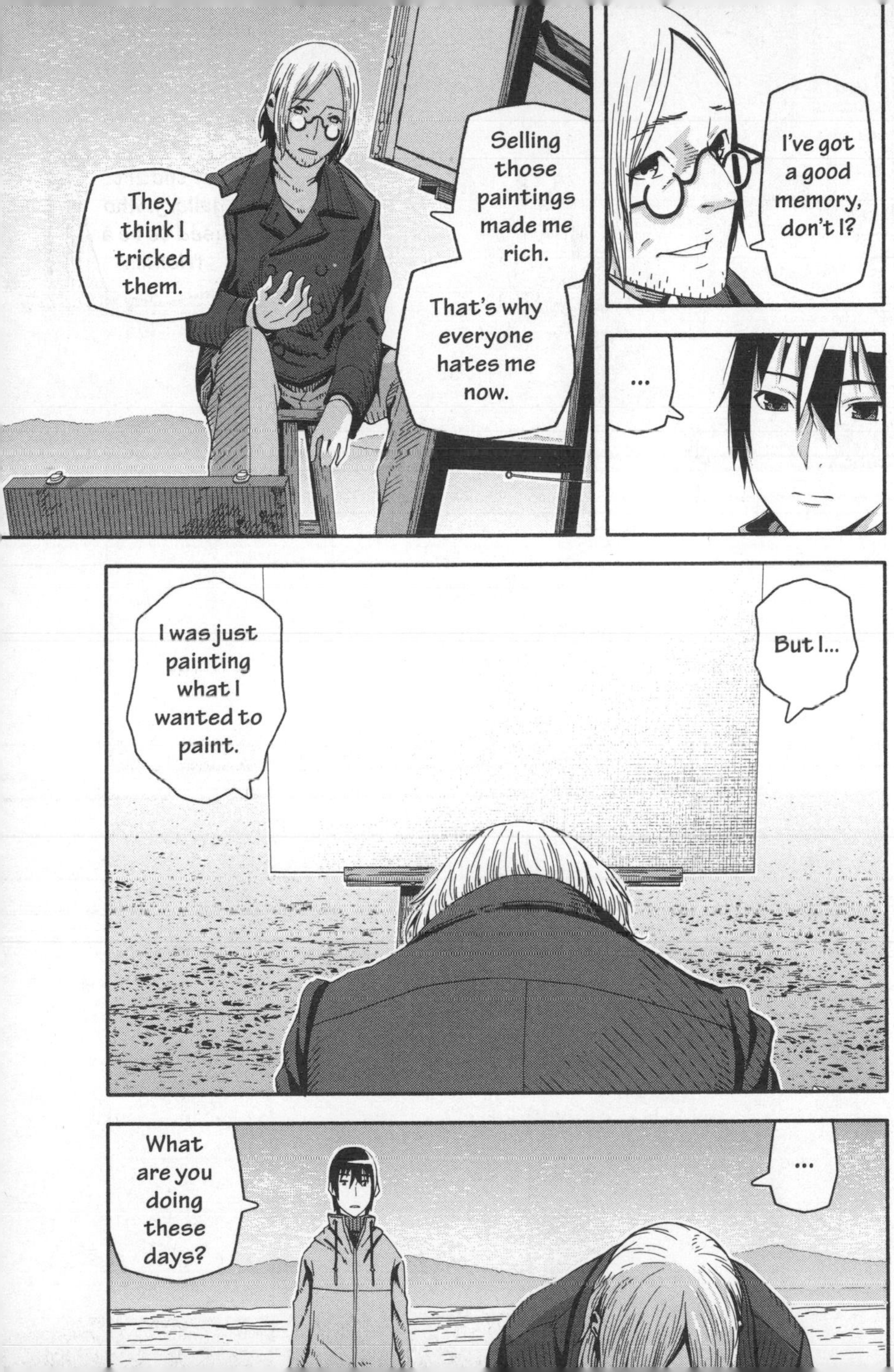
I've got a good memory, don't I?
...
Selling those paintings made me rich.
That's why everyone hates me now.
They think I tricked them.
But I...
I was just painting what I wanted to paint.
...
What are you doing these days?

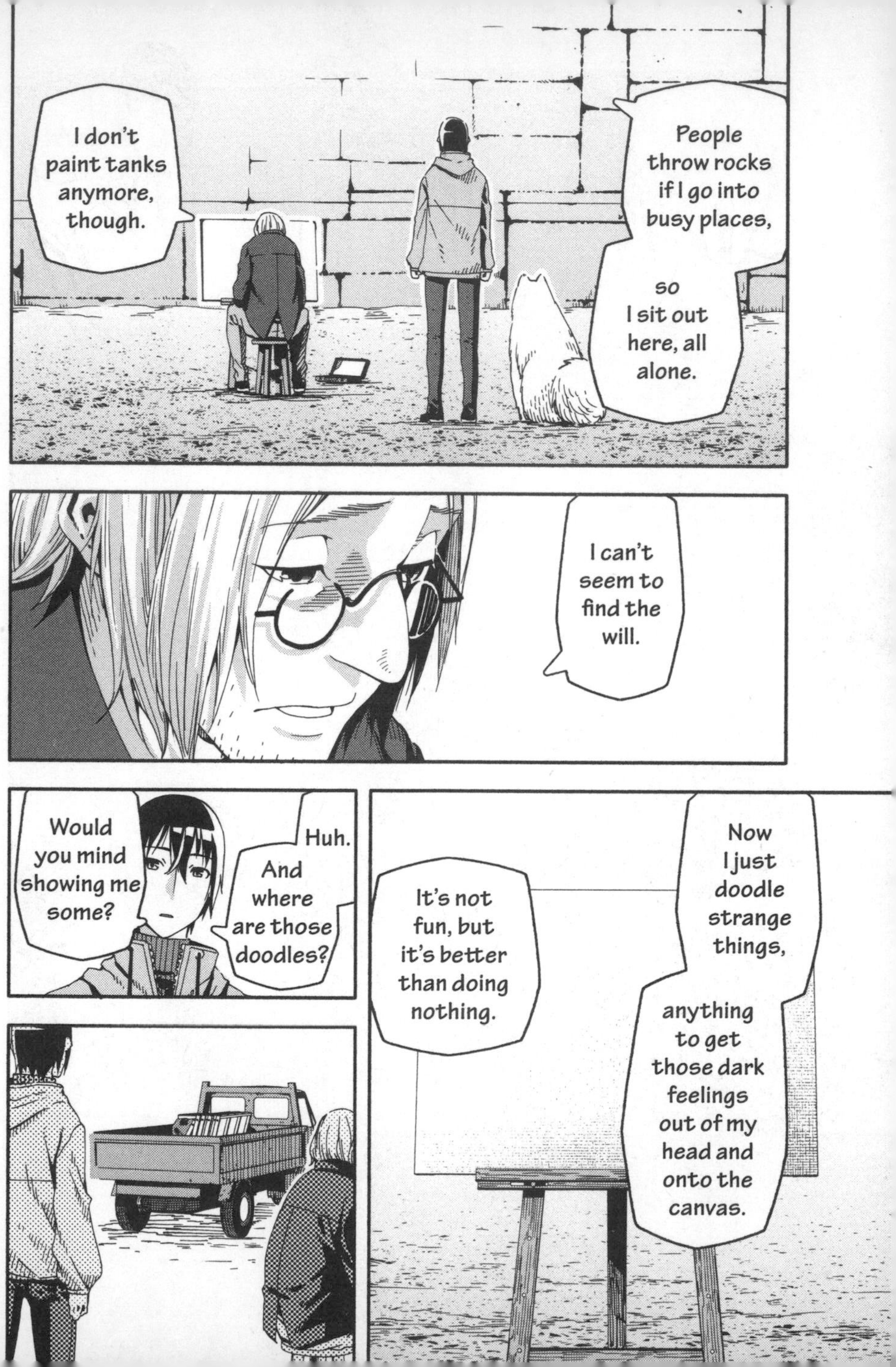
People throw rocks if I go into busy places,
so I sit out here, all alone.
I don't paint tanks anymore, though.
I can't seem to find the will.
Now I just doodle strange things,
anything to get those dark feelings out of my head and onto the canvas.
It's not fun, but it's better than doing nothing.
Huh. And where are those doodles?
Would you mind showing me some?

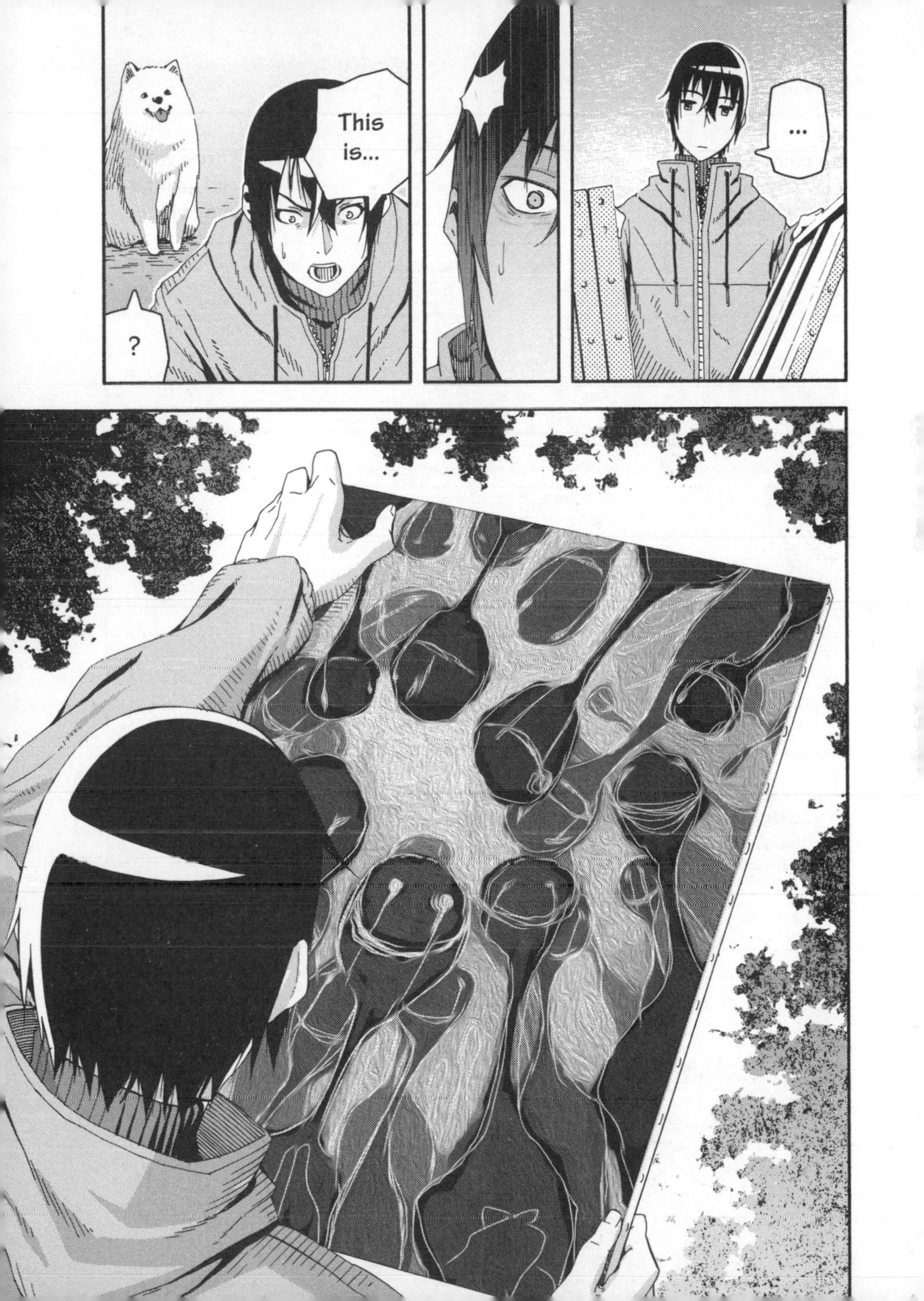
...
This is...
?

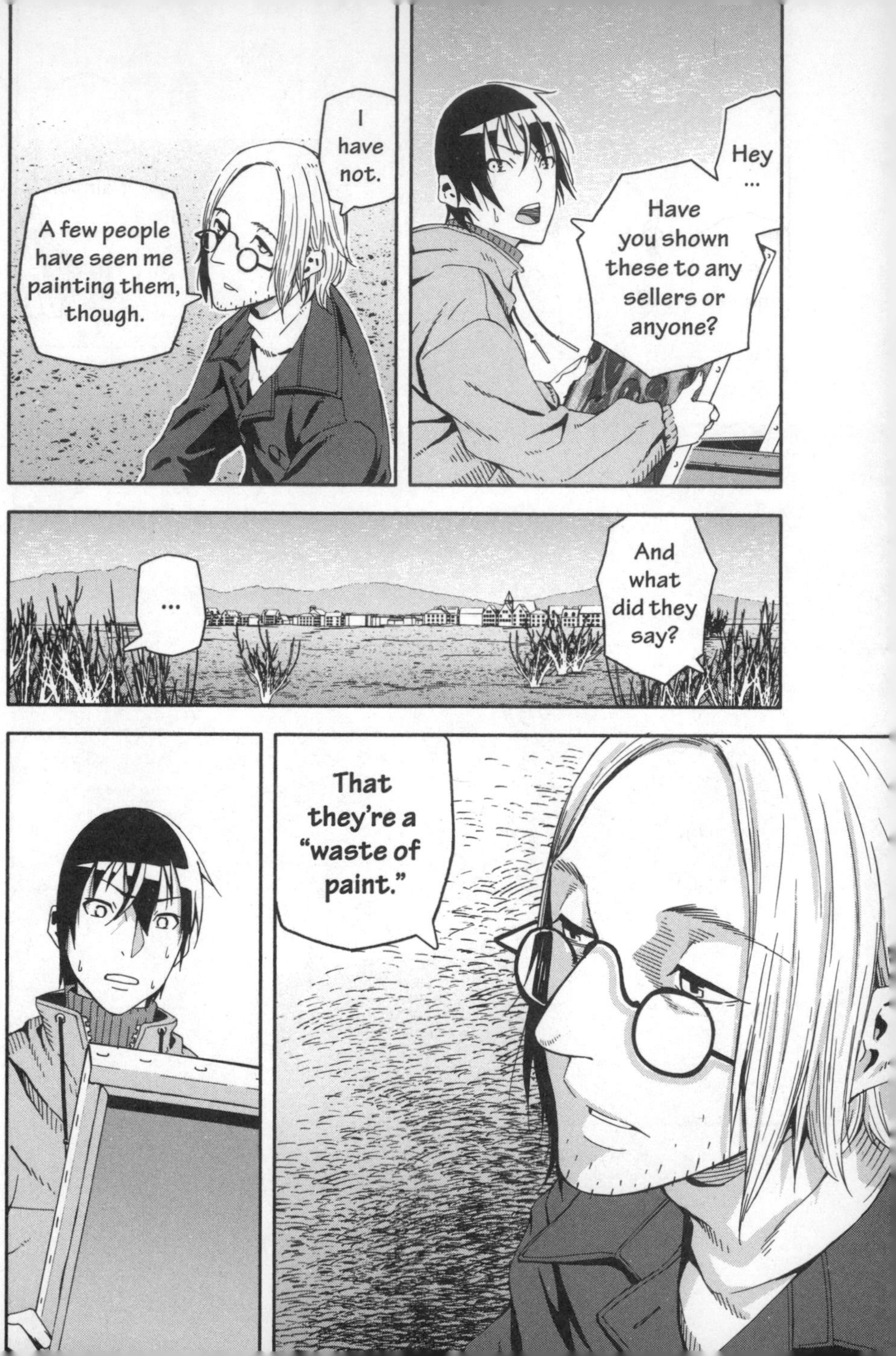
Hey ...
Have you shown these to any sellers or anyone?
I have not.
A few people have seen me painting them, though.
And what did they say?
...
That they're a "waste of paint."

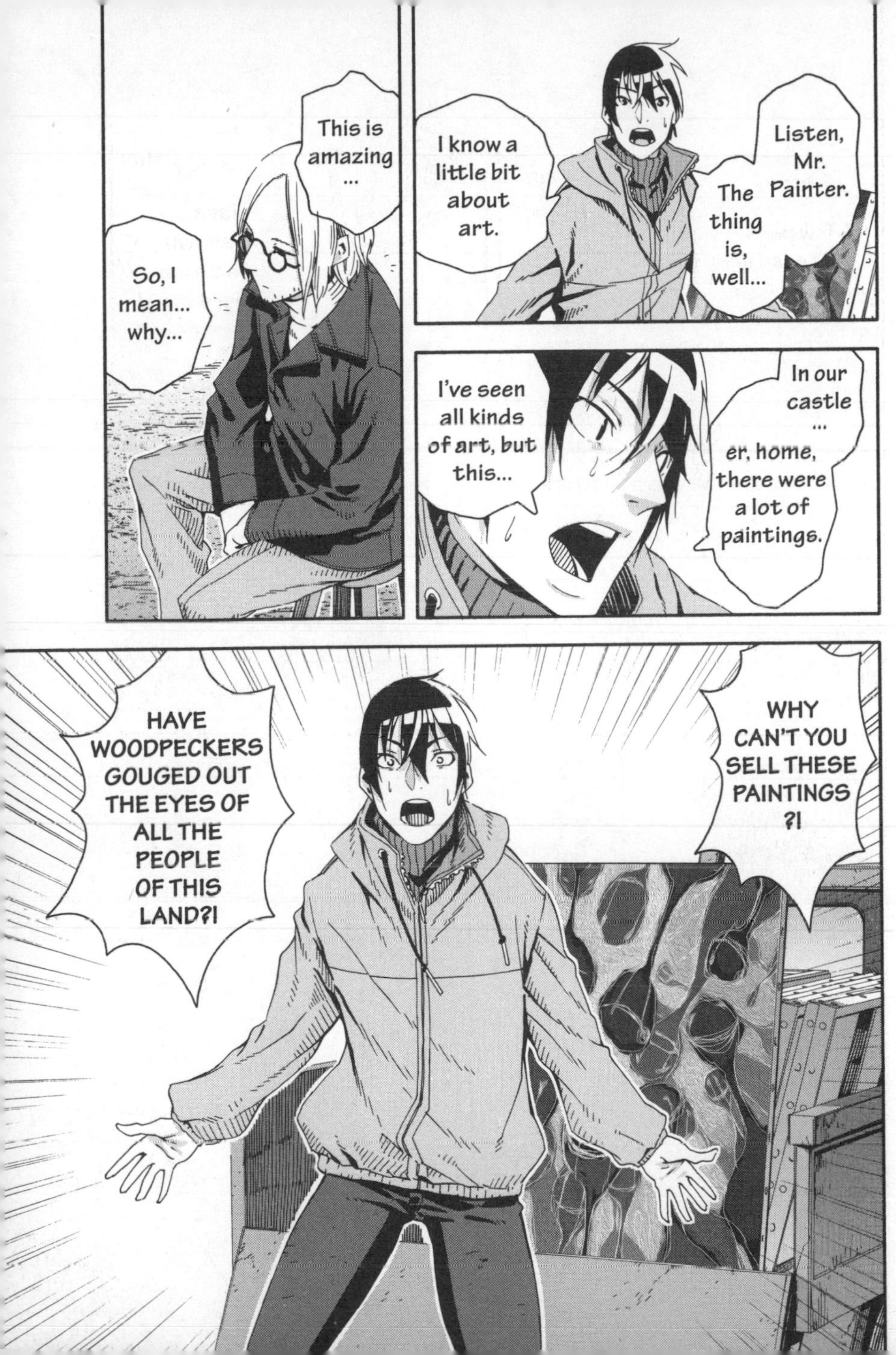
Listen, Mr. Painter.
The thing is, well...
I know a little bit about art.
In our castle ...
er, home, there were a lot of paintings.
I've seen all kinds of art, but this...
This is amazing ...
So, I mean... why...
WHY CAN'T YOU SELL THESE PAINTINGS ?!
HAVE WOODPECKERS GOUGED OUT THE EYES OF ALL THE PEOPLE OF THIS LAND?!

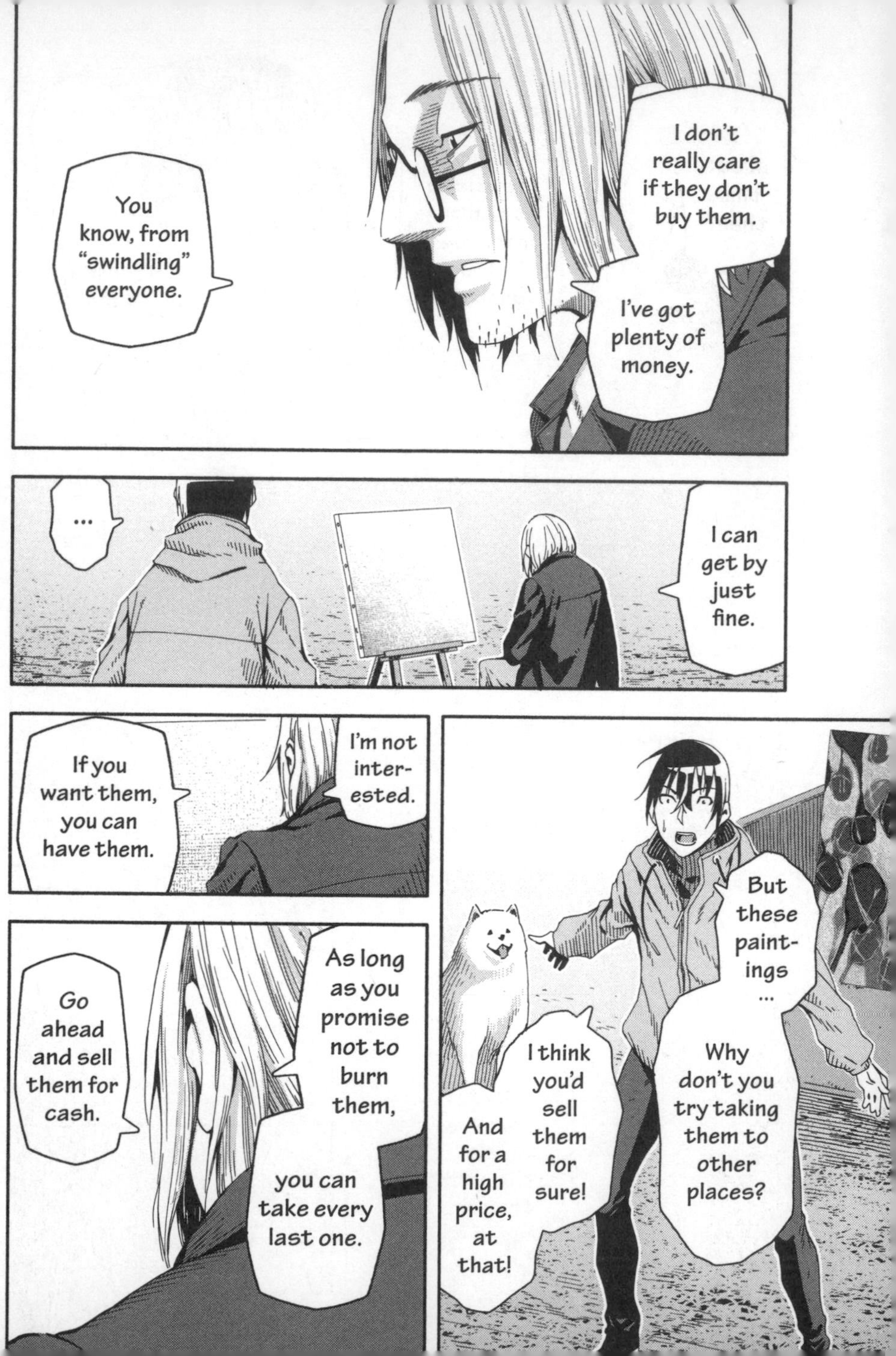
I don't really care if they don't buy them.
I've got plenty of money.
You know, from "swindling" everyone.
I can get by just fine.
...
But these paintings...
Why don't you try taking them to other places?
I think you'd sell them for sure!
And for a high price, at that!
I'm not interested.
If you want them, you can have them.
As long as you promise not to burn them,
you can take every last one.
Go ahead and sell them for cash.

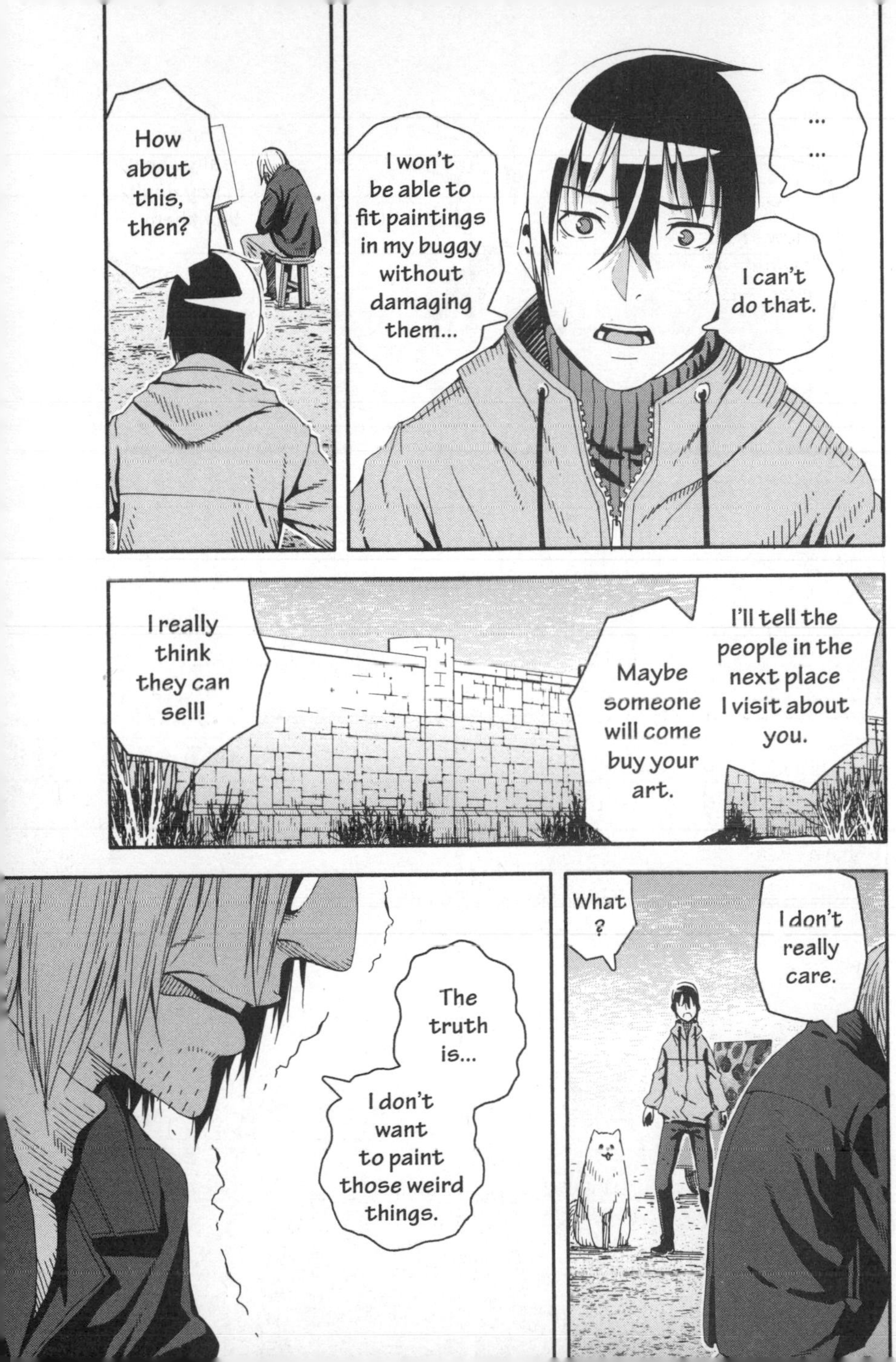
......
I can't do that.
I won't be able to fit paintings in my buggy without damaging them...
How about this, then?
I'll tell the people in the next place I visit about you.
Maybe someone will come buy your art.
I really think they can sell!
I don't really care.
What?
The truth is...
I don't want to paint those weird things.

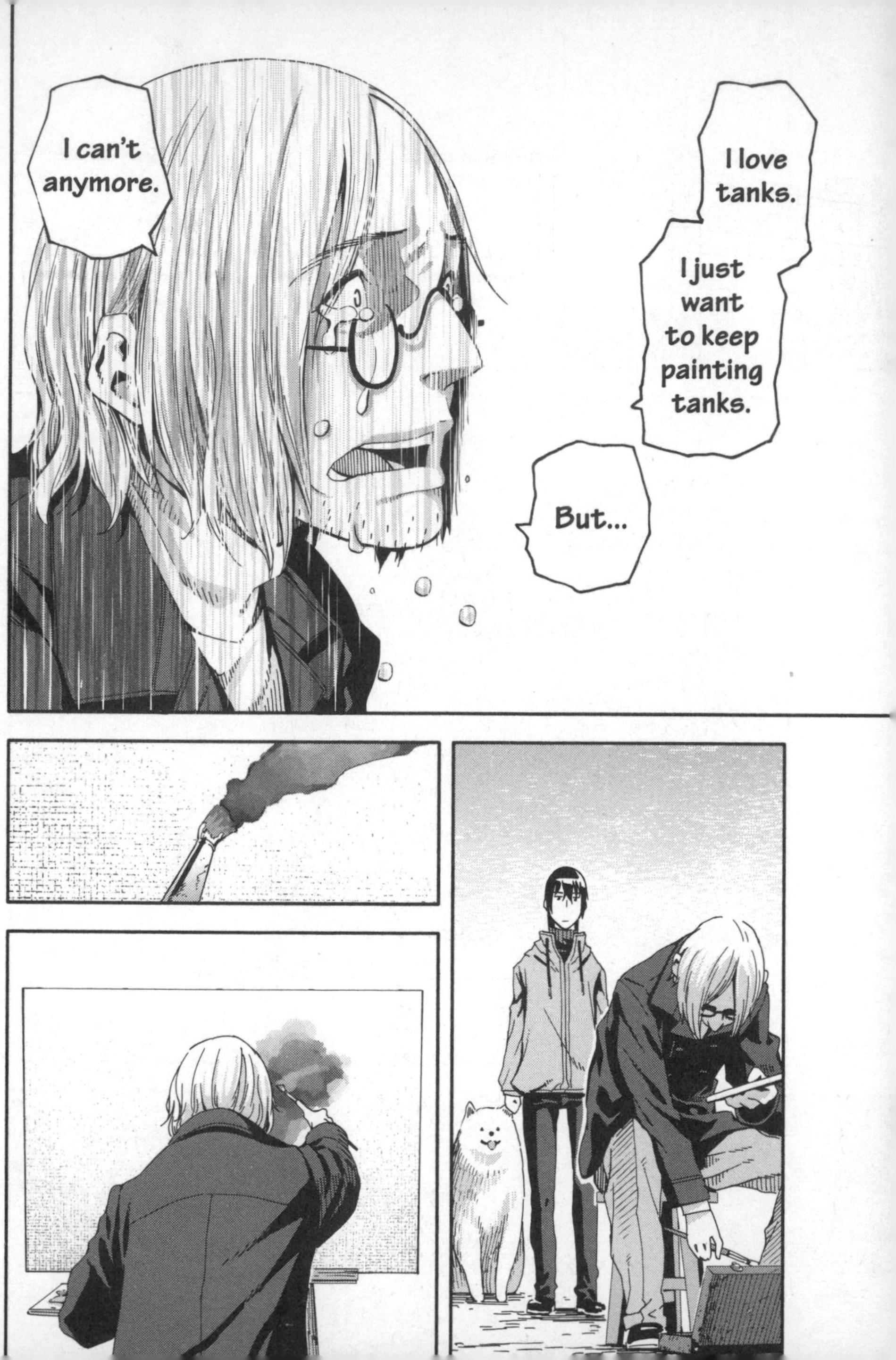
I love tanks.
I just want to keep painting tanks.
But...
I can't anymore.

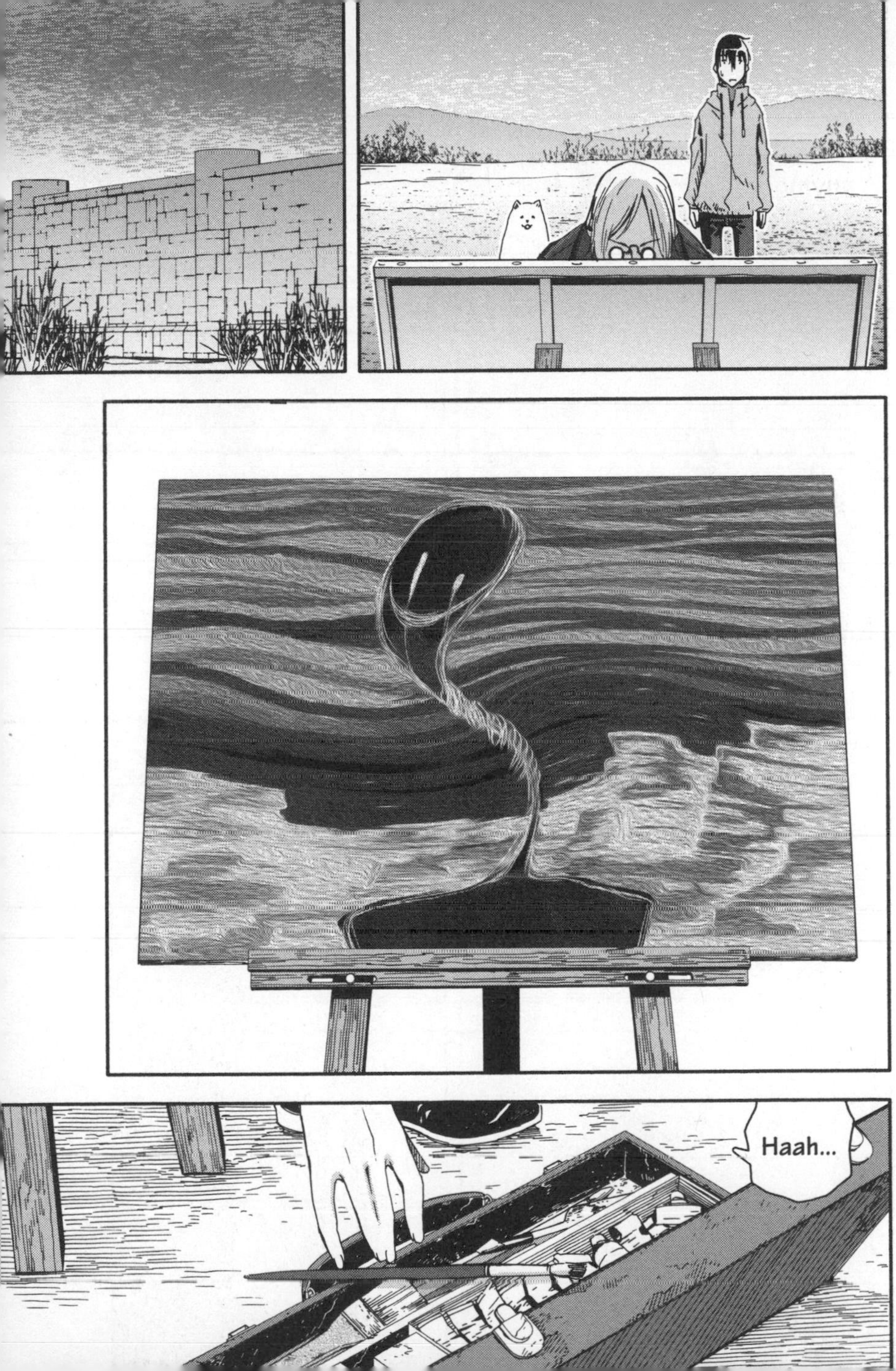
Haah...

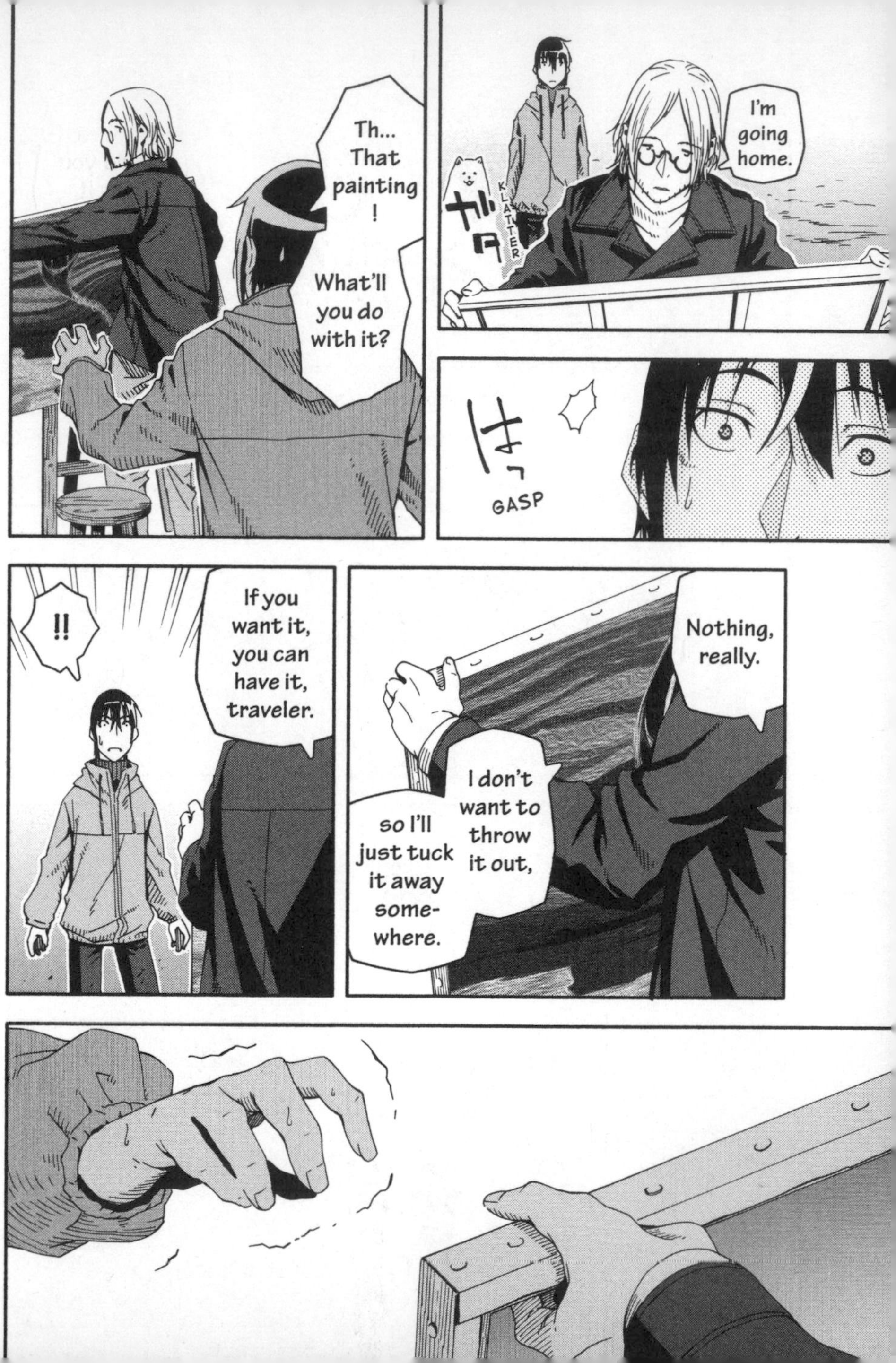
I'm going home.
KLATTER
GASP
Th... That painting!
What'll you do with it?
Nothing, really.
I don't want to throw it out,
so I'll just tuck it away some-where.
!!
If you want it, you can have it, traveler.

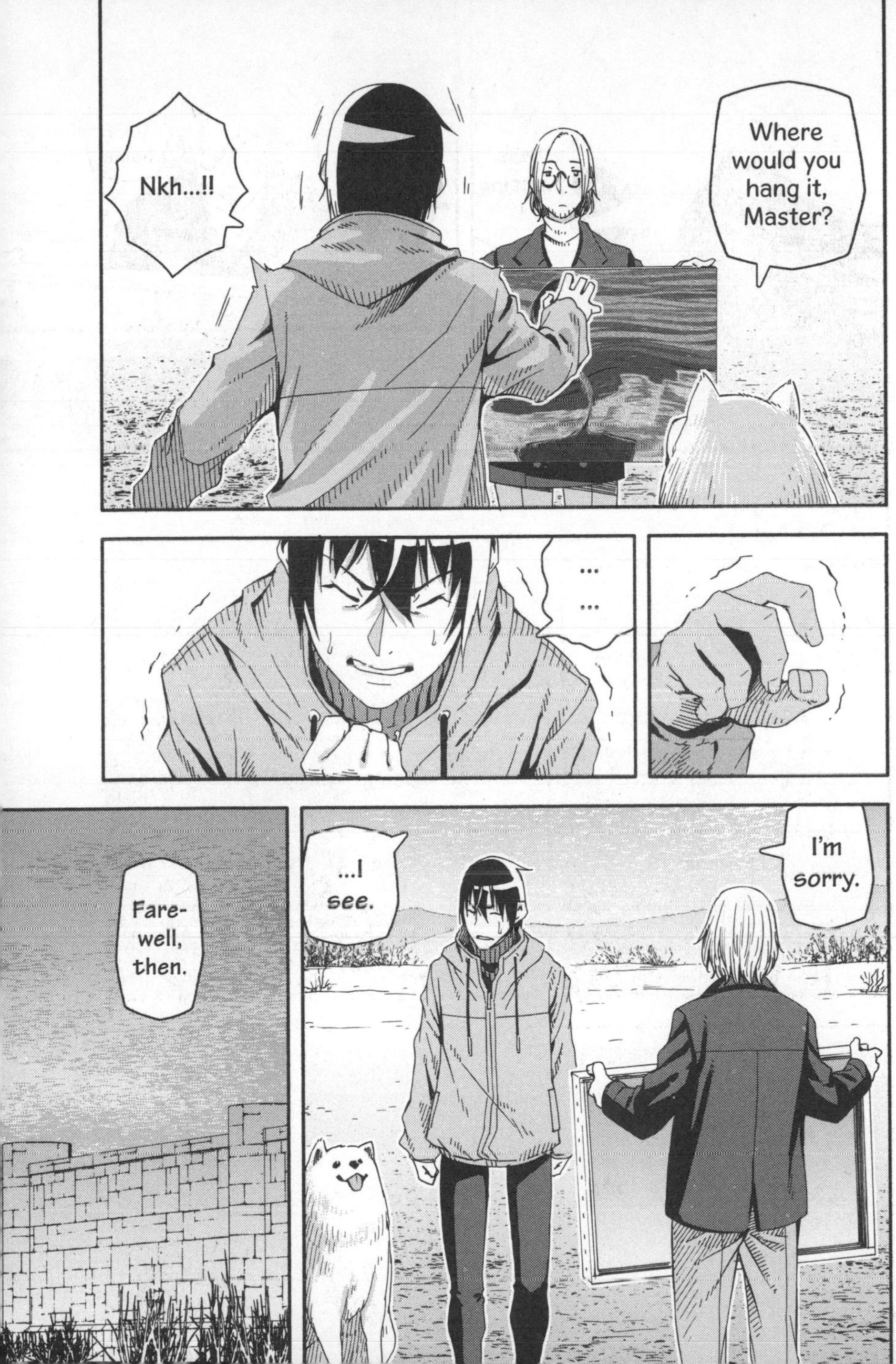
Where would you hang it, Master?
Nkh...!!
...
...
I'm sorry.
...I see.
Fare-well, then.

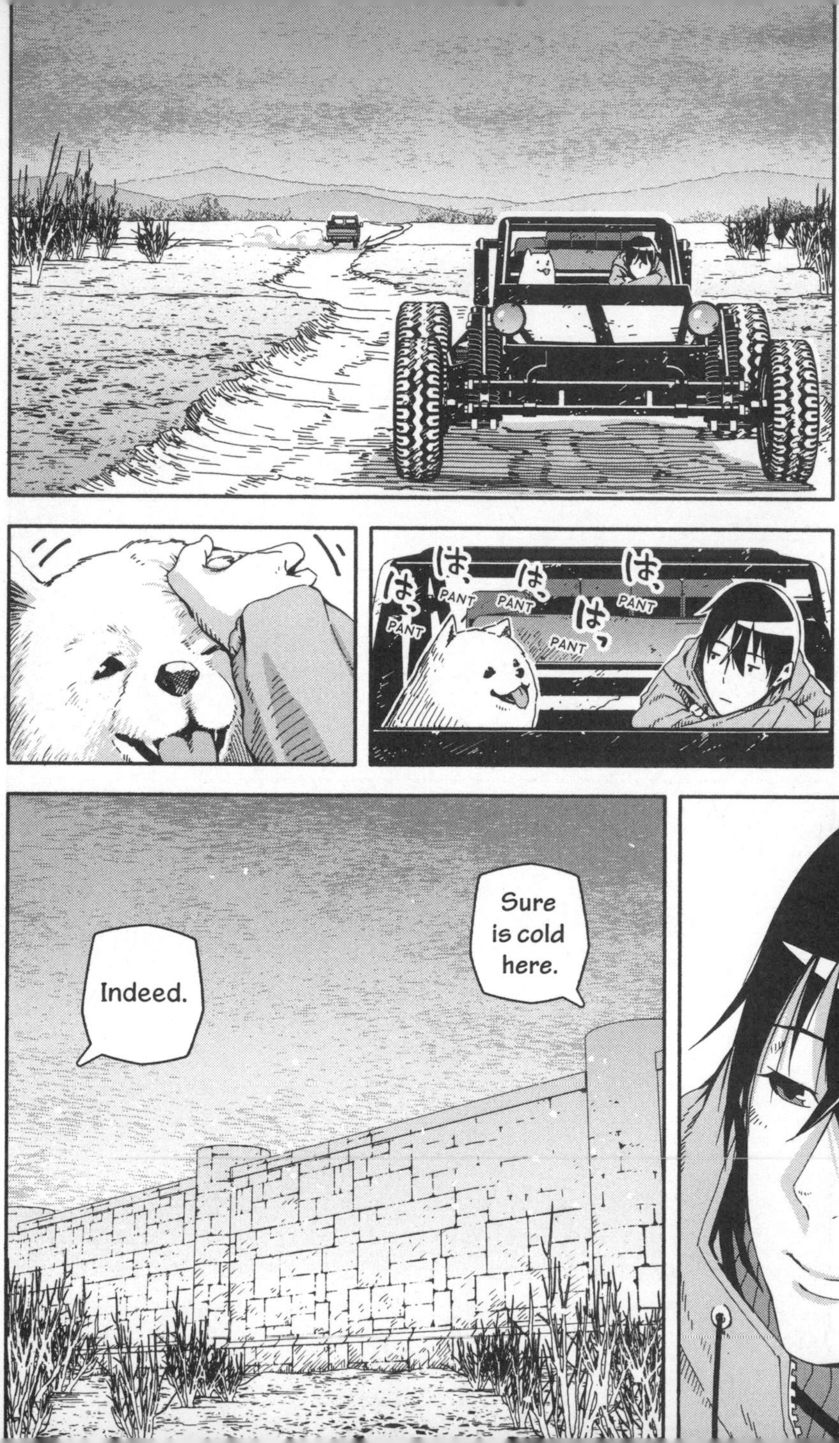
は、
PANT
は、
PANT
は、
PANT
はっ
PANT
はっ
PANT
Sure is cold here.
Indeed.

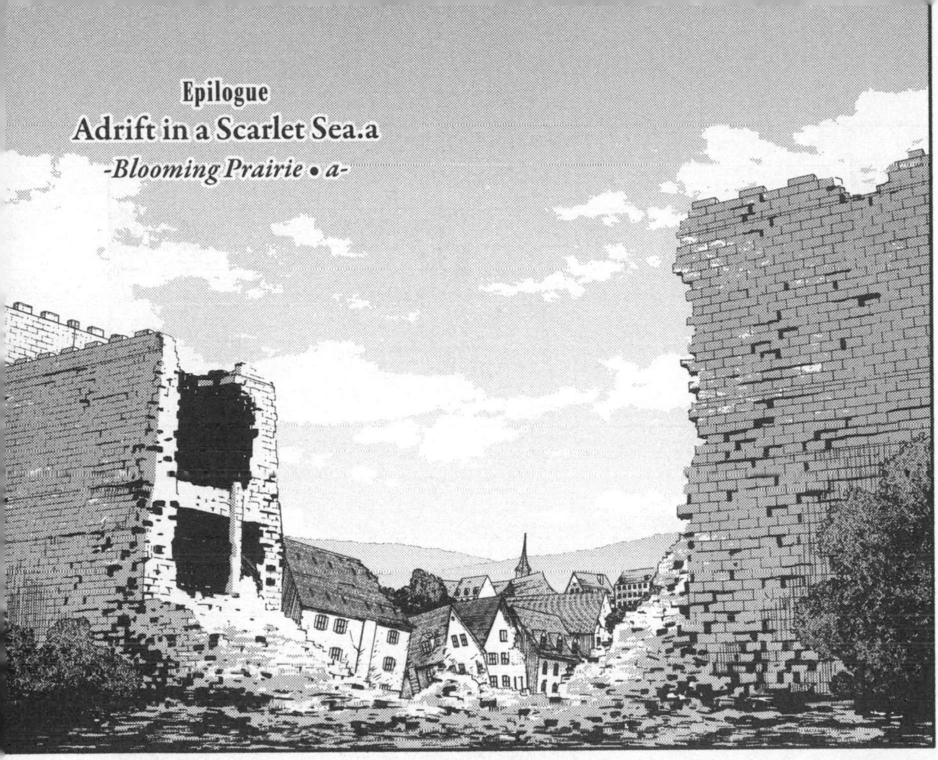
Epilogue
Adrift in a Scarlet Sea.a
-Blooming Prairie • a-

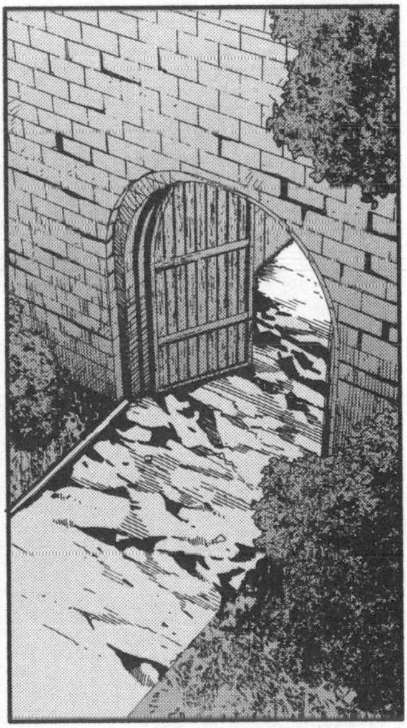

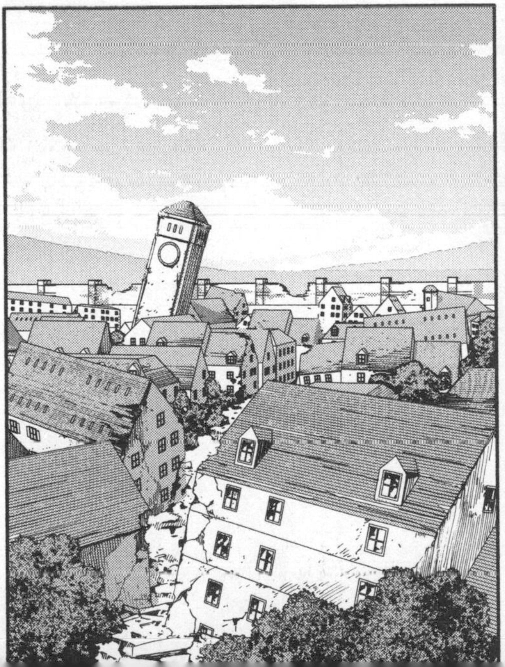

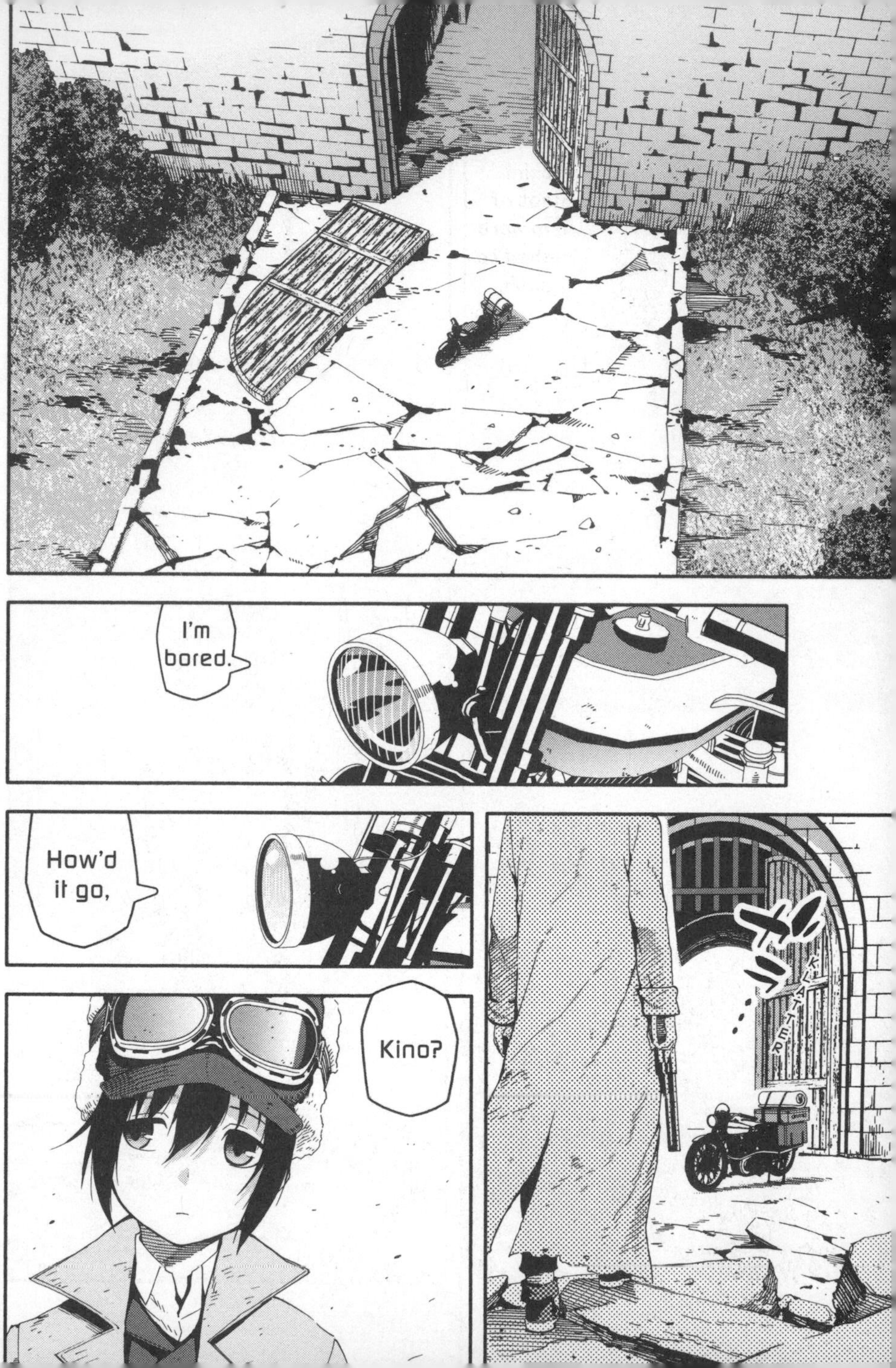
I'm bored.
KLATTER
How'd it go,
Kino?

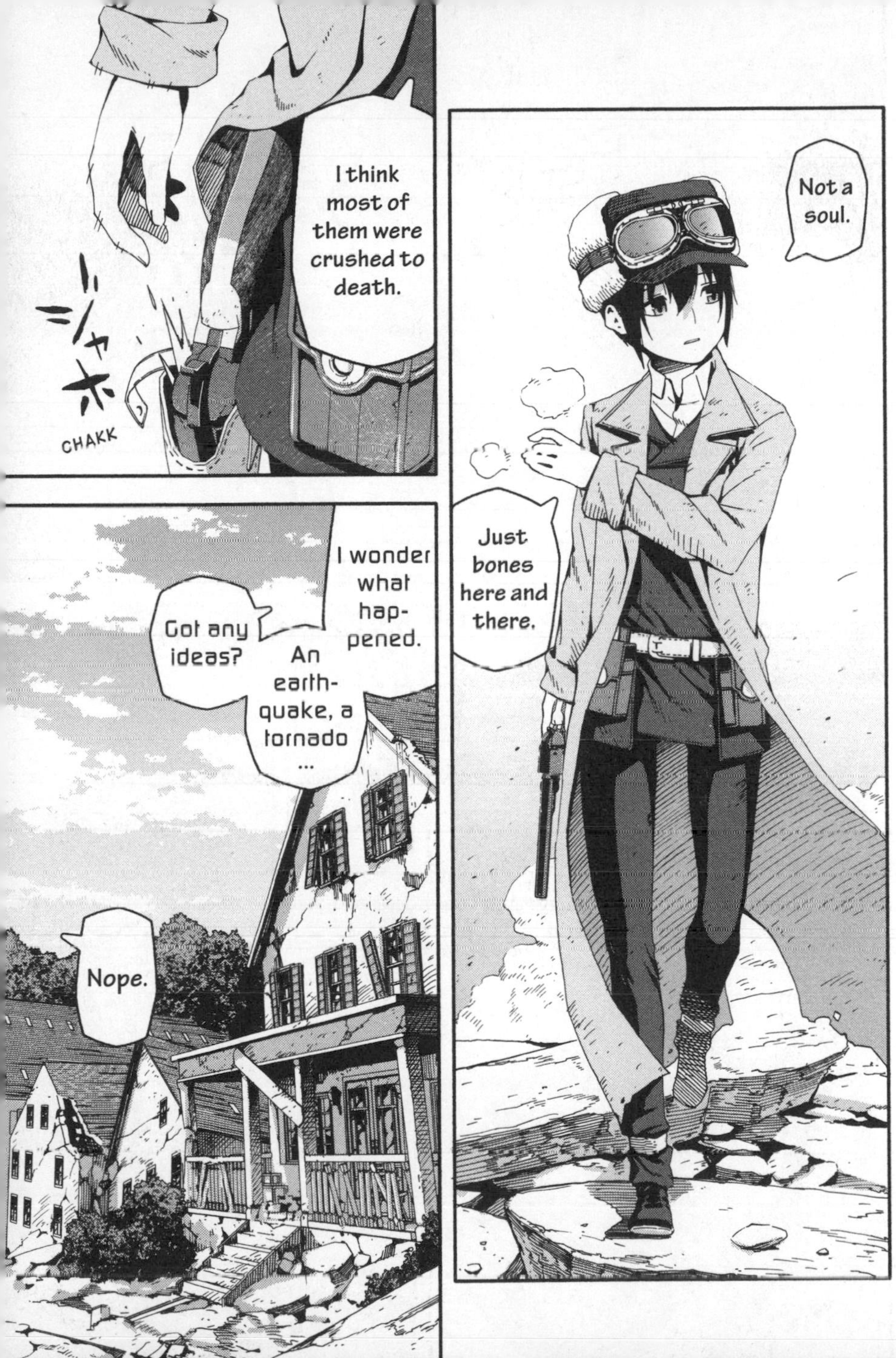
Not a soul.
Just bones here and there.
I think most of them were crushed to death.
CHAKK
I wonder what hap-pened.
Got any ideas?
An earth-quake, a tornado ...
Nope.

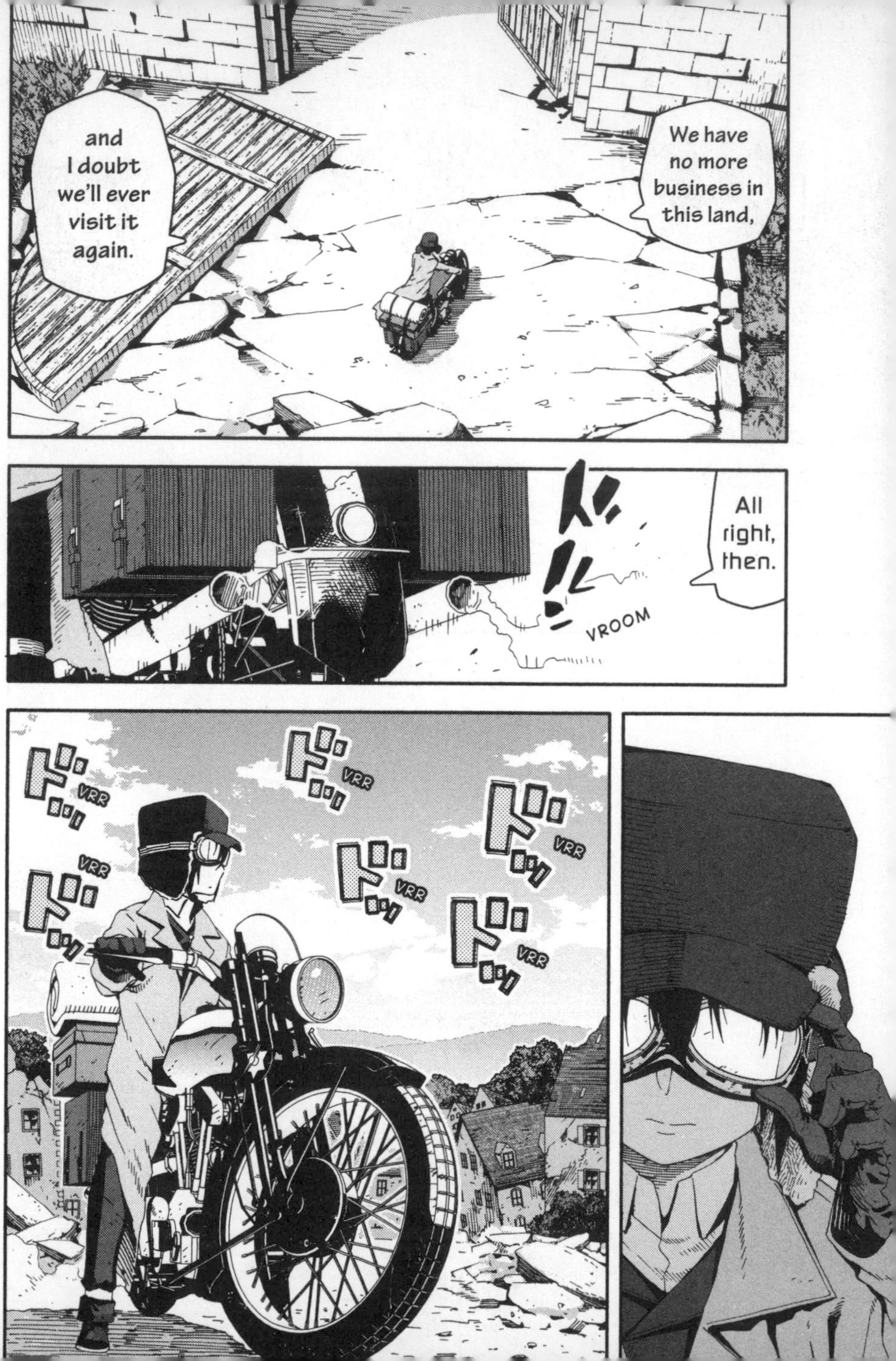
We have no more business in this land,
and I doubt we'll ever visit it again.
All right, then.
VROOM
VRR
VRR
VRR
VRR
VRR
VRR

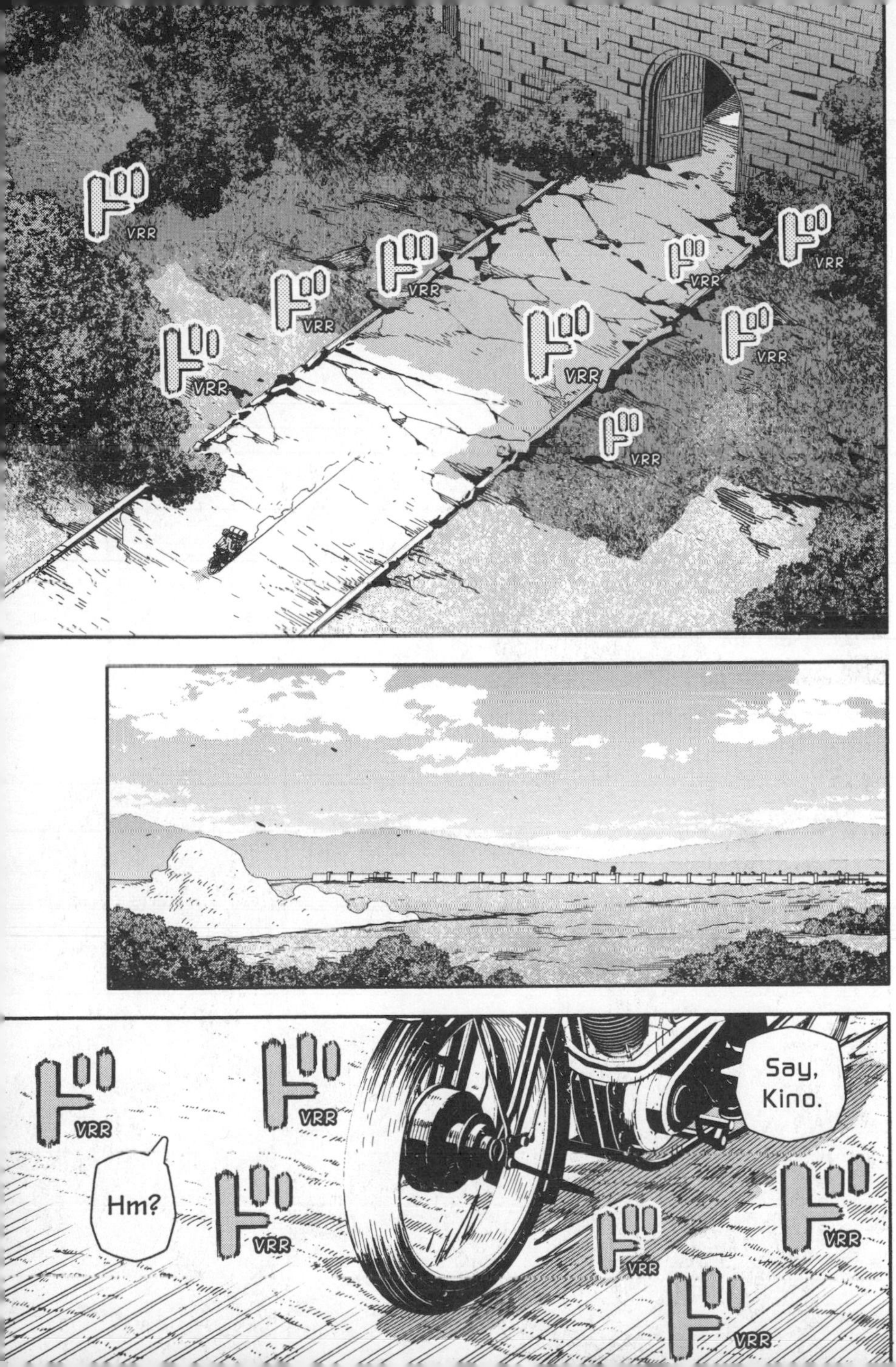
VRR
VRR
VRR
VRR
VRR
VRR
VRR
VRR
VRR
VRR
Say, Kino.
VRR
VRR
VRR
VRR
VRR
Hm?
VRR

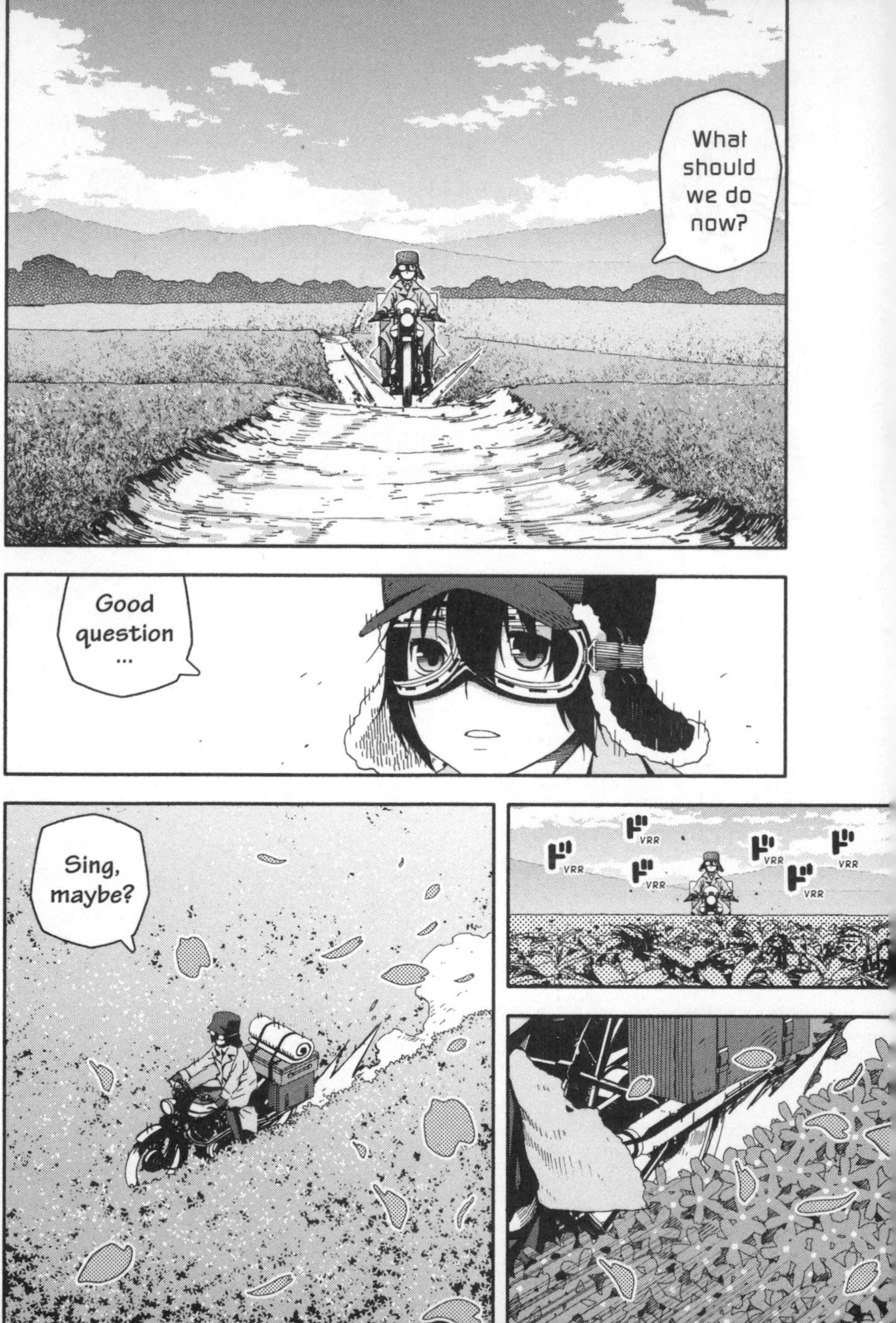
What should we do now?
Good question ...
ド VRR
ド VRR
ド VRR
ド VRR
ド VRR
ド VRR
Sing, maybe?

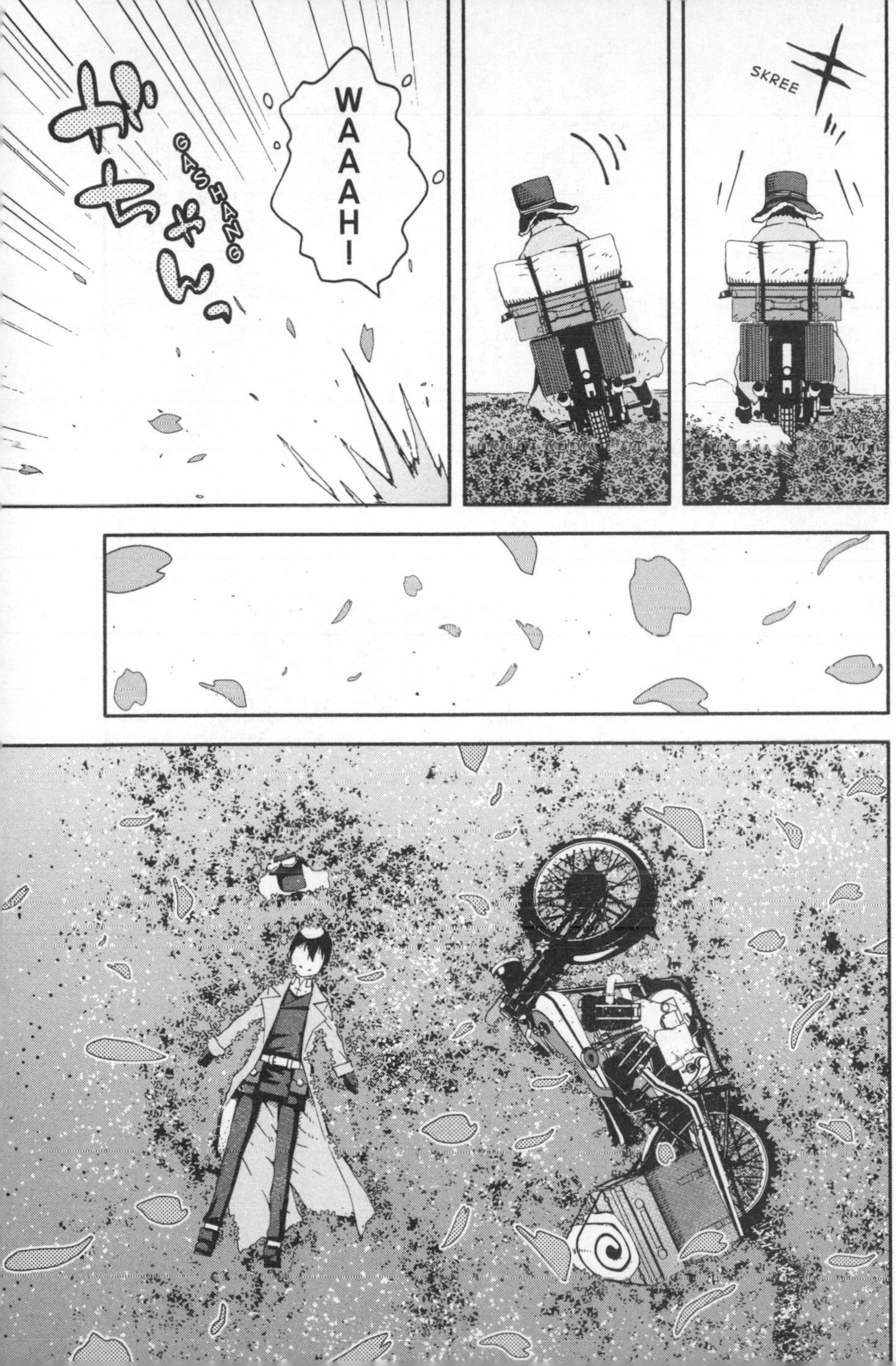
SKREE
WAAAAH!
GASHANG

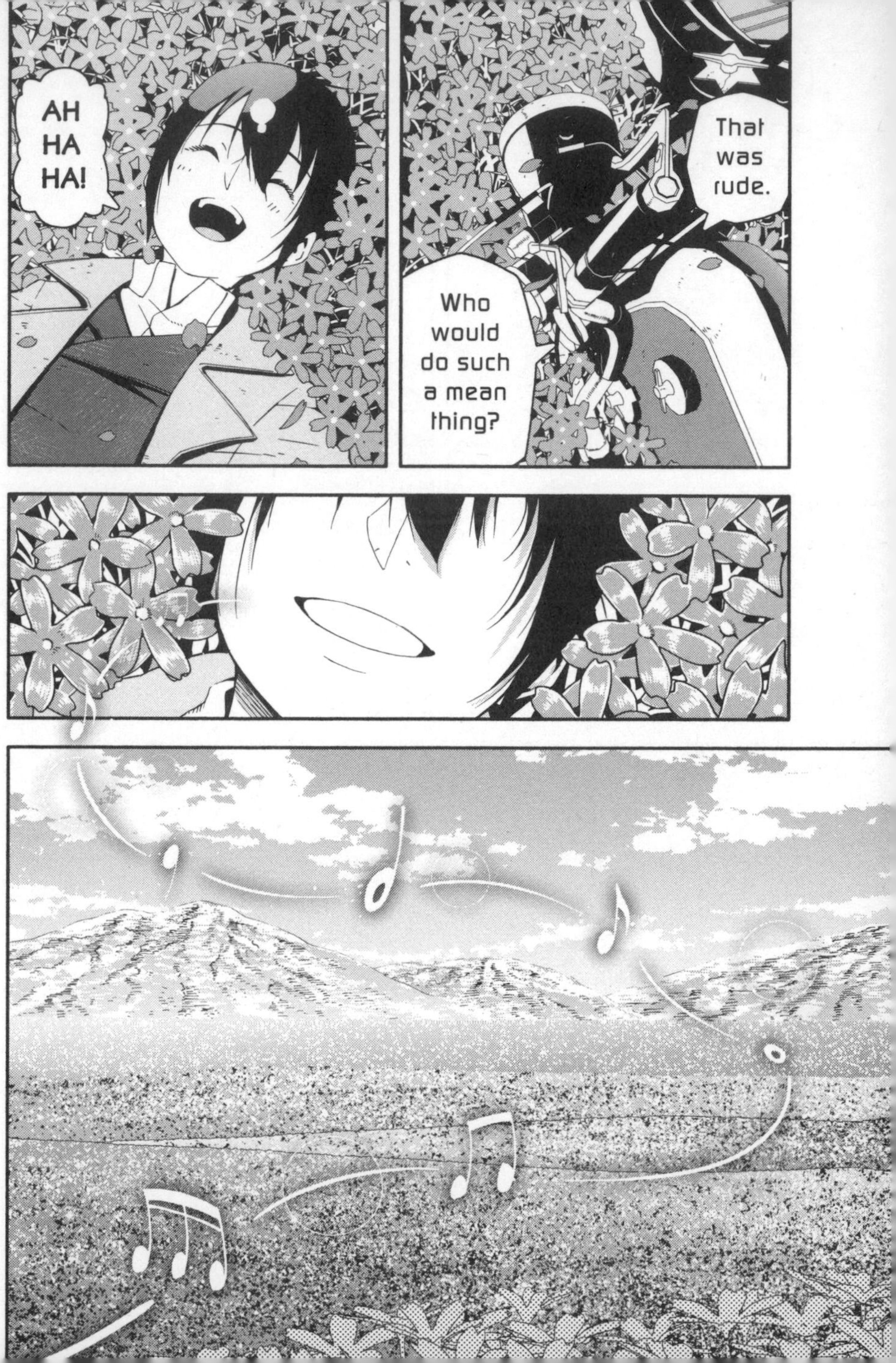
That was rude.
Who would do such a mean thing?
AH HA HA!

Kino's Journey

→ The Beautiful World ←

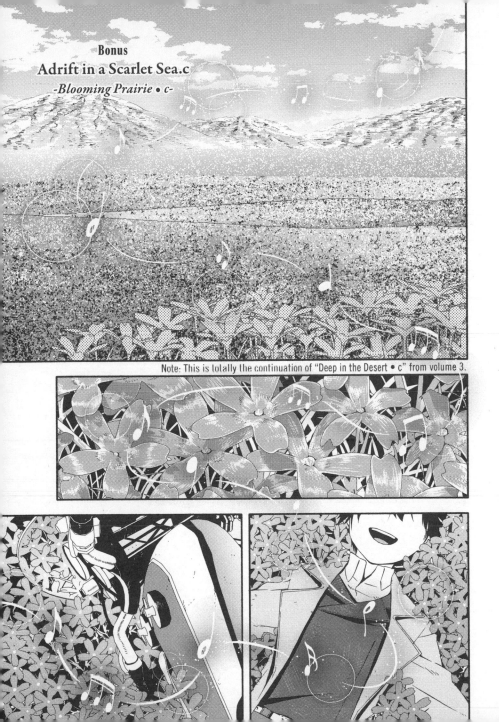

Bonus
Adrift in a Scarlet Sea.c
-Blooming Prairie • c-

Note: This is totally the continuation of "Deep in the Desert • c" from volume 3.

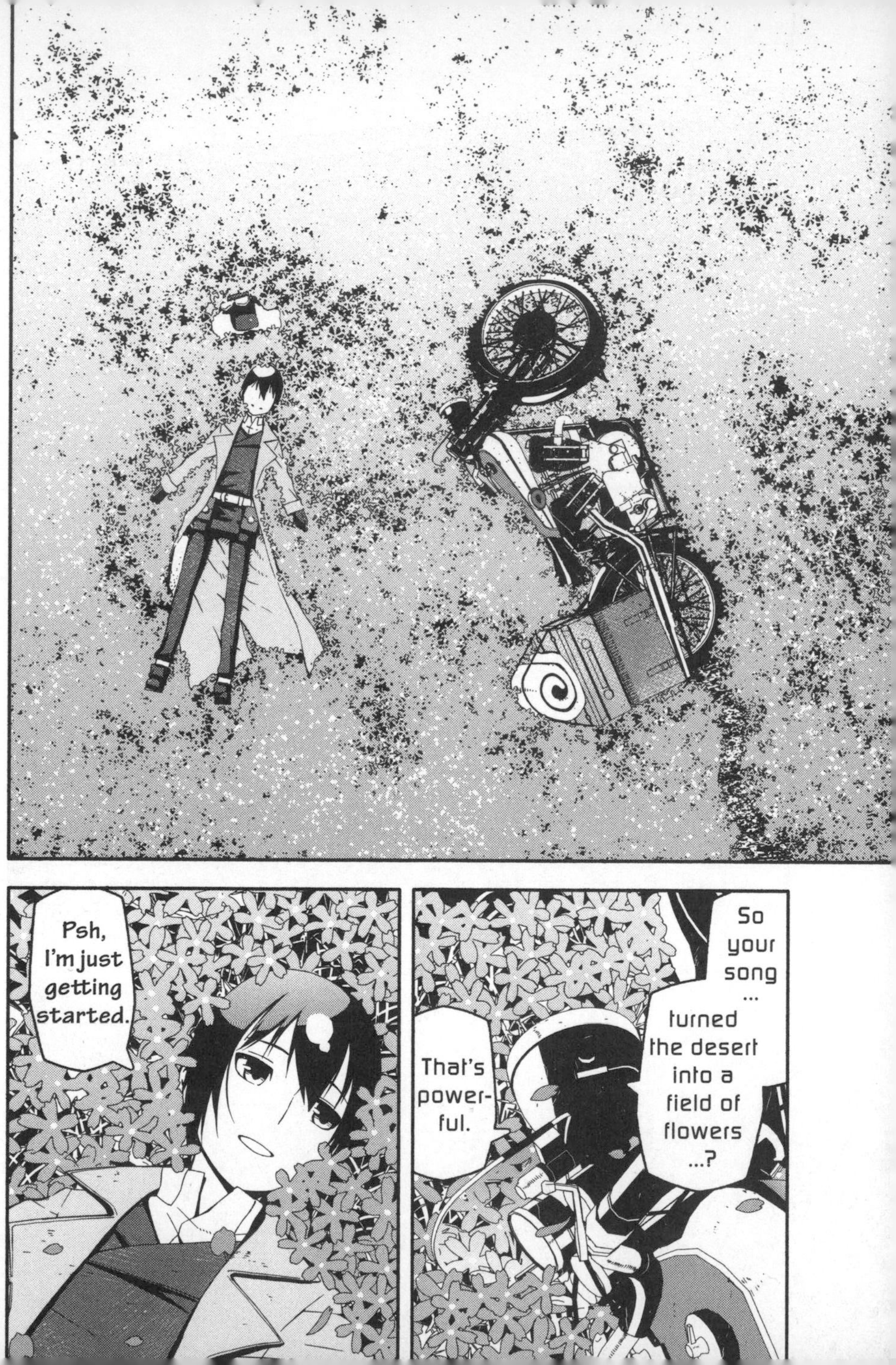
So your song ... turned the desert into a field of flowers ...?
That's power-ful.
Psh, I'm just getting started.

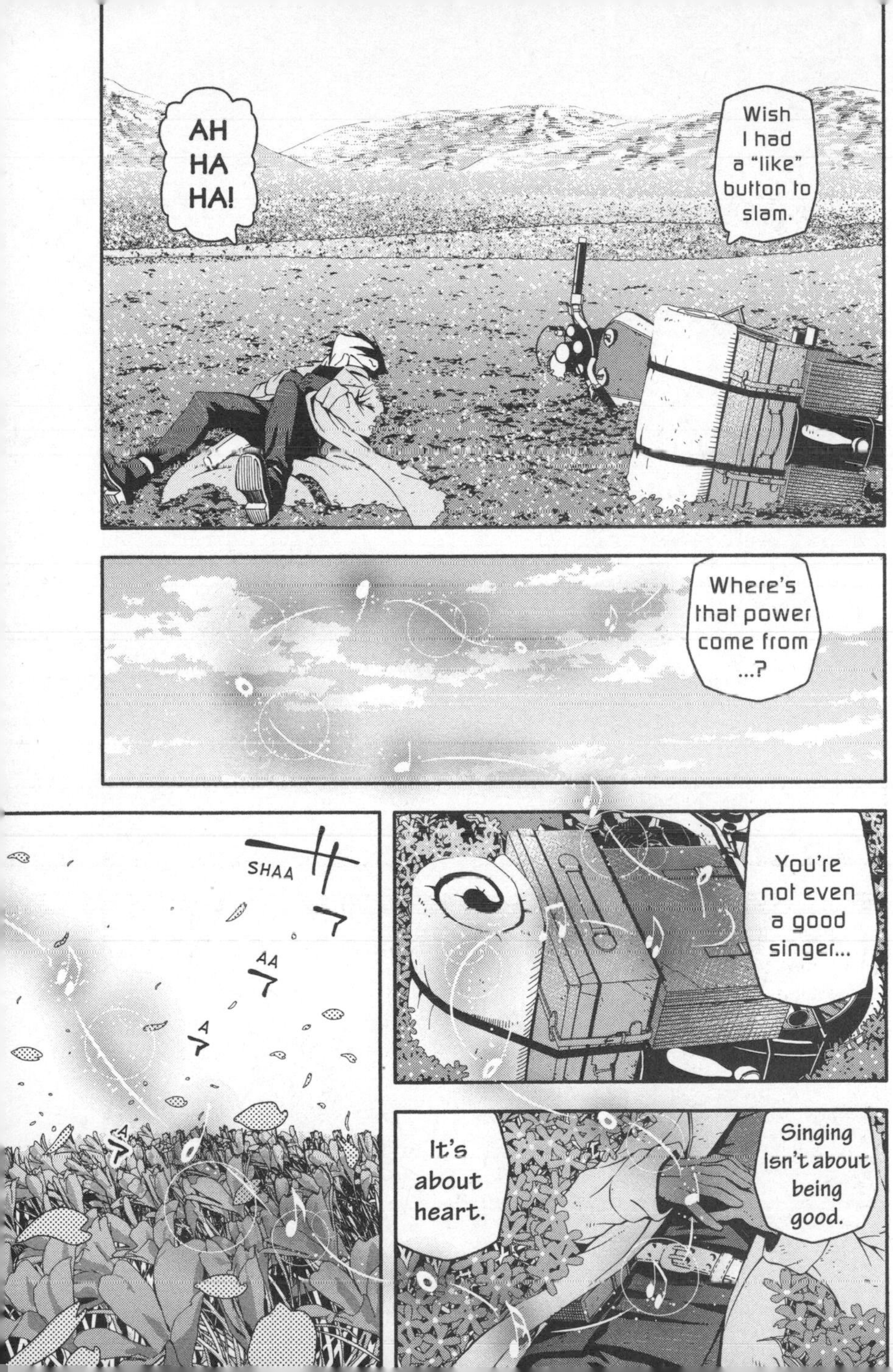
Wish I had a "like" button to slam.
AH HA HA!
Where's that power come from ...?
You're not even a good singer...
Singing isn't about being good.
It's about heart.
SHAA
AA
A
A

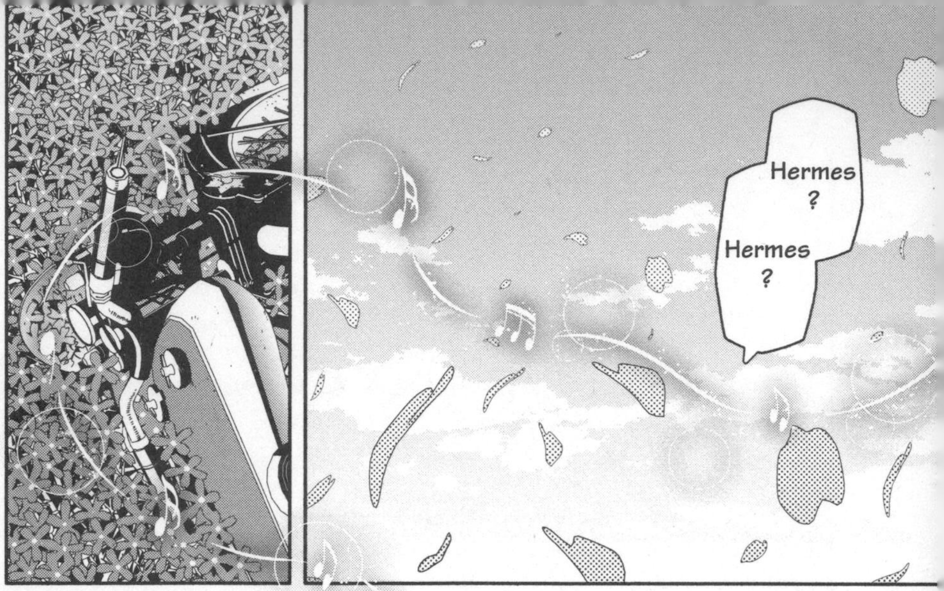
Hermes? Hermes?

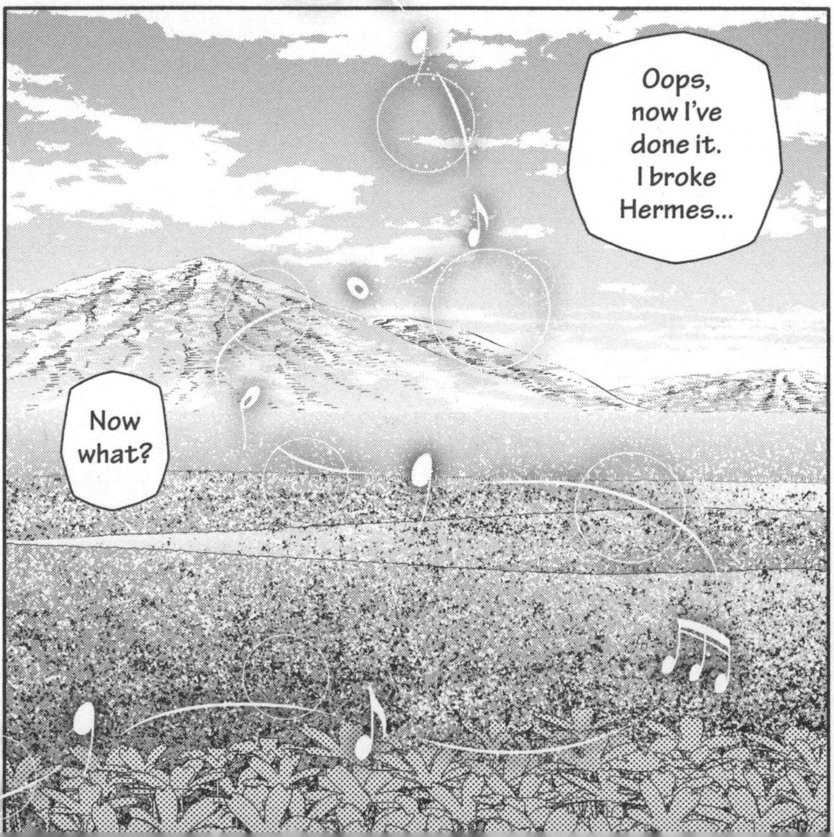
Oops, now I've done it. I broke Hermes...
Now what?

When will the engine sing again?